Cowper's Poetry

A Critical Study and Reassessment

Cowper's Poetry)

A Critical Study and Reassessment

BY

VINCENT NEWEY

Senior Lecturer in English Literature
in the University of Liverpool

BARNES & NOBLE BOOKS
TOTOWA, NEW JERSEY

First published in the USA 1982 by
BARNES & NOBLE BOOKS
81 ADAMS DRIVE
TOTOWA, NEW JERSEY, 07512

Copyright © 1982 by
Liverpool University Press

ISBN 0-389-20079-4

First published 1982

Library of Congress Cataloging in Publication Data

Newey, Vincent.
  Cowper's poetry.

  (Liverpool English texts and studies; 20)
  Includes bibliographical references and index.
  1. Cowper, William, 1731–1800 – Criticism and interpretation.
  I. Title. II. Series: Liverpool English texts and studies.

(Totowa, N.J.); 20.
PR3384.N4   1982   821'.6   82–6843
ISBN 0-389-20079-4   AACR2

Text set in Baskerville 11/12pt
Printed and Bound in Great Britain at
The Camelot Press Ltd, Southampton

Then they took him up, and carried him through the air to the door that I saw in the side of the Hill, and put him there. Then I saw that there was a way to Hell, even from the Gates of Heaven, as well as from the City of Destruction. So I awoke, and behold it was a dream.

(Bunyan, conclusion to *The Pilgrim's Progress*)

When I have thought myself falling into the abyss, I have been caught up again; and when I have thought myself on the threshold of a happy eternity, I have been thrust down to hell ... I have no expectation but of sad vicissitude, and ever believe that the last shock of all will be fatal.

(Cowper to the Rev. John Newton, 1788)

Our literature echoes with the sound of chains, breaking the larger silences of the dungeon. Victor Brombert sums up: 'Oneiric moods, the descent into a private hell, immurement within the confines of the mind, the oppression of madness ...' We discern the shape of our experience in the shape of prison life.

(W. B. Carnochan, *Confinement and Flight*)

Contents

Introduction

Cowper's immense early reputation was rooted much more in the appeal of his Evangelicalism, conservative morals and peculiar 'Englishness' than in a response to his strictly literary or intellectual qualities. Above all, he became the favourite of what Carlyle called 'the religious classes'—to such an extent that his works found a place in thousands of homes which admitted no other volumes except the Bible, Milton, and *The Pilgrim's Progress*. The grounds of this popularity and standing have, needless to say, almost entirely dissolved. Yet it remains that Cowper *is* a poet broadly of the first order, both in himself and his literary-historical importance; and the basic aim of this book is, quite simply, to offer a new, detailed, and thorough study of his achievement and its significance. The decline of his wide readership, the general neglect of his writings in recent literary criticism, and the persistence of old and often unhelpful critical assumptions all conspire, however, to involve us in a conscious act, not only of reinterpretation, but of rehabilitation. The time is singularly ripe for a fresh assessment of what Cowper does and what he has to offer.

It will be obvious that I have no sympathy with two very common views of Cowper: the traditional belief, endorsed by a long succession of good biographies, that his poetry is of interest mainly as case history or an adjunct to his fascinating life, and the notion that, as D. J. Enright contends in a well-known guide to English literature, 'it is not easy to find much to say about Cowper's poetry . . . : for the greater part its virtues are as obvious as its weaknesses'.[1] In what I take to be the prevalent attitude, Cowper writes with a transparent naturalness, 'a simple dignity'[2]—a man of piety and humane instincts, who, turning to poetry to escape depression, became by chance the acknowledged champion of Evangelical Christianity, sometimes popular humorist (everyone remembers

John Gilpin), and one of our most accurate delineators of rural landscape. Only in 'The Castaway' is he generally granted true imaginative force: 'with a madman's lucidity he expresses his conviction that he is damned ... Such "nakedness of senti-ment", the intensity of despair, is rare in poetry'.[3]

Cowper's whole poetry is a great deal more complex, problematical, and rewarding than people think. And it is also more 'modern' in one rather clear respect—its often patent psychological character. As Donald Davie has argued, Cowper was in some ways a staunch exponent of the neo-classical conception of literature as rhetorical 'product', the art of addressing an educated audience on matters of shared social and cultural concern. Yet objective intention is constantly being overtaken and displaced in his work by private impulse and motive, so as to give rise to a current of self-revelation which not only lays open the recesses of his mind but constitutes a quest for identity and psychic integration. *The Task* itself is, whatever else, a trial of the spirit, a struggle for balanced and fruitful being-in-the-world. The famous celebra-tions of nature represent at bottom the triumph of outgoing sensibilities over an acute proneness to solipsism and despair.

Now, there are special reasons why Cowper's poetry should thus express inward tensions and a continuing search for creative relations with the external world. He was a life-long victim of melancholia and knew from early experience the 'descent into a private hell, ... the oppression of madness'.[4] The other strong underlying influence is the Calvinism which first affected him during his recovery at Dr. Cotton's *Collegium Insanorum* in 1763 and was later fostered by his friendship with John Newton at Olney. Innate affliction and a religion based on the fierce doctrines of election, predestination and reprobation combined to confront Cowper directly with the problem of his own condition, though contrary to the emphasis of much biography his work is no more a mirror of recurrent pessimism and fears of damnation than a medium through which he strove to surmount these pressures, even at times, as we shall see, making a bid for spiritual assurance.

Despite its particular origins, however, the more one con-templates this psychological, or therapeutic, side of Cowper's poetry the more it seems to exhibit what was subsequently to become a shared theme, a dynamic centre of consciousness. Cowper's was the first strenuously subjective poetic vision, the first to feed upon and put forth 'the mystery within' (Shelley); but more than this, it pursues a question which has continued to reverberate loudly across our literature and thinking ever since the Romantic period—a question felt, so to speak, along the blood. As Keats put it when propounding his famous non-Christian scheme of salvation, 'How then are Souls to be made? How then are these sparks which are God to have identity given them—so as ever to possess a bliss peculiar to each one's individual existence? How, but by the medium of a world like this? . . . a World of Pains and Troubles.'[5] While Cowper's situation, as it is presented in his poems and letters, does have specific links with that of the Christian, or more precisely Puritan and Bunyanesque, pilgrim whose life is subject to dogma and the inscrutable will of Providence, it also perceptibly foreshadows (as indeed does the experience of the Puritan himself) the familiar predicament of 'modern man', who, in the felt absence of a uniform culture and inviolable framework of common belief within which he may unselfconsciously exist, must find out for himself whether life is meaningful or meaningless, and must, if possible, forge a personal wholeness out of a response to self and the world beyond self. The religious tenets and morals to which Cowper devoted a whole series of long poems, the Moral Satires, might of course be described as 'a framework of common belief'. The point is, however, that in Cowper religion is essentially something taken over rather than something given; a philosophic system personally adapted as a bulwark against hopelessness and feelings of insecurity, which served him well for a time but in the long run (and here one thinks especially of 'The Castaway') could do nothing to solve a deep-seated apprehension of how large and indifferent the universe is, and how alone is each person in it. Even so public a poetry as the Moral Satires forms part of a mental journey in which the perils of isolation and despondency are met and countered—in which various resources, ranging from sheer resignation and the use of available schemata to a cultivation of an ennobling interchange between the mind and nature, are successfully, though never conclusively, opposed to an awareness of disorder, dereliction and vulnerability. To put it another way, Cowper is, like Wordsworth and Coleridge, a forerunner of the psycho-historian Philip Rieff's twentieth-century 'psychological man' in whom 'the new centre, which can be held even as communities disintegrate, is the self', existing where 'there is no longer an effective sense of communion, driving the individual out of himself', nurturing or failing to nurture his 'well-being' and 'personal capacity' in a response to 'destruction without and to the chaos within'.[6]

With Cowper Rieff's type-figure steps right to the fore, giving shape and expression to an emergent presence in English literature. Other transitional poets—Gray and Goldsmith—we shall consider at the appropriate time. Suffice it for the moment to say that even in mainstream Augustanism there is a discernible movement towards a sense of the individual's need to adjust via his own resources to the loss of corporate identity and values. We see it in Pope's journey from ceremonial chronicler of the civilizing potential of his age in 'Windsor Forest', through diagnosis of a new amoral acquisitiveness in the *Moral Essays*, to beleaguered witness at the dissolution of Christian-humanist tradition in the last Book of *The Dunciad*; or, differently, in Johnson, whose socio-cultural principles and trust in the superintendence of Providence are hard pressed by an intense and gloomy vision of life as a 'state of universal uncertainty, where a thousand dangers hover about us' and the demon of madness stalks us from within.[7] And if we want a point of reference at the other end of the spectrum, who better than Eliot, for whom, at least in that poem which has assumed a centrality in the minds of a generation, the unavoidable spectacle is of a 'waste land' in which the individual can find no rest or healthy stimulation either from without or within? His characters' greatest problem is the ability, or inability, to 'connect'—'I can connect/Nothing with nothing'; and the same burden is carried by the authorial imagination itself, which moves homelessly through the poem, falling back into itself to encounter the mad oneiric confusion of 'bats with baby faces' crawling 'downward down a blackened wall', 'upside-down-in-air' towers and 'reminiscent bells', or travelling outwards into a landscape of unlovely, violent and intractable materials—'trams and dusty trees', 'synthetic perfumes,/

Unguent', the 'automatic' typist's bored and permitted rape—
that resist the desire for fertile creative reciprocity.[8] Cowper's
own experiences of the prison-house of futility and imaginative
disablement, and his victories in breaking out, will be among
my primary concerns in later chapters. He was not, like Yeats
and Eliot (and Philip Rieff), a professional mourner at the
wake for cultural coherence, nor so conscious in his articulation
of the difficulties and opportunities of the artist-individual
thrown back upon his own devices—but he knew very well in
his bones what was coming.

One important book on Cowper, Morris Golden's *In Search of
Stability* (New Haven, 1960), does examine the poetry from a
psychological angle but is limited to a consideration of the ways
in which such mental preoccupations as imprisonment 'intrude
themselves upon and shape some of the poems'. It is Golden's
avowed policy to avoid the critical and literary questions
'which would be essential in any full-scale analysis of Cowper's
achievement'.[9] Most of the other specialist studies concentrate
on the poet's life and milieu, so that the analytical interpreter of
Cowper has all the obvious advantages and disadvantages of a
relatively free hand. I am conscious, however, of my strong
indebtedness to two very different statements: the section on
parts of *The Task* and *Olney Hymns* in Patricia Meyer Spacks's
The Poetry of Vision: Five Eighteenth-Century Poets (Cambridge,
Mass., 1967), which contains the best close reading of Cowper's poetry, and Donald Davie's seminal defence of the
language of later eighteenth-century poetry in *Purity of Diction in
English Verse* (1952). W. N. Free's *William Cowper* (Twayne's
English Authors Series, New York, 1970), a general account of
the life and works, includes some helpful critical commentary.
The monograph of the same name by Norman Nicholson
(1951) is still, I think, the best introduction to Cowper.
Although they appeared after most of this study was written, I
have profited from Richard Feingold's excellent chapters on
The Task in *Nature and Society; Later Eighteenth-Century Uses of the
Pastoral and Georgic* (1978), and have incorporated my detailed
response to them in chapter 6.

Finally, a word should be said about the material covered,
for although Cowper was past middle age when he published
his first volume in 1782, he left all told a surprisingly large body

of verse, composed on and off throughout his lifetime. I have
regrettably omitted his work as translator, including the once
famous blank-verse translation of Homer, which, for all its
literalness, does often rise to an ideal rapport with the 'plain
and simple sublimity' of the original and is of historical
importance as a deliberate and successful rival to Pope's
version. With this one exception, I have tried to deal with every
aspect of Cowper's achievement and career. To an extent his
strength lies in his consistency, so that we shall necessarily
observe, for example, a repeated commitment to the virtues of
pure and logical English and a courageous willingness to face
again and again the same insoluable riddles of the human
condition. But there is as much startling variety as judicious
continuity: to read Cowper is, so to speak, like peering into a
kaleidoscope of limitless subtle and shifting patterns and
effects. *The Task* (1785), the fullest single expression of his
genius and poetic personality, must naturally take pride of
place in any essay on his work. Yet it is not usually realized that
he also prospered in perhaps as wide a range of lyric and
narrative modes as any other poet, from the congregational
hymn to *jeux d'esprit* like *The Ballad of John Gilpin*, hard-hitting
'protest songs' in support of the Anti-slavery Movement to
urbane complimentary verses which make model performances
in the conduct of personal and social relationships, eloquent
responses to great national events to the solitary introspective
utterances of 'To Mary', 'On the Receipt of my Mother's
Picture' and 'The Castaway'. That I shall concentrate on this
last group of shorter poems and their extension of the
confessional dimension of *The Task* will not, I trust, prevent me
from doing justice to the others and *their* particular qualities.
The eight Moral Satires, which formed the bulk of the Volume
of 1782, present a special problem, pervaded as they are by
those attitudes that made Cowper's name with the stricter
'religious classes' of the time. Nevertheless, to term them
'merely dull and rather naive versifications of Calvinist
doctrine'[10] is a gross misrepresentation. Not only is it extremely
difficult, as Gilbert Thomas has demonstrated, to find anything
precisely Calvinist in them, but, more to the point, they
frequently develop a vein of lively discourse, a sophisticated
one-way conversation with the reader on such general topics as

literature, politics, and contemporary manners. Most of all, they are an essential stage in Cowper's maturation, embodying signal new departures as well as recognized dead-ends. The author of *The Task*—the unique poet of nature and retirement, of selfhood and the interior life, and of the public world too—would have been impossible without them.

The preliminary chapter on the history of Cowper's reputation and approaches to his work was written in the belief that by understanding a writer's status in the past we come better armed for discussing him in the present. In preparing it I owe much to Mrs. Norma Russell's *Bibliography of William Cowper to 1837* (Oxford, 1963) and Lodwick Hartley's *William Cowper: the Continuing Revaluation* (Chapel Hill, 1963), which contains an extensive annotated list of books and articles since 1895.

All references to Cowper's poems are taken from *The Poetical Works of William Cowper*, edited by Sir Humphrey Milford (4th edn., revised Norma Russell, 1971). For the correspondence I have used whenever possible the substantial selection in Brian Spiller's *Cowper: Poetry and Prose* (Reynard Library, London, 1968); otherwise quotations are from the old standard edition, *The Correspondence of William Cowper*, edited by Thomas Wright (4 vols., London, 1904).

I am grateful to Miss Rachel Trickett for her generous and varied help; to my colleagues Bernard Beatty and Brian Nellist, who brought their usual incisiveness to bear in many conversations about Cowper; to Mrs. Norma Russell, Mr. Graham Midgley, Professor Kenneth Muir, and the late Professor Kenneth Allott, all of whom read the manuscript at an early stage and made suggestions for its improvement; and especially Professor Philip Edwards for his invaluable support and assistance in relation to so many aspects of this book. To the Chairman and Committee of the Liverpool University Press, and to Mrs. Rosalind Campbell, Secretary of the Press, I owe thanks for their perceptive advice and for the humane efficiency with which the process of publication was conducted. Without the expert aid of our typists, Mrs. Joan Welford, Mrs. Margaret Mosquera, and Miss Cathy Rees, I should still be struggling in a morass of sometimes barely decipherable pages.

My deepest debt is to my wife and family. This volume is for them: they made it possible.

Chronology

1731   (15 November) William Cowper born at the rectory, Great Berkhamstead, Herts., son of the Revd. John Cowper, Chaplain to George II, and Ann, daughter of Roger Donne of Ludham Hall in Norfolk.

1737   (13 November) Death of Cowper's mother.

?1738–?40 A boarder at Dr. Pittman's school at Market (Markyate) Street, on the boundary of Beds. and Herts.

?1740–?42 Lives in London at the house of the oculist, Mrs. Disney, undergoing treatment for serious eye trouble.

1742   (April) Enters Westminster School.

1748   (29 April) Admitted to the Middle Temple. Writes first extant poem, 'On Finding the Heel of a Shoe', in imitation of John Philips's mock-heroic *The Splendid Shilling*.

1749   (May) Leaves Westminster, where he had formed friendships with Vincent Bourne, fifth-form master, and fellow-pupils Robert Lloyd, Charles Churchill, George Colman the elder, and Sir William Russell. Other contemporaries include Warren Hastings and Cumberland. After Westminster, spends nine months at Berkhamstead.

1750–?53 Articled to a solicitor, Mr. Chapman of Ely Place, Holborn; pays frequent visits to the house of his uncle Ashley Cowper in Southampton Row, where he falls in love with his cousin Theadora, the Delia of the lyrics written at this time.

1753   Abandons hope of marrying Theadora because of his uncle's persistent opposition to the match. (November) In residence in the Middle Temple; first mental breakdown, from which he recovers after a stay in Southampton.

1754   (June) Called to the Bar. Member of the Nonsense Club, a small circle of literati including George Colman and Robert Lloyd.

1756   Contributes papers to *The Connoisseur*, a literary periodical edited by Colman and Bonnell Thornton. (9 July) Death of Cowper's father.

1757   Admitted to the Inner Temple.

1759   Appointed to the sinecure post of Commissioner of Bankrupts.

1763   Is offered the Reading Clerkship and the Clerkship of Committees in the House of Lords, positions in the patronage of Ashley Cowper, but is then allowed to exchange them for the Clerkship of the Journals which, though less remunerative, could be performed in private. His uncle's right of nomination being challenged, Cowper breaks down under the threat of examination at the bar of the House and is sent to Margate to recuperate. Returns to London in the late summer but immediately suffers a relapse. (November) Twice attempts suicide; a committee of the House of Lords dismisses charges of corruption in connection with his exchange of offices. (December) Again attempts suicide and is taken to Dr. Cotton's *Collegium Insanorum* at St. Albans.

1764   (July) Recovery, accompanied by religious conversion.

1765   (June) Leaves St. Albans; adopts 'Dick' Coleman, young son of a drunken cobbler; resigns Commissionership of Bankrupts, so becoming entirely dependent on friends and relatives for an income; settles in lodgings at Huntingdon. (November) Moves to the house of the Revd. Morley and Mary Unwin.

1766   At Huntingdon with the Unwins; begins to write his autobiographical *Memoir*.

1767   (July) Death of Morley Unwin. (October) Cowper and Mrs. Unwin arrive at Olney, Bucks., as guests of the Revd. John Newton.

1768   (February) Takes up residence at Orchard Side, Olney, with Mrs. Unwin and her daughter.

1769   Increasing friendship with Newton. The Unwins' son, William, becomes rector of Stock in Essex.

1770   (20 March) Death of Cowper's brother, the Revd. John Cowper, Fellow of Benet College (Corpus Christi), Cambridge. C. afterwards writes *Adelphi*, an eye-witness account of his brother's spiritual triumphs during his last illness.

1771   Begins work on the *Olney Hymns* in collaboration with John Newton.

1772   Engaged to be married to Mrs. Unwin.

1773   (January) Engagement broken off during an attack of severe depression. (February) Has a dream in which he is visited by a voice sentencing him to eternal damnation, 'before the recollection of which all consolation vanishes, and, it seems to me, must always vanish' (Letter to Newton, 16 October, 1785). (April) Moved by Newton to the Vicarage. (October) Once more tries to commit suicide.

1774   (May) After recovery returns to Orchard Side.

1779   (February) Publication of *Olney Hymns*.

1780   (June) Newton goes to London as vicar of St. Mary Woolnoth. C. composes a number of shorter poems and (December) begins to write *The Progress of Error* and *Truth*. Starts friendship with the Revd. William Bull, dissenting minister of Newport Pagnell.

1781   (January) Publishes anonymously the verse essay *Anti-Thelyphthora*, refuting his cousin Martin Madan's defence of polygamy. Writes *Table Talk*, *Expostulation* and *Charity*. (July) First meeting with Lady Austen. (August) Begins *Retirement*.

1782   (March) Publication of his first volume, *Poems, by William Cowper, of the Inner Temple, Esq.* Begins translations of the French Quietist, Madame Guion. (October) Writes *John Gilpin*, which is published anonymously in *The Public Advertiser* in November.

1783   (October) *The Task* begun at the suggestion of Lady Austen.

1784   End of friendship with Lady Austen; first acquaintance with the Throckmortons of Weston Hall near Olney. (October) *The Task* completed and sent to the publisher, Joseph Johnson. (November) Finishes *Tirocinium* and begins the translation of Homer.

1785   'The Poplar Field' and other poems appear in *The Gentleman's Magazine*. (July) *The Task* published. (October) Resumes correspondence with Lady Hesketh, with the result that she and 'Anonymous' (probably Theadora, her sister) send him financial help.

1786   Lady Hesketh becomes tenant of Olney vicarage. (November) C. moves to The Lodge, Weston Underwood. (29 November) Death of the Revd. William Unwin.

1787   Fourth period of derangement.

1788   Writes ballads against slavery. (September) Starts trans-
        lating the *Odyssey*.

1790   (January) First visit from his young kinsman John Johnson
        ('Johnny of Norfolk'). (February and May) Writes 'On the
        Receipt of my Mother's Picture' and 'Sonnet to Mrs.
        Unwin'. C. is considered for the Laureateship, left vacant
        by the death of Thomas Warton.

1791   (July) Translation of Homer published, bringing Cowper
        £1,000 and the copyright. (September) Agrees with Joseph
        Johnson to edit Milton. (December) Mrs. Unwin para-
        lysed by a stroke.

1792   (May) Is visited by William Hayley, who is working on a
        life of Milton; Mrs. Unwin has a second seizure. (1
        August–17 September) C., Mrs. Unwin, and John John-
        son stay with Hayley at Eartham Place, Sussex. (Autumn)
        Collapses again into a state of acute depression, and comes
        under the influence of the Olney schoolmaster Samuel
        Teedon, interpreter of dreams.

1793   (Autumn) Mrs. Unwin's condition deteriorates; C. com-
        poses the stanzas 'To Mary'. (November) Hayley comes to
        Weston in the hope of helping Cowper's recovery; Lady
        Hesketh arrives to manage his household.

1794   The fifth and last breakdown begins. (April) Granted a
        pension of £300 per annum by the King, largely through
        Hayley's efforts. (May) Mrs. Unwin's third stroke.

1795   Cowper and Mrs. Unwin taken by John Johnson to
        Norfolk, first to North Tuddenham and Mundesley (July–
        October) and then Dunham Lodge, near Swaffham.

1796   (October) Finally settles in Johnson's own house at East
        Dereham. (17 December) Death of Mrs. Unwin.

1797   Begins revising the translation of Homer.

1799   (8 March) Completes revision of Homer. (12 March)
        Writes 'Montes Glaciales'. (20–25 March) Writes 'The
        Castaway'.

1800   (January) Falls ill with dropsy. (25 April) Death of
        Cowper. (2 May) Buried at East Dereham parish church.

I

Approaches to Cowper

There are good reasons for accepting Norman Nicholson's contention that 'from the end of the eighteenth century to nearly the middle of the nineteenth, William Cowper was probably the most widely read—at least, in England—of any English poet'.[1] The standard *Bibliography* lists well over a hundred editions of his poems in Britain, and almost fifty in America, between 1782 and 1837, the year in which Southey completed the monumental *Life and Works of Cowper*. By all accounts his first collection, in 1782, made no great stir, though the attention it received from the literary reviews suggests that Samuel Greatheed was exaggerating when he claimed that it was practically unknown outside the small circle of John Newton's religious friends.[2] *The Task*, however, was an immediate and universal success. According to Southey no poem had won fame for its author more quickly, and by 1812 Crabb Robinson could report that the publisher Joseph Johnson had earned a profit of around £10,000 from the sale of Cowper's verse.[3]

But, as Byron saw, Cowper 'lived at a fortunate time for his works':[4] he was, whatever else, the champion of reformed Christianity and humanitarian values during a period when the tide of the Evangelical Revival, expressed as much in the moral zeal of men like Wilberforce as in the Wesleys' call to salvation, was at its highest. In 1812 Francis Jeffrey estimated the size of the middle-class reading public at about 200,000, as against 20,000 more cultured, presumably upper-class, readers, and Carlyle no doubt had the former category in mind when remarking in 1829 that Cowper was still the favourite poet of 'the religious classes'.[5] A more solid guide to the basis of Cowper's immense popularity is the fact that Southey's professional edition sold only 6,000 copies, compared with

Notes and References begin on page 323

32,000 for the rival *Life and Works* (1835) by the Revd. T. S. Grimshawe, which had been produced specifically for the Evangelical market and advertised from the pulpit.[6]

With Cowper, then, we are more than usually aware of the possible gulf between popular regard and genuine literary merit and standing; and there was always the danger that his close links with a religious movement—and a particular branch to boot, namely the Calvinistic 'Methodism' of Whitfield and Newton—might hamper recognition of his artistic and imaginative qualities. Byron himself in fact condemned him for the very piety which recommended his writings to so many, calling him 'that maniacal Calvinist and coddled poet' and on one occasion denying him the title of poet altogether.[7] Comments like Hannah More's (the corollary of Byron's) that he was an author who could be safely given to young ladies for Sunday reading, seem likelier still to send us into full retreat from his work.[8] Moreover, even if we forget religion and think more generally of the contemporary setting, then again Cowper's early reputation will hardly tell in his favour: his was an age, after all, which virtually ignored Blake and applauded *The Rolliad*, Hayley's *Triumphs of Temper*, and Erasmus Darwin's *Botanic Garden*.[9]

However, while Cowper's original success may thus be seen to work against his future status in certain respects, encouraging signs and helpful material do emerge among the responses of the reviewers, some of whom welcomed him, at times fervently, as a wholly fresh *poetic* voice and were ready to celebrate his virtues, including his moralism, on considered literary grounds. The salient points are worth recalling.

The 1782 volume—consisting chiefly, we remember, of the eight rhymed discourses known later as the Moral Satires—had its detractors, above all *The Critical Review*, which spoke vaguely of 'flat and tedious' matter and 'weak and languid' verses.[10] But Hazlitt was wrong to say that 'the Monthly Reviewers' quoted from these poems only 'to shew that Cowper was no poet', for *The Monthly Review* itself was entirely favourable in its remarks, declaring Cowper a poet *sui generis* who had achieved a wholly original blend of satire, humour and devout reflection, all in a style that was at once both lucid and vigorous and far superior to the efforts of those (unfortunately nameless) modern versifiers that confined themselves 'like pack horses to the same beaten track and uniformity of pace' with bells 'jingling along in uninterrupted unison'.[11] Again and again the reviewer (Edmund Cartwright) reaches the same enthusiastic conclusion: Cowper far outstrips all other latter-day imitators of Pope, not only on account of the earnestness of his subjects and uncomplicated vitality of the couplets, but because the poetry everywhere expresses an individual personality—'Hence his very religion has a smile that is arch, and his sallies of humour an air that is religious.'

In 1785 *The Task* was praised by all, but especially *The Monthly Review* and *The Gentleman's Magazine*. The latter, after designating Cowper 'the poet of nature and humanity', goes on to illustrate at length his various merits: his 'natural and unforced language' and the uncommon 'harmony and variety' of his blank verse, the realism and beauty of his vignettes of rural life and scenery, his 'benevolence', and the interest of his introspective, at times melancholy, frame of mind.[12] Samuel Badcock in *The Monthly Review*[13] is a livelier, if sometimes over-rhapsodic, critic. He begins by condemning what he calls the 'vacant insipidity' of recent poetry, and then proceeds to commend *The Task* in terms of the neo-classical theory that art should instruct through pleasure. Cowper is 'always moral, yet never dull: ... He frequently entertains by his comic humour; and still oftener awakens more serious and more tender sentiments ... by descriptions that sooth and melt the heart, and rouse and terrify guilt in its closest retreats.' His style, 'seldom rich and ornamented, yet ... vigorous and animated', carries the thought 'to the heart with irresistible energy'. But informing and uniting every part of the poem are the author's own 'noble and generous mind', 'tender, virtuous and good' character and 'enraptured imagination'—which have finally become for Badcock the most important ingredients in Cowper's appeal. To a work so rich in *feeling*, he concludes, a critic can in the end only respond with fervour, laying aside perforce his habits of cool inspection.

These reviews bring home to us just how positively Cowper's resourceful moralism and 'plain' but forcible style were valued in his own day. What is being approved in this, of course, is his adherence to, and reassertion of, long-established Augustan ideals. 'Natural and unforced language', 'seldom rich and ornamented, yet ... vigorous and animated': for analogies we need go no farther than Denham's famous eloquent petition for the gift of fluent, purposeful, and moderated force, in lines so often quoted in the eighteenth century:

> O could I flow like thee, and make thy stream
> My great example, as it is my theme!
> Though deep, yet clear, though gentle, yet not dull,
> Strong without rage, without ore-flowing full.
>   (*Cooper's Hill*, ll.189–92)[14]

And Badcock's, or Cartwright's, persistent interest in the fact that Cowper has something useful to say and never subordinates matter to manner so as to court 'vacant insipidity' can likewise be tracked back quite easily to the *Essay on Criticism*, where Pope attacks the 'tuneful fools' who 'haunt Parnassus but to please their ear,/Not mend their minds; as some to Church repair,/Not for the doctrine, but the music there' (ll.341–3).

These, the basic 'late-Augustan' features of Cowper's poetry —which, as we shall see, were ones he himself always prized—were subsequently to find fewer and fewer advocates; and it is very much to the point that *The Monthly Review* and *The Gentleman's Magazine*, where they figure most prominently, were the two oldest surviving periodicals, both with a reputation for rearguard critical opinions.[15] But it is abundantly clear, too, that even here the emphasis does ultimately fall on what may, if loosely, be called 'Romantic' qualities—on the way Cowper's poetry is so patently rooted in the activity of the individual's feelings and imagination, and in a love of nature and mankind. One notices how often the reviewers stress the presence of Cowper's 'self' within and behind the poetry of *The Task*, or focus directly upon its autobiographical content: '... all who read him must be curious to know him and his communications, and grieve that such a writer, such a man, ever had an arrow in his side'.[16] When Badcock praises Cowper for bearing his message 'to the heart with irresistible energy' he recalls fairly precisely Pope's implicit belief in the superiority of spontaneous 'wit', which strikes directly at the affections, over any attachment to 'correctness' or the primacy of reason:

And snatch a grace beyond the reach of art,
Which without passing thro' the judgment, gains
The heart, and all its ends at once attains.
                    (*Essay on Criticism*, ll. 155–7)

Yet 'the heart' plays a much greater role in Badcock's article than this. Morality itself becomes for him a question of 'tender sentiment', of sensibility rather than sense. Nor is he beyond allowing himself to be helplessly carried away by the sheer delight of reading Cowper, in whose company he had 'got on fairy ground, and *had eaten Lotus*'. Such relish for the enchantments of poetry would certainly have been too much for the subscriber who wrote to *The Gentleman's Magazine* complaining that their reviewer, and apparently the author of *The Task* himself, underestimated the importance of the intellect![17]

The picture which begins to form, of a poet mirroring and contributing to a transitional phase within the literary-historical process, is brought into much sharper focus by Alexander Knox's outstanding appraisals of Cowper in *The Flapper*, a Dublin periodical, during 1796. First, however, something should be said about Cowper's standing with other poets and imaginative writers. The evidence suggests that he was, on the whole, greatly respected—at least until the nineteenth century was well under way. Burns, for example, thought him by far the best poet since Thomson and referred to *The Task* as 'a glorious poem',[18] while Blake (who was eventually to provide the illustrations for Hayley's *Life and Writings of Cowper* in 1803) compared him favourably with Milton. He was not only Jane Austen's favourite poet, but the authority to which she instinctively appealed in support of her ideals of social stability, good sense and civilized conduct, those traditional virtues which she opposed to metropolitan corruptness and the new acquisitive commercialism.[19] If Jane Austen's relation to Cowper casts him in a decidedly conservative role, Coleridge judged him quite simply 'the best of modern poets', the first to reconcile 'the heart with the head' and unite 'natural thoughts with natural diction'—formulations which put in a nutshell an idea generally present in the reviews of *The Task*.[20] In due course we shall explore Cowper's actual influence on the first generation of Romantics as a model of new ways of writing and of experiencing the world. All that need be said here is that they took him much more seriously than their immediate successors. Where there is censure it is in the second generation—in Byron (who did nevertheless sometimes borrow from Cowper), or Leigh Hunt, who decided that Cowper 'was alone, not because he led the way, but because he was left on the road side'.[21] He could never have meant much to poets of such a different order as Shelley or Keats (though again Keats seems to have been struck by some ideas and phrases).[22] The truth is that Cowper was by this stage losing ground with more sophisticated readers, which he was to regain in some measure during the Victorian period. Hazlitt is usually a good test of received opinion, and he, writing in 1818, admits that Cowper is 'a genuine poet, and deserves all his reputation' only after warning his audience that 'there is an effeminacy about him, which shrinks from and repels common and hearty sympathy'.[23]

It is Alexander Knox's ability to theorize about Cowper's peculiar originality that sets his critique so decisively above anything else that was written about his poetry in these early decades.[24] Although he was a theologian and friend of John Wesley, Knox refers only once, in a fine parting flourish, to specifically religious sources of inspiration—'His imagination as well as his language . . . heightened by his deep acquaintance with the Holy Scriptures'—and concentrates, rather, on Cowper's power of stimulating, even in the relatively unlettered, an awareness of the miracles of the commonplace, a fresh and salutary interest in the events everyday enacted in nature and in human life:

> We wonder at the interest we now for the first time take in what we have so often seen without any pleasurable sensation, and wonder still more that such an effect should be so easily produced; we observe . . . an execution as artless as the conception is vigorous.

Cowper 'thinks with the wise' but speaks to all men, describing in 'a language intelligible even to the vulgar . . . what the village swain has contemplated in common with the philosopher'. We notice at once that the reviewers' routine tribute to Cowper's plain and natural style has been replaced by a more speculative

and idealistic attitude which attributes to *The Task* (for that is
the poem under consideration) a democratizing and educative
function. Behind this view lies an obvious allegiance to certain
traditional religio-moralistic assumptions—traditional, that is,
to Methodism and Dissent. Cowper is, for Knox, a version of
the popular preacher, a literary counterpart to Wesley,
ministering to the interior needs of all classes of society but
especially the lower ones. When the student-minister in Mark
Rutherford's *The Revolution in Tanner's Lane* is told after his first
sermon that 'in the villages we cannot be too plain' he is being
instructed in one of the foremost rules of his profession; and it is
in the same novel, which portrays the life of a rural community
in the earlier part of the nineteenth century, that we learn—
from a passing, and therefore all the more persuasive, observation—that Cowper did indeed exercise a positive ennobling
influence among the less articulate, who were sometimes
'touched by dawn or sunset' and prompted by the stars to
'unanswerable interrogations' although they knew no other
literature save Dr. Watts and Pollok's *Course of Time*.[25] Knox
and Rutherford help us to put our finger on something
important in Cowper's achievement: no poet, except perhaps
Wordsworth, did as much to sensitize the ordinary human
imagination. He appealed, like the preacher, to the soul, but on
a more secular plain, encouraging deeper, fuller and more
sympathetic relations with the world. He taught pleasure,
insight, and humane instinct where otherwise there might have
been none.

To Knox, then, Cowper was the new sublime. He mentions
Longinus's *On the Sublime* at one point and may well have had in
mind from the beginning the key dictate of that popular
treatise, that 'at all times, and in every way, what transports us
with wonder is more telling than what merely persuades or
gratifies us'.[26] But Longinus, and his latter-day disciples such
as Joseph Warton ('Men love to be moved, much better than to
be instructed'), were concerned with grandeur and amplification—what Dr. Johnson calls 'that comprehension and ex-
panse of thought which at once fills the whole mind, and of
which the first effect is sudden astonishment, and the second
rational admiration'.[27] Knox, on the other hand, prefers milder
stimulants, and so adapts the Longinian concept of art's

emotive sources and potential to a belief in the poetry which deals quietly, faithfully, in familiar things. Instead of reducing the reader 'to the sterile pleasure of inactive contemplation', as Pope in Knox's view often does, Cowper 'inspires' him with 'a power of thinking for himself' and, discounting the refinements of the intellect, excels in forming 'ideal pictures ... with nearness to nature and fact ... and in expressing what he himself feels so as to make others participate in his feelings'. In all of this Cowper displays the indefinable creative 'soul' by which 'a poet chiefly differs from a common man'.

As these quotations indicate, Knox's position, and occasionally his phrases, are very close to those of the Preface to *Lyrical Ballads* (which first appeared some four years after the *Flapper* articles). Knox and Wordsworth are both committed (for there is much of the legislator in Knox) to poetry that chooses incidents from common life, relates them in a selection of the language really used by men, and casts over them a colouring from the writer's own spirit whereby they are presented to the mind in an unusual way. Knox's Cowper is nothing more or less than—to cite again Wordsworth's memorable phrases—'a man speaking to men' but endued 'with more lively sensibility ... and a more comprehensive soul'.[28] The ultimate effect of his poetry is

> ... to restore the mind to its safe and natural habits and to awaken ... those capacities of guiltless delight which, though still existing in the soul, are too frequently benumbed by the opiates of luxury.

This hardly measures up to Wordsworth's incisive defence of his own attempts to prove that 'the human mind is capable of being excited without the application of gross and violent stimulants'; and neither does 'the opiates of luxury' have the urgency of his conviction that the tempo of urbanization threatened to subdue the mind 'to a state of almost savage torpor'. Yet the stance is remarkably similar.

The similarity does, of course, suggest the possibility of direct influence. In the present context, however, the point is that it prompts awareness of the vital literary-historical significance of Cowper's cultivation during the 1780s of a gift for lending depth and novelty to things commonly known but commonly overlooked. Reading Knox, we feel that without Cowper's example Wordsworth and Coleridge could never have aimed so confidently—with such assurance that what they were doing was both worthwhile and achievable—at, in Coleridge's words, 'awakening . . . attention from the lethargy of custom, and directing it to the loveliness and the wonders of the world before us'.[29] These words return us, moreover, to Knox's and Cowper's religious leanings. Not the least of those traditions of Protestant thought which Cowper carried over into mainstream literature was a thoroughgoing appreciation of the underlying profundity of everything in the Creation, expressed according to the principle that 'it is the sensibility of the soul [and not the reason] that must receive what this world can communicate to it; it is the sensibility of the soul that must receive what God can communicate to it'.[30]

Cowper's main advocate in the first part of the nineteenth century was the poet Bowles. After Knox his comments are a notable disappointment, his effusive admiration for Cowper's 'affecting and beautiful pictures' of nature and 'common circumstance' ('how clothed with the light and hues of heaven . . . brightening into the sunshine of the most exquisite and living poetry') being the less convincing because it is the hinge of a partisan, and by any standard shallow, attack on Pope as the poet of 'artificial life', during the prolonged debate over Pope's merits known as the Bowles–Byron controversy.[31] Hazlitt, we recall, had mixed feelings about Cowper. To him the alternative poetry is not so much Pope's as Thomson's, whose *Seasons* he finds greatly superior to the more elegant descriptions of a writer who peers at nature 'over his clipped hedges, and from his well-swept garden-walks'.[32] This looks forward to the way in which Cowper was later to suffer from comparison with the bolder 'sublimity' of Romantic poetry. Walter Bagehot's essay in the *National Review* in 1855, for example, draws a straight contrast between Cowper and Wordsworth, much to the former's disadvantage.[33] What Cowper 'has really left us', in Bagehot's opinion, 'is a delicate and appreciative delineation of the simple essential English country'; in his poetry 'Nature is simply a background, . . . a space in which the work and mirth of life pass and are performed'. Cowper sketches 'the object before him, and there he leaves it', Wordsworth is never satisfied 'unless he describe the reflected high-wrought feelings which that object excites'.

Bagehot's aim is to put Cowper in perspective. That he felt it necessary to do so, and could automatically offer a serious comparison with Wordsworth, bears witness of course to Cowper's still continuing popularity. But this Bagehot attributes to the modest scope of his talents and subject-matter, and to his adoption by the 'still considerable portion of the English world' which rejects all other poets for 'distracting the soul from an intense consideration of abstract [theological] doctrine'. Cowper's name is a household word—and here, in the end, Bagehot becomes rather less slighting—because he dresses in a 'sober suit of well-fitting expressions' what the English really prefer, their native scenery, the 'gentle round of "calm delights"', the 'petty detail of quiet relaxation'. No poet is 'more exclusively English', a 'possession . . . on which we can repose . . . even in the acute crises of life'.

There is no mention in Bagehot of Cowper's shorter poems, some of which had passed into that body of verse which was read and known almost as a matter of course—the patriotic and declamatory stanzas of 'Boadicea' and 'Toll for the brave', *John Gilpin*, the best of the hymns, and those poems, 'The Castaway' and others, which record with singular frankness the experiences of a mind deeply conscious of a personal tragic destiny. The Brontë sisters, Elizabeth Barrett Browning, Tennyson, and Sainte-Beuve all testify to the tense pathos and cathartic power of this last group, Sainte-Beuve to the point of self-identification: 'venez à moi, mes chères Muses, mes morts chéris en qui je me réfugie avec transports contre les injures du présent, Théocrite, Parny, Cowper, vous qui avez souffert aussi, consolez moi'.[34] This apart, Bagehot's essay gives a fair idea of Cowper's position in the second half of the century. Edition after edition, cheaply printed or ornately produced for presentation, commanded big sales; and there was among the critics a steady regard for his accurate and urbane portrayals of the English countryside and 'life's daily round', often accompanied by a connected sense of the relative limitations of his vision. And that, I think, is still the usual view—much more the rule than the exception. One notices, for instance, how precisely Bagehot is echoed by D. J. Enright: 'For sharp and

appreciative observation of nature Cowper is often excellent'
but he never 'rises to [Wordsworth's] direct and powerful
vision'.[35] But the fact is that the twentieth century seems to
have cared more for Cowper the man than for Cowper the poet.

Biography flourished from the start, largely under the
impetus of argument over the causes of his madness, instigated
by the assertion of the Anglican press that Cowper's affliction
was a terrible warning against the effects of strict Calvinism.
(As might be expected, when Hayley attempted a balanced
interpretation of the facts in his *Life* he was immediately
accused of bias by both parties.)[36] A later extension of this
debate then brought a whole succession of writers into dispute
about the relation between Cowper's religion and inspiration,
so that we find Hugh I'Anson Fausset claiming that Cowper's
creativity was disastrously restricted by his need to use poetry
as a medium for governing his dread of a tyrannical God, and,
at the other extreme, Norman Nicholson and Gilbert Thomas
believing (more justifiably) that Evangelicalism was the
catalyst which released his latent sympathy with Man and
Nature.[37] This polemic, together with a general interest in his
life, has inevitably distracted attention from his specifically
literary endeavours and achievements. Indeed, so great has
been the preponderance of biography and biographical-cum-
historical interpretation that Fausset's opening announcement
that 'Cowper's life offers more of an adventure in understanding than his poetry' appears entirely plausible. Excellent
though they sometimes are when discussing the poetry,
Thomas's *William Cowper and the Eighteenth Century*, M. J.
Quinlan's recently reprinted *William Cowper, a Critical Life*
(Minneapolis, 1953) and W. N. Free's *William Cowper*, the
latest book to be devoted solely to Cowper, have Fausset's
assumption built into their very titles.

It is true that knowledge of an author's life, environment,
and milieu will often cast valuable light on his work, and that
Cowper strongly invites the use of such knowledge. The world
of his poetry is coloured always by the circumstances which
shaped his real existence, most of all by the mental instability
that had driven him to the seclusion of Olney. No comprehensive critical study can properly ignore such important 'external' factors, or the unusually rich background material that

reaches us from his own pen and from those who knew him. His prolific correspondence and autobiographical *Memoir* take us deep into the recesses of his personality: nowhere is there a finer web of intimate self-revelation.[38] Nevertheless, it is wrong to say that Cowper's poems are 'but an echo of his life', and wrong to imply that they offer comparatively little 'adventure in understanding'; for they possess in abundance that autonomous, self-sufficient life which it is the primary function of criticism to explain and evaluate (a function, let it be said, that was first seriously promoted by contemporaries of Cowper, in Alexander Gerard's *Essay on Genius* (1774) and other antecedents to Coleridge's insights into the processes of imaginative creation and the organic nature of literary form). But this is to present premature conclusions. We must be content at this stage with saying what would be taken for granted when beginning to tackle perhaps any other poet; namely, that it will be in Cowper's works, if anywhere, and pre-eminently in his poetry, that his experiences and situation take on profound or universal significance, having been enriched by the imagination, ordered by the intellect, made communicable by art. It will be there that his fullest self becomes operative and expressed; there that any formative interaction goes on between personality and environment—*formative* because identity and 'outer' phenomena (intellectual influences as well as physical settings) are, both of them, re-created and changed in the process of composition. The poetry mixes reverberations from and complex orchestration of the life rather than being its 'echo': its Cowper is more, not less, than the 'biographical' Cowper.

It remains to look briefly at the few recent critics who have been ready to defend Cowper's achievement as poet. D. J. Enright's essay—which is important since it is, I think, the only one liable to fall into the hands of readers not already searching for material on Cowper—starts with the guarded judgement that 'although he is unlikely to enjoy any future vogue, he has something to offer which will never fall entirely out of fashion or out of date'.[39] This problem of Cowper's durability, of the extent to which he can still appeal in spite of the radical decline of his popularity, naturally looms large in the minds of his admirers. Morris Golden solves it by an appeal to the 'permanence' of the emotional tensions and drives transmitted by his poetry—a desire for freedom and a need for authority, a yearning for both solitude and society—which 'have their counterparts in all of us': 'we admire and react because what we are reading is a sympathetic and terribly honest portrayal of man's fate, organized around and culminating in a vision of what all men have sought—the final balance of all conflicts, a perfect and eternal stability'.[40] Yet in so far as the purpose of Golden's fine study of this powerful psycho-drama is to show Cowper's lasting relevance, his intentions are subverted by his refusal to say anything precise about the ways in which the poet's preoccupations are formulated—that is, about his art, which is surely essential to any consideration of whether or not he is worth reading, or indeed readable at all. Where Cowper *is* argued for on a more critical basis, however, the result can be positively discouraging. Lodwick Hartley, for instance, sums up, in a chapter entitled 'The Aspect of Permanence', with the statement that 'the ability to set down what one sees or experiences with sincerity, simplicity and accuracy is a first-rate artistic gift no matter what the size of the canvas happens to be'.[41] We are back with Bagehot. In the second half of the twentieth century such terms of praise could never be more than a weak apology. Here is Hartley again: Cowper 'simply looked about him ... what he saw of beauty and peace he took to himself with quiet delight. What he saw of suffering and pain he took to himself with warm compassion.'[42] Alexander Knox was infinitely more persuasive.

Both Hartley and Enright have a healthy consciousness of Cowper's neglect: as the latter puts it, even 'his admirers have made little attempt to justify Cowper the poet'. But neither goes very far towards meeting the requirements of a revaluation, being largely satisfied with generalizations about a quiet if individual voice, the freshness and realism of his descriptions, his humane and sometimes witty moralizing. To be fair, Enright intends only a mild recommendation, and executes it brilliantly. Hartley, on the other hand, appears to know, and admit, that he has undersold the poet he set out to reinstate, when he makes a last desperate bid to tip the balance by rearranging one of Cowper's letters as if it were free-verse!

The scene has changed little since these two essays despite

P. M. Spacks's analysis of Cowper's complex vision of the natural world and Free's balanced discussion of the private and public elements in Cowper's work, although there have been one or two signs lately that the former may at last be having an effect among American scholars.[43] One thing is certain: the older view of Cowper, established by Bagehot and endorsed by repetition right down to the present, needs to be displaced by an adequate sense of the intricacy, force, and essential modernity of much of what Cowper wrote. To talk of his 'charming, tender, and unsophisticated' verses (Enright), or, to push on into the current decade, of his 'relaxed, confident and rhetorical' thinking or leisurely disposition of 'particular incidents and details',[44] is hardly likely to ensure his survival as, in Leavis's still effective phrase, a 'living classic'. Such judgements do not begin to go far enough, giving the false impression of an undemanding, unambitious poet. Believing like Bagehot that we have in Cowper a possession which is exclusively English, Edmund Blunden predicted in 1931 that 'our most natural interpreter . . . of the things we go out to see', our 'harmonist of country life', would probably be 'even more beloved in the future than he is now'.[45] Needless to say, this has proved a poor prediction of future literary taste. If Cowper is *only*, or indeed mainly, what Blunden, Hartley, Enright, and their successors say he is, then the likelihood is that he will fall increasingly into the category of a museum-piece. To be sure, as one sympathetic editor has remarked, whether Cowper is out of fashion or not doesn't affect his merits;[46] but the crux of the matter is precisely what those merits are—or what they can be seen to be when the poetry is tested in accordance with the analytical procedures we have come to favour as ways of appreciating and assessing literature, something which has so far rarely been attempted with Cowper.

The full significance, as I see it, of P. M. Spacks's contribution to the understanding of Cowper will emerge in later chapters. Her starting point, however, is the simple fact that Cowper is one of 'the most neglected of our poets' and 'the neglect is of analysis rather than . . . of attention', which leads her to avoid broad generalization—the usual refuge of Cowper criticism—in favour of urging the poetry to speak for itself in all its minutiae of style and content. She discovers in *The Task* an

evolving progress towards personal faith and fulfilment, traceable as much in the local texture of the poem as in its larger
movements and patterns: the act of perception, motivated at
first by Cowper's preacherly desire to honour God via the
richness and variety of the Creation, expands ultimately, in
moments of climactic imaginative intensity, into an act of 'such
total worship that it involves the poet's entire sensibility—his
desire for peace, for beauty, for piety' and brings him to 'his
ideal state of faith and ease'.[47] As its title suggests, her book
implies that Cowper is best understood in relation to those
contemporaries and immediate predecessors who were likewise
preoccupied with 'vision', with ways of 'seeing' and 'imagining'
the world and especially nature—in relation, that is, to
Thomson, Collins, Gray, and Smart. In this, as in such other
respects as its omission of all the shorter poems except a few of
the hymns, *The Poetry of Vision* gives an incomplete and
one-sided view of Cowper—Donald Davie makes an equally
good, if brief, case for linking him to the neo-classicism of
Goldsmith, Watts, Prior, and Dr. Johnson, thus placing him
within a tradition of cultured 'sobriety'.[48] But Spacks has her
finger firmly on the pulse of what is most central and most
original in Cowper's major poem: his discovery of nature as a
means of grace, a radical accomplishment which had profound
repercussions in English poetry. That, together with his
attendant loss of faith in corporate life and ideals, both religious
and socio-political, and his struggles in the toils of isolation,
desperate self-consciousness, and potentially deadly imaginings will be our overruling concern.

2

Cowper the Poet: an Outline

The tendency among critics to underestimate the subtlety of Cowper's poetry is nowhere more apparent than in statements about *The Task*. I am not sure that Spacks is right to illustrate this point by reference to anything as old as Walter Bagehot's remark that in Cowper nature is 'simply a background ... a space in which the work and mirth of life pass and are performed', or J. A. Roy's description of *The Task*, in 1914, as 'the conversation of one dowered with no special gifts of intellect, ... a quiet man of humour and austerity with an intensely human hand-grip'.[1] Fausset, for whom Cowper 'never strove to discipline ideas to facts or to interpret facts ideally', is safer evidence; and to this can be added, say, the very recent critic who talks of 'a long desultory poem' in which Cowper sets down unashamedly and at random 'his own simple pleasures, activities and experiences'.[2]

Some of these views are more obviously inadequate than others. The most cursory reading of *The Task* will show that Cowper treated nature as an object of direct contemplation, and not 'simply a background'. But they all lose credibility when tested in relation to specific passages, where we regularly find intentions and effects well beyond the scope of any companionable conversationalist or casual verse diarist, if only a belief on Cowper's part in the importance of his concerns, or a marked agility in his response to the life around him, or the finely and firmly wrought texture of the verse and expression. We meet everywhere in Cowper a committed artist bent on influencing a wide audience, but one who also develops a close, personal and complex involvement in his subject-matter. He frequently 'interpret[s] facts ideally', if by this we mean

Notes and References begin on page 326

investing the bare material of factual and visual observation with 'ideal' life and meaning derived from the intellect, emotions, and imagination. Of course, without such qualities Cowper would hardly be a poet at all; at least, no more of a poet than, for instance, his virtually forgotten disciples Thomas Gisborne and James Hurdis, both of whom had quite as good an eye for the actual appearances of nature.

Cowper's powers of natural description are an obvious starting point. The following representative lines come from a section of *The Task* in which he seeks to convince 'inattentive man' of the divine energy eternally at work in the Creation:

> Where now the vital energy that mov'd,
> While summer was, the pure and subtile lymph
> Through th' imperceptible meand'ring veins
> Of leaf and flow'r? It sleeps; and th' icy touch
> Of unprolific winter has impress'd
> A cold stagnation on th'intestine tide.
> But let the months go round, a few short months,
> And all shall be restor'd. These naked shoots,
> Barren as lances, among which the wind
> Makes wintry music, sighing as it goes,
> Shall put their graceful foliage on again,
> And, more aspiring, and with ampler spread,
> Shall boast new charms, and more than they have lost.
>
> (VI,134–46)

While this does not belie the traditional idea that *The Task* is notable for its 'plainness' and fluency ('... he seems to have avoided nothing so much as the stiff pomposity so common to blank verse writers'),[3] it would be better characterized as a poetry of 'moderate difficulty', of the kind recommended by Alexander Gerard at the beginning of his *Essay on Taste* (1759):

> Even plainness and perspicuity becomes displeasing in an Author, when it is carried to excess, and leaves no room for exercising the reader's thought: and though great obscurity disgusts us, yet we are highly gratified by delicacy of sentiment, which always includes some degree of it, occasions a suspense of thought, and leaves the full meaning to be ... comprehended only on attending.[4]

Coleridge expressed much the same preference, and may well
have had Cowper in mind, when complaining that in Wordsworth's *Descriptive Sketches* 'the novelty and struggling crowd of
images, acting in conjunction with the difficulties of the style,
demanded always a greater closeness of attention than poetry
(at all events, than descriptive poetry) has a right to claim'.[5]
We see what Gerard and Coleridge mean: there can be
something distinctly appealing about a writer who makes
demands on our comprehension and perceptiveness—'rouses
the faculties to act' (Blake)—without constantly putting us
under strain. This said, however, the thing to note as we turn to
the passage is that there *is* a sustained and substantial activity
to be registered and explored.

In the first part of the extract Cowper's language is basically
one of exact definition, including terms reminiscent of the
concrete, rational idiom of science ('subtile lymph', 'stagnation', 'intestine'). Yet it is used not only to identify the processes
of nature in precise detail, but also to convey the peculiar 'feel'
of these processes. Although Cowper never takes us to the very
heart of natural phenomena as Keats does,[6] so that we
experience them from the inside, sensuously, he does possess an
exceptional gift for making us intimately aware of their hidden
life. In the opening sentence, in fact, diction and rhythm enact
the event so perfectly that the creative activity of the poet seems
to become the activity of nature itself. The long, muted vowels
and gentle but persistent movement of the verse, which checks
at 'mov'd', hovers, and then finds gradual release under the
pressure of this verb into a momentum of its own, do not so
much portray as *embody* the steady continuity of the pulse of leaf
and flower. The imperceptible becomes perceptible, almost
tangible, as 'meand'ring' makes present both the shape and
inner motion of the veins. We are conscious, all along, not
simply of how the poet perceives things, how they appear from
without, but of their essential quality, what they are. There
follows in the next sentence one of Cowper's favourite devices,
informal personification, which allows him to establish winter's
distinctive character, positively 'unprolific', and impart to his
verbal landscape the vividness of 'icy touch' and vigorous
weight of 'has impress'd'; but here too, where the writer's skill
is most noticeable, the spirit of nature seems to inhabit the

poetry, slowing its delicate 'tide', impoverishing the scene, imposing a 'cold stagnation'.

Clearly, the conventional interpretation of such lines—that Cowper is fashioning a faithful and graphic word-picture—will not do. Precedence cannot be so easily assigned, for in effect the energies and hand of the artist are at one with the energies and hand of nature. Instead of 'depiction' or 'delineation', we need to speak, somehow, of a merging, a coalescence, of Art and Nature. Another good example would be where (at lines 142–3) the wind whistles tunefully through the verse, passing away in a half-line ('sighing as it goes') in which the simultaneous lengthening and fading of the rhythm is nothing but the rush of nature's 'wintry music'. In analysis Cowper's sensitivity and technical expertise become manifest; he has a singularly controlled and instinctive rapport with the living universe. But it is impossible all the same to put aside the impression that the poetry is drawing life directly from, and bearing celebrative witness to, a field of forces external to the poet's self. We have at once both an act of constructive perception, a tribute to human capability, and the very workings of an autonomous Power, seemingly unmediated.

We can more conveniently project some of the implications of these fusions of potential opposites (Art and Nature, self and external forces) after we have looked further into the style of the passage. For whatever its subtleties it is plainly a style which shares (in Eliot's famous words) 'the virtues of good prose'. In keeping with Cowper's stated predilection for 'the familiar style', the art of making 'verse speak the language of prose without being prosaic',[7] there is no departure from normal linguistic usage, no dislocation of syntax, no idiosyncrasy. The pursuit of a poetic idiom remote from common use would have been as alien to him as to Dr. Johnson, for whom Gray's Odes, rooted in the notion that 'the language of the age is never the language of poetry', were not merely obscure but objectionable, so much glittering nonsense.[8] Clarity, sober elegance, 'purity' were the standards Cowper, an educated and educating poet, kept characteristically in mind—ideals which are social and moral as well as literary, and which he held in common with many of the more authoritative critics of the day, including (besides Johnson) Gerard, Hugh Blair and, later, Coleridge, whose radical embrace of the imagination did not prevent him from taking great pains to expound the civilizing value of poetry composed in 'pure and genuine mother English', free from the defects of 'arbitrary and illogical phrases' and the glare of 'fantastic' images.[9] Blair had a particular respect for the author guided by 'simplicity', in whose work you see 'not the writer and his labour, but the man in his own natural character'.[10] Cowper is an excellent instance of this exemplary type: 'the man in his own natural character', dedicated to cultured sobriety, about whom there is nothing ostentatious or theatrical.

Yet Blair's designation fits Cowper just as well in another sense—that of an individual recording his own responses, insights and thoughts in his own inimitable manner. And that manner, unelaborate though it is, has a marked metaphorical dimension. In Cowper 'plainness' does not exclude the advantages of figurative expression, especially as it serves to 'interpret facts ideally' and articulate patterns of meaning.

'Sleeps' (l.137), for example, is a prolepsis, introducing the idea of nature's cyclical progress: winter is a time, not simply of paralysis, but of *rest* before ampler renewal. The verb can function in this way, and with such precision, because of the partial personification of summer's 'vital energy' in the previous sentence, although it does so all the more effectively, too, because it stands out in a brief syntactical unit—'It sleeps'—which invites us to pause and concentrate. In the personification of winter itself we see a clichéd 'figure' deformalized, and enlivened by the activeness of 'touch' and 'impress'd', both of which exemplify Cowper's ability simultaneously to recover and employ the full original force of commonplace words. Thus both the link and the opposition between the seasons—the necessary, recuperative stasis of winter and life-supporting energies of summer—find memorable poetic statement at no expense to economy or logic.

In the second half of the passage Cowper relies more openly on metaphoric suggestion, to evoke the paradoxes of the season as a whole, a period of desolation and strange beauty, bleakness and life, sadness and hope. Firstly, he withdraws from the 'natural'/poetic rhythms in which his own voice has been submerged, in order to communicate—by means of repetition ('months ... a few short months'), capped by the grand inclusiveness of 'all shall be restor'd'—his mounting expectation of future renovation. Then follows a cluster of swiftly-changing images, the embodiment of his mobile response to a single object, the 'naked shoots': the impression of defenceless-ness in 'naked' is immediately modified by that of weapon-like strength in 'lances', while by another more extreme trans-formation the branches become a musical instrument played upon by the wind.[11] In this moment of perceptual complexity we have a conspicuous display of the process of give and take, the flexible and balanced interplay, between poet and nature which fills Cowper's poetry with so much vital authenticity, and which is on occasion so intimate that the gap between, on the one side, response/formulation and, on the other, the life of the Creation disappears. The initiative is taken first by the poet, who enhances nature, as an object of contemplation, by drawing attention to the nakedness of the shoots and by the unusual comparison in the simile of the lances. The position is reversed with the entry of the wind's 'wintry music', for, as we have already seen, in spite of the human terms of reference ('music', 'sighing') the effect is of a natural phenomenon making itself felt and heard; art gives way to nature, the poet yields to its stress, content to capture its accent. We listen to the 'music' of the wind, a real 'sighing'; the central paradox of the season, its mingling of beauty and sad desolation, is experi-enced first-hand, not as a mimic and interpretative perform-ance of style.

A final point. The passage is in a sense one large and meaningful image—a representation of the *discordia concors* of the natural universe as a whole. The various details of life and inactivity, motion and pause, relationship and opposition, all held within a progression from past to future, form ultimately an emblem of the harmonious diversity of the Creation—a concept enforced, moreover, by the curious fact that even as our focus is fixed upon the single object (a tree, or group of trees) we are encouraged to 'see' the wider landscape of which they are but an element, the landscape, that is, of river or stream ('meand'ring', 'stagnation', 'tide') and abundant vegetation (are the 'leaf and flow'r' and the 'shoots' those only of the tree, or of nature more generally?).

Now, behind Cowper's interest in this concept and in what he has just previously called 'the constancy of nature's course' (l.122) lies an intention to demonstrate the immanence and benign authority of God. He moves from God to nature and then back again to God:

> From dearth to plenty, and from death to life,
> Is Nature's progress when she lectures man
> In heav'nly truth; evincing, as she makes
> The grand transition, that there lives and works
> A soul in all things, and that soul is God.
>
> (VI,181–5)

It is here, in Book VI of *The Task*, that the Evangelical and preacherly bias of Cowper's approach to nature is at its strongest, in his inclination to treat all things as *logos* according to the conventional assumption that (in John Newton's words) 'They who know God ... may find both pleasure and profit in tracing his wisdom in his works.'[12] The reader is pressed first and last to profit in orthodox religious terms from what he has witnessed in the landscapes of summer and winter; to see the miracles as God's miracles, the design as the workmanship of the Artificer Divine, the movement from dearth to plenty as a lecture in heavenly truth.

On the other hand, Mark Storey misleads in stating categorically that Cowper's 'concern was seldom with nature for what it was: what mattered ultimately were the lessons to be drawn from it'.[13] The last thing Cowper could be accused of, where nature is involved, is rigid didacticism. His work shows remarkably little of the rationalizing habit so common in Newton and other religious meditators, who raid the Creation mechanically for useful doctrinal analogies such as (from the Newton passage cited above) that between 'the magnitude ... of the sun' and 'the Sun of righteousness, the source of light and life'.[14] There is perhaps one example of this mode of reading the Book of Nature in the lines recently quoted, where the phrase 'from death to life' (l.181), a conventional Christian formula, threatens to tie the foregoing experience of nature to simple illustrative and dogmatic ends—ends which would be unjustified in view of the fact that Cowper has registered winter less as 'death' than as a specific kind of life. But the danger passes when he shifts to a more general conclusion—'there lives and works/A soul in all things ...'—that is at the very least satisfactory so long as one is careful not to indulge a special disregard for a belief in God. In any case, if we have learned anything at all from analysing a passage of natural description it is that Cowper's wish to honour God and draw lessons from His Creation did nothing to undermine or restrict his capacity for engaging with nature as it is. Although, overall, he put God first, his nature poetry is itself as much a celebration of that capacity, of the self, as of the Creation or the Artificer Divine. Where now the vital energy that moved? There on the page, made to exist by the poet himself. Cowper's attack in Book I on those who 'Prefer to the performance of a God/Th'inferior wonders of an artist's hand' (ll.418–19) contains a verbal confusion that suggests he was subconsciously aware of a paradox running through the poem; for *wonders* are really superior to any *performance*, and the creative miracles of *The Task* always in a sense belong to, and elevate, the poet-artist rather than the God to whom he theoretically grants primacy. Yet our analysis also revealed a self-abnegation in favour of fidelity to, and celebrative respect for, the very processes of nature, which were for Cowper 'the soul in all things', God himself. In contemplating the Creation he achieved a balance, a bringing together on equal terms, a fluent interaction, of Art and Nature, self and God, satisfaction and duty, action from within and receptivity to influences from without. As we shall see, it is a balance which had to be struggled for, and which is a psychological as well as poetic high-point in his work, representing both an escape from an earlier restrictive allegiance to religio-moralistic aims and a way of supplying the felt absence of fullness, grace, and repose in his life from the strength of the subjective spirit in its sympathetic dealings with a divine and active universe.

We shall be looking next at the darker side of Cowper's personality and being-in-the-world which made his intercourse with nature such a stabilizing and saving factor in his existence; but whatever its personal motivation and significance this intercourse, this reciprocity, amounts to nothing less than a new aesthetic. In the giant of the former age, Pope, the ideal relationship of man to his natural environment had been one of

respectful improvement leading to the common social good—
as in the image of the Man of Ross's irrigation schemes which
copy and release nature's abundance, '... clear and artless,
pouring thro' the plain/Health to the sick, and solace to the
swain'.[15] In Cowper the ideal is of the isolated individual
communing with the power and presences of nature, which are
God; seeking, and finding, food for the spirit in an act of private
meditation.

*   *   *   *   *

Death-in-life, damnation, confinement, vulnerability, hang-
ing-on—such themes are no less characteristic of Cowper than
the happy contemplation of nature. The lines on the paralytic
in Book I of *The Task* are as good an example as more obvious
choices like 'The Castaway' or 'Lines written during a Short
Period of Insanity', and offer a better counterpart to the
passage we have already discussed:

> It is the constant revolution, stale
> And tasteless, of the same repeated joys,
> That palls and satiates, and makes languid life
> A pedlar's pack, that bows the bearer down.
> Health suffers, and the spirits ebb; the heart
> Recoils from its own choice—at the full feast
> Is famish'd—finds no music in the song,
> No smartness in the jest; and wonders why.
> Yet thousands still desire to journey on,
> Though halt, and weary of the path they tread.
> The paralytic, who can hold her cards,
> But cannot play them, borrows a friend's hand
> To deal and shuffle, to divide and sort,
> Her mingled suits and sequences; and sits,
> Spectatress both and spectacle, a sad
> And silent cypher, while her proxy plays.
> Others are dragg'd into the crowded room
> Between supporters; and, once seated, sit,
> Through downright inability to rise,
> Till the stout bearers lift the corpse again.

These speak a loud memento. Yet ev'n these
Themselves love life, and cling to it, as he
That overhangs a torrent to a twig.
They love it, and yet loath it; fear to die,
Yet scorn the purposes for which they live.
Then wherefore not renounce them? No—the dread,
The slavish dread of solitude, that breeds
Reflection and remorse, the fear of shame,
And their invet'rate habits, all forbid.

(I,462–90)

Inasmuch as it continues impressions of incapacity, torpor and joylessness from the earlier part of the passage the sketch of the paralytic and her surroundings (ll.472ff.) is a moral *exemplum*, a cautionary picture of the debility produced in man by the dull round of frivolous social pleasure—by the sort of environment which Cowper attacks just before and after the quotation in references to the fashionable world of people 'self-imprison'd in their proud saloons' (l.414), victims of 'gaiety that fills the bones with pain,/... the heart with woe' (ll.504–5). It is part of the general ethical design mentioned by the poet in a letter to William Unwin when claiming that *The Task* had a more regular plan than might be initially apparent, which was 'to discountenance the modern enthusiasm after a London life, and to recommend rural ease and leisure, as friendly to the cause of piety and virtue'.[16] The atrophy of the paralytic and the other 'corpses' shows in extreme form the sickness of body and soul that Cowper tends always to associate, accusingly, with 'the town'. It symbolizes the consequences of an *unnatural* existence. This prescriptive moralism is not, however, the sole, nor indeed primary, constituent of the passage. There is also a strong human interest. Things just happen in *The Task*—a sudden imaginative insight, an unexpected shift of perspective; so here, in the portrait of the broken votaries of pleasure, Cowper fixes on, and is fixed by, a tragic scene, the essence of which he concentrates in a few sharply expressive strokes so as to produce a universal image of death-in-life, an unforgettable revelation of the fundamental human experience of irrevocable isolation, helplessness, immurement in the confines of a futile, automatic survival. In the end it is his subjects' state of being—or non-being—that most interests him, not the moral implications of their choice of life; a concern with experiential and psychological truth more or less displaces didactic intent.

We have only to recall Gay's simplistic contrast between the fevered sullenness of the 'courtly dame' and cheerful good-looks of the 'rural maid' in *Rural Sports*, or (a nearer parallel) Young's bizarre comic portrait of the 'languid lady' who is so crippled by indolence that she must eat 'by proxy' and 'lolls, reels, staggers, till some foreign aid/To her own stature lifts the feeble maid', to appreciate Cowper's sensitivity and his 'humanization' of conventional satiric attitudes and subjects.[17] Pope's moving satire on women of fashion in the second Moral Essay:

> Beauties, like Tyrants, old and friendless grown,
> Yet hate to rest, and dread to be alone,
> Worn out in public, weary ev'ry eye,
> Nor leave one sigh behind them when they die...[18]

are an altogether different matter of course from Gay and Young, a subtle blend of censure and sympathy. Yet in its own graver way Cowper's understanding of the impotence of the devotees of false pleasure ('Spectatress both and spectacle, a sad/And silent cypher ...') is no less keen, his sense of how people cling slavishly to the familiar ('... can hold her cards,/But cannot play them') no less incisive. He peers just as seriously and feelingly into the prison-house, not only of 'proud saloons', but of the self.

The description could well be based upon a scene Cowper once witnessed in London, or during his visits to resorts like Margate and Brighton (which he condemned as places of 'idleness and luxury, music, dancing, cards ...');[19] but although it possesses the graphic realism of a picture drawn from first-hand observation, this finally matters less than Cowper's ability for generalizing the particular, for raising the concrete and literal to a representative status and significance. I have remarked already that the paralytic herself becomes an emblem, a 'spectacle', of hopeless isolation—an isolation made all the more shocking by her efforts to join in the rituals of her society, to play the cards. The cards, with their 'mingled suits and sequences', suggest the nature of life itself, unpredictable, beyond her or any man's control, a game of chance. Those two remarkably compact and pregnant phrases, 'Spectatress both and spectacle' and 'sad/And silent cypher', express the full horror of a fate to which all men are potentially exposed: the nightmare condition of silence and immobility, of exchanging proper identity for the role of passive onlooker. The setting, on one level so recognizably mundane, develops in Cowper's imagination the features of a hell-on-earth, a receptacle of lost souls and corpse-like bodies attended by 'bearers' who are no more free or alive than those they serve. And, as in the passage on winter, we should not let the seeming casualness of the 'familiar style' shut our eyes to Cowper's skill with words and rhythm: the arresting undertone of elegiac solemnity kept up by the measured pace of the verse and repeated alliteration on 's', 'p' and 'd' sounds; the use of energizing verbs, some ('borrows', 'dragg'd', 'sit') combining a descriptive with an interpretative function (we notice, for example, how 'borrows' signals in a word the paralytic's half-contact with life), some ('ebb', 'recoils', 'breeds') enlivening abstract argument by their metaphorical cogency; the pointedness gained from partial repetition ('Spectatress ... spectacle', 'once seated, sit') and more generally from straightforward, hard-hitting syntactical structures. All this, and especially the constant figurative content of the style, brings poetic and conceptual substance to what would otherwise be merely relaxed circumlocution, an exercise in the art of talking around a conventional issue.

But anyone who has read the passage carefully will realize that there is a problem. Perspicuity, fluency, and control are words one could apply to this instance of Cowper's 'familiar style' with very little confidence. There is no perfectly logical development of meaning throughout the passage as a whole, simply because Cowper is in two minds, undecided whether to settle for the negative or positive implications of his subject— that is, whether to stress the 'sickness' of those who 'desire to journey on' or to respect in them the human instinct to persist in the face of adversity and survive at all costs. The lines—

> Yet thousands still desire to journey on,
> Though halt, and weary of the path they tread.

and—

>   Yet ev'n these
>   Themselves love life, and cling to it, as he
>   That overhangs a torrent to a twig.

could bear either inference. Or is Cowper merely concerned with the pitiful *fact* of their predicament? The truth is that all three things are going on simultaneously; an inability in Cowper to take up a single-minded stance towards his subject gives rise to a composite, and enigmatic, effect in the poetry. (The one critic ever to have considered this passage highlights this effect, but only by blandly ignoring it, and everything else except the moral comment on the dangers of false pleasure.)[20] Or, to put it another way, *The Task* depends on the author's 'flow of consciousness', and the stream does not always run smooth and clear. This is particularly noticeable in the final movement of the passage. 'They love it [life], and yet loath it': is it man's zeal for life and resistance to death that matters to the poet, or the fact that some men can find no joy in life? Is he celebrating the spark of life or condemning a worthless life? They 'fear to die,/Yet scorn the purposes for which they live': the emphasis now appears to switch to the bitter irony that life, which no one can renounce, can be a curse from which the only escape is death, or suicide. Then there is a further complication of response in the final sentence—'No—the dread,/The slavish dread of solitude . . .'. Here Cowper points critically once more to the life of false pleasure, breeding place of heart-sickness and 'invet'rate habit', but, as in the preceding *exemplum*, the urge to admonish or condemn, the moral thrust of the poetry, is outweighed by the force of his insight into a representative human situation—a state where redemptive actions are impossible, where the individual is entrapped by his own feelings, by dread, by fear, by habit. By this stage the original alternative of a life close to nature, 'where Flora reigns' (l.455), has been forgotten, the poet having found his way into a web of uncertainty and complex reactions at the centre of which emerges the dark reality of irremediable despair.

Uncertainty and complex reactions: this is of course formally reflected in the style. Instead of the more lucid, progressive structuring of the winter passage, we have an accumulation of

relatively short and loosely connected units, which, though
highly effective in producing points of intensity, creates overall
an effect of strain and indecision. Qualification, extension, and
changes of direction, signalled by the use of semicolons and
dashes, and the words 'yet', 'but', and 'and', are frequent, so
that while the style does remain broadly 'conversational',
subtlety and ease of communication give way to the immediate
claims of tense, veering imaginative and mental experience.
Seen objectively, the comparative lack of poise may seem an
aesthetic flaw; it is nevertheless a measure of the peculiar
honesty—the unpremeditated authenticity—of Cowper's engagement with his subject. Some poets, of which the Byron of
Don Juan is a supreme example, can turn their subjects over in
their hands at will, holding them up in changing lights for the
reader's inspection and delight. Cowper is not like that. His is a
more spontaneous and more precarious 'flow of consciousness'.
Often things come suddenly upon him, or he is halted by some
unexpected recognition, or struggling for direction. And we feel
the effort. We are allowed right into his journeying mind.

But no mind travels quite at random or in territory it has not,
somehow, known before; and the subject of the paralytic
episode is one in which Cowper always had a deep interest. It is
hardly surprising in view of his own past that he should have
penetrated to the roots of, and struggled with, the experience:

> I never went into the street, but I thought the people
> stared and laughed at me ... They who knew me seemed to
> avoid me; and if they spoke to me they seemed to do it in
> scorn.

> I slept generally an hour in the evening, but it was only to
> be terrified in dreams; and when I awoke, it was some time
> before I could walk steadily through the passage into the
> dining room. I reeled and staggered like a drunken man.
> The eyes of man I could not bear ...

> I spent the rest of the day in a kind of stupid insensibility;
> undetermined as to the manner of dying, but still bent on
> self-murder, as the only possible deliverance.

This is from the account in the autobiographical *Memoir* of the
period of derangement brought on by having to stand a public

examination for the post of Keeper of the Journals.[21] Being cut
off and reduced to a silent spectacle, clinging to yet loathing life,
the toils of desperation—Cowper had knowledge enough of
such states.

It has been pointed out that the man writing the *Memoir* and
The Task is a model of sanity rather than a study in psychic
aberrancy.[22] All the same, the relation between the poetry and
the affliction described in so much detail in the *Memoir* is not a
simple case of the poet drawing on personal history from a safe
distance for his materials and psychological realism. For one
thing, Cowper had never truly thrown off the burden of that
affliction; the weight of conscious misery made itself felt even as
he was at work on *The Task* in the winter of 1784:

> I looked back upon all the passages and occurrences of it
> [the old year], as a traveller looks back upon a wilderness
> through which he has passed with weariness and sorrow of
> heart ... For, more unhappy than the traveller with whom
> I set out, pass through what difficulties I may, through
> whatever dangers and afflictions, I am not a whit nearer
> home, unless a dungeon may be called so ... The weather
> is an exact emblem of my mind in its present state. A thick
> fog envelops everything, and at the same time it freezes
> intensely. You will tell me that this cold gloom will be
> succeeded by a cheerful spring, and endeavour to encour-
> age me to hope for a spiritual change resembling it—but it
> will be lost labour. Nature revives again; but a soul once
> slain lives no more.[23]

In this, one of his many evocations of the pilgrimage motif
traditional to the Puritan vision of the individual's being-in-
the-world, Cowper conceives of his own life as a direct anti-type
of the progress of the elect soul. Unlike Christian in *The
Pilgrim's Progress*, for whom dangers and difficulties are necessary stages along the route to the Celestial City, he is the forlorn
traveller whose way leads nowhere unless it be to the 'dungeon'
(it is Bunyan's word too) of Despair, or the pit of Hell.[24] He
rejects in advance the encouragements of his spiritual guide,
Newton, who filled for him the roles of Bunyan's Evangelist,
Interpreter, and Faithful: nature is of consequence only in so
far as it emblematizes and feeds his insensible inner gloom, and

the standard consolation to be gleaned from her Book, that all things revive, is dismissed in favour of an acceptance of the sentence passed on him in his 'fatal dream' of 1773, *Actum est de te, periisti* ('It is all over with thee, thou hast perished').[25] Indeed, so black is the mood of this letter that if one had to cite a single character from *The Pilgrim's Progress* analogous to its author it would be the 'man of despair' shut up in the iron cage at Interpreter's House, who transforms all thought, of past, present, and future, of the self and the outer world, into fuel for his conviction that he is doomed to suffering in life and afterwards eternal damnation.[26] And this same dark side of Cowper's personality haunts the poetry. Though there is no palpable self-reference at all in the lines on the paralytic, they are inhabited by the daemon of his private desert places which produces, and broods on, morbid versions of reality. They are neither one of the 'horrible visions' of personal torment and death that, according to the *Memoir*, visited him during his stay in Dr. Cotton's asylum ('my prison-house') nor a paranoid projection such as he recounts when recalling how in the course of his madness he bought a ballad from a street-vendor because he thought it was written on him, but they do clearly signify a related propensity for perceiving life in the image of his own sufferings, as a landscape of disease, loneliness, and despair.[27] Moreover, the humane, generalized perspective of the passage is, as we have seen, accompanied by an undercurrent of excited, puzzled involvement in that landscape as Cowper comes face to face with what are, at bottom, representations of his fearful affliction and fate. There are always these two perils for Cowper: that his mind and imagination would generate only a life-denying pessimism, and that he would be overwhelmed by the pressure of gloomy self-centredness. His poetry is in large measure the story of his battle against them.

The melancholy preoccupations of the episode of the paralytic—death-in-life, insecurity, the terrible impasse of mere instinctive survival—emerge regularly in his poetry and letters, sometimes in direct personal utterance (of which the 'Lines written during a Short Period of Insanity', with their bitter sense of being 'buried above ground', is the extreme case) and sometimes more objectively, as in the portraits of Crazy Kate in *The Task* or the depressive in *Hope* ('Expressive of his mind, /His

eyes are sunk, arms folded, head reclin'd'). They persist to the
very end of his career, where he is gripped by the castaway's
ultimately futile struggle against a malign Fate:

> For then, by toil subdued, he drank
> The stifling wave, and then he sank.
> (ll.47–8)

'The Castaway' is an impressive poem, not least because
Cowper transcends the painfulness of his theme by plunging
wholeheartedly into it. Yet it bears striking witness all the same
to the fact that only in death did he find lasting release from the
insistent claims of cheerless and self-conscious vision. The
unselfconscious joy that he found in the contemplation of
nature was not an answer to those claims, but a counterpoise—
the reactive assertion of healthier capacities.

Writing to Newton in 1788 about the restlessness of his inner
life, Cowper complained that:

> When I have thought myself falling into the abyss, I have
> been caught up again; when I have thought myself on the
> threshold of a happy eternity, I have been cast down to
> hell. . . . I have no expectation but of sad vicissitude, and
> ever believe that the last shock of all will be fatal.[28]

This statement is interesting as evidence of his basic conviction
that his life's journey would inevitably end with his being
hurled down into the 'way to Hell' which in *The Pilgrim's
Progress* descends 'even from the Gates of Heaven', from the
very threshold of the Celestial City, but what immediately
concerns us is that the pattern he describes—a constant
swinging to and fro that will end in sudden and decisive
darkness—applies just as well to his work as to his spiritual
condition. Both in the poetry as a whole and more locally in *The
Task* and other individual poems, we are aware of a ceaseless
alternation between reverse sides of the poet's personality—
between the 'two natures' in man, 'joy the one,/The other
melancholy' (Wordsworth). The two passages we have considered in detail, which on one level further the public theme of
town versus country, are in essence representative of dominant
psychological polarities, of opposite ways of experiencing the
world which run through the entire corpus. The outgoing

celebrant of nature and nature's God, who loses himself in the
minutiae and processes of 'pow'r divine', won no victory over
the self-haunted explorer of God-forsaken landscapes and
states of dereliction. His imagination found its final abode in
the fated struggles of a drowning castaway; his last act of all was
to concede the inescapability of death and damnation.

Yet despite this oscillation and lack of progression *The Task*
itself did yield positive, and indeed invaluable, psychological
gains, for its composition offered Cowper the opportunity not
only of experimenting with the therapeutic advantages of
contemplating nature but of organizing a satisfactory personal
identity by reference to the time-honoured ideal of the sequestered man. The praise of happy seclusion by Vergil, Horace,
and the English Augustans helped him to accept his enforced
retirement at Olney (which he calls elsewhere his 'sepulchre')[29]
as a blessing:

> He is the happy man, whose life ev'n now
> Shows somewhat of that happier life to come;
> Who, doom'd to an obscure but tranquil state,
> Is pleas'd with it, and, were he free to choose,
> Would make his fate his choice; whom peace, the fruit
> Of virtue, and whom virtue, fruit of faith,
> Prepare for happiness; bespeak him one
> Content indeed to sojourn while he must
> Below the skies, but having there his home . . .
>
> (VI,906–14)

The 'He' is Cowper—the self placed, therapeutically, in a
welcome station. Of course, it is evident that the poet has not
discovered complete peace of mind: the words 'doom'd' and
'fate' in particular betray an irrepressible sense of deprivation,
even as it is being smoothed and held in check. Furthermore,
this lingering resentment over his fated obscurity does, I think,
compound our initial difficulty in respecting what amounts to a
rejection of the human potential for full participation in this life
and this world, a rejection so emphatic that retirement becomes
less an image of optimal civilized being than an escape into
dreams of a 'happier life to come'. Cowper is a prisoner
still—making the best of a bad job. Yet making the best of
things was important to him: his use of the theme of rural

retreat—which, as we shall see, he developed over the length of two very substantial poems, *Retirement* and *The Task*—was a necessary stabilizing strategy, and a successful one in that it allowed him to see alienation as privilege, confinement as good fortune.

His cultivation of heightened perception has a similar personal significance. P. M. Spacks shows that in the later stages of *The Task* Cowper asserts that a sound relation with God is a necessary precondition for heart-felt enjoyment of nature:[30]

> Acquaint thyself with God, if thou would'st taste
> His works. Admitted once to his embrace,
> Thou shalt perceive that thou wast blind before . . .
>
> (V,779–81)

He had, however, expressed this idea in full as early as *Retirement*, where he interprets the melancholic's recovery from psychic paralysis in terms of a saving intervention by God leading in turn to knowledge of God and exceptional sensitivity to the Creation, now a paradise of 'delights unfelt before' (ll.341ff.). Thus the ability to appreciate nature's gifts was always for Cowper a touchstone of one's spiritual condition, and in exercising that ability in himself he was, in effect, proving his own state of grace. Prey though he was to recurrent dejection, accompanied by an incapacity to be renewed in the presence of nature—'Nature revives again; but a soul once slain lives no more'—the poetry of the 1780s is primarily a poetry of faith and hope, in which the gift of perceptual power counters melancholy's phantoms not only by bringing a rich harvest of active delight but also by operating as a sign of personal wholeness and God's favour.

*　　*　　*　　*　　*

The confessional and psychodramatic elements of Cowper's poetry are the life-blood of his originality. We cannot go too far, however, before facing the thorny problem of his often austere moralizing. He did after all consider himself to be first and foremost a teacher of virtue and orthodox religion, his earnest declaration that the 'sole drift' of the Moral Satires was to correct 'a dissolute age' being echoed in his assertion that the purpose of *The Task* was to strike at 'vice, vanity and folly' and 'allure the reader . . . to the reading of what may profit him';[31] and there can be no denying that a good proportion of his verse is assiduously didactic—the sort of thing for which the modern reader can be expected to have little sympathy. The standard critical response to such passages as I have in mind is that 'the poet as contriver has . . . superseded the poet as expresser of felt, perceived or imagined reality'.[32]

That sounds reasonable enough:

> The pulpit, therefore (and I name it fill'd
> With solemn awe, that bids me well beware
> With what intent I touch that holy thing)—
> The pulpit (when the sat'rist has at last,
> Strutting and vap'ring in an empty school,
> Spent all his force and made no proselyte)—
> I say the pulpit (in the sober use
> Of its legitimate, peculiar pow'rs)
> Must stand acknowledg'd, while the world shall stand,
> The most important and effectual guard,
> Support, and ornament, of virtue's cause.
>
> (II,326–36)

Here Cowper writes as though Newton were at his shoulder, and if there is any feeling in the passage it is not so much the 'solemn awe' of which he speaks as an awkward determination to say what is right for a man of his persuasion. He is both too dogmatic and too guarded, the insistent tones of the preacher, heard especially in the punched-out reiteration of 'the pulpit', being interrupted by the over-calculated parentheses of a 'believer' afraid lest he should undersell his sacred theme. The style is extremely shaky—not because Cowper is grappling with a difficult intellectual issue or (as in the episode of the paralytic) caught up in the insoluble riddles of the human condition, but because his excessive concern with conveying the correct attitudes and message undermines his good sense in the use of the idiom of the language. 'Proselyte' is an intelligent word but so exposed as to sound pretentious. The pun on 'touch'—which may well not be deliberate—seems out of place in an expression of awe-struck piety. There is a similar intrusive double-meaning in the first 'stand' of the last line but two, which verges on the comic in visualizing the physical presence of the pulpit, while at the same time the figurative energy of this verb is dissipated, as opposed to being tellingly discharged, in a succession of stock images ('guard', 'support', 'ornament')— where, moreover, the verse levels out tamely instead of mounting to the promised climax. Only in the brief satiric picture of the 'strutting' satirist does the poetry come to life, yet the whole point of the aside is to reject satire as a worthless expense of effort. But although we may feel that Cowper would do better to write more in the vein he condemns the image itself is hardly satisfactory. Blatantly dismissive—does *Pope* merely 'vapour' in an 'empty school'?—it will, like the passage as a whole, convince none but the converted. Ironically, it is Cowper himself who will win no proselyte.

It would be a great mistake, though, to write off Cowper's formal moralism *in toto*. He is much better when observing contemporary manners and offering opinions natural to a person of his class and Christian background—as in the comments on modish preachers a little later in Book II:

> Perverting often, by the stress of lewd
> And loose example, whom he should instruct;
> Exposes, and holds up to broad disgrace
> The noblest function, and discredits much
> The brightest truths that man has ever seen.
> For ghostly counsel; if it either fall
> Below the exigence, or be not back'd
> With show of love, at least with hopeful proof
> Of some sincerity on the giver's part;
> Or be dishonour'd, in th' exterior form
> And mode of its conveyance, by such tricks
> As move derision, or by foppish airs
> And histrionic mumm'ry, that let down
> The pulpit to the level of the stage;
> Drops from the lips a disregarded thing.
>
> (II,551–65)

The slowness and suspension in the structure of this passage is not the defect that Spacks makes it—'a contrived complexity' with 'no corresponding complexity of thought'.[33] Admittedly, it skirts close to the pitfall always lying in wait for writers of blank verse: as Wordsworth notes, in a résumé of Dr. Johnson's thoughts on the matter, in this medium the language may suffer undue 'distortion' to keep it out of prose, and 'if once the natural order and connection of the words is broken, and the idiom of the language violated, the lines appear manufactured, ... cold and vapid'.[34] But Cowper clearly stops short of the brink. In employing the diction and phrasing of polite discourse in a gradual movement towards the planned anti-climax of 'disregarded thing' he satisfies one of his own main criteria for poetic excellence—'to marshal the words ... in such an order as they might take in falling from the lips of an extemporary speaker, yet without meanness'.[35] And the movement within 'suspension' is a progression in meaning, since each unit of the passage adds to the catalogue of pastorly shortcomings. As for the words themselves, the mixture of intellectual and more colloquial English—'exigence', 'histrionic'/'back'd', 'foppish', 'mumm'ry', and so on—not only makes a good conversational blend on its own account, but helps to enforce the poet's point by setting a serious, deliberately thoughtful language over against impressions of empty affectation; if 'ghostly', 'exigence', or 'histrionic', for example, belong all to Cowper, 'foppish', 'mumm'ry', and 'thing' catch, in their very tone, the nature and atmosphere of the behaviour he is attacking, while yet representing a wit and polish totally absent from the fashionable world of mindless posturing. In contrast to the objects of his reproof, Cowper has something to say; and he says it undramatically but with flair. This is not a poetry to get excited about—but that of course is its intention: for Cowper excitement goes with theatrical superficiality.

Spacks's main objection to such sections of *The Task* is that Cowper puts too much weight on outward appearances: 'exterior forms assume a disproportionate importance', both in the poet's own procedures and in his concern with 'modes of conveyance' ('show of love', 'hopeful proof of some sincerity'). Now, although this view usefully throws into relief the complex life of passages like those we considered earlier, where style is a register of perceptual and psychic process, it does less than justice to the interest in exterior forms, which was wholly

purposeful and part of a responsible socio-cultural idealism
that Cowper shared with many of his contemporaries. In his
remarks on bad preaching he aligns himself with a tradition
that valued above all 'those [whether poets or preachers] who
address their productions to the plain sense and sober judgement of their readers' (Crabbe), and that could equate vapidity
not with lack of feeling and imagination but 'a deviation from
propriety' owing to 'extravagance' and a penchant for 'novelty'
(Goldsmith).[36] As Donald Davie shows, one of the commonest
characteristics of the eighteenth century, from Pope right
through to the early Wordsworth, is the instinct to see style, no
less than facts or sentiments, in an ethical light;[37] and Cowper's
own manner in this passage, a literary/conversational counterpart of the 'decent, solemn, chaste' delivery he recommends in
the true preacher (ll.397ff.), is a significant act in itself, an
exercise in social and moral conduct. If like Spacks we find the
manner 'impoverished', then that is not because of any
inherent artistic deficiency or perverseness on Cowper's part
but a decline in the status of such conduct and the Christian-
humanist virtues to which, in Cowper, it automatically refers.

Cowper was indeed a prophet of that decline. Though linked
to a traditional ethos, his moral attitudes are aggressively
rather than confidently conservative, as of one fighting to
defend ground that is already in the process of being lost. He
felt that the centre could not hold, that things were falling apart
across the whole spectrum of contemporary life. That clergy-
men 'let down/The pulpit to the level of the stage' was to him
the clearest indication of rottenness in the very foundations of
society; in speaking out against 'sacerdotal mismanagement'
he is not blandly airing a narrow Evangelical prejudice, but
expressing a genuine sense of national crisis, of a breakdown
which he detected elsewhere in the 'solemn farce' of latter-day
politics and education (we notice the same image of theatrical
pretence), the widespread neglect of 'piety and virtue', the
modern enthusiasm among the upper classes for a corrupt
'London life', a voracious appetite in the reading public for
'childish fiction'.[38] Inevitably, religious and moral fervour
caused him to over-react, so that at times he parades his
misgivings like a Jeremiah awaiting the imminent collapse of
the kingdom:

> the old castle of the state,
> That promis'd once more firmness, so assail'd
> That all its tempest-beaten turrets shake,
> Stand motionless expectants of its fall.
>
> (V,525–8)

or gets carried away in diatribes against 'gain-devoted cities', in which the not unimpressive tone of passionate (and desperate?) defiance, flung full in the face of the acquisitive commercial spirit, hardly compensates for the surrender of all finesse of thought and style:

> Thither flow,
> As to a common and most noisome sew'r,
> The dregs and feculence of ev'ry land ...
> ... Rank abundance breeds
> In gross and pamper'd cities sloth and lust,
> And wantonness and gluttonous excess.
>
> (I,682–4,686–8)

But this strong element of overstatement and one-sidedness lessens neither Cowper's sincerity nor the reality of the historical situation to which he was responding. Even his most puritanical rhetoric bears a relation to things that were actually happening around him: the attack on metropolitan excess stands at one extreme of a living contemporary debate on the pros and cons of urbanization, on the other side of which we find, for example, Arthur Young's equally biased enthusiasm for the 'energy of consumption' or Paolo Balsamo's praise of extravagance on the economic grounds that 'it is evident that 100,000 people ... scattered into many villages, consume much less than if they were gathered into one town, for the reason of luxury which increases in proportion to the number of individuals united together; and which ... in spite of all the loud complaints of the moralists against it, must be acknowledged very useful to society'.[39] The course of history carried Balsamo's amoral secularism to victory, yet his own reference to 'the moralists'—and he is as likely to have Cowper in mind as anyone else—suggests that they were very much a presence to be taken into account.

To its first readers *The Task* must also have seemed an immensely topical poem in its reaction to political events. The

Gordon Riots in late 1780, the loss of the American colonies in
1782 ('the perfidy of France/That pick'd the jewel out of
England's crown' [*Task*, II,264–5]), roaring inflation, violent
anti-government protest on the streets of the capital while
Parliament was spending its energies discussing game laws,
turnpike trusts, and (November 1783) the Fox/North India
Bill which was aimed at extending patronage on a massive
scale—such was the background to Cowper's anxieties over the
fate of the 'castle of the state', most of which he wrote down
during 1783, right in the midst of a general uncertainty which
prompted one M.P. to exclaim that England was 'more than on
the brink of ruin'. In the same year George III contemplated
resigning, so bad did he consider the country's plight. What
was needed in the King's view was 'to restore that sense of
religious and moral duties in the kingdom, to the want of which
every evil that has arisen owes its source'. Cowper would have
agreed with him, as with his cry of 'liberty and virtue' and
hatred of 'the degenerate mercenary sons of slavery who sought
and held office':[40]

> But th'age of virtuous politics is past,
> And we are deep in that of cold pretence.
> Patriots are grown too shrewd to be sincere,
> And we too wise to trust them. He that takes
> Deep in his soft credulity the stamp
> Design'd by loud declaimers on the part
> Of liberty, themselves the slaves of lust,
> Incurs derision . . .
> For when was public virtue to be found
> Where private was not? . . .
> 'Tis therefore sober and good men are sad
> For England's glory, seeing it wax pale
> And sickly . . .
>   (V,493–500,502–3,509–11)

Thus Cowper spoke for all 'sober and good men', with a frank,
strenuous, muscular integrity that signals the standard by
which the age of 'cold pretence' and 'soft credulity' is being
judged. This quality is characteristic: his gaze is steady, trained
responsibly on things of consequence, whether he is talking
about politics or the state of the clergy, or, at the other end of

the social scale, the effects of 'enclosure' of common land, the collapse of cottage industries, and a patronizing but inadequate system of 'poor relief', as in the sketch of the Olney cottagers, once prosperous, now 'Ill clad and fed but sparely . . .'[41]

> choosing rather far
> A dry but independent crust, hard earn'd,
> And eaten with a sigh, than to endure
> The rugged frowns and insolent rebuffs
> Of knaves in office . . .

(IV,408–12)

Cowper's 'moral satire' has, on the whole, lasted well; much better than that of his rival for contemporary popularity, Charles Churchill, to whose 'genius' he paid unstinted tribute in *Table Talk*.[42] For all his brilliance we soon weary of Churchill, either because he lashes indiscriminately at everything in sight (*The Times* is an incomparably eclectic exposé of the vices and follies of metropolitan life) or because his concerns were, in the end, the wonder of a day (his pugnacious defence of the radicalism of John Wilkes in *The Duellist*, for example). He is in a way Cowper's direct opposite: Churchill 'the profligate person' feasting his wit on the feuds, hypocrisy, and heady restlessness of 'the town', and Cowper the provincial recluse and clear-sighted guardian of the values of reformed Christianity and classical humanism, exemplar of that same peculiarly English tradition which finds concentrated expression in Milton and the Wordsworth of the political sonnets and *The Excursion*. If we sometimes gasp at Churchill's fiery magic, in the long run we respect Cowper more, not just for his greater sense of what really mattered in the corporate life of the times, but—whatever we may think of his faith in the universal panacea of a return to 'religious obligation'—for his unswerving defence of honesty, self-knowledge, freedom, and the dignity of man.

But there is something else, more to the point in an assessment of Cowper's place in literary history and the psycho-historical process. When all is said in defence of his moral qualities, it remains that his poetry is among the most pointed examples of, in Raymond Williams's words, 'that separation of virtue from any practically available world which is a feature of the later phases of Puritanism and still later Romanticism'.[43] It is not merely that his simple creed of duty and good blinds him to the complexities of political circumstances, so that (in the passage quoted) he can attribute the misfortune of a nation grown 'pale and sickly' to its leaders' lack of 'private virtue'—as if such matters were ever that straightforward. His whole vision of society is of a world in which virtue is doomed, isolated, or cut off from any active sphere, and which the sober and upright man can only lament, never negotiate with. In the lines on the Olney cottagers, honest labour has become quite simply the victim of an irreclaimably pernicious system administered by 'knaves'; the other passage suggests that there are percipient men 'too wise to trust' the motives of 'shrewd' politicians, but they are granted no influence whatsoever in the political order itself, which is described as a conspiracy between the 'cold pretence' of false patriots and the 'soft credulity' of those they rule. In recognizing that the problems of the countryside are essentially economic, by that telling detail of the 'dry but independent crust' which is barely enough for survival, and in seeing that politics operate through an interplay of shrewd pretence and credulity, Cowper does put his finger on certain social realities; yet he cannot look beyond them to any workable remedy, or reach any accommodation with them. All he can do is stand back and contemplate—idealistically but helplessly—the 'pale and sickly' body of a diseased nation.

This inability to locate value anywhere in 'the world' is of course offset by gains in other areas, other directions, of which the greatest is undoubtedly Cowper's special relationship with nature. I would like to draw this section to a close, however, by noting a more basic concomitant of his practical alienation from society—the capacity to create poetry out of the potential void of alienation itself. He learned to take inspiration from the experience of being in a world of his own. 'Yardley Oak' (1791) is the perfect example.

Raymond Williams seizes eagerly on this poem for a 'reflection' which 'seems to catch the dialectic of just the change that was being widely experienced' with the quickening pace of agrarian and industrial 'revolution':[44]

> Nature's threads,
> Fine passing thought, ev'n in her coarsest works,
> Delight in agitation, yet sustain
> The force that agitates, not unimpair'd,
> But, worn by frequent impulse, to the cause
> Of their best tone their dissolution owe.
>
> (ll.80–5)

'This sense, of a dissolution within a lively and productive exercise, is exact'; Cowper was uniquely attuned to the rhythm of an age which saw a decisive shift from an older feudal organization of the countryside to an aggressive capitalism preoccupied with 'production'. A cruder Marxist than Professor Williams might also have made much of the fact that the oak itself, which has grown 'hollow' and 'rotten', stood at the centre of the Yardley Estate of the Earls of Northampton—a possible symbol of the eventual death of a landowning aristocracy whose recent 'engrossing' activities were creating the conditions by which it would in the long term decay. But we shall not get the full measure of the poem, even as an historical document, by tying it to socio-economic trends. It is about dissolution on various levels: in nature; in the State, whose structure 'by the tooth/Pulveriz'd of venality, a shell/Stands now and semblance only of itself' (ll.122–4); in orthodox religion whose one-time champion finds himself tempted to 'kneel and worship' a 'thing'—not because it is God's handiwork but because it offers food for the Fancy; in the self, for a connection is at once established between subject and poet, himself a 'shatter'd veteran' of 'three-score winters' (ll.3–4); and in poetry, since 'Yardley Oak' is a private fragment, a spasmodic and improvised piece, in which the poet is content to sing for and to himself alone—'with hearers none'

> I will perform
> Myself the oracle, and will discourse
> In my own ear such matter as I may.
>
> (ll.141–3)

With the sense of dissolution, then, comes withdrawal, and with withdrawal a lively and productive exercise *of the mind*. A poem like 'Yardley Oak' is not primarily about the external world at all, but the poet's momentary and personal experience. It is addressed to no audience; rather, it is something to be overheard. It is a new kind of lyric—peculiarly modern in its deliberate subjectivity, which verges at times on cryptic solipsism yet testifies to the sheer creative resilience of the self in isolation.

There is one very specific precedent for Cowper's retreat from an impossibly corrupt world into the realms of privacy and selfhood: the Book of Jeremiah, in which we watch the struggle for salvation being turned inwards from the community to the soul of the individual, in the prophet's quest for a personal faith against the background of a collapsing framework of religion and law. This direct biblical influence must be noted. Yet Cowper is also fulfilling trends from the immediate past, with its increase of authorial self-consciousness linked to consciousness of social and cultural dissolution. The obvious instances are still the best: *The Deserted Village*, a lament for the destruction of personal happiness and of 'sweet Poetry' itself ('first to fly where sensual joys invade') in a stricken land where 'wealth accumulates and men decay'; Gray's *Elegy*, in which the poet finally turns from what Leavis called 'the normally and centrally human as manifested on the common-sense social surface of life' to dramatize his own uneasy sense of isolation and sensibility at once unique and burdensome in the portrait of the romantic outsider 'muttering his wayward fancies' only to himself, 'drooping, woeful wan, ... crazed with care';[45] Pope, whose supreme efforts to envision an age of progress and good polity to rival the Rome of Vergil's *Georgics*, in 'Windsor Forest' or the celebration of the good works of power and money at the end of the 'Epistle to Burlington':

> Bid Harbors open, public Ways extend,
> Bid Temples, worthier of the God, ascend ...

yield to the sublime disillusionment which leaves him at last, in Book IV of *The Dunciad*, the chronicler of a grotesquely immoral Order.[46] Cowper the poet was no less pessimistic about society than the author of *The Dunciad*; and he was in a sense more emphatically cut off from the public world, for there is nothing in his work truly comparable to the way Pope's imagination thrives on the materials of a botched civilization as if in answer to his fears that all art is doomed. In Cowper art's response to an inimical environment lies not so much in an inventive exploitation of that environment as in an exploration of the mind itself, in all its strength and all its vulnerability, especially within the context of nature and those 'rural virtues' which had been in Goldsmith a desert of lost hopes. His legacy to the first generation of Romantics was nothing so simple as realistic observation. It may be that he stands directly behind Wordsworth's uncompromising break with a dehumanizing contemporary world where men crave 'extraordinary incident' and 'frantic ... and idle literature', and the mind has been reduced to 'almost savage torpor' by 'great national events and the increasing accumulation of men in cities': the remarks come very close to Cowper's attack on an age given over to 'luxury' and 'childish fiction'.[47] More important, however, he taught the direction in which poetry could grow once the break has been made. Wordsworth's poetry is permeated by the same inward pressures as Cowper's—a proneness to solipsism, morbid reciprocity, the loss of 'genial spirits'. Even when exploring the vulnerability of others he is projecting, and facing, the problems of his own individual existence: in *The Ruined Cottage* Margaret's decline into mental and physical atrophy—brought on by her obsessive longing for her husband's return, which fixes her to one 'wretched spot'—is, like Cowper's portrait of the paralytic, an image of the poet's own possible fate, of that 'madness' on which he had just reflected in 'Lines, left upon a Seat in a Yew Tree' in the (self-)description of one who, cut off from his fellow men, was doomed always to 'sigh,/Inly disturbed'.[48] The mind can be a prison. But, as Cowper had shown, it might also flourish when 'wedded to this goodly universe'.

*   *   *   *   *

In one of the most astute of all brief statements about the poetry of the second half of the eighteenth century Donald Davie, disagreeing with 'the many critics' who assume that 'the Augustan order, in moral conduct and in art, was thrown down

by individuals who experienced surges of feeling too powerful
to be accommodated in the Augustan system', argues that the
pre-Romantics—Collins, Gray, Goldsmith, Cowper—were in
fact distinguished by low vitality, while the impregnable
Augustan, Dr. Johnson, was a figure of monumental energy:

> One comes to think, indeed, that it was enervation, not
> energy, which fretted most under the Augustan dispensa-
> tion. The Augustan chains were chafed away; they were
> not broken. It was harder to be Augustan if you did not feel
> enough, than if you felt too much.[49]

This properly encourages us to recognize incisive originality,
the power to establish new modes of thought and expression,
where we might least expect it—in authors about whom there is
nothing spectacular, refugees from the busy world whose
faithful companions were 'weariness and sorrow of heart'
(Cowper) and 'low spirits' (Gray).[50] Cowper's own genius was
far from urgently revolutionary. He was not the kind to strike
out ardently into fresh territory, with the missionary zeal of a
Wordsworth or a Shelley. His conservatism as a man—he was
pleased to be known as Squire Cowper by the villagers of
Olney—was matched by that of his critical opinions: contrary
to common belief he did not condemn Pope for making poetry
'a mere mechanic art', but rather the senseless 'warblers' who
had Pope's tune by heart, the very types indeed that Pope put
down for 'tuneful fools' in the *Essay on Criticism*.[51] Coming late
to authorship, by accident rather than vocation, he styled
himself an *amateur* practising the pen 'as a gentleman performer
does his fiddle'.[52] Yet this same poet left his mark indelibly on
almost everything to which he turned his hand, and in the case
of the subjective/reflective lyric and poetry of natural description made decisive innovations. Not without cause did
Coleridge name him 'the best of *modern* poets'.

But Davie's formula is unsatisfactory for two reasons. For
one thing, who would now talk so categorically of an 'Augustan
dispensation', a 'system', founded on temperance, candour,
and a belief that 'the passions must be controlled by rational
good sense'?[53] No one, it is certain, who has responded to the
mercurial and corrosive irony of *Tale of a Tub*, or to Prior's racy
elegance, or the intense imaginative sympathies—extended

even to the sordid and perverted—of *The Rape of the Lock* and *The Dunciad*. There were, to be sure, prevalent ideals such as Donald Davie describes, and Cowper and Johnson continued to uphold them right to the end of the century; but they never amounted to a system which held writers in chains. Augustan literature is characteristically free-ranging, passionate, as alert to the claims made upon the imagination by vice and disorder as to the ultimate demands of current morality. What is truly apparent in the later part of the century is a transference of the proper sphere and subject of creative activity from society and human life in general to the individual, often (in poetry at any rate) the author himself. Goldsmith, Gray, and Cowper present a much more moral view of the world than Pope, Swift, and Prior, but it is, precisely, a view from a distance, of a world all but lost to art. By and large their poetry is an expression, and sometimes a conscious exploration, of their own condition. Johnson even, though admittedly he would have thought it improper to make his private feelings the subject of a poem, sounds frequently enough the theme of the individual cut off from any satisfactory corporate life, restlessly seeking happiness like Rasselas, wisely resigned to the vanity of the world like Imlac, or victim of his own fantasies like the insane astronomer who thinks he can control the weather.[54] His one great poem, *The Vanity of Human Wishes*, is not at all an engagement with and criticism of an actual period or structure of society, as Pope's satires are, but a vision, deeply personal, of each man's aloneness and insecurity in a life ruled by 'unnumber'd maladies', where the only resource is prayer and patient acceptance of 'whate'er [God] gives'.

No poetry reflects as strongly as Cowper's the emergence of the cut-off individual actively involved in the problems of his own existence; and the second weakness in Davie's statement is that it allows for only one facet of his personality as it is displayed in and determines that involvement. For all his proneness to 'sorrow of heart', low vitality, there was a streak of egotism in Cowper whereby he valued his difference from others both as poet and sufferer. In retrospect he insisted that the independence and originality of his work be recognized: 'My descriptions are all from nature: not one of them second-handed. My delineations of the heart are from my own experience: not one of them borrowed or in the least degree conjectural.'[55] 'I am of a very singular temper', he wrote to Lady Hesketh, 'and very unlike all the men that I have ever conversed with.'[56] This is far as can be from the timid Cowper of Lord David Cecil's biography; and the same tough, assertive self-consciousness surfaces in the poetry itself, in unflinching confrontations with the full horror of his 'case':

> Hatred and vengeance, my eternal portion,
> Scarce can endure delay of execution,
> Wait, with impatient readiness, to seize my
> 　　　　　Soul in a moment . . .
>
> Man disavows, and Deity disowns me:
> Hell might afford my miseries a shelter;
> Therefore hell keeps her ever hungry mouths all
> 　　　　　Bolted against me.
>
> Hard lot! encompass'd with a thousand dangers;
> Weary, faint, trembling with a thousand terrors;
> I'm called, if vanquish'd, to receive a sentence
> 　　　　　Worse than Abiram's.
>
> *Him* the vindictive rod of angry justice
> Sent quick and howling to the centre headlong;
> *I*, fed with judgment, in a fleshly tomb, am
> 　　　　　Buried above ground.
> 　　('Lines written during a Short Period of Insanity')

It is remarkable that Cowper was not silenced by his terrors, but could articulate and bring them under control so magnificently. Instead of overwhelming him, his miseries have become the occasion for highly original poetic statement—and, moreover, a source of personal stature, not only because he faces up to them but because he sees them as something unique, extravagant, greater than the 'sentence' of that classic victim of divine vengeance, Abiram, who was cast down *quickly* to hell. To be 'buried above ground' may indeed be worse than being locked up in hell, but not when one can embrace the agony with such vigour, and especially not when one can find some status in the experience, even if only the perverse status of extreme isolation, incredible privation. Not that Cowper wrote easily about his torments: we hear in the strange, discordant rhythms of the sapphic metre the stress and strain of a mind moving compulsively in the nightmare world of its most distressing illusions. Yet the fears and imaginings, the painful pressures from within, are, at the same time, disciplined, not least by the restraint imposed in observing the rules of such a difficult, unnatural verse-form.

These 'Lines' were written in exceptional circumstances, just after Cowper had tried to drown himself in the Ouse in 1773, and nowhere does he tread so fine an edge between self-command and frenzy, or between art and hysteria. It is nevertheless but one of a group of poems in which he must master fierce psychic energies, even as he draws inspiration from them. At times he 'did not feel enough', at others he 'felt too much'; though spiritual death, the cold gloom of non-being, was what he most complained of, in practice his need was almost as much to govern the fires as to keep the wraith of feeling alight, to give shape to powerful emotion as to maintain a free, vital and outgoing spirit. Both sides of his poetic personality will emerge as we follow him through the Moral Satires to *The Task* and his shorter poems.

3

The Moral Satires
and *Retirement*

Table Talk, which comes first in the volume of 1782, is in a way the odd poem out among the Moral Satires, being the only one to move to any real extent in the realm of public affairs. Indeed, no poem in English concerns itself more directly with pressing political issues: the catastrophic course of the war against the American colonies; the efforts of George III to maintain the position of the Crown, which Cowper hotly defends; the mild conduct of the magistrates during the Gordon Riots, which he deplores as a threat to the security and freedom of the individual; the plight of England at a time when the Armed Neutrality of five European states, led by Russia, left her more or less completely isolated, where the image of the 'stricken deer' is used without any of the personal meaning it was later to take on:

> Poor England! thou art a devoted deer,
> Beset with ev'ry ill but that of fear.
> The nations hunt; all mark thee for a prey;
> They swarm around thee, and thou stand'st at bay.
> Undaunted still, thou wearied and perplex'd,
> Once Chatham sav'd thee; but who saves thee next?
>
> (ll.362–7)

If we add, say, an extract from the passage on the Gordon Riots:

> Let active laws apply the needful curb
> To guard the peace that riot would disturb;
> And liberty, preserv'd from wild excess,

Notes and References begin on page 330

Shall raise no feuds for armies to suppress.
(ll.314–17)

it becomes clear that Cowper had needed the minimum of
practice to find a distinctive rhetoric in which to deal with
current events. He was a born verse-journalist, able to capture
and share in the mood of the times, when anger at the
behaviour of the magistrates during the Riots was widespread
and the death of Chatham on the floor of the Lords—'the chief
actor died upon the stage' (l.341)—had already entered the
national consciousness as a symbol of the passing of England's
greatness.[1] Yet he is not merely dressing facts and popular
sentiments in fine phrases, but strongly, independently upholding a moral and ideological position. As in comparable parts of
The Task,[2] *style* is of the utmost importance, the poet's manner
being inseparable from a responsible mode of thinking that lays
stress on those virtues of 'sober zeal' and 'integrity' for the want
of which, so he claims, things were in danger of falling apart.
There could be no more obvious example of this characteristic
conflation than the four lines last quoted, whose easy but
disciplined vigour is the straight counterpart of the freedom-
with-stability, rooted in the application of 'needful curbs' and
avoidance of 'wild excess', for which he is pleading in his
reaction to administrative incompetence.[3]

Apparently Cowper led off with *Table Talk* because of its
topicality—because it was, as John Newton put it, more '*ad
captum plebis*' than the other satires, which, with the partial
exception of *Conversation* and *Retirement*, treat specifically religious issues. But there may have been another reason. The
discussion of poetry that takes up a large section of the poem
constitutes something of a personal manifesto. The entire series
is written according to serious principles and considered
objectives, whatever the immediate subject.

Cowper clearly saw himself as raising the whole level of
poetic endeavour in the later eighteenth century, where all has
been reduced to an idle game, mere 'push-pin play':

Manner is all in all, whate'er is writ,
The substitute for genius, sense, and wit . . .
The man that means success should soar above

A soldier's feather, or a lady's glove;
Else summoning the muse to such a theme,
The fruit of all her labour is whipt-cream.

$$(ll.542-3,548-51)^4$$

None of the accused are named, and it seems that Cowper's purpose is, at least in part, to build a case for his own poems—*The Progress of Error*, an attack on the subversion of Christian faith by science and rationalism, and *Truth*, a sermon against pride and justification by works, had already been written—by forcing a generalized picture of the superficiality of modern literature. Yet this element of polemical overstatement makes his own aims no less clear and discriminating. He will shun the 'clockwork tintinabulum' of fastidious, empty rhyming and pursue instead a bolder, more substantial style that

                              plows its stately course
Like a proud swan, conq'ring the stream by force;
That, like some cottage beauty, strikes the heart,
Quite unindebted to the tricks of art.

$$(ll.522-5)^5$$

Neither will he misuse his talent to beguile the rich with 'flowing numbers' and 'float a bubble on the breath of fame' (ll.740–9). So far so good: the desire to soar above effeteness and dilettantism—to purify the art and 'ends' of poetry—sounds promising. The trouble starts when he begins describing the exact nature of his intentions, which are prompted in fact not only by an opposition to wilful misapplication of 'the pow'rs of genius' but by a sense of the same problem as haunted so many of his contemporaries, namely, the difficulty of finding anything new for the Muse to say or do.[6] 'What'er we write, we bring forth nothing new', he says; but there is still religion, hitherto neglected, about whom 'The flow'rs would spring where'er she deign'd to stray,/And ev'ry muse attend her on her way' (ll.716ff.). We agree that it would be 'new indeed' to see a bard wholeheartedly dedicating his gift to God the giver, 'to trace him in his word, his work, his ways'—with some alarm, however, in view of the warning signs that have already emerged in *Table Talk* itself, where the mantle of religious poet, though but half put on, has seemed designed only to constrict the flow of creative and intellectual energies. The muscular vigour of Cowper's hard-hitting response to national crisis, in a debate between *virtus* and enfeeblement and 'wild excess', had soon given way to a despairing lament for the sins and punishments of a godless people, 'a land, once christian, fall'n, and lost'. With the embrace of an outright religio-prophetic role comes the rejection of all intercourse with the 'world', except as something to be castigated and endlessly, repetitively, 'given up':

> ... they frolic it along,
> With mad rapidity and unconcern,
> Down to the gulf from which is no return.
>
> (ll.463–5)

There can be no real future as poet of public life for the outright religionist, though he may, as Cowper does, swing back from time to time to a more engaged, if still unproductive, *moral* stance.

Just as worrying is the reductionism apparent in Cowper's view of the literature of the past. Horace, for example, becomes the leader of a bacchanalian riot, profaning the 'sacred wires' of, in a very strict sense, *heavenly* poesy; after which it is hardly surprising that the Restoration in England should be dismissed as no more than a school for 'rank obscenity' (ll.608–9,620ff.). So rigidly are religio-moralistic criteria adhered to that the metrical psalms of Sternhold and Hopkins are presented as the last word in poetic excellence. Indeed, Cowper seems to see how comical this may appear. 'Hail Sternhold, then; and Hopkins, hail!' is a wry intrusion of the poet's breezy interlocutor; but the poet himself goes on to argue for, not against, the initially half-jocular proposition—yes, 'One madrigal of theirs is worth them all' (ll.759ff.). Without making too much of such understandable bias in Cowper's critical opinions, it does plainly show how drastically anti-literary his chosen course— his Evangelicalism—could be at this stage of his career. When it comes to pursuing that course in a poem like *Expostulation* his piety issues in a torrent of zealous condemnation washing into every conceivable nook and cranny of the nation's sinful state, so that, far from being redeemed, poetry grows bloated and incontinent on an excessive diet of righteousness. The warnings we get from *Table Talk* are at times all too thoroughly confirmed.

As I suggested earlier, Cowper was not alone in his pessimism about the fate of poetry. But his horizons were narrower, and nearer, than those of the Sensibility poets who shared his view that the present was enfeebled, 'laggard', in comparison with the past. Collins, Gray, the Wartons looked back, trembling but in emulative hope, to Greece and the Middle Ages, to Shakespeare and the English Renaissance. Paul Sherwin writes that their urge was 'to level the . . . temple of the Augustans'; and one thinks of Joseph Warton's strictures on Pope's sacrifice of Fancy to Judgement, or the Advertisement in which he announces his revolutionary intent: 'The Author . . . is convinced that the fashion of moralizing in Verse has been carried too far, and as he looks upon *Invention* and *Imagination* to be the chief *Faculties of a Poet*, so he will be happy if the following Odes . . . bring back Poetry into its right Channel.'[8] To Cowper, poetry had run in exactly the right channel in the reign of Queen Anne; for him, English letters had reached their zenith in Addison's 'sublimity and Attic taste', the 'droll sobriety' of Arbuthnot and Swift, and the Pope who first 'gave virtue and morality a grace' (*Table Talk*, ll.642–61). His desire was not to demolish the Augustan temple but to preserve it, though on very special terms already to some extent implicit in the fact that he praises his immediate predecessors more or less exclusively for claiming 'the palm for *purity of song,*/That lewdness had usurp'd and worn so long' (ll.636–7). He wished, as the proper way forward, to sanctify the temple to the glory of God and Christian virtues.

The Augustan connection is further emphasized in the picture of the ideal poet near the end of *Table Talk*:

> Fervency, freedom, fluency of thought,
> Harmony, strength, words exquisitely sought;
> Fancy, that from the bow that spans the sky
> Brings colours, dipt in heav'n, that never die;
> A soul exalted above earth, a mind
> Skill'd in the characters that form mankind;
> And, as the sun in rising beauty dress'd,
> Looks to the westward from the dappled east, . . .

An eye like his to catch the distant goal,
Or ere the wheels of verse begin to roll;
Like his to shed illuminating rays
On ev'ry scene and subject it surveys ...
(ll. 700–7, 710–13)

This does acknowledge Invention, Fancy and the sublime
status of the poetical character, whereas it is customary for
Cowper rather to lay all the stress on perspicuity (the need to be
'as clear as possible'), communication, the writer's duty to
reproduce and refine the spoken language ('to marshal the
words ... in such an order as they might naturally take in
falling from the lips of an extemporary speaker, yet without
meanness, harmoniously, elegantly')—on certain basic tenets,
that is, of the latter-day neo-classical school of Kames and
Hugh Blair.[9] But the passage from *Table Talk* is complementary
to, not a contradiction of, his usual position. Although the poet
is afforded majestic faculties and 'a soul exalted' there is
nothing to suggest that he dwells apart from other men in
splendid isolation, glorying in autonomous, transcendent and
self-justifying powers of creation; nothing in other words to
place Cowper among 'Romantic' critics such as Warton, or
Richard Hurd who flatly asserted that 'the poet has a world of
his own, where experience has less to do, than consistent
imagination', that poets are 'lyars by profession' and demand
from their readers, not belief, but involvement in their 'air-
formed visions'.[10] Cowper's poet deals in palpable truths, to
which he brings the freshness of poetic 'colouring' and a
spirited elegance of expression; he does not weave compelling
fictions or even transform his materials, but sheds 'illuminating
rays'—embellishes and clarifies—the scenes and subjects that
stretch before him in the world of human experience. And none
of this would have seemed at all exceptional to Pope—from
whose *Essay on Criticism* Cowper appears in fact to have culled
his essential critical ideas in *Table Talk*. Wherever we turn in
the *Essay* we find parallels and semi-parallels of thought and
imagery: praise for the 'easy vigour' that overleaps the 'rules'
and 'gains/The Heart'; scorn for the tuneful fools who haunt
Parnassus 'but to please their ear,/Not mend their minds'; the
'true Expression' that

> like th' unchanging sun,
> Clears and improves what'er it shines upon,
> It gilds all objects, but it alters none.
>
> (ll.315–17)[11]

Donald Davie is right to maintain that Cowper's views were 'far more the consummation of one tradition than the prelude to another'.[12]

In his practice as 'satirist', Cowper actually observes neo-classical precepts more rigidly than Pope, who after all takes as much delight in spinning the 'air-formed visions' of *The Rape of the Lock* (a poem 'made of nothing', 'a double-refined essence of wit and fancy', Hazlitt called it)[13] as in producing the epigrammatic discourse of the *Essay on Criticism* itself. The expression that clears and improves without altering, and the language which is 'the dress of thought', are universally present in the Moral Satires—as might be expected from a writer who was in touch too with the Puritan tradition, where it was assumed that style should be severely useful, a vehicle for revealing absolute truth, undistorted and unobscured.[14] Of course, everything so far quoted from the poems shows that the 'dress' may not only fit well with the 'thought' but be indistinguishable from it, as Hugh Blair also reminds us when speaking of style as 'a picture of the ideas which rise in the mind, and of the manner in which they rise there; and hence ... it is, in many cases, extremely difficult to separate the Style from the sentiment. ... Style is that sort of expression which our thoughts most readily assume.'[15] Mostly, however, the 'sentiment' of the Moral Satires is very straightforward and the 'expression' impersonally functional: Cowper the popular preacher pushes the Augustan style to a new level of plainness in an attempt to convey simple ideas to a relatively unsophisticated audience.

Truth stands at the centre of this design in its appeal for men to accept the unambiguous teachings of Scripture, 'Heav'n's easy, artless, unincumber'd plan' (l.22); and at the heart of *Truth* lies the passage much admired by Hazlitt, in which the simplicity and contentment of the Olney lacemaker is set above the anxious reasoning of a Voltaire:[16]

Yon cottager, who weaves at her own door,
Pillow and bobbins all her little store;
Content, though mean; and cheerful, if not gay;
Shuffling her threads about the livelong day,
Just earns a scanty pittance; and at night
Lies down secure, her heart and pocket light:
She, for her humble sphere by nature fit,
Has little understanding, and no wit,
Receives no praise; but though her lot be such,
(Toilsome and indigent) she renders much;
Just knows, and knows no more, her Bible true—
A truth the brilliant Frenchman never knew;
And in that charter reads, with sparkling eyes,
Her title to a treasure in the skies.
Oh, happy peasant! Oh, unhappy bard!
His the mere tinsel, hers the rich reward . . .

(ll.317–32)

All is transparent in the extreme—style, meaning, the poet's
unquestioning acceptance of the superiority of faith over
philosophy. We miss at once the agility and compression of
Pope's verse: instead of complex, developing argument, there is
a series of individual details and comments loosely accumulat-
ing to press home a single, preconceived idea. The syntax and
idiom are more those of the prose writer than the poet, though
rhyme and balance ('Content, though mean . . .', 'His the mere
tinsel . . .') help to formalize, and so check, the sentimentality of
the portrait. The images ('charter', 'tinsel', 'treasure'), drawn
from the common fund of Evangelical phraseology, seem
automatic and a little quaint but are too distinct to sound trite
or clichéd. All in all, the lines work well as an expression of a
particular set of religious and humanitarian assumptions, the
only positive stylistic fault being the ungainly word-play in 'her
heart and pocket *light*'. It would be wrong in the end to see them
as a pale imitation of Pope; rather, the Augustan manner has
been deliberately evacuated of all density, all elaborateness, in
an effort to celebrate a new ethos grounded in the virtues of
Faith, Simplicity, and Innocence. Even when praising the
'clear and artless' character and works of John Kyrle, the Man

of Ross, Pope had insisted on introducing—at the risk of
blatant incongruity—the highest available language of tribute,
the elevated terminology of classical panegyric:

> Pleas'd Vage echoes thro' her winding bounds,
> And rapid Severn hoarse applause resounds . . .
> ('Epistle to Bathurst', ll.251–2)

Cowper's exemplar, on the other hand, is one from which all
considerations of stature, and of social usefulness, are excluded
(for whatever it is that the lacemaker 'renders', it cannot be for
the good of others). With the pursuit of Augustan sobriety in
the service of Evangelical attitudes goes, inevitably, a rejection
of the Augustan 'heroic' and the Augustan concern with the
active life of society.

No pale imitation of Pope. On the other hand, for all its
obvious decency and serious intent this 'purifying' of Augustanism represents in retrospect not so much a meaningful
reorientation of the style and function of poetry as a diminu-
tion—a disavowal of both art and the intellect. Attempting to
bring forth something new out of his legacy from the immediate
past, Cowper dilutes what he has received, veering dangerously
towards complete attenuation.

It needs saying, however, that not even *Truth* is all like this.
The 'plain style' is capable of variation; and there are times
when ideological concern falls away or is subsumed in an
immediate play of mind and personality, an expressive process
in which we can fluently participate:

> Yon ancient prude, whose wither'd features show
> She might be young some forty years ago,
> Her elbows pinion'd close upon her hips,
> Her head erect, her fan upon her lips,
> Her eye-brows arch'd, her eyes both gone astray
> To watch yon am'rous couple in their play,
> With bony and unkerchief'd neck, defies
> The rude inclemency of wintry skies,
> And sails, with lappet-head and mincing airs,
> Duly, at clink of bell, to morning pray'rs.
> To thrift and parsimony much inclin'd,
> She yet allows herself that boy behind.

The shiv'ring urchin, bending as he goes,
With slip-shod heels, and dew-drop at his nose;
His predecessor's coat advanc'd to wear,
Which future pages yet are doom'd to share;
Carries her bible, tuck'd beneath his arm,
And hides his hands, to keep his fingers warm.

$$(ll. 131-48)$$

Oddly enough, this unmistakably Cowperian skit is intimately based upon an existing work and presents an entirely stock 'character'. Norman Nicholson likens it to Cruikshank, and it does indeed have its source in visual portraiture—Hogarth's picture of the sanctimonious prude from the series *Four Times of the Day*.[17] The original is followed so faithfully that one is tempted to talk of 'reproduction'; but that would be to deny what immediately strikes us—the poet's felt presence as observer and interpreter. In translating the given material from one medium to another Cowper creates an inimitable blend of comedy and reproof wherein we are aware simultaneously of both the seer and the scene.

As with much of Cowper's best poetry, his moral attitudes emerge naturally during an act of contemplation and response in which the reader is allowed to share. Criticism of the prude's strait-laced hypocrisy is everywhere implied, nowhere stated, contempt in the opening couplet, for example, being communicated by a spontaneous emphasis of the speaking-voice, an amused and almost casual tone that wins our confidence at once: 'She *might* be young some forty years ago.' Appearances and actions are then left—or rather *made*—to speak for themselves: the stiffness of 'pinion'd' (the figure grows bird-like), 'erect', and 'arch'd' first raises a graphic impression of the woman's overwrought puritanism, before the verse wanders with her gaze to catch her ambiguous interest in the nearby lovers (the double meaning of 'astray' is a perfect touch). The grotesque humour shades gently into grotesque pathos with the introduction of the page, whose condition, though comic, serves to sharpen the satire by showing that it is another's flesh his mistress mortifies and not her own—a point already prepared for by the suggestions of ostentation in her dress and manner. We see what the early critics meant when they designated Cowper a poet *sui generis* offering an original combination of the *utile* and the *dulce*, and spoke of the *dulce* not simply as something which sweetened the pill of instruction but as a reflection of the author's genuine delight in the human landscape.[18]

This mode of portraiture—which proves Cowper was himself no mere strait-laced moralist—occurs throughout the longer poems, enlivening stretches of abstract argument. *Conversation* is full of it: the thumb-nail sketch of the athletic philosopher, for instance, whose

> nimble nonsense takes a shorter course;
> Flings at your head conviction in the lump,
> And gains remote conclusions at a jump . . .
> (ll.152–4)

or of pipe-smoking sages who 'drop the drowsy strain,/Then pause, and puff—and speak, and pause again' (ll.247–8). It has been often pointed out that Cowper lacked the animus and knowledge of mankind necessary for the writing of high satire—'Cowper is an instance of a thinker too far apart from the great world to apply the lash effectually' (Leslie Stephen).[19] All the same, no one has left us more memorable pictures of men's *lesser* vices than these miniature masterpieces of semi-indignant mimicry, composed with so personal a touch that we are not at all surprised at Wordsworth's conspicuous failure to produce anything except lifeless copies.[20] Though, like the *exemplum* of the lacemaker, they do nothing to redeem Augustanism, and indeed represent a weakening of satiric high-seriousness in comparison with the sketches of Pope's Moral Essays or *The Dunciad*, their brilliance does much to save the Moral Satires as a general reading experience. They are the genial counterpart of the spirited sobriety of the topical sections of *Table Talk*—the independent but out-going poet embracing the life around him.

The moral satires are above all, however, poems of religious statement. The general drift of the arguments is predictable: defence of revealed religion against deism and natural religion; the Protestant emphasis on faith as opposed to works and church ritual; the Calvinist preoccupation with the corruptness of our nature and earthly environment, and the consequent need to subject our energies to the service of God and inner salvation.²¹ Lost in life's 'giddy maze', a man's only hope and true happiness lie in directing his gaze patiently, via the Word, towards Christ and 'the place of [hope's] ethereal birth'; this, made explicit in *Hope*, is the underlying theme of the more doctrinal of the Moral Satires, as it is of Newton's eloquent apostolic work, *Cardiphonia* (1781), from which Cowper undoubtedly took his lead:

> What a poor, uncertain, dying world is this! What a wilderness in itself! How dark, how desolate, without the light of the Gospel and knowledge of Jesus! It does not appear so to us in a state of nature, because we are then in a state of enchantment, the magic lantern blinding us with a splendid delusion ... yet we [the undeceived] can discern, beyond the limits of the wilderness, a better land, where we shall be at rest and at home.²²

But from an interpretative point of view, the interesting thing is not so much the theme itself as the unevenness of the poetry in which Cowper expresses it. Everywhere in *Cardiphonia* there is a bite, a stringency, which leaves us convinced that everything Newton says or ponders has the same importance, the same strong hold on his consciousness, whether he is referring to the 'delusions' of this 'uncertain, dying world' or affirming the consolations of 'the Gospel and knowledge of Jesus'. In Cowper, we have a mixture of the personal and relatively objective, the felt and unfelt. In particular, the brighter facets of the Christian's being-in-the-world tend to appear as inert *concepts*, as something borrowed, sifted and carefully set down:²³

>   scripture is the only cure of woe.
> That field of promise, how it flings abroad
> Its odour o'er the Christian's thorny road!
> The soul, reposing on assur'd relief,
> Feels herself happy amidst all her grief...
>   (*Truth*, ll.452–6)

The detachment, specially noticeable here because Cowper is actually dealing with sensuous and emotional states, is a recurrent feature of the poems. So too is the conversion of reality into a set of manageable abstractions, couched in an easily manipulated language. Again and again we meet the answering of woe with comfort, struggle with repose, grief with happiness, images of stifled growth, tempest or ill-favoured journey being neatly compensated by ones of fertility, peace, and progress. The promises of scripture plough up 'the roots of a believer's care' and kill the 'weeds' that bind a sinner's brow; man may find himself tossed on the waves of anxiety, 'His ship half founder'd and his compass lost', but 'Hope, as an anchor firm and sure, holds fast/The Christian vessel, and defies the blast'.[24] It is clear, I think, that for the author of the Moral Satires religion was not a living or lived reality but a scheme, a 'construct', by which life could be ordered, rationalized, accepted. Once this is realized, we can no longer see the Moral Satires purely as a public act: the creating mind comes into focus—a mind relying, for stability and a stable view of experience, upon the formulae and set consolations of a given creed. They are not only about the well-being of Poetry or of men but the well-being of the poet himself. We become aware of a confessional dimension.

The more 'felt' and impressive insights are provoked by this dying world itself, with its ineluctable evidences of self-deception and waste, the inevitability of loss, man's enslavement to time and his own folly. The object of *Hope*, for example, is to discredit pessimism by insisting that Christian hope is a 'remedy' for every ill (ll.111ff.), but it is the dull pain, the gnawing discontent, of unenlightened existence that captures Cowper's keenest sympathy:

> [Life is] A painful passage o'er a restless flood,
>   A vain pursuit of fugitive false good,
>   A scene of fancied bliss and heart-felt care,
>   Closing at last in darkness and despair . . .
>   Youth lost in dissipation, we deplore,
>   Through life's sad remnant, what no sighs
>   restore;
>   Our years, a fruitless race without a prize,
>   Too many, yet too few to make us wise.
>   (ll.3–6,23–6)

> [Life 'without a plan']
>   Serves merely as a soil for discontent

To thrive in; an incumbrance, ere half spent.
Oh! weariness beyond what asses feel,
That tread the circuit of the cistern wheel;
A dull rotation, never at a stay,
Yesterday's face twin image of to-day.

(ll.97–102)[25]

In the second passage, we find Cowper not only imaginatively at home with the mood of selfconscious weariness but oneirically interior to the condition of restless confinement within a circuit of unprogressive being. The adventurous, strange, and yet thoroughly confident image of the asses at the wheel, the 'tread' and 'dull rotation' of the verse-rhythm, the final suspension of time and motion in the see-saw balance of 'Yesterday' and 'to-day', are the pledge of an experiential authenticity singularly lacking in the previously quoted lines on the scriptural 'field of promise'. The beginning of *Hope* is in fact an attack on false 'philosophers' who, blind to the light of Christianity, paint 'things terrestrial' in the dismal hues of their own hardened disillusionment. But Cowper is of their party without knowing it, in that he is more fully attuned to their perspectives than to those of Hope itself, inwardly more an inhabitant of their wilderness than of the happy sphere in which Newton wants to locate him when presenting him in the Preface to the Moral Satires as one brought out of darkness into a cheerful and gracious dawn.[26]

The Moral Satires were to Newton the exemplary product of a 'happy deliverance' from affliction afforded by God to one who had long 'lived without God in the world'.[27] It would be more accurate to say that they are in part the fruits of such a deliverance and in part a *stabilizing process*, a therapeutic act. Their sombre landscapes, of the kind we have just considered, are plainly inspirited by, and a projection of, the same psychic energies, the same potential for finding life meaningless and the world a dungeon or waste land, as had surfaced in Cowper's bouts of 'madness'—energies which, though controlled, still constitute a palpable threat. Religion itself, whatever it had meant to him during his conversion, is now the property of the intellect: the conscious mind's attempted answer to psychological danger, an ideology clung to and cultivated in an effort to possess a philosophy, a view of things, which would indeed bring the 'peace and solid hope' that Newton believed to be his friend's future. The ideology failed him, for he writes just as the Moral Satires were published:

> No man upon earth is more sensible of the unprofitableness of a life like mine than I am, or groans more heavily under the burthen; but this too is vanity, because it is in vain; my groans will not bring the remedy, because there is no remedy for me.[28]

Newton's prediction had proved false. Again in the grip of life-weariness, the poet specifically rejects the wisdom put forward in the Moral Satires, as irrelevant to a case like his—'... there is no remedy for me'. His is again a life 'without a plan', 'an incumbrance'; the sensibility of unprofitableness, which has been discharged into a repudiative dramatic context, had flowed back to the centre of his own waking consciousness. And the return to despair really comes as no shock to us. That the consolations of Faith and Hope are in the Moral Satires comparatively unfelt—what Newton himself might have designated as 'acquired' rather than 'experimental'[29]—makes them seem all along a somewhat precarious structure which might easily give way under an assault from those darker feelings that reside, still active, within the elegiac passages of *Hope*.

One passage at the climax of *Hope* is of outstanding interest in connection with this, the psycho-confessional element in the Moral Satires. The poet enters the poem; for Cowper clearly has his own past self in mind when describing the figure who was at first 'happy' ('politely learn'd' and of a 'gentle race', gay at the 'toilette of the fair', to the fore in 'masculine debate'), until the sudden onslaught of dread-full, conscience-stricken despondency:

> Alas, how chang'd!—Expressive of his mind,
> His eyes are sunk, arms folded, head reclin'd;
> Those awful syllables, hell, death, and sin,
> Though whisper'd, plainly tell what works within;
> That conscience there performs her proper part,

And writes a doomsday sentence on his heart!
                                    (ll.688–93)

'Forsaking, and forsaken of his friends', the sufferer dwells in
the nightmare world of his own fixed thoughts, of a monomania
whose symptoms are physical emaciation and inarticulateness,
and whose effects are the loss of perceptual pleasure ('beauty
has no charms') and the transformation of external life, the
'music' and the 'laughter', into sounds that ring 'like madness
in his ear'. 'We receive but what we give' (Coleridge, 'Dejection'): the shattered personality readily projects its own discord
into the world around him, making of it a madhouse, from
whence in turn there can come no healing influences. 'His grief
the world of all her pow'r disarms', says Cowper with simple
directness (l.704). At the same time the melancholic grows
abnormally sensitive to the passage of time, though time is also
suspended in one endless moment of apocalyptic terror:

> His hours no longer pass unmark'd away,
> A dark importance saddens every day;
> He hears the notice of the clock, perplex'd,
> And cries—perhaps eternity strikes next!
>   (ll.698–701)

But then his realization of the precious truth that 'God's holy
word' is 'the fountain whence alone/Must spring the hope he
pants to make his own' prepares the way for a 'bright reverse',
which Cowper proceeds to portray in an extended simile
depicting the ecstasy of a condemned prisoner released at the
hour appointed for his execution:

> He drops at once his fetters and his fear;
> A transport glows in all he looks and speaks,
> And the first thankful tears bedew his cheeks.
> Joy, far superior joy . . .
> Invades, possesses, and o'erwhelms, the soul
> Of him, whom hope has with a touch made whole.
>   (ll.725–8,730–1)

The gift of perception is renewed, with manifold increase of
power:

> ... 'tis God diffus'd through ev'ry part,
> 'Tis God himself triumphant in his heart!
> Oh! welcome now the sun's once hated light,
> His noon-day beams were never half so bright.
> Not kindred minds alone are call'd t'employ
> Their hours, their days, in list'ning to his joy;
> Unconscious nature, all that he surveys,
> Rocks, groves, and streams, must join him in his praise.
>
> (ll.734–41)

The individual reborn not only regains his place in the society of men ('kindred minds') but enjoys a privileged intercourse with nature and with God. His being-in-the-world is far superior to the old, prior to the onset of affliction, because it has a profound spiritual dimension. The deity is both felt without and present within, 'triumphant in his heart'. Though properly subservient to God, a worshipper still, he is yet at one with Him, sharing in His Spirit and creative might as he leads 'all that he surveys', else silent, in a chorus of praise to the Creator. The fuller potentialities of self are liberated and realized in the service of Other, from whom they derive.

This episode is an important manifest anticipation of the familiar Romantic concern with the terrors of morbid alienation and the glories of ennobling communion between Nature and highest minds. Cowper's penetration of the experience of mute, uncreative and seemingly unalterable 'grief'—a 'grief/ Which finds no natural outlet, no relief' (Coleridge)—is remarkable; and his framing of the idea of grace in terms of a concept of the One Life within us and abroad is truly prophetic. What is significant in relation to the Moral Satires themselves, however, is that the passage is a shaping of personal experience—that bound up with the presentation of a public *exemplum* is an act of self-revelation involving therapeutic strategies.

It needs to be recognized first how perfectly the details tally in outline with those of Cowper's life. He, like his subject, was 'politely learn'd'—a student of the classics and modern literature; he came of 'gentle race', for his paternal ancestors included the first Lord Chancellor of England, while on his mother's side he could trace his descent back to the poet Donne and Henry III; much of his spare time as an aspiring lawyer had been spent in 'masculine debate' at the Nonsense Club. The subsequent collapse is of course a recollection of the suicidal depression that had put him into Dr. Cotton's asylum in 1763. The autobiographical *Memoir* gives exactly the same picture of physical paralysis, disorientation and imprisonment within the self:

> A numbness seized upon the extremities of my body, and life seemed to retreat before it ... No convicted criminal ever feared death more, or was more assured of dying ... At every stroke my thoughts and expressions became more wild and indistinct; all that remained clear was the sense of sin, and the expectation of punishment.[30]

And the autobiography and the poem are even closer to one another in their descriptions of the happy release:

> ... seeing a Bible there, [I] ventured once more to apply to it for comfort and instruction ... Immediately I received strength to believe, and the full beams of the Sun of Righteousness shone upon me ... Unless the Almighty arm had been under me, I think I should have died with gratitude and joy. My eyes filled with tears, and my voice choked with transport, and I could only look up to heaven in silent fear, overwhelmed with love and wonder ... To rejoice day and night was all my employment.[31]

Cowper the poet, then, is plainly drawing on his life-experience, on events and feelings which retain a living presence in his mind and memory, a sort of vivifying virtue; and in so doing he achieves, for one thing, a degree of realism and immediacy unknown in the religio-moralistic writings he is imitating. There is nothing in Newton's *Cardiphonia* or *Autobiography* like his friend's capacity for communicating the *nature* of inward experience out of the depths of active remembrance and imagination. Beside the poetry of the passage from *Hope* and the poetic prose of the *Memoir*, his accounts of even the most tremendous occasions during his own conversion seem tame— the reflections of an assured rationalist who knows the import-ance of his theme, but in contrast to Cowper, feels it no longer:

> I dreaded death now, and my heart foreboded the worst, if the Scriptures, which I had long since opposed, were true. Still I was but half convinced, and remained ... in a sullen frame, a mixture of despair and impatience.[32]

It is much the same with James Hervey whose *Meditations and Contemplations*, which played a crucial part in Cowper's recovery at the St. Albans' asylum,[33] shows a thoroughgoing concern with the states of unselfconscious happiness, sudden affliction and superior joy that form the three main landmarks of the standard Puritan/Evangelical call to salvation. The following are two relevant examples, the first being a random instance of many probable detailed influences on Cowper and the second an extract from Hervey's long monitory description of the drama of conversion:

> ... they are counting the tedious hours, telling every striking clock, or measuring the very moments by their throbbing pulse.[34]

> ... when divine grace dissipates the delusive glitter which dazzled his understanding ... then he begins to discern the things which belong unto his peace. Some admonition of scripture darts conviction into his soul, as the glimmering of a star pierces the gloom of night ... this is, possibly, succeeded by some afflictive dispensation of providence ... [finally] scenes of refined and exalted, but hitherto unknown delight, address him with their attractions ...[35]

The *Meditations* supplied the basic material, but it is in Cowper filled out by material from the poet's own past and transformed into something richer and more compelling—a train of powerful images embodying emotional extremities, ranging from the gravely poignant 'His hours no longer pass unmark'd away,/A dark importance saddens every day' to the stark melodramatic energy of 'A transport glows in all he looks and speaks,/And the first thankful tears bedew his cheeks'. It has sometimes been claimed that Evangelical 'literature' was largely responsible for preparing the way for the Romantic elevation of feeling over reason.[36] There is a good deal of truth in this (one might refer in the present context to the difference between the Evangelical theme of spiritual change and its Augustan counterpart, the neo-classical theme of *quantum mutatus ab illo*, which not only stops short of 'rebirth' but, as in Oldham's lines on Butler or Pope's on the death of Villiers, centres on outward circumstance, the fall from riches to rags, the vicissitudes of fortune);[37] and we need look no farther than Cowper for the mediation of religio-psychological perspectives into the mainstream of poetry. So boldly and unequivocally do the above couplets respect the primacy of feeling that the impersonal subjects ('dark importance', 'transport' . . .) and active verbs ('saddens', 'glows', 'bedew') make the individual into a receptacle for a relentless process over which he has no control.

Personal experience is not only expressed and dramatized in this episode, however. It is also organized and accounted for. More accurately, Cowper is repeating from the *Memoir* a conception of his existence that was itself an ordering, an interpretation founded upon a traditional Puritan/Evangelical *topos* which he had seen preached, so encouragingly, in Hervey. Within the pattern thus provided and adopted, sickness of mind is a profitable condition, an 'afflictive dispensation of providence' (Hervey) preceding enlightenment and, in the end, 'Joy, far superior joy.'[38] Madness—which Cowper first suffered before, not after, his acquaintance with Calvinism—becomes part of a divine plan, a shattering of the self so that it can be made anew. In *Hope* he is doing more than offering that plan for the edification of others; he is recovering a commitment to its presence in his own life, and regaining contact with his own former strength.

One cannot pretend that the stabilizing strategies of Puritan meditation are consciously applied in the Moral Satires: the poet neither sets himself deliberately to sustain a belief in his state of grace by recalling special occasions which (in Bunyan's words) 'bring fresh into my mind the remembrance of . . . my support from Heaven, and the great grace that God extended to such a Wretch as I', nor writes on purpose to 'consider how wonderfully one thing has been connected with another', so that he might press forward in good spirits, in the knowledge that 'nothing befell [him] without a cause'.[39] Only in the *Memoir* does he join the ranks of those who had trod 'the walks of self-examination' with the precise aim of discovering Order and Unity in their lives. Nevertheless, there is much of this, the self-confessing and self-assuring spiritual autobiographer, in the poems; setting out, quite unrealistically, to restore Poetry by claiming it for religion, he finished up producing a poetry as substantially about himself as anything. Even the celebration of the Olney lacemaker's utter simplicity and instinctive trust in God and the Bible may be read as personal statement—the articulation of Cowper's ideal life of innocence, faith, and unchallengeable hope. But our poet is no 'happy peasant' blessed with ready-made repose: he must constantly rediscover it for himself. It is worth offering one further example, another of his many brief portraits and narratives dealing with the salvation of the individual. We have just seen him recapturing the 'reality' of his own rebirth, pushing through memories of monomaniacal dereliction, to an image of the self free, favoured and secure. There is a similar episode in *Truth* (ll.238–82), where the traveller moves 'hopeless' through the violent storm—'Now flashing wide, now glancing as in play,/Swift beyond thought the lightnings dart away'—until he is brought to the refuge of 'some mansion, neat and elegantly dress'd', a place of 'warmth, security, and rest':

> Think with what pleasure, safe, and at his ease,
> He hears the tempest howling in the trees;
> What glowing thanks his lips and heart employ,
> While danger past is turn'd to present joy.
>
> (ll.253–6)

So fares it with the sinner, lashed by the foaming waves of conscience and by a fear of death, for whom God prepares a peaceful home:

> The book shall teach you—read, believe, and live!
> 'Tis done—the raging storm is heard no more,
> Mercy receives him on her peaceful shore.
>
> (ll.274–6)

The God who can destroy at a stroke can at a word make whole. Again the consoling pattern of events; again the carefully structured insistence on a happy outcome; again the link with the poet's own experience, especially when we recall that storm imagery was his characteristic means of emblematizing personal distress, as in the lines 'To Newton' of 1780, which conclude 'I tempest-toss'd, and wreck'd at last,/Come home to port no more.' The passage might serve as an epitome of what so often goes on just beneath the didactic surface of the Moral Satires: Cowper the poet-traveller, the mental pilgrim, is journeying through externalized and objectified images of his 'afflictions', his private hell, and reaches always some point of rest, some compensating vision or formula. Cowper's 'mansion' is the framework of Faith which he inherited from Newton, Hervey, and others—a philosophy of life which embraces suffering, promises peace, and brings stability. Yet whereas the fictional traveller is rescued from without, by a dispensation of Providence ('. . . God replies;/The remedy you want I freely give'), the poet is in fact building a refuge for himself, though out of existing materials. His psychological gains are, at bottom, made on his own initiative, and are his own triumph.[40]

But 'triumph' is perhaps too strong a word, and certainly applies only to *loci* within the poems. Overall the Moral Satires are, more specifically, a holding operation. As we have seen, there is always the danger of *peripeteia*: the landscape of the poems, which is the landscape of the poet's mind, is full of dark apprehensions and darker possibilities—the traveller who finds no rest, the disease that kills, the Providence that does not relent, and in *Table Talk* (and *Expostulation*) the socio-political world in crisis. This tragic sense—the shadow side of Cowper's vision—is of course an asset to the poetry; and it is here, paradoxically, that his religion had a positive effect on his creativity. Instead of regretting his contact with Calvinistic Methodism on the grounds that its fatalism unhinged his mind, we should be thankful that it gave communicable shape, and a substance, to what might otherwise have been but vague intimations of desolate privacy and collective meaninglessness. The elegiac theme, the feeling that man is ultimately at the mercy of inscrutable and irresistible forces, the uncertainty of life and the elusiveness of repose—all these can be traced back to the writings of radical Protestantism; to Bunyan, Newton and Hervey, who, along with Prior's *Solomon* and Johnson's essays and *The Vanity of Human Wishes*, offered a channel for Cowper's inborn 'melancholy' to run in.[41] For all his self-possession, even Newton was not immune to the trials of a troubled imagination. He suffers 'some little faintings', mo-

ments when he cannot be sure that he will dwell peacefully in
the bosom of the Lord: 'May it be your experience and mine!',
he concludes one apparently consolatory letter of *Cardiphonia*,
after preaching the 'light and cheerful progress' of God's
chosen.[42] Religion was never so simple a matter for real people
as for the lacemaker. Far from simply isolating Cowper from
the tensions and problems of living, it sensitized his awareness
of them, much to his advantage as poet.

On the other hand, it is plain that in so far as they are a
determined exposition of the 'truth, beauty and influence of the
religion of the Bible' (Newton's Preface) the Moral Satires did
require Cowper to keep a tight rein on his 'natural character'.
One straightforward manifestation of this is his embarrassment
over the 'worldliness' of *Table Talk*, which he allowed Newton
to explain away in the Preface, as a necessary concession to
popular taste.[43] Similarly, he declares in *Truth* that learning is
the greatest of the snares that bar the 'path to bliss' (l.301) and
in the 'conversion' episode in *Hope* discredits the cultivated life
as worthless 'earthly pleasure', in contrast to the life-saving
allegiance to 'God's holy word'. Yet the educated curiosity
about literature and politics which pervades *Table Talk*, and is
the product of a mind 'politely learn'd' and strong in 'masculine debate', is what we might expect from an interesting writer.
The influence of Newton, his own conscience, and above all the
attractions of a faith that 'can alone exclude despair' (*Hope*,
l.751) led him partially to suppress his personality, and placed
severe restrictions on his mind and art. And no doubt Cowper
would have willingly paid any price for the key to the mansion
of complete 'security and rest'. Had he actually been able to
possess that key in the form of strict religious dedication,
psychic struggle would have ceased, but so too would poetic
growth and experiment.

As it turned out, he did not end up in the cul-de-sac into
which he seems to have stepped. The customary explanation
for the difference between the poems we have been discussing
and the freer atmosphere of *Retirement* is that Lady Austen
arrived to break Newton's dominance over his spiritual 'ward'.
Her *joie de vivre* was, it is certain, responsible to a degree for
releasing Cowper's own more genial spirits, but he had already
found the way forward. A new Cowper is prophesied in the final

'movement' of the conversion episode in *Hope*, where, in an incipient advance of consciousness, he recognizes the emotional,
spiritual, and creative potential of interaction between self,
which is inspired by God, and the active universe, which is
God's greater habitation—'God himself triumphant in his
heart'/'God diffused through ev'ry part.' Contrary to the usual
conception of the individual's being-in-the-world in these
poems, the possessor of 'far superior joy' is active and at liberty,
perceiving the brightness of the sun, *calling* others to share his
delight, *surveying* nature and *prompting* her to join him in his
praise, rather than being the passive recipient of odour from the
'field of promise', or being shut up in 'some mansion, neat and
elegantly dress'd' which has been prepared by 'the Almighty
arm'. For the first time Cowper sees perception as a sign of
grace, and the Creation as a proper object of contemplation. A
state is envisioned which preserves Faith and the ultimate
supremacy of God yet allows for the fuller exercise of the
subjective spirit. That state, tried out and further defined in
Retirement, lies at the very heart of Cowper's future achievements in poetry and the pursuit of 'salvation'.

*   *   *   *   *

The hub around which the wheels of verse revolve in *Retirement*,
however, is Cowper's habitual sense of the condition of
*un*creativeness. Midway through the poem we meet a particularly graphic representation of death in life, where physical
enervation points inwards to psychological stasis:

> Look where he comes—in this embow'r'd alcove—
> Stand close conceal'd, and see a statue move:
> Lips busy, and eyes fixt, foot falling slow,
> Arms hanging idly down, hands clasp'd below,
> Interpret to the marking eye distress,
> Such as its symptoms can alone express.
>
> (ll.283–8)

There follows a comparison between past and present which,
like the conversion passage in *Hope*, recalls the *quantum mutatus
ab illo* motif as expressed in James Hervey's *exempla* of sinners
brought low.[44] But Cowper now isolates two aspects of the 'sad

suffrer's' dark estate: loss of language and the ability to communicate with other men, and weakness of the senses in the presence of nature. The tongue that could 'argue, . . . jest or join the song' lies silent; the 'brisker' and the 'graver' strains both 'fail beneath a fever's secret sway' (ll.289–96). Neither nature untouched by man ('heathy wilds', 'soft declivities with tufted hills') nor nature humanized ('waters turning busy mills', 'Parks in which art preceptress nature weds') affects the 'faded eye' or rouses the 'wounded spirit' (ll.331–42). In the end it is insisted upon that the power to heal belongs to God alone (l.341), but responsiveness to the Creation assumes immense importance, not only as a source of pure delight but as a manifestation, and therefore proof, of God's favour; for when He retunes the strings of the personality, which his 'chast'ning hand' has slackened,

> Then heav'n, eclips'd so long, and this dull earth,
> Shall seem to start into a second birth;
> Nature, assuming a more lovely face,
> Borrowing a beauty from the works of grace,
> Shall be despis'd and overlook'd no more,
> Shall fill thee with delights unfelt before,
> Impart to things inanimate a voice,
> And bid her mountains and her hills rejoice;
> The sound shall run along the winding vales,
> And thou enjoy an Eden ere it fails.
>
> (ll.355–64)

An opening reference to 'virtuous and faithful HEBERDEN', the psycho-physician who had looked after Cowper during his attacks of suicidal depression in London, indicates that the poet is thinking once more of his own past restoration. He holds to the same optimistic developmental 'construct' as in *Hope*. More importantly, he has made his exceptional sensitivity to nature—a faculty he has already displayed in the poem—into a sign of personal grace. It is true that, at this point, Cowper apparently considers transcendent bliss, the return to pre-lapsarian joy, to be the unrepeatable experience of the new convert: 'And thou enjoy an Eden *ere it fails.*' Yet heightened 'seeing' and 'feeling' are just as surely taken as certain evidence of continuing spiritual wholeness.

So emphatically did Cowper come to associate such perception with inner well-being that it was his impotence before nature which finally convinced him that the end was near and he was irrevocably doomed. 'We shall meet no more' is how he ends his penultimate letter to Lady Hesketh in 1798, after reflecting on his blindness to 'delightful scenes' which he would once have taken in with relish. Anticipating Coleridge's lament in 'Dejection', the blankness of the eye and the dull pain within make nature but a series of soul-less images:

> In one day, in one moment I should rather have said, [nature] became an *universal blank* to me . . . with an effect as difficult to remove, as blindness itself. . . . Why is scenery like this, I had almost said, why is the very scene, which many years since I could not contemplate without rapture, now become, at the best, an insipid wilderness to me? . . . The reason is obvious. My state of mind is a medium through which the beauties of Paradise itself could not be communicated with any effect but a painful one.[45]

'I may not hope from outward forms to win/The passion and the life, whose fountains are within' ('Dejection', ll.45–6). Cowper had in effect recognized this disturbing truth—that in our life alone does nature *live*—when depicting the melancholic's relation to the world around him in *Retirement*: the stars 'Shine not, or undesir'd and hated shine,/Seen through the medium of a cloud like thine' (ll.351–2). Now he applies it directly to himself: he sees only sterile forms, which for all their known beauty—'an object still more magnificent than any river, the ocean itself, is almost immediately under the window'—can do nothing to lift the cloud of flat despondency. He is spiritually dead—which is also to say, of course, that the poet in him has died. Even within the letter itself, the brisker and the graver strains of his earlier encounters with nature, in verse and prose, have been exchanged for almost careless, matter-of-fact statement.[46]

Thus Cowper bids a resigned farewell to the capacity on which his happiness and his hopes for a 'happy eternity' had crucially depended. Perceptual power and receptivity had been necessary for the existence of his nature poetry, but it can be said with equal truth that the poetry had existed for their realization: in recording elevated experiences of the Creation he was both calling upon *and* actualizing an ability with which he identified the state of grace—as well as pursuing the lesser goal of sensuous gratification. In a sense, in practice, this makes him a proto-existentialist, the agent of his own prosperity, transferring active responsibility for the individual's welfare from an absolute God and the total scheme of things to the resourceful individual himself, his will and creativity. Yet the more audacious step of actually denying God and living without Him would never have occurred to Cowper. He was troubled by no such conscious temptation as faces Coleridge in 'The Eolian Harp', where the poet retreats from guilty, 'unhallow'd' thoughts of animated nature's 'one Life', 'one intellectual breeze,/At once the Soul of each', to safer, more conventional praise of the Christian God 'Who with his saving mercies healed me'.[47] To the author of *Retirement* nature was always the workmanship and the expression of the Deity himself; and the Deity remains very much the acknowledged source and end of his creative acts. 'Unassisted sight no beauty sees' (1.56), but eyes that have been opened to 'the Sov'reign we were born t'obey' receive the full magnificence and meaning of nature. For them 'an atom is an ample field', the 'invisible in things scarce seen reveal'd' (ll.60-1). They trace the 'signature and stamp of pow'r divine' in all things, from the minutest objects, 'insect forms', to the spacious heavens:

> The sun, a world whence other worlds drink light;
> The crescent moon, the diadem of night;
> Stars countless, each in his appointed place,
> Fast-anchor'd in the deep abyss of space—
>
> (ll.81-4)

There is clearly more to Cowper's contemplation of nature, however, than static recognition of the Artificer Divine. Already we feel the poet's joy as he reaches outward into the spectacular but harmonious profundity of the 'universal frame'; and in the next section, rather than merely arguing from nature up to nature's God, he is led, via the act of inspired perception, to a felt awareness of the individual's capacity for purification, loss of self, and identification with the Deity:

Absorb'd in that immensity I see,
I shrink abas'd, and yet aspire to thee;
Instruct me, guide me, to that heavn'ly day
Thy words more clearly than thy works display,
That, while thy truths my grosser thoughts refine,
I may resemble thee and call thee mine.

(ll.93–8)

'I shrink abas'd, and yet aspire to thee': the self is belittled, yet
is recompensed in the present moment by an influx of spiritual
aspiration which raises confident thoughts of oneness with God
and possible sublimity. In a way, moreover, Cowper has even
now attained a closeness to God, and a resemblance to Him. To
immerse oneself in the miraculous life of nature is to gain entry
to the divine Presence diffused through all, while the poetic
creation itself, Cowper's own making and ordering, is a
counterpart or, to use Coleridge's words, 'repetition in the
finite mind of the eternal act of creation in the infinite I AM'.[48]
In the following lines we see, indivisibly, an image of the
wondrous skill of 'pow'r divine'—'Contrivance intricate, express'd with ease' (l.55)—and an image of the delicate
muscular perfection of Cowper's poetry:

The shapely limb and lubricated joint,
Within the small dimensions of a point,
Muscle and nerve miraculously spun,
His mighty work, who speaks and it is done . . .

(ll.57–60)

The 'signature and stamp' carried by the verse is simultaneously that of creator and Creator; self-assertion and self-
fulfilment blend with a respectful sense of the greater Power, in
the contemplation of nature. When later in *Retirement* Cowper
prays that, in poring over nature's page, he may 'feel an heart
enrich'd by what it pays' (l.209), he is supplicating for what has
already been accomplished. There have been ample returns for
his investment in studying nature: it affords access to Beauty,
Order, and the divine Presence; it nourishes, and refines, Life
and Hope; it satisfies emotional, aesthetic, and intellectual
needs; it brings forth the poetic genius. Above all, in an
enactment of the exalted 'reciprocity', the give-and-take, the

asking and having, which Cowper sees as a privilege of the reborn soul, it allows for an ideal balance, or interactive union, between self and God—who is, effectively, removed from His distant heaven and placed familiarly in the world around us. Though, as we have seen, Cowper does at times, like Coleridge, suggest that the 'passion and the life' has its mainspring within man himself, the *ideal* for both poets is of course a cyclical interaction between inner and outer, whereby nature answers to and further enlarges the asking capacities of the individual. We notice, for example, that the 'rebirth' passage in *Retirement* includes a couplet pointing specifically to a two-way relationship: 'Shall be despis'd and overlook'd no more,/Shall fill thee with delights unfelt before.' (Cf. 'Frost at Midnight', ll.63–4 and 'Dejection', stanza viii. Needless to say, the 'ideal balance' referred to above has its counterpart in modern psychology—notably the Jungian concept of ego-Self identification/reconciliation.)

Now this discovery of the rich rewards of contemplating nature takes place within the context of an equally important discovery of the advantages of retirement itself. There had been hardly a poet in the eighteenth century who had not in some way or other sung the praises of a sequestered life; so popular was the theme that even Johnson, averse in private to all 'the common cant about solitude', yet thought fit to rehearse the conventions in a superbly weighty lyric:

> From false caresses, causeless strife,
>> Wild hope, vain fear, alike remov'd,
> Here let me learn the use of life,
>> Then best enjoy'd, when most improv'd.
>
> Teach me, thou venerable bow'r,
>> Cool meditation's quiet seat,
> The gen'rous scorn of venal pow'r,
>> The silent grandeur of retreat.
>> ('Stern winter now, by spring repress'd', ll.25–32)[49]

But no one thought as assiduously or diversely about the benefits of that life as Cowper himself. Who was more likely to weigh the gains than one for whom rural retreat had long been an actual necessity and way of life? Counting his blessings of leisure, peace, and the freedom to undertake 'the great pursuit' of self-knowledge and knowledge of Providence, he becomes one of the favoured few who have escaped 'custom's idiot sway', looking out upon the world's ignoble strife, not from behind the narrow loopholes of a cramped seclusion, but from a speculative height, a *superior position*:

> We find a little isle, this life of man;
> Eternity's unknown expanse appears
> Circling around and limiting his years;
> The busy race examine and explore
> Each creek and cavern of the dang'rous shore,
> With care collect what in their eyes excels,
> Some shining pebbles, and some weeds and shells; . . .
> The waves o'ertake them in their serious play,
> And ev'ry hour sweeps multitudes away;
> They shriek and sink, survivors start and weep,
> Pursue their sport and follow to the deep.
> A few forsake the throng; with lifted eyes
> Ask wealth of heav'n, and gain a real prize—
> Truth, wisdom, grace, and peace like that above, . . .
> And unregrett'd soon are snatch'd away
> From scenes of sorrow into glorious day.
>
> (ll.148–68)

This is characteristic: the poem everywhere avers the positive and special status not only of retirement but also of the poet-retiree, Cowper in an assumed role.

Cowper had not in fact chosen to 'forsake the throng' at all. He had been forced to leave it by his temperamental incompetence in the sphere of routine action, and there were times when his refuge seemed like a grave:

> It is no attachment to the place [Olney] that binds me here, but an unfitness for every other. I lived in it once, but now I am buried in it, and have no business with the world on the outside of my sepulchre; my appearance would startle them, and theirs would be shocking to me.[50]

These remarks, addressed to Mrs. Newton as recently as 1780, no doubt reflect the poet's desolation at the Newtons' permanent departure from Olney and may also show an underlying resentment about his own inadequacy in comparison with

Newton's success in the active life, of which the latter's new promotion to the living of St. Mary Woolnoth was ample proof. It is possible then to interpret *Retirement* as an expression of restored confidence. But it would be a mistake to stop there. The important thing is the act of formulation and the advantage, long-term as well as immediate, that accrues to Cowper from that act. In certain moods he was capable of finding only a terrifyingly perverse logic in his life, a pattern of endless torment: '*I*, fed with judgment, in a fleshly tomb, am/Buried above ground' is a fiercer version of his complaint to Mrs. Newton of being shut up in the 'sepulchre' of Olney. In *Retirement*, on the other hand, he takes hold of it in such a way as to give it value; which is also to say that he gains control over his discontent. His enforced withdrawal from the world becomes a welcome dispensation; incompetence becomes superiority; the tomb is exchanged for a summit, or a calm recess. That Cowper can still regard retirement, in passing, as a defeat—a result of unsuitability for 'the tumult half the world enjoys' (ll.175–6)— perhaps betrays a lingering anxiety concerning the circumstances of his own 'choice' of life. Similarly, the last part of the poem is crowded with references to the possible dangers of solitude. Guez de Balzac's recommendation of the state is given only qualified approval, for what seems a sanctuary may prove a hell:[51]

> A sepulchre in which the living lie,
> Where all good qualities grow sick and die.
>
> (ll.737–8)

Good company and good books are necessary not merely to improve retirement but to guard against inevitable brooding, since 'A mind quite vacant is a mind distress'd' and 'a thousand plagues [may] haunt the breast' (ll.757ff.). In so carefully defining the drawbacks of the sequestered life and supplying answers to them, Cowper is subduing the uneasy thoughts that haunt his own consciousness. He is, in the fullest sense of the phrase, working things out in *Retirement*—moderating tensions, taking stock, achieving a position vis-à-vis his predicament which stabilizes the personal present and brings the possibility of future advance.

Not that the 'little isle' passage, recently quoted, in itself

holds out much promise of either psychological or poetic
progression. The overriding impression is of stasis, the poet's
superior vantage-point suggesting neither visionary/sublime
nor satiric/legislative potential, but a fixed moral and emotional distance from the world's stage, which is sweepingly reduced
to a scene of futile 'play' as the busy race hunt childishly for
pretty pebbles and shells. Though Cowper avoids the self-
effacement of Gray, who in a similar context throws away all he
has gained from putting on the identity of the sober contemplative by making the sportive insects cast him as but a 'Poor
moralist', a 'solitary fly',[52] he buys his stature and sense of
privilege at the expense of trivializing all forms of active
endeavour. He stands aloof, waiting to be snatched away into
heaven's glorious day. There seems to be a real chance that he
might have become a mere escapist, inert, wrapped up in selfish
dreams of apartness and divine repose. But he did not. The
sequestered life was rich in creative opportunities which he
exploited to the full. Of these, the contemplation of nature was
at once the most attractive and most meaningful to him; and it
is to nature that he returns immediately after the 'little isle'
passage, in lines which characteristically blend celebration and
desire, tribute to nature's harmonies with a satisfied longing for
peace and stimulation:

> the deep recess of dusky groves,
> Or forest where the deer securely roves,
> The fall of waters, . . .
> The clouds that flit, or slowly float away,
> Nature in all the various shapes she wears,
> Frowning in storms, or breathing gentle airs,
> The snowy robe her wintry state assumes . . .
>   (ll. 181–3, 192–5)

There follows an act of poetic dedication, as Cowper calls on
nature to be henceforth 'the great inspirer of my strains' (l.202).
His future opens up before him: a bard dwelling in profitable
isolation, student of the eternal language of the Book of Nature,
who while teaching others of God's 'bright perfections' will find
his own 'heart enrich'd by what it pays'.

At the same time, however, *Retirement* shows Cowper to be
also, in his own distinctive way, a successful student of *human*

nature, in his astute analysis of 'the deficiencies and the mistakes of thousands who enter on a scene of retirement, unqualified for it in every respect and with such designs as have no tendency to promote either their own happiness or that of others'.[53] The bourgeois craze for 'country living', for example, provides material for some of his most enduring satire:

> Suburban villas, highway-side retreats,
> That dread th'encroachment of our growing streets,
> Tight boxes, neatly sash'd, and in a blaze
> With all a July sun's collected rays,
> Delight the citizen, who, gasping there,
> Breathes clouds of dust, and calls it country air . . .
>
> (ll.481ff.)

In this observant response to an incipient social trend we glimpse our own happy–unhappy relationship to the town and 'urban growth', and our own willing 'suburban' 'imprison-ment' ('neatly sash'd') and illusions of freedom. The accom-panying paragraphs on the retired statesman, the 'disincum-ber'd Atlas of the state', belong more particularly to the eighteenth century but make an incisive study in capricious-ness and the Ruling Passion. We are led stage by stage from the politician's initial enthusiasm for the wholesome sight of his patrimonial fields to his eventual boredom and return to the scenes of his former triumphs:

> The prospect, such as might enchant despair,
> He views it not, or sees no beauty there;
> With aching heart, and discontented looks,
> Returns at noon to billiards or to books,
> But feels, while grasping at his fading joys,
> A secret thirst of his renounc'd employs.
> He chides the tardiness of ev'ry post,
> Pants to be told of battles won or lost,
> Blames his own indolence, observes, though late,
> 'Tis criminal to leave a sinking state,
> Flies to the levee, and, receiv'd with grace,
> Kneels, kisses hands, and shines again in place.
>
> (ll.469–80)

The interesting thing about this sketch, apart from its

humorous ironies, is that it turns a major Augustan convention
upside down. It calls in question the idealism that had
surrounded the figure of the retired gentleman-politician in a
host of poems including Dryden's 'To my honour'd kinsman',
Pope's 'Epistle to Robert, Earl of Oxford', and Johnson's
translation of Robert Freind's epitaph on Sir Thomas Hanmer,
the last of which conveniently groups the usual formulae:

> Age call'd at length his active mind to rest,
> With honour sated, and with cares opprest;
> To letter'd ease retir'd, and honest mirth,
> To rural grandeur, and domestick worth . . .
>
> (ll.35–8)

Cowper's portrait has all the same details but a quite different
tenor. His tone, which is equivocal from the first ('Ye groves,
the statesman at his desk exclaims,/Sick of a thousand
disappointed aims'), grows more and more sceptical, amused,
knowing:

> What early philosophic hours he keeps,
> How regular his meals, how sound he sleeps!
>
> (ll.429–30)

The customs and character of his statesman read like travesties
of those praised by Johnson: the few choice friends of Horatian
tradition, for instance, become associates whom he can treat
with his customary contempt, men that 'come when call'd' and
'listen with applause'. But the end-effect of all this is by no
means a repudiation of the basic assumptions of the poetry of
rural retreat, though these assumptions are placed in a
searching and realistic light. As in Horace's famous second
Epode (the *Beatus ille* from which this poetry largely stems),
where the words of celebration belong to the money-lender
Aphius who decides after all to remain town-usurer, Cowper's
dramatic/satiric setting actually re-validates the moral and
psychological claims of retirement. The fickleness of the
statesman, like that of Aphius, supplies a measure by which its
true value and use—and the knowledgeable sincerity of the
author, the poet behind the lines—can be more fully understood. And much the same could be said of the other satirical
episodes in *Retirement*—the bankrupt lord fleeing to the country

to evade his debtors, or the pensive lover in whom Cowper ridicules the sentimentalism of pastoral 'complaint'. The introduction of critical perspectives, present in Horace but excised in a thousand latter-day poems of happy seclusion,[54] is part of a process by which fresh depth and sharper definition is given to an old artistic stock-in-trade. In Cowper retirement is not so much a shared ideal, taken for granted or reproduced for common consumption, as something personally thought about, anatomized, known, and lived by the poet-individual himself. It is justified anew in terms of authorial insight—along with the authorial therapeutic need to value and earn respect for an unsought isolation.

It was important to Cowper, however, that retirement *was* a common ideal. His confidence and his development of a fruitful identity and sphere of activity would not have been possible without the support of an available and honoured tradition,[55] and of two predecessors in particular.

The epigraph to *Retirement* takes us right back to the *Georgics*, where Vergil celebrates the lives of both the contented husbandman (*O fortunatos nimium, sua si bona norint,/agricolas!*) and the poet living as a quiet spectator of nature; and Cowper would have been equally well acquainted with Horace, the great advocate of cultured retirement, and, in leaving Rome for the blest seclusion of his Sabine farm, its classic exemplar.[56] But Cowper's real forebears are nearer home. After the upheavals of the Civil War, and as the practice of imitating and translating Latin authors grew, Horace's urbane prescription for happiness, often merging with the Vergilian idea of the country as a place of innocence reminiscent of the Golden Age, soon became established as a standard contrast to the rigours and turmoil of political and metropolitan life. No one had repeated the prescription more gracefully than the 'ingenious' Cowley, 'courtly though retir'd', to whom unstinted tribute is paid in *The Task*: happy the man who

> has a moderate Minde and Fortune, and lives in the conversation of two or three agreeable friends, with little commerce in the world besides, who is esteemed well enough by his few neighbours that know him, and is truly irreproachable by anybody, and so after a healthful quiet

life ... goes more silently out of it than he came in, (for I would not have him so much as Cry in the *Exit*).[57]

In such words, from the essay 'Of Obscurity', Cowper would have found encouragement enough for accepting, and taking pride in, his retreat from the world; the perfect model on which to base his own criteria for a prosperous life. It is with Cowley in mind, if anyone, that he offers his final definition of genuine retirement, where he cherishes all that his ageing statesman had perverted or ignored. As the bard of Chertsey had discovered 'rich amends/For a lost world in solitude and verse' (*Task*, IV,729–30), so will the recluse of Olney enjoy the peace of 'silent bow'rs', seeking employment in poetry:

> And while I teach an art too little known,
> To close life wisely, may not waste my own.
> (*Retirement*, ll.807–8)

'May not waste my own': usefulness and profit are of much greater concern to Cowper than to Cowley—understandably so, since the latter had, prior to his 'exile', built up a store of fame in the political arena. The poet of *Retirement* has one eye on his place in the external world, envisaging himself as teaching others by precept and his own example. Yet there is some warrant in 'Of Obscurity' even for this desire for the honest returns of doing good ('I love and commend a true good Fame, because it is the shadow of Virtue'), as there is throughout Cowley for Cowper's emphasis on the need to cultivate the mind by friendship ('Friends, not adopted with a school-boy's haste,/But chosen with a nice discerning taste') and reading among 'writers of the abler sort',

> ... such as, in the zeal of good design,
> Strong judgment lab'ring in the scripture mine,
> All such as manly and great souls produce,
> Worthy to live, and of eternal use...
> (ll.697–700)

These things are so commonplace within the tradition, though, that in the end one is struck as much by the way both Cowley and Cowper put them to individual use as by the fact that the later poet drew inspiration from the other. At every turn in

Cowper traditionalism bears the firm impress of an independent personality—as in his insistence on the quality of manly sobriety in literature. Who else would have introduced into a description of the pastimes of the sequestered man an attack, itself more soberly than urbanely humorous, on contemporary fiction—novels that 'Belie their name, and offer nothing new' (ll.709ff.)—and 'learn'd philologists' who chase

> A panting syllable through time and space,
> Start it at home, and hunt it in the dark,
> To Gaul, to Greece, and into Noah's ark.
>
> (ll.692–4)

The other presence behind *Retirement* is of course Thomson. Echoing Vergil in placing the sequestered man alongside the labourer in a setting of rural peace, pleasure, and virtue, *The Seasons* offers what is probably the clearest succinct restatement by any English poet of the concept of *otium* and innocence:

> The happiest he! who far from public rage
> Deep in the vale, with a choice few retired,
> Drinks the pure pleasures of the rural life . . .
> Here too dwells simple truth, plain innocence,
> Unsullied beauty, sound unbroken youth
> Patient of labour—with a little pleased,
> Health ever-blooming, unambitious toil,
> Calm contemplation, and poetic ease.
>
> ('Autumn', ll.1235–7, 1273–7)[58]

The most important parallel, however, is Thomson's interest in retirement as a condition favourable to mental harmony and spiritual growth, where remembering no doubt Vergil's reference to the pleasures of philosophic and religious enlightenment (*Felix qui potuit rerum cognoscere causas . . . /fortunatus et ille, deos qui novit agrestis*), he describes how contact with nature keeps the passions 'aptly harmonized', the mind 'serene and pure', until a state is attained in which the individual can join with angelic voices in singing exaltedly of 'nature . . . nature's God' and at the height of rapture may 'feel the present Deity, and taste/The Joy of God, to see a happy World'.[59] So close is this to what we have seen of Cowper's treatment of the 'experiential' benefits of the life of solitary contemplation that we find him taking his cue from the immediate past even when most conspicuously departing from it into new modes of subjective response. But depart he did. John Chalker points out that Thomson's sense of the 'psychological benefit' that springs from the contemplative life close to nature renders his attitude 'far more immediate and emotionalized ... than anything suggested by Vergil';[60] but, judging by Chalker's quotations, beside Cowper Thomson is on the whole rather disengaged and cerebral in his approach. Here is Thomson returning 'again to the psychological influence of the woods':[61]

> These are the Haunts of Meditation, these
> The scenes where antient Bards th'inspiring Breath,
> Extatic, felt...
> Oft, in these dim Recesses, undisturb'd
> By noisy Folly, and discordant Vice,
> Of Nature sing with us, and Nature's God.
>> ('Summer', ll.409–11,440–2)

Thomson's was a less 'inward' and less self-conscious art than Cowper's. An intimate sensibility and unmistakably personal probing of the emotional and spiritual advantages of retreat seep through even when he is, technically, considering the retirement theme very much from the outside, in lines which blend a faint anticipation of Wordsworth's 'Immortality Ode' with recollection of the conclusion to Cowley's 'Of Obscurity':

> (Happy the man called away from 'cities' and the
>> 'works of man' ...)
> To regions where, in spite of sin and woe,
> Traces of Eden are still seen below,
> Where mountain, river, forest, field, and grove,
> Remind him of his Maker's power and love.
> 'Tis well if, look'd for at so late a day,
> In the last scene of such a senseless play,
> True wisdom will attend his feeble call,
> And grace his action ere the curtain fall.
>> (ll.27–34)[62]

The country is a paradise where the depressed and tainted spirit recovers, through mere proximity to natural objects, its unfallen state of peace, security and willing obedience to God.

This happy man, this imaginary 'life', is any individual who is granted the blessing of 'true wisdom', yet the *exemplum* is also part of a process in which the Evangelical 'monitor' is at bottom the 'sad suff'rer', leading actor in a 'senseless play' of Fate, taking hold of his situation and himself, opening up regions of private salvation. If Thomson offers a poetic statement of the psychological value of retirement, Cowper's relation to the subject is itself, from the very beginning, psychological.

*   *   *   *   *

Retirement ends on a note of achievement and anticipation, mixed however with a strain of anxiety. First the poet lists the 'unnumber'd pleasures' that 'religion does not censure or exclude' (ll.783ff.), as if intent on establishing the options open to him in his life and writing. Gardening, humanitarian acts ('share the joys your bounty may create'), the study and enjoyment of God's Creation in all its sensuous delights and 'matchless workings', the sister arts of poetry and painting ('to lay the landscape on the snowy sheet')—each is allowable, and each was to find a prominent place in *The Task* and in the life of which it is a reflection. Cowper has found a definite field of action, without offending against the 'rules' of religion. The nature of his worry changes, however, when he begins to look more closely at himself vis-à-vis the outside world:

> Me poetry (or, rather, notes that aim
> Feebly and vainly at poetic fame)
> Employs, shut out from more important views,
> Fast by the banks of the slow winding Ouse;
> Content if, thus sequester'd, I may raise
> A monitor's, though not a poet's praise,
> And while I teach an art too little known,
> To close life wisely, may not waste my own.
>
> (ll.801–8)

The concern is twofold: that he is no poet, and that he is cut off after all from the 'more important views' of the world beyond his refuge ('shut out' suggests *exclusion*, 'fast' *enchainment* as well as stability). To look for recognition as a 'monitor' is a reaction to both anxieties; though no poet, he may be a teacher and to teach is to have a place in the world. Here, in his desire to be of some consequence to a society from which he is excluded, Cowper again reminds us very much of Gray, who, we remember, rewrote the ending to the *Elegy* so as to attribute to himself, the melancholy man, the communal, and exemplary, virtues of charity, sincerity, and wisdom: 'Large was his bounty and his soul sincere . . .' (l.121). Like Gray, Cowper cannot, for all his praise of retirement, be content simply to pursue 'the silent tenour of his doom' far from 'the madding crowd's ignoble strife', his mind trained on the promise of 'eternal peace', but must seek at last to justify his existence to himself in terms of wider usefulness.[63]

Taking a hint from Roger Lonsdale's discussion of the *Elegy*,[64] we might link Gray and Cowper together as poets caught in a kind of limbo between two great dispensations— neither urban, urbane, worldly Augustans, confident of their place and function in society, nor Romantics with solid assurance of the merits of solitude and selfhood. But although it is basically accurate, this is too neat a characterization and too loose a linking. For one thing, Gray never committed himself, as Cowper did, to a belief that the true object of art was to legislate for mankind, and indeed all his poetry after the *Elegy*—the Norse and Celtic odes—was a programmatic attempt to divorce poetry from Life and Society and turn it into a vehicle for learned and scrupulous aetheticism. Cowper took a more traditional view—a view which is in fact as crucial to the thinking of the Romantics as to that of Augustans like Pope or Johnson. His wish to be a 'monitor', a socio-moral force, has its counterpart of course in Wordsworth, whose epic of self-discovery, *The Prelude*, was intended only as an 'ante-chapel' to the 'gothic church' of *The Excursion* (and beyond it the philosophic poem *The Recluse*). Yet from a twentieth-century viewpoint Cowper and Wordsworth seem to have got their priorities the wrong way round. The 'sage of Rydal', celebrant of the collective wisdom of the Anglo-Catholic Church, has been displaced by the confessional Wordsworth. And contrary to his hopes at the end of *Retirement* it is not the 'monitor' in Cowper that vindicates the poem but the stylist, the enter-tainer, and above all the artist-individual with his personal needs and unique imaginative vision. We value it because in it we catch poetry at the point of discovering that belief in solitude and selfhood which we are to some extent wrong to consider the overriding motivation of Romantic literature, but which was in the long term its most important legacy.

THE TASK

4

Ut mens poesis:
Cowper and the Description
of Nature

With what enchantment Nature's goodly scene
Attracts the sense of mortals; how the mind,
For its own eye, doth objects nobler still
Prepare...
(Akenside, *Pleasures of the Imagination*)[1]

The Task began as a diversion, at Lady Austen's playful request
for a blank-verse poem on the subject of 'the sofa'. So the story
goes.[2] And indeed the work opens with a mock-heroic account
of the 'progress' of seating in the burlesque manner of John
Philips's *The Splendid Shilling* (1701) (a work Cowper had
imitated in his first extant verses, 'Written at Bath on finding
the Heel of a Shoe'). But great contests spring from trivial
things. By the end of Book VI Cowper had taken on a whole
series of modes, from the satiric to the meditative/reflective, the
Miltonic sublime to the conversational, and had embraced
practically the entire spectrum of contemporary English life—
social, political, religious, aesthetic, commercial, rural, metropolitan, domestic. *The Task* is usually classified as a 'didactic-
descriptive' poem within the same 'tradition' as *The Seasons*,
Dyer's *The Fleece*, Gay's *Rural Sports*, or—to move from the
'Georgic' to the 'graveyard' school—Young's *Night Thoughts*;
and to relate it thus to a loose assembly of what are themselves
largely unmethodical writings is as near as we shall get to any
categorization of its literary form. It could perhaps be more
aptly termed a national poem; for there is no more generous
literary treatment in poetry of the character and concerns of an

Notes and References begin on page 335

age. As we shall see, however, even this aspect of the poem is
crucially influenced by the underlying 'egotism', the compulsive 'self-centredness', of Cowper's genius, and it is still the
relationship of mind and nature, retirement as deprivation and
privilege, the problems of individual existence, which most
positively occupy and express that genius. It is not merely for
convenience that we must make these themes the centre of our
discussion of a work that seems at times intractably various.

*   *   *   *   *

Cowper's own guidance on how to read *The Task* is unhelpful.
In explaining to Newton that his aim was to teach religion and
virtue, he asks us to view the poem as primarily didactic, the
fulfilment of his decision at the end of *Retirement* to bid for 'A
monitor's, though not a poet's, praise'.[3] In practice of course
his responsiveness to life and nature is too great for him ever to
become an out-and-out preacher, his subjective, imaginative,
and perceptual involvement in his subjects too willingly
sustained for *The Task* to be, except occasionally, simply a
moral tract. Indeed, the best known passages from the poem
are not so much preceptive as autobiographical:

> I was a stricken deer, that left the herd
> Long since; with many an arrow deep infixt
> My panting side was charg'd, when I withdrew
> To seek a tranquil death in distant shades.
> There was I found by one who had himself
> Been hurt by th'archers. In his side he bore,
> And in his hands and feet, the cruel scars.
> With gentle force soliciting the darts,
> He drew them forth, and heal'd, and bade me live.
> Since then, with few associates, in remote
> And silent woods I wander, far from those
> My former partners of the peopled scene;
> With few associates, and not wishing more.
> Here much I ruminate, as much I may,
> With other views of men and manners now
> Than once, and others of a life to come.
> I see that all are wand'rers, gone astray
> Each in his own delusions; they are lost
> In chase of fancied happiness, still woo'd

And never won. Dream after dream ensues;
And still they dream that they shall still succeed.
And still are disappointed ...

(III,108–29)

There *is* a familiar lesson in this: Christ makes the injured spirit whole and calms the troubled breast. Yet the purpose of the passage is not to celebrate the Redeemer. Christ's healing power, like his suffering, is something assumed by the poet, and his real importance is as an agent in a personal history—or more accurately an element in a reconstruction of a personal history. What Northrop Frye calls the 'direct identification in which the poet himself is involved'—that is, Cowper's identification with the stricken deer—situates the passage within Frye's Age of Sensibility, with its instinctual subjectivism;[4] but no other exponent of that mode—Collins, Smart, or Gray—speaks so *deliberately* of himself. Past and present are both organized, and in a way that purposefully transforms adversity into advantage. Evacuated of all terror and all joy (and there is terror and joy enough in the *Memoir*), Cowper's great mental crisis becomes, in an act of tranquil retrospection, the occasion of a life-giving intervention by Christ leading on to a state of wise and favoured seclusion. The balanced mind reaffirms its equilibrium by revisiting the past and finding there not only misfortune but good fortune, not only vicissitude but a sequence issuing in peace ('not wishing more') and superior knowledge, both of this life and 'a life to come'. The role of passive victim, indeed all passiveness, is consigned to former times. 'I was a stricken deer', 'deep infixt', 'was charg'd'—the passive verb-forms give way to the active, 'I wander', 'I ruminate', 'I see', as Cowper at once creates and confirms a stable personal identity. It is others now who are the victims— the prey of their own endless dreaming. It is they who are 'mad'—inhabitants of one vast asylum, engaged in innumerable odd and pointless games. Some write of wars and feats of heroes little known, 'and call the rant/An history'; some play tricks on nature, 'giving laws/To distant worlds, and trifling in their own'.

Thus Cowper comes to perceive his flight from the world as an escape from a general insanity. He, and his few like-minded associates, are the truly healthy ones. This is itself of course a species of illusion—imagery of wandering and then of futility used to construct a therapeutic, 'saving' fiction. But such events are wholly positive, not only psychologically but in producing a poetry of the individual life, a poetic drama of mind. And worrying though Cowper's seemingly outright rejection of the world's 'wisdom' may be, his real attitude is in fact neither complacent nor aggressive: his 'pity' at the sight of 'the learn'd . . . most of all deceiv'd' (ll.182–4) is challenged by a certain poignancy, an undertone of sadness, a holding-back, when he is describing his own way of life. 'In remote/And silent woods I wander' . . . 'Here much I ruminate, as much I may': there is in the voice a sense of isolation, of solitariness as well as superiority, which acknowledges the precariousness of a 'contentment' rooted in apartness. For all the one-sidedness of its view of mankind, the poetry is thoroughly, and complexly, human.

    Gilbert Thomas advises us that *The Task* is 'remarkably objective for the work of one prone to introspection'.[5] On the contrary, it is remarkably subjective and 'inward' for one who aimed at objectivity. While it is true that the 'stricken deer' passage is somewhat exceptional in the transparency of its 'confession', the quality and life of the poem as a whole largely derive from the immediate presence, overt or implied, of authorial consciousness and self-consciousness. To recall again Frye's seminal essay, it is 'Longinian' rather than 'Aristotelian', 'psychological' rather than 'aesthetic', 'literature as process' rather than 'literature as product'.[6] This is so even in the more formal delineations of landscape with which this chapter will be primarily concerned—the passages normally talked about in discussions of Cowper as nature poet, where the custom is to describe them merely as 'eye-dominated' and 'realistic', skilful and accurate portrayals of the external world.[7]

*   *   *   *   *

In a simple sense Cowper's descriptions of nature are always equally personal. When Samuel Rose accused him of imitating another poet in the line 'God made the country, and man made the town' he defended himself with a degree of impatience that is surprising in view of the conventionality of the sentiment: 'Nothing is more certain, than that when I wrote the line. . . . I had not the least recollection of that very similar one, which you quote from Hawkins Browne.'[8] He was clearly proud of the fact that his responses to the natural world were never 'second handed', but based on direct experience and genuine love:

> . . . the country wins me still.
> I never fram'd a wish, or form'd a plan,
> That flatter'd me with hopes of earthly bliss,
> But there I laid the scene.
> (IV,694–7)

The man that expects hereafter to be imprisoned in a dungeon where nothing but misery and deformity are to be found, has a peculiar pleasure in contemplating the beauties of Nature and sees a thousand charms in meadows and the flowers that adorn them, in blue skies and skies overhung with tempests, in trees and rocks, and in every circumstance of rural life that are lost upon a mind in security . . . Oh! I could spend whole days and moonlight nights in feeding upon a lovely prospect! My eye drinks the rivers as they flow . . .[9]

Long-standing, sensitized by misery, a conscious source of 'nourishment', Cowper's interest in nature could never have been merely aesthetic, still less a convenience for coaxing the reluctant reader into the reading of what might profit him.

So, in the address to city-dwellers that rounds off Book I the poet's instinctive feeling for the 'beauties' and consolations of familiar scenes, amply communicated by the unstressed intimacy with which he relates the objects of nature, at once enforces and outweighs the thrust of moral argument:

> Our groves were planted to console at noon
> The pensive wand'rer in their shades. At eve
> The moonbeam, sliding softly in between
> The sleeping leaves, is all the light they wish,
> Birds warbling all the music. We can spare
> The splendour of your lamps; they but eclipse
> Our softer satellite. Your songs confound

Our more harmonious notes; the thrush departs
Scar'd, and th'offended nightingale is mute.
                                                    (I,760–8)

One of the main theses of John Barrell's important book on
Clare and landscape poetry is that for various reasons—the
influence of painting, the socio-economic idea of land as
property, the growth of consumerist attitudes at large—
eighteenth-century nature-poets characteristically 'subjected'
nature to themselves, made it 'passive under the eye', and
prevented 'the particular things within it from asserting
themselves at all';[10] and a distinction is later drawn between
the way Cowper *does* sometimes reveal the particularity of a
thing, which is 'to heap it with details' at a leisurely pace, and
Clare's (obviously preferable) method of 'fix[ing] the object
with one or two striking images'.[11] Yet Cowper is in fact well
able to realize a particular feature of nature by one or two
striking images, as here in 'sliding softly' and 'sleeping leaves',
phrases whose effect is not at all to 'subject' nature or make it
'passive' but to allow for, respect, and enhance its peculiar life.
The opening sentence suggests of course that man puts nature
to his service: 'Our groves *were planted* to console...'. But nature
participates in his efforts; the moon-beam shines softly, almost
approvingly, through the groves, while the birds sing harmoniously. The whole drift of the passage is to reject the activities,
the 'art' (songs and lamps), which offend or shut out nature in
favour of a balanced relationship in which nature yields its
psychological and aesthetic benefits, of quietness and beauty,
to the heart that loves her.

While Cowper never imposes on nature, however, his view of
it *is* noticeably selective and shaped. There is no place in his
poetry for the beauty that has terror in it—at least until the last
decade, when in the poem on the Ice Islands and 'The
Castaway' he comes to confront the darker forces of a universe
which by then he sees as uncaring, even spectacularly
malevolent.[12] The one section of *The Task* dealing with threat
and violence treats them mechanically as signs of God's wrath
towards sinful man, after the fashion of Jeremiah and popular
verse-sermons like Benjamin Stillingfleet's *Thoughts Occasioned
by the Late Earthquakes* (1750); the pseudo-Miltonics capture the

strangeness of the events, the tortured motions of the earth, but the poet himself remains uninvolved even when the images might be expected to touch the most sensitive areas of his psyche:

> and the fixt and rooted earth,
> Tormented into billows, heaves and swells,
> Or with vortiginous and hideous whirl
> Sucks down its prey insatiable.
>
> (II, 100–3)[13]

As a rule Cowper seeks the gentle, benign face of nature. Though this may be understood in terms of contemporary aesthetics, as a preference for the 'beautiful' over the 'sublime', for the qualities of delicacy, 'smallness' outlined within Burke's influential treatise,[14] it is also clearly, and deeply, rooted in character and temperament, as the poet saw when writing from Eartham in Sussex of 'woods like forests and hills like mountains, a wildness in short that rather increases my natural melancholy'.[15] Yet the nature-poetry of *The Task* is not simply a reflection of a particular aversion but the active fulfilment of a related need for stimulation and repose—for temperate joy and tranquil restoration. Thus, in another passage from Book I, Cowper begins with the proposition that nature, this time rural sounds, can 'exhilarate' and 'restore' and then proceeds to solicit from her just the 'charms' he most desires—soothings, serenity, genial promptings of the spirit:

> Mighty winds,
> That sweep the skirt of some far-spreading wood
> Of ancient growth, make music not unlike
> The dash of ocean on his winding shore,
> And lull the spirit while they fill the mind;
> Unnumber'd branches waving in the blast,
> And all their leaves fast flutt'ring, all at once.
> Nor less composure waits upon the roar
> Of distant floods, or on the softer voice
> Of neighb'ring fountain, or of rills that slip
> Through the cleft rock, and, chiming as they fall
> Upon loose pebbles, lose themselves at length
> In matted grass, that with a livelier green

Betrays the secret of their silent course.
Nature inanimate employs sweet sounds,
But animated nature sweeter still,
To soothe and satisfy ...
                    ... [Even] kites that swim sublime
In still repeated circles, screaming loud,
The jay, the pie, and ev'n the boding owl
That hails the rising moon, have charms for me.
                              (I, 183–99, 203–6)

'Mighty winds' and the 'dash of ocean' become a source of
composure and the kite, bringer of death, becomes a source of
pleasurable mild sensation, tracing patterns of delight. Without in any way misrepresenting nature Cowper takes exactly
what he craves, the mental state of activity-in-repose, excitement without fear. There is a strategy at work, but nothing like
that so emphatically isolated by Barrell—the effort to control
nature encouraged by the 'Whig, and mercantile, ideology in
eighteenth-century England [which] saw nature as something
to be conquered, and forced to give up her riches'.[16] Of course,
Cowper has few rivals—Coleridge being the closest in time—in
his fidelity to the sights, sounds and movements of rural nature:
the leaves 'fast flutt'ring, all at once', the kites swimming their
'still repeated circles', the rills that 'slip', 'chime', and 'lose
themselves' in grass which 'Betrays the secret of their silent
course' are all living presences, dictating the speed, rhythms
and texture of the verse which embodies them.[17] But at the
same time nature does appear and speak as the poet *likes*. To
say, however, simply that nature is made to act in a psychologically appropriate way would not be enough. The closing
phrase, '. . . have charms for me', implies a claim of privilege
dependent on desert, similar to that made by Coleridge in 'This
Lime-tree Bower' for the 'gentle-hearted' Lamb, the poet's
other self, to whom, in his pure and wise receptivity, 'No sound
is dissonant that tells of Life';[18] and throughout the passage the
overriding impression is of that relationship in which nature
rewards the mind that respects and is open to her gifts. A
relationship experientially as well as philosophically present,
for in the uplifted surprise of 'all at once', the eager satisfaction
of being let into the secret of the stream's hidden flow, the

heart's leaping at the sight of the kites' lofty grace, are registered the immediate responses of one whom nature soothes and keeps awake to Beauty. Cowper speaks of nature 'fill[ing] the mind'. With what? Nothing, so far as we can tell, but peace, delight, and its own image. Certainly, it is not, as we might expect from the Evangelical Cowper, with thoughts of Christ or of God the Creator. What is celebrated—and it is fundamental to Cowper's conception of stable being—is the blessings and blessed moods of a living attachment to Nature itself. We are witnessing, in other words, a radical displacement of religious sensibility, a 'naturalization' of Faith.

The general similarity between Cowper's position here and that of Coleridge and Wordsworth in 'This Lime-tree Bower' and 'Tintern Abbey' is striking. But although, like them, he values nature, not for its appeal to the outer eye, but for its influences upon the inner self, his vision seemingly lacks the temporal and ontological perspectives whereby they see their intercourse with nature within the context of their lives and 'being' as a whole. To Coleridge, present joy is food for future years—'Beauties and feelings, such as would have been/Most sweet to my remembrance even when age/Had dimm'd mine eyes to blindness . . .' (ll.3–5); and the perception arrived at by Wordsworth is of the link between our early, primitive impulses and our most sophisticated thoughts and feelings, between youth and age, 'sense' and 'moral being'.[19] However, in the first descriptive section of *The Task*, of which the passage on rural sounds is an extension, Cowper has already connected past and present, so as to stress the continuity as well as the changes in his relation to nature. A reflective and autobiographical frame surrounds his most quoted delineation of landscape—the 'prospect' of the Ouse valley. Leaving the confusions and torpor of the city, where curates doze (orthodox religion put to sleep?) and the nurse 'snores the sick man dead' (conventional healing set aside?), he begins by recalling, 'nor without regret', his rural excursions as a child in love with nature, who literally provided sustenance for his 'boyish appetite', 'scarlet hips and stony haws . . .' (ll.109–22). He then contrasts these coarser pleasures, as Wordsworth does, with the more sober, contemplative 'relish' of his later years, but, again like Wordsworth, emphasizes the abiding strength of his responses (though 'life

declines') and nature's power to answer them.[20] He finds his
joy intensified by the presence of Mary Unwin, long the 'dear
companion of my walks', whom he calls to witness the sincerity
of his praise for nature and the genuineness of his raptures—as
Wordsworth asks Dorothy, his 'dear, dear Friend', to testify to
his zeal and 'warmer love' for scenes 'More dear, both for
themselves and for thy sake':[21]

>   . . . nor yet impair'd
> My relish of fair prospect; scenes that sooth'd
> Or charm'd me young, no longer young, I find
> Still soothing and of pow'r to charm me still.
> And witness, dear companion of my walks,
> Whose arm this twentieth winter I perceive
> Fast lock'd in mine, with pleasure such as love,
> Confirm'd by long experience of thy worth
> And well-tried virtues, could alone inspire—
> Witness a joy that thou hast doubled long.
> Thou know'st my praise of nature most sincere . . .
> How oft upon yon eminence our pace
> Has slacken'd to a pause, and we have born
> The ruffling wind, scarce conscious that it blew,
> While admiration, feeding at the eye,
> And still unsated, dwelt upon the scene.
> Thence with what pleasure have we just discern'd
> The distant plough slow moving, and beside
> His lab'ring team, that swerv'd not from the track,
> The sturdy swain diminish'd to a boy!
> Here Ouse, slow winding through a level plain
> Of spacious meads with cattle sprinked o'er,
> Conducts the eye along its sinuous course
> Delighted. There, fast rooted in his bank,
> Stand, never overlook'd, our fav'rite elms,
> That screen the herdsman's solitary hut;
> While far beyond, and overthwart the stream
> That, as with molten glass, inlays the vale,
> The sloping land recedes into the clouds;
> Displaying on its varied side the grace
> Of hedge-row beauties numberless, square tow'r,
> Tall spire, from which the sound of cheerful bells

Just undulates upon the list'ning ear,
Groves, heaths, and smoking villages, remote.
Scenes must be beautiful which, daily view'd,
Please daily, and whose novelty survives
Long knowledge and the scrutiny of years.
Praise justly due to those that I describe.

(I, 140–50, 154–80)

Taking the 'prospect' by itself, we can, for the time being, agree with the critics who present Cowper as an adept exponent of the principle of *ut pictura poesis*.[22] The final image of the stream inlaying the vale 'as with molten glass' (ll.169–70) suggests that nature's effects are analogous to those of art, and in the description itself Cowper carefully constructs a design of the kind a painter might produce. Myrddin Jones is more specific: 'The extract is laid out in the form of a landscape of the school of Claude'.[23] But whether or not he has a particular model in mind—which I doubt—it is certain that Cowper proceeds in accordance with the contemporary taste for painterly structures and detail, a taste reflected for instance in his own favourite theorist, Hugh Blair, who advises that 'a true poet makes us imagine that we see it [the object or scene] before our eyes; he catches the distinguishing features; . . . he places it in such a light that a painter could copy after him'.[24]

In his pioneering study of techniques of composition in eighteenth-century nature-poetry C. V. Deane remarked that, lacking the total impact of a painting, descriptive verse depends for its success largely on the poet's skill in revealing the sequence and spatial relationships of objects.[25] Cowper is expert at this type of 'progressive' organization, the reader being led through degrees of perspective by the key adverbs 'there', 'here', 'beyond', the topographical adjectives 'distant', 'sloping', and 'remote', and the central line of the river which connects the succession of salient features. The slowness with which he 'maps' the landscape allows us time to take in and combine the various details as we are guided in a semi-circular sweep from the near-distant ploughman to the meadowland stretching into the foreground, back along the course of the river to the arresting detail of the elms, and then on to the rising ground that leads in turn to the horizon diversified with a group

of sights on a diminished scale. Words like 'lab'ring' (l.161) and
'winding' (l.163) supply action without disturbing the overall
impression of orderliness, while man and animals appear
simply as another ingredient in the picture—as if Cowper were
consciously following the recommendations of Lessing, who
ruled that hints of movement were invaluable for preventing
flatness in descriptive poetry, and Hugh Blair, who advised
poets to introduce figures into their pictures, as painters did, for
the sake of variety.[26]

Nor is this the only evidence suggesting that it was the *visual*
joys of nature that attracted Cowper, or that he strove to
subordinate it to the aesthetic needs of the observer. Josephine
Miles has shown that 'eye', 'see', 'art', and 'beauty' are among
his favourite words;[27] and among the descriptions of Book I
even the relative confusion of the forest is made to yield a neat,
picturesque beauty—*picturesque* in a strict sense, indicating not
only, in the words of the leading publicist of this concept, 'that
kind of beauty which would look well in a picture', but also a
preoccupation with the distinctive colours, shapes and attitudes of individual objects in the scene:[28]

> Nor less attractive is the woodland scene,
> Diversified with trees of ev'ry growth,
> Alike, yet various. Here the gray smooth trunks
> Of ash, or lime, or beech, distinctly shine,
> Within the twilight of their distant shades;
> There, lost behind a rising ground, the wood
> Seems sunk, and shorten'd to its topmost boughs . . .
> (I,300–6)

The 'charms' of the different trees are sharply specified—
'poplar, that with silver lines his leaf', 'ash far-stretching his
umbrageous arm', 'Of deeper green the elm'—before the
perspective opens out once more to take in the panorama of hill
and valley, 'a spacious map', bounded on either side by woods
and river, where—

> The Ouse, dividing the well-water'd land,
> Now glitters in the sun, and now retires,
> As bashful, yet impatient to be seen.
> (I,323–5)

The 'here–there' arrangement, the ideal of *discordia concors*

('Alike, yet various'), and above all the simile of the 'bashful' mistress, recall the opening of Pope's 'Windsor Forest' in which the groves part admit and part exclude the light, 'As some coy nymph her lover's warm address/Nor quite indulges, nor can quite repress' (ll.19–20). Yet the whole tenor of Pope's contemplation of the 'chequer'd scene', with its 'order in variety', had been different. For Pope the landscape had borne a quite definite social significance, as a symbol of natural harmony-in-abundance of which the peace and plenty of Stuart England was a microcosmic extension. In Cowper the human need for *perceptual* order is paramount, and is both reflected in and satisfied by an art-conscious mode of presentation. Art-conscious, and sometimes literature-conscious too:

> The sheep-fold here
> Pours out its fleecy tenants o'er the glebe.
> At first, progressive as a stream, they seek
> The middle field; but, scattered by degrees,
> Each to his choice, soon whiten all the land.
> (I,290–4)

This recalls Pope's description, in the Pastoral 'Spring', of how the shepherds 'Pour'd o'er the whitening vale their fleecy care' (l.19), which itself draws upon a stock poetic diction. 'Fleecy' was standard in periphrases for sheep, while 'pour' and 'whiten' were commonly employed in this way, on the model of Vergil's *fundere* and *albescere*.[29] Cowper's lines are undoubtedly an accurate, indeed excellent, record of a phenomenon he had observed for himself, rather than an instance of the servile application of conventional phraseology that so irritated the 'naturalists' Joseph Warton and John Aikin in their attacks on contemporary nature-poets,[30] but the language inevitably formalizes the event, and by evoking a tradition of similar descriptions makes our experience of the event all the more an experience not only of nature but of art as well.

When all is said, however, the most important thing is Cowper's presence within his poetry. By this I do not mean simply that he writes always with his eye and mind firmly on the object. That goes without saying: 'fleecy tenants', for instance, tells us just what the sheep are in themselves (covered in wool), in relation to the sheepfold ('tenants'), and in relation

to society (givers of fleeces), while nothing could be so
unerringly observant as such sights as that of the sunken wood
'shorten'd to its topmost boughs'. I am thinking, rather, of a
pervasive, sustained, and at times highly complex, presence of
'self', as exemplified in full in the Ouse Valley episode. It is this
that sets Cowper crucially apart from other eighteenth-century
descriptive poets.

.   The difference is apparent even at the relatively straightforward level of emotional engagement. Here is the popular John
Scott of Amwell, one of Cowper's models:

> How beautiful,
> How various is yon view! delicious hills
> Bounding smooth vales, smooth vales by winding streams
> Divided, that here glide through grassy banks
> In open sun, there wander under shade
> Of aspen tall, or ancient elm . . .
>
> (*Amwell, a descriptive poem*, 1776, ll.258–63)

Cowper transcends such writing in his 'prospect' not only
through a greater specificity of detail and location[31] but in the
authenticity of his simple sensuous responses. Scott's assertive
language actually tells us very little either about nature or the
poet's feelings towards nature: the repetition of 'smooth'
merely underlines the vagueness of the term, while 'beautiful',
'various', and the over-emphatic 'delicious' speak more of
rhetorical effort than heart-felt enthusiasm. 'Admiration, feeding at the eye,/ *And still unsated*', 'The . . . swain *diminish'd to a
boy!*', '*spacious* meads', 'Conducts the eye . . ./ *Delighted*', 'never
overlook'd, our fav'rite elms', 'hedge-row beauties *numberless*',
'the sound of *cheerful* bells/ *Just undulates* upon the . . . ear': in
Cowper description combines with intimacy of response, the
latter being communicated sometimes by explicit statement
('Delighted'), sometimes as an inflexion of the voice (the gentle
lift in tone at 'numberless', the chuckle of naive glee and
surprise in 'diminish'd to a boy!', the freer breathing of
'spacious'), sometimes by suggestions of conscious, pleasurable
familiarity ('our *fav'rite* elms'), sometimes in the very informality with which things are so exactly defined ('*just* undulates', or
elsewhere the trees that '*screen* the herdsman's *solitary* hut').
Then there is that least easily analysed of Cowper's characteris-

tic qualities, the pause and cadence, the accessible, unaffected, freely structured 'music' of the verse. The painterly arrangement and the stress upon the 'eye'—'Here Ouse, slow winding through the level plain/Of spacious meads with cattle sprinkled o'er,/Conducts the eye along its sinuous course/Delighted ...'—do not prevent the poetry from also being an embodiment of the movements of the perceiving mind. The sights, motions and atmosphere of nature engage—one might say pass into—the poet's own sensitive, receptive spirit, so that their portrayal is, simultaneously, a portrayal of the self absorbed in and by the thing it contemplates.

According to Barrell, Cowper treats landscape as something remote, 'apart from the observer ... something *over there*'.[32] But this is to overemphasize the matter of physical perspective. He may be positioned on an 'eminence', looking from afar and with the apparent detachment and habits of a connoisseur of art, yet in the final analysis he is extraordinarily close to nature—much closer not only than John Scott but than Thomson:

> Meantime you gain the height, from whose fair brow
> The bursting prospect spreads immense around;
> And, snatch'd o'er hill and dale, and wood and lawn,
> And verdant field, and darkening heath between,
> And villages embosomed soft in trees,
> And spiry towns by surging columns marked
> Of household smoke, your eye excursive roams—
> Wide-stretching from the Hall in whose kind haunt
> The hospitable Genius lingers still ...
>
> (*The Seasons*, 'Spring', ll.950–8)

We should, to be sure, credit Thomson with somewhat greater feeling for the life of nature than Barrell allows when stressing its domination by 'the poet's eye' and the arrangement into Claude-like 'lateral bands';[33] the prospect *bursting* and *snatching*, the villages *embosomed soft* in trees, or the mountains that *dusky rise*, grant the objects an identity of their own and not merely the status of components in a preconceived visual design. But there is none of the 'reciprocity' so typical of Cowper, who is gently led by nature and gently nourished with pleasure—conducted by slow-winding Ouse, treated to a display of beauties numberless ('Displaying on its varied side ...'—the

verb is active, nature willingly exhibits its charms), visited by
the bells' sound that undulates upon the ear (the *list'ning* ear,
suggesting that the individual too makes a willing effort, a
contribution to the process whereby the landscape pleases),
blown upon, 'scarce conscious', by the ruffling wind. Far from
either controlling or being controlled by nature, Cowper both
acts and is acted upon, both gives and receives. At times indeed
there is in this episode a strength of harmony between self and
nature unusual even for Cowper. We may take, for example,
the word 'Delighted' (1.166), which could grammatically define
either 'Ouse' or 'eye'; man and nature come inseparably
together in a moment of shared delight, the former delighting to
receive what the latter delights to give. Always, of course, man
must consciously bring himself to nature, taking an initiative
rooted in personal capacity, a 'relish of fair prospect' (1.141).
That done, however, nature readily offers food and makes him
seek for more: having climbed the 'eminence' (ll.154–5), a
deliberate act of going to nature, Cowper is blown on by the
wind (ll.155–6), the spirit of nature, and 'feeds' entranced on
the beauties of the scene, which in turn cause him, 'still
unsated', to 'dwell' further on the landscape (ll.157–8), to ask
for more.

There is one last point about the passage that needs
emphasizing, not least because it has a bearing on the quality of
Cowper's descriptions in general. The Ouse valley is not
somewhere visited for the first time but a familiar place
revisited; and it is as much a locus of the mind, or memory, as a
physical spot. It is made known at once that Cowper journeys
habitually to the spot—'*How oft* upon yon eminence our
pace/Has slacken'd to a pause . . .'—and the joys he finds there
are in part directly dependent on feelings and expectations
formed by the regularity of his comings: only an ear that has
heard the faint, just-undulating, bells before would *listen* for
them at all, while the elms, fast-rooted in the river's bank as if in
solid separateness from humanity, have become through the
years objects of love and a constant, unfailing source of
pleasure—'Stand, never overlook'd, our fav'rite elms'. The
toning of the passage as a whole—that effect of intimacy and
heart-felt response—is the simultaneous expression of long-
standing and undiminished accord, of an involvement with the

genius of the place that is at once old and forever new. Thus feeling comes in aid of feeling—not via any mere recollection of previous pleasurable occasions, nor simply from the increase of joy brought by the sympathetic presence of Mrs. Unwin, but from the affective power, the inwrought legacy, of former moments of significant experience. And that is not all. The passage represents, in a special way, an actual recovery of the past. For beneath the painterly design is another structural development: we begin with memories, but then shift, almost imperceptibly, from a past to a present tense ('has slacken'd', 'have ... discern'd', 'swerv'd' etc./'Here Ouse ... *Conducts*'), with the customary adverb of pictorial-spatial organization, 'Here', functioning, unusually, in a temporal as well as loco-descriptive role so as to signify the point at which remembrance becomes immediate perception. The poetry is less a description than a meditation, an act of and in the mind. In recalling those times when he has sought nature and been rewarded by her, when he has lingered at her shrine and been embraced by her influence (the 'eminence', the mention of 'praise' and 'raptures', and the slowing of the step all suggest reverence and holiness), Cowper is also entering a sacred recess of the heart—entering it contemplatively and imaginatively, for that physical slackening 'to a pause' is a mental slackening too and a prelude to a trance-like state in the writer—whence he draws both creative inspiration and ease and refreshment for the spirit. 'From nature doth emotion come, and moods of calmness ...'; 'So feeling comes in aid/Of feeling, and diversity of strength/Attends us, if but once we have been strong'; the 'vivifying Virtue' of 'spots of time', whence our minds 'Are nourished and invisibly repaired': Wordsworth gave sophisticated shape to the 'philosophy' which grounds well-being and creation in the subtle interplay between past and present and self and nature, but Cowper was the first to practise and establish it in achieved form.[34]

*   *   *   *   *

All Cowper's nature-poetry is, in Robert Langbaum's now standard phrase, a 'poetry of experience'. The section of *The Task* we have just been considering possesses, indeed, every one of the distinguishing features of that 'genre' as they are listed by Langbaum when discussing its emergence in Wordsworth and Coleridge, and in 'Tintern Abbey' in particular: the autobiographical content; the use of an extraordinary perspective of which Cowper's looking *down* at the distant plough, and not conventionally across at its front view and on a level plane, is a perfect example;[35] the presence in the object or scene of the poet's 'perceiving consciousness'; the grounding of value and the validity of an idea 'in perception . . . [and] the genuine experience of an identifiable person', and not in a publicly accepted order of values and ideas; the observer not so much learning as becoming something—'Each discovery of the external world is a discovery of himself—[of] an individual existence or identity'.[36]

The last two of these aspects demand comment. Firstly, Cowper is just the poet we might expect to centre value in a public, or at least objective, order or system of beliefs—in that his loyalty is ultimately to God and religion. But while it is true that Book I sometimes refers to nature as God's handiwork ('the performance of a God', 'God made the country'), the whole thrust of the poetry lies towards a celebration of nature itself and the benefits of a close relationship with it. 'Scenes must be beautiful, which, daily view'd, / Please daily ... / Praise justly due to those that I describe': God, as we shall see, re-enters Cowper's vision later in the poem, but for the moment nature is all in all to him. And this celebration is not a matter of conforming to and confirming a set of fixed, received verities. 'The love of Nature, and the scene she draws' (l.412) is in essence a philosophy personal to the poet, subjectively developed, the validity or falseness of which can be judged only by how convincingly or unconvincingly it is presented within the poem, and not by any standards of absolute truth. Moreover, it is of course a philosophy very firmly related to the poet's discovery of himself. We saw at the beginning of this chapter that Book I of *The Task* ends with the poet secure in the bosom of the countryside, confidently dismissing 'the world' and its riches in favour of the greater wealth of a life amid 'fields and groves'. Out of his encounters with nature he has discovered an identity, an individual existence—which is at last defined, partly by what it is not (that is, being borne around in 'chariots and sedans', living a life of idle luxury), partly by reference to what it is (a life-in-nature, amid the groves' consoling embrace and the soothing/exhilarating visitations of the moon and warbling birds), and partly by the tone of calm assurance with which he rejects the 'element' of the gay ('... possess ye still/Your element') and talks about his own ('Our groves were planted to console ...'). *The Task* is a history of the imaginative and psychological life of an identifiable person—which offers, however, a new model for poetry and for prosperous 'being'.

And the model emerges always against a background of felt socio-cultural dissolution. The image of 'empire' as a 'mutilated structure, soon to fall' (l.774) which occupies the very last lines of Book I caps a whole cluster of images of incoherence and collapse, not least in religion itself, for the very observance of God's authority and the authority of holy writ has been contemptuously usurped in an invasion of materialist goals and secular ritual:

> Advancing fashion to the post of truth,
> And cent'ring all authority in modes
> And customs of her own, till sabbath rites
> Have dwindled into unrespected forms,
> And knees and hassocks are well-nigh divorc'd.
>   (I,744–8)

If Cowper teaches us—and his immediate successors—anything, it is the possibility of finding value when value is no longer to be found in the public world, where luxury 'plagues' not only the metropolis ('so fair/May yet be foul') but the land, the 'country' (l.770), of which it is the heart. In Goldsmith's *The Deserted Village*, we may recall, 'sweet Poetry' is driven out by 'degenerate times', fleeing with the virtues of 'piety', 'loyalty', and 'faithful love' before a torrent of 'hastening ills', amoral capitalism, the headlong pursuit of 'wealth'. In Cowper the Muse is not exiled but rusticated. She finds more than sufficient sustenance in the other mighty world of eye and ear—in nature and the language of the sense. Many had gone to nature for their inspiration before, of course—Thomson, the Wartons, Akenside—but never, I think, with this accompanying sense of other possibilities being closed, or fast closing, and of the need to keep creatively, spiritually, and morally alive in an age hostile to creativity, spirituality, and moral sensibility.

Aliveness is the hallmark of Cowper's poetry of nature, and the meaning resides primarily in *that*—in the experience—rather than any stated or even implied beliefs and ideas. This is perhaps more immediately apparent in the quick succession of random, brief, and varied exchanges that form the middle section of Book I, a journey through the wonderland of familiar scenes:

> Descending now (but cautious, lest too fast)
> A sudden steep, upon a rustic bridge
> We pass a gulph, in which the willows dip
> Their pendent boughs, stooping as if to drink.
> Hence, ancle-deep in moss and flow'ry thyme,
> We mount again, and feel at ev'ry step
> Our foot half sunk in hillocks green and soft,
> Raised by the mole . . .
>
> (I,266–73)

> Refreshing change! where now the blazing sun?
> By short transition we have lost his glare,
> And stepp'd at once into a cooler clime.
> Ye fallen avenues! once more I mourn
> Your fate unmerited, once more rejoice
> That yet a remnant of your race survives.
> How airy and how light the graceful arch,
> Yet awful as the consecrated roof
> Re-echoing pious anthems! while beneath
> The chequer'd earth seems restless as a flood
> Brush'd by the wind. So sportive is the light
> Shot through the boughs, it dances as they dance,
> Shadow and sunshine intermingling quick,
> And dark'ning and enlight'ning, as the leaves
> Play wanton, ev'ry moment, ev'ry spot.
>
> (I,335–49)

> We tread the wilderness, whose well-roll'd walks,
> With curvature of slow and easy sweep—
> Deception innocent—give ample space
> To narrow bounds. The grove receives us next;

Between the upright shafts of whose tall elms
We may discern the thresher at his task.
Thump after thump resounds the constant flail,
That seems to swing uncertain, and yet falls
Full on the destin'd ear . . .

(I,351–9)

There is in this no principle, design, or goal external to the poetic-psychological-experiential event—whether of *ut pictura poesis*, Popean *discordia concors*, or Evangelical reading in the Book of Nature. It is the pure and vital being-with-nature, and the value this automatically assumes, that matter. At a basic level, of course, the poetry simply elevates experience *per se*. The word 'descending' at the beginning of the first extract, followed by the typically spontaneous aside of 'but cautious . . .', does not so much plot the contours of the landscape as locate the poet within it and make *us* interior to *his* perceptions and sensations. We are sympathetically engaged with an act of sympathetic 'seeing' and 'feeling'. At the same time, however, we are aware of the elevation of a particular way of relating to the natural world, and a particular mode of articulation. The familiar Cowperian ingredients take a specially rich but lucid form. There is no distance, no gulf or barrier, between the poet and nature: he sinks into 'hillocks green and soft', delighting in the feeling of raw contact with the earth. In contrast to thus being received downward by the earth, as he presses from without, he finds himself in the second extract enclosed by nature, being uplifted (both in the direction of his gaze and emotionally, in spirit) by her awesome grace and prompted to a swift analogy with the human world (the 'consecrated roof') that bears witness to the felt sacredness of the spot rather than turning it into a metaphor for a man-made object, a church, or for an abstract idea (ll.341–3). He is then transfixed by the miracle of the dancing light, the intermingling shadow and sunshine—so transfixed that all he can do is excitedly articulate that miracle, in a sportive, dancing, harmoniously restive verse which 'gives' no more and no less than is 'given'. Finally, he is received into the grove, where another miracle is revealed, this time the miracle of rural labour, whose never-failing skill, like the previous reference to art's 'deception innocent' in creating pleasing illusions, forms an exact image of the poet's own craftsmanship, reminding us that however inspired, however 'uncalled', the events, he makes a crucial contribution to their shape and quality. In places Cowper may, to be sure, seem to invite that criticism which was levelled at existing meditative-descriptive poetry by Coleridge, who came to dislike even Bowles, his early favourite, for his 'perpetual trick of moralizing everything', of connecting natural appearances 'by dim analogies, with the moral world'.[37] We note, for example, the lament for the 'fate unmerited' of the 'fallen avenues' in the middle passage, while the other two extracts both continue with moral reflections, the first with a comparison between the mole's 'hillocks' and the disfigurements wrought by the great ones of mankind (ll.274–5), the third with thoughts of man's 'primal curse', which in the case of the thresher's toil has been 'soften'd into mercy' and made the pledge of 'cheerful days, and nights without a groan' (ll.364–6). Yet these 'analogies' are but minor incidents in a mental journey dominated by an experiential involvement with nature which clearly exhibits that union of mind and perceived object, self and nature, which Coleridge himself demands of the poet, whose 'heart and intellect should be combined, intimately combined and unified with the great appearances of nature, and not merely held in solution and loose mixture with them, in the shape of formal similes'.[38] Nor, on closer scrutiny, are the incidents really out of the main course of the journey, since each expresses, and further defines, just that relationship which is being carried on in the passages of description—a relationship in which the individual does *not* destroy or disfigure nature, in which the 'primal curse' of man's self-consciousness and separation from nature is put off (at the Fall 'Earth felt the wound', 'nature gave a second groan'),[39] and in which there is generated an inner well-being that is indeed a 'pledge' of 'cheerful days, and nights without a groan'. For, to take up the last point, in walking with nature as he does, a welcome visitant who never fails to rise to, and is never disappointed by, what is offered of cruder sense-impression ('half-sunk in hillocks . . .') or finer miracle (that *grace-full* moment beneath the arch, where he stands awe-struck in the presence of nature), he makes possible that confident sense of

secure and favoured 'being' which is made manifest at the end
of Book I.

Discussing the 'new scheme of poetry' introduced by Denham's *Cooper's Hill* about the middle of the seventeenth century,
Dr. Johnson quotes the popular lines with which we are already
familiar:

> O could I flow like thee, and make thy stream
> My great example, as it is my theme!
> Though deep, yet clear; though gentle, yet not dull;
> Strong without rage, without ore-flowing full.

and comments, 'Most of the words thus artfully opposed are to
be understood simply on one side of the comparison, and
metaphorically on the other'; that is, in Langbaum's words, the
river stays 'a rhetorical device, an analogy'—rather than being
an indivisible part of an articulated experience in which
thought and feeling, and meaning and response, are fused.[40]
Denham, of course, everywhere *intends* the landscape to be a
rhetorical device, an emblem:

> [Windsor] above the Valley swells
> Into my eye, and doth it self present
> With such an easie and unforc't ascent,
> That no stupendious precipice denies
> Access, no horror turns away our eyes:
> But such a Rise, as doth at once invite
> A pleasure, and a reverence from the sight.
> Thy mighty Master's Embleme, in whose face
> Sate meekness, heightened with Majestick Grace
> Such seems thy gentle height . . .
>
> (ll. 40–9)

This is extremely fine poetry, but very different from Cowper's.
What is, on one side, the embodiment of an aesthetic and
emotional apprehension of the scene, signifying nature's power
to inspire 'pleasure' and 'reverence', becomes on the other a
ceremonial strategy for celebrating kingly 'height' and gracious
majesty. In Cowper there are no such dichotomies and
equations. To him, nature is never an 'example' or a 'theme';
neither are his 'raptures', as he puts it, ever 'conjur'd up/To
serve occasions of poetic pomp' (I, 151–2)—especially not

occasions of socio-political idealization. Whereas Denham's 'O
could I flow like thee' postulates a unity between the inherent
properties of the perceived object and the experiencing,
creating 'I', Cowper actually unites them, moving actively in
an active world, blending his energies with the energies of
nature, producing a poetry that is at once an expression of an
active self and of 'the life of things'. His 'scheme of poetry' is
clearly one that overrides the 'dissociation of sensibility' which
Langbaum, in the wake of Johnson and Eliot, complains of in
such poems as *Cooper's Hill*: so meaningful is his concrete
experiencing of and interaction with 'the life of things' that
meaning derived from conventional knowledge, rational thinking, and traditional ideals becomes unnecessary. The message
is in the medium, the poetic-experiential event, and is, as M. H.
Abrams puts it when describing Wordsworth's own position,
'that the mind is creative in perception, and an integral part of
an organically interrelated [and dynamic] universe'.[41]

On the evidence of his one description in *The Task* of the
process of composition, Cowper was seemingly unaware of the
innovative form of his meditative-descriptive writing. Poets
strive merely

> T'arrest the fleeting images that fill
> The mirror of the mind, and hold them fast,
> And force them sit till he has pencill'd off
> A faithful likeness of the forms he views;
> Then to dispose his copies with such art,
> That each may find its most propitious light,
> And shine by situation . . .
>
> (II,290–6)

The traditional neo-classic metaphor of the mirror (which can
be traced right back into Renaissance concepts of art as
imitation),[42] the phrases 'pencill'd off' and 'faithful likeness',
the stress on artful disposition of 'copies', all conspire to equate
poetry with its 'sister art' of painting and can only have
encouraged the habit among his early readers of valuing his
poetry for its mimetic realism and pictorial qualities (a habit
reflected in that appetite for illustrations of his work which
caused Lady Hesketh to wish that the *words* were more often
appreciated).[43] It is important to note, of course, that 'mind' is

granted a central place in poetic creation—but it is seen more as a passive receptacle for exterior 'forms' than a locus for organic interplay between inner and outer. Cowper failed to see what Coleridge saw when commenting, perhaps with Cowper the 'best of modern poets' in mind, that 'Images, however beautiful, though copied faithfully from nature, ... become proofs of original genius only so far as they are modified by a predominant passion . . . when a human and intellectual life is transferred to them from the poet's own spirit'.[44]

Cowper's poetic practice achieves more than he was aware of. This is also true with regard to the philosophic implications of his dealings with nature—though to a much lesser extent, for he was manifestly conscious of offering, if not quite a creed of 'natural piety', then at least a formula for individual well-being. There are, if we seek nature, infinite chances for man, every man, to be renovated: 'sweet Nature' pleases 'ev'ry sense'—

> The air salubrious of her lofty hills,
> The cheering fragrance of her dewy vales,
> And music of her woods—no works of man
> May rival these; these all bespeak a pow'r
> Peculiar, and exclusively her own.
> Beneath the open sky she spreads the feast;
> 'Tis free to all—'tis ev'ry day renew'd;
> Who scorns it starves deservedly at home.
>
> (I,428–35)

Cowper always includes inner, as well as physical, health and strength among nature's gifts. Just previously, for example, he has referred to 'pow'rs of fancy and strong thought' and the avoidance of a 'vapid soul' as the special right of her devotees (ll.393,401). Now the hymnological idiom—not 'sweet Jesus' but 'sweet Nature', a 'pow'r/Peculiar' like 'peculiar grace', refreshment freely offered and every day renewed as in the Olney hymn, 'Joy and Peace in Believing', Christ feeds his children from boundless stores of love—begins to shift the idea of nature's active beneficence onto a religious plane, suggesting an incipient 'naturalization' of Christian impulse and thinking. We shall look more deeply into this process of 'naturalization' in the next chapter, when considering the deepening of the process itself in later parts of the poem and also Cowper's eventual return to God via the doctrine of 'the light of nature' (i.e. God 'being understood by the things that are made, even his eternal power and Godhead').[45] Already, however, he has put religion in a new dress, the dress of sensitivity to the beauty and 'fresh'ning impulse (1.376) that lie about us: 'The love of Nature, and the scene she draws.' He does not deny the supernatural, God and Christ, but says in effect that nature is enough—sufficient to sooth, uphold and nourish the individual. The appeal of such a faith is obvious: it opens religion to all, as in the primitive Christianity of St. Paul, and requires the sanction neither of externally framed laws nor of the reason. In Book VI of *The Task* we shall find passages that prove beyond a shadow of a doubt that the 'philosophy' of what Geoffrey Hartman calls Wordsworth's 'credal lyrics'—'Lines written in early Spring', the Matthew poems, and so on—derives directly from Cowper; a philosophy based in a rejection of 'the head' and a belief in man's capacity to be constantly restored and 'taught' in the presence of nature.[46] But Book I is itself an invitation, by precept and example, to 'come forth into the light of things' to 'drink at every pore/The spirit of the season'.[47] In the hymn 'Joy and Peace in Believing' Cowper had affirmed that 'Sometimes a light surprizes/The Christian when he sings;/It is the Lord who rises/With healing in his wings' (ll.1–4), but to the poet-singer of *The Task* the charms of familiar scenes and a gentle vistation by the sun's 'sportive . . . light' in the temple of fallen avenues are all the feeling and all the light he needs.

In anticipating the Wordsworthian view of nature as the 'open secret' or 'commonplace mystery' Cowper was making a positive assault on the despiritualizing tendencies of an Enlighted Age, when the magic circle joining Self and World, Heaven and Earth, had been unLocked, *genius* was reduced to *genus*, and God became a mere Mechanic Cause. To say this is, of course, to respond to the universal historical significance of what is in essence a personal story. Every encounter with nature invests Cowper's own life with value; every one is a trial and triumph of his own spirit; every one nourishes and affirms the aliveness of the inner man—that worthier self established in his accounts of the recovery of the dead-in-life melancholic.

The shadow side of his psyche is present too, imaging darker possibilities—the non-being of the paralytic, the madness of Crazy Kate, the unsatisfied longings and death of the mariner starved of nature's food:

> his very heart athirst
> To gaze at Nature in her green array,
> Upon the ship's tall side he stands, possess'd
> With visions prompted by intense desire:
> Fair fields appear below, such as he left,
> Far distant, such as he would die to find—
> He seeks them headlong, and is seen no more.
>   (I,448–54)

This is a particularly interesting instance of Cowper's tragic awareness; for it envisions the reverse-state of his ontological ideal of gentle communion with a benign nature—the sense of both nature and imaginative/creative power as disastrously parasitic (the mariner craves for nature, creates it, and dies of his imaginings, as Kate is consumed by her 'delusive fancies' that her long-lost lover will return [ll.539ff.]). It underpins the ideal but is also the poet's dream of its dangers, of how death might come to one dependent upon it. Thus Cowper's 'natural faith' and optimism are challenged from within: the dialectic of the imagination, the drama of mind, persists.

Yet authorial psycho-drama often goes with the expression of historical truth. There is Carlyle, for example, in whom we find the same emphases as dominate Cowper's consciousness and response to the world. The latter's desperate rejection of the materialism of 'gross and pamper'd cities', where men roundly abrogate the 'total ordinance and will of God' and science, usurping religion, parades 'her eagle eye,/With which she gazes at yon burning disk/Undazzl'd and detects and counts his spots' (I,686ff.), clearly prophesies the Victorian's condemnation of the spiritual paralysis that set in during 'The Unbelieving Century' of the Enlightenment when the world became a 'Machine' and 'God's absolute laws ... Moral Philosophies'.[48] Less obvious, but no less real, is their shared interiorization of the Christian Hell. Though Cowper talks of being imprisoned 'hereafter' in a world of 'misery and deformity', his real concern was the prison-house of the self in the here and now—be it the private hell that he recalls in the *Memoir* when remembering his moments of paranoia ('I never went into the street, but I thought the people stared and laughed at me ...') or the extravagant urges of his heart-sick mariner. Carlyle felt that in his 'age of Downpulling and Disbelief' the very notions of Heaven and Hell had been pulled down, but he knew well enough the interior darkness of the 'Everlasting No', the solitary experience of a 'Universe ... all void of Life, of purpose, of Volition', and knew also what he called the 'detestable state of enchantment' whereby the world appears a spectral, 'discordant, almost infernal' Dance of Death.[49] To the scepticism they perceived around them and to their own subterranean despair both writers opposed one and the same answer—the religion of Nature. *The Task* declares what Carlyle asserts in *Sartor Resartus*: 'O Nature! ... Ha! why do I not name thee God? Art thou not the "Living Garment of God"?'.[50] The Church is dying?—then worship in the temple of Nature; miracles are discredited?—but Nature is a miracle. Both men were individuals seeking a personal faith, yet they were just as surely men of their times—men of the same epoch, for Cowper stands at the inception of the tradition of post-Enlightenment Romanticism to which Carlyle gives late expression. The materialist made an idol of profit and wealth; the Deist exiled the Divinity to the reaches of space; Locke, encoding the philosophic implications of Newtonian physics, said that the world of our ordinary perception was largely illusory, that the only objective reality consisted of matter inhabiting space. Against these postures the Romanticist, from Cowper to Carlyle and beyond, protests by appealing to his own concrete experience of 'the life of things', renewing the reality both of spirit and Spirit. That Carlyle or Wordsworth did this is common knowledge. That Cowper did it has been left unsaid.

*   *   *   *   *

The characteristics and qualities of Cowper's descriptions of nature as we have witnessed them in the course of this chapter, are by no means confined to isolated occasions. They are pervasive, though variously expressed. We may usefully conclude with another important example, from much later in the poem:

> 　　　　　　　　　　　　. . . how the frost
> Raging abroad, and the rough wind, endear
> The silence and the warmth enjoy'd within!
> I saw the woods and fields, at close of day,
> A variegated show; the meadows green,
> Though faded; and the lands, where lately wav'd
> The golden harvest, of a mellow brown,
> Upturn'd so lately by the forceful share.
> I saw far off the weedy fallows smile
> With verdure not unprofitable, graz'd
> By flocks, fast feeding, and selecting each
> His fav'rite herb; while all the leafless groves,
> That skirt th' horizon, wore a sable hue,
> Scarce notic'd in the kindred dusk of eve.
> To-morrow brings a change, a total change!
> Which even now, though silently perform'd
> And slowly, and by most unfelt, the face
> Of universal nature undergoes.
> Fast falls a fleecy show'r: the downy flakes,
> Descending, and with never-ceasing lapse,
> Softly alighting upon all below,
> Assimilate all objects. Earth receives
> Gladly the thick'ning mantle; and the green
> And tender blade, that fear'd the chilling blast,
> Escapes unhurt beneath so warm a veil.
>
> 　　　　　　　　　　　　(IV,308–32)

The customary realism is there from the start, for the four planes of the landscape, alternately light and dark, correspond to the four actual areas of land-use of a type of eighteenth-century agricultural landscape—the green meadows, the brown arable lands, the fallows grazed by sheep, and the sable woodland in the far-distance. Then, in a versatile switch from a broad to a concentrated perspective, Cowper achieves a remarkably complete account of an individual phenomenon with very few strokes, the minimum of fuss and a maximum effect. The adjectives 'fleecy' and 'downy'—'stock' epithets revivified—function precisely to supply a sense of the delicate texture, the soft 'feel' of the snow, while the verbs and faintly lingering participles—'Fast falls ... Descending ... never-ceasing ... alighting ...'—enact the relentless yet gentle descent of the shower, its motions and silent 'music'. In the single word 'lapse' the three ingredients of this very fine word-picture come momentarily together—the hint of sen-suousness, the movement, the melody that lies in the absence of sound.

But what is it then that sets this poetry apart from the work of Cowper's disciple, James Hurdis, who shared his aptitude for responsive portrayal of natural phenomena?—

> Few flakes of ev'ry size float through the air,
> As undetermin'd or to rise or fall;
> Caught by the circling eddy of the breeze,
> Lo! now they mingle all in rapid dance,
> And with a sweep descend. A feathery shower
> Of flakes enormous follows, 'lighting soft
> As cygnet's down ...
>
> (*The Favourite Village*)[51]

Certainly, Cowper captures the rhythms of the event more easily, and orchestrates them more smoothly, than Hurdis does here, where, relatively speaking, the verse struggles to an extent both against flatness (the first line) and against over-statement ('feathery ... 'lighting soft/As cygnet's down')—although the details of the 'circling eddy' and 'rapid dance' could not be fresher or better controlled. This, however, is a difference of degree rather than kind. More significant is the emblematic content of Cowper's vision of nature. Unlike Hurdis, he is interested in the 'order' of things as well as in phenomena, things themselves. The references to harvest, flocks and the system of rotation remind us of the profitable relationship between mankind and his environment, while the balance and variety, the *discordia concors*, of nature itself appears in a whole series of details—the sheep feeding on seemingly useless weeds, the seasonal cycle suggested in the movement from green meadows, through golden harvest, autumnal fallows, leafless groves, and winter snow back to a sense of the future spring in the image of the embryonic life of 'the green/And tender blade', the slender shoot being protected from the fierceness of winter by winter's own warm veil. Impressions of independence and connection, mutability and enduring process, conflict and kinship, difference and sameness (the flakes 'assimilate' all objects) combine to produce a notably full representation of organic Life and Unity.

Charles Ryskamp says of the passage that 'in his overt emphasis on moral and general ends [Cowper] remains with the Augustan poets', and the Augustan poetry Ryskamp has in mind is Pope's 'Windsor Forest'.[52] But there is really no *overt* emphasis on moral ends at all, despite the emblematic dimension; and the similarities with Pope are limited to the general idea of order-in-variety and a few resemblances of phrasing ('lately wav'd', 'verdure', 'sable'). The urge towards the symbolic, so strong in 'Windsor Forest', is entirely muted in Cowper, as can be seen by comparing the latter's understated suggestion of a benign nature in 'the weedy fallows smile . . .' with Pope's eager evocation of the concern for human need in the image of cornfields 'nodding' to 'tempt the joyful reaper's hand' (l.40). It may be that in framing his picture of nature's harmonies Cowper has at the back of his mind what is elsewhere very much to the front—the perfect workmanship of 'the great Artificer of all that moves' (VI,207). Yet there is no explicit religio-philosophic goal replacing the socio-philosophic aims of Pope's landscape-painting. The interest lies not so much in the meaning of the landscape as in the landscape itself—and in the act of perceiving, for we are made aware, as nowhere else in the eighteenth century, of the contemplative and sentient poet, of contemplation and sentience as valuable ends in themselves. Nature may be 'unfelt' by 'most', but the poet's sensibility is everywhere at work in a response to the 'feel' of things—the fadedness of the fields, the fleeciness of the snow, the miraculous totality of the change from variety to uniformity, the soft-falling and -settling flakes. Cowper's respect for the independent life of nature is as strong as ever, yet the richness of that life is supplied to a large degree from his own feelings. If, in the final lines, 'green', 'chilling', and even 'tender' direct attention to the intrinsic qualities of natural phenomena, 'fear'd' and 'unhurt'—indeed the whole conception that inanimate nature is *itself* sentient—signal the working of an acute human sensitivity, a special intimacy carried to the

very point of identification with the object. The life of nature is
in two senses expressed from within—as a landscape of the
meditating mind and, at last, from a position of interiority in an
act of sympathetic 'projection'. (Perhaps 'warm' is the best
measure of this interiority: snow, which we think of as cold,
becomes from the imagined point of view of the blade of grass a
warm protective blanket.) There could be no surer example of
the organic interrelation of mind and an organically interrelated universe.

In the comments that precede this passage, Cowper's claims
are all for the value of meditation itself, even meditation of the
most undirected, 'indolent' kind:

> such a gloom
> Suits well the thoughtful or unthinking mind,
> The mind contemplative, with some new theme
> Pregnant, or indispos'd alike to all.
> Laugh ye, who boast your more mercurial pow'rs,
> That never feel a stupor, know no pause,
> Nor need one; I am conscious, and confess,
> Fearless, a soul that does not always think.
> Me oft has fancy, ludicrous and wild,
> Sooth'd with a waking dream. . . .
> 'Tis thus the understanding takes repose
> In indolent vacuity of thought,
> And sleeps and is refresh'd. . . .
>
> (IV,278–87,296–8)

Taken together with the vision of nature's 'variegated show',
there is more to the statement than a defence of the homely
pleasures of day-dreaming, though this is included as Cowper
refers to the 'brittle toys' woven by his fancy while he pores over
the 'sooty films' that play upon the bars of the fire. On the one
hand, of course, he argues for the restorative effect—the
refreshment—of quiescent 'vacuity of thought', thus extending
to the raw play of imagination ('In the red cinders ... with
poring eye/I gaz'd, myself creating what I saw') the therapeutic gains that he habitually makes from the imaginative
exploration of nature. Yet this is part of a larger theme—the
opposing of the 'unthinking mind' or 'mind contemplative' and
the 'mercurial powers' of the intellect so as to imply the

superiority of the former as an agency for knowing the world. When first setting up this opposition Cowper leaves us asking, 'But just what is the *use* of cultivating "a soul that does not always think"?', and 'How, exactly, *is* the understanding "refresh'd" in moments of thoughtless silence?'. The contemplative act that occurs in the 'silence and warmth' of the poet's 'calm . . . recess' gives the answer: it is souls like this in moments like this which most fully apprehend, come to know and enter into, natural life and natural process. Thus his challenge of the boastful analytical intelligence's professed hold on truth is substantiated by a practical demonstration of truth revealed through non-intellectual means—the revelation of a living organic reality that is the reverse of the material reality of empirical science. True knowledge of the 'beauteous form of things', says Wordsworth, comes only when we bring 'a heart/That watches and receives'; or as Goethe phrased it, 'The man who wants to know/organic truth and describe it well/seeks first to drive the living spirit out . . .'.[53] Cowper's 'ends' are those of all post-Enlightenment Romanticism—the elevation of the inward process by which we spontaneously grasp, through observation aided by intuition, the wholeness and spirit of 'all objects'.

But it is 'Frost at Midnight' that most conveniently underlines this centrally Romantic orientation of *The Task*. The links between Coleridge's poem and the lines from Book IV do not, as Humphrey House contends,[54] consist simply in certain similarities of detail—most prominently the low-burning fire into which the idling spirit projects its own dreams—or in the 'personal' meditative toning of the 'conversational' style, but extend to the whole meaning of the poetic act. In neither case is the idea of nature as God and nature as educator the point of the poetry—though Coleridge's hopes for his son's spiritual growth through intercourse with a divinely inspired natural world, the manifestation of the 'God . . ./. . . who from eternity doth teach Himself in all, and all things in himself', articulate a concept that *The Task*, especially Book VI, did much to popularize. Coleridge's prophecy of Hartley's future union with natural process is a step towards his own present discovery, or rediscovery, of that process; for in describing the seasons, all of which will be sweet to the child beloved of nature,

he returns to his original vision of the frost with an enlarged
sense of the numinous quality, harmonies, and (since it now
includes the child) beneficence of nature's 'ministry':

> whether the eave-drops fall
> Heard only in the trances of the blast,
> Or if the secret ministry of frost
> Shall hang them up in silent icicles,
> Quietly shining to the quiet Moon.
>
> (ll. 70–4)

The poem has its culmination, its 'ultimate point', in a
revelation of the miracle of awareness as well as the miracle of
natural process and permanence, and above all a revelation of
the mysterious ties between the unthinking, wisely passive
mind and the spirit without. The opening paragraph records a
state in which the mind is separate from nature and playing
over the surface of things—conscious of the 'secret ministry' of
the frost outside, vexed by the calm and extreme silentness,
constructing 'dim sympathies' between the film that flutters on
the grate and the life of the idling spirit, remarking how that
spirit interprets the life of objects as its own mood demands.
The end of the poem celebrates an advance into communion.
And that is exactly what Cowper's passage does; in talking of
how he pores over the dying cinders, 'amus'd', creating images
or reading 'some stranger's near approach', he describes an
inferior mental activity which highlights the later profound,
though quiet, accord with living organic reality. Coleridge's
final vision of the frost is the counterpart of Cowper's vision of
the tender blade beneath the mantle of snow: both are
epiphanies, upholding the act of sentient knowing as opposed
to the act of knowing analytically which requires that we
'murder' the object, seeing it as something unalive, something
unlike ourselves. They insist, that is, upon an anti-scientific
view of the universe, and upon recognition of the 'companionable' powers of mind and nature—so 'companionable' in
Cowper's case that the object is imbued with the same feelings,
the same fear and senses, as man. Since in the poetic process,
and especially such an effort of 'identification' with the object,
we contemplate the manifest aliveness of self, the living organic
reality we are made aware of is one that includes consciousness.

5

Contemplation as a Means of Grace

Intercourse between self and nature, a living apprehension of a living organic reality, remains of primary importance throughout *The Task*. The more we read of the poem, however, the more impressed we are by the variousness of this 'intercourse'—the variety of ways in which Cowper sees, responds to, and connects with the natural world. His concern was not to develop any one specific mode of perceiving nature but to perceive, and experience, it as widely and fully as possible, within the general limits supplied by his preference for its milder forms. Spacks, for example, draws our attention to the panorama of animal life in winter near the beginning of Book V, which embodies a whole series of perspectives and techniques.[1]

Some readers will doubtless share her impression that the middle section is 'almost pure convention, in language and in concept':

> Now from the roost, or from the neighb'ring pale,
> Where, diligent to catch the first faint gleam
> Of smiling day, they gossip'd side by side,
> Come trooping at the housewife's well-known call
> The feather'd tribes domestic. Half on wing,
> And half on foot, they brush the fleecy flood,
> Conscious, and fearful of too deep a plunge.
> The sparrows peep, and quit the shelt'ring eaves
> To seize the fair occasion. Well they eye
> The scatter'd grain; and, thievishly resolv'd
> T'escape th'impending famine, often scar'd,
> As oft return—a pert voracious kind.

Notes and References begin on page 337

Clean riddance quickly made, one only care
Remains to each—the search of sunny nook,
Or shed impervious to the blast.

(V,58–72)

The conventionality lies of course in the emphatic use of the pseudo-Miltonic syntax and phraseology so common in mid-eighteenth-century descriptive verse (from 'diligent to catch' right through to 'the search of . . . shed impervious'), in the periphrases of 'feather'd tribes domestic', 'fleecy flood', and 'pert voracious kind', and in such formulations as the seemingly inert personification of 'smiling day'. The style carries with it the familiar idea—highly developed in *The Seasons*—of the interrelatedness and diversity of all created life, including man himself, which is all the more discernible in the winter landscape because of sentient nature's increased individuality and increased dependence on human help. The farmyard birds and the sparrows are portrayed in all their separateness, not least by the simple categorizing phrases 'feather'd tribes domestic' and 'pert voracious kind', both good examples of that element of exact generic designation which John Arthos and others have shown to underlie the apparently vague idiom of the eighteenth-century language of natural description.[2] On the other hand, any hint of 'classification' will inevitably suggest the greater whole of which the 'tribe' or 'kind' is an integral part, while in Cowper's passage the 'species' are also linked by the instinct for survival—'the one only care' for food and shelter. At the same time, moreover, the behaviour and appearance of the lower forms of nature are characterized in such a way as to emphasize their similarity to, and ties with, mankind: they 'troop' and 'gossip' like the housewife who feeds them, are 'fearful' and responsive to the main chance, act 'thievishly', and possibly remind us of 'pert voracious' children. There can be no denying the truth of Spacks's summary remark—which is actually rather different from her reference to 'almost pure convention'—that the lines operate in terms of 'well-established poetic patterns . . . which will reinforce the reader's sense of some vast natural harmony'.[3] A harmony indeed in which the poet is himself included, for the passage is, whatever else, a typical act of sympathy on Cowper's part. The tone, that of a genial observer involved in yet detached from the 'drama' enacted in the winter landscape, suggests a duality mirroring the revealed concept of kinship and distinction.

Yet are pattern and concept more important here than the manifest presence of the perceiving and creating mind? I think not. We are as much aware as ever not only of scene and its philosophic meanings but of the poet's immediate and fluent engagement with the life of nature—a creative act of perception, experiential interrelation and ontological release. And as always it is this psycho-kinetic ingredient which distinguishes Cowper's poetry from that of other exponents of the 'didactic-descriptive' tradition. *The Seasons* offers a comparable description of the reactions of animals to the hardships of winter, where the 'fowls of heaven' seek out the 'winnowing store', the 'brown inhabitants' of the wilds invade the garden out of 'fearless want', and the 'bleating kind/Eye the bleak heaven, and next the glistening earth,/With looks of dumb despair . . .', while the redbreast pays his annual visit to man:

> hopping o'er the floor,
> Eyes all the smiling family askance,
> And pecks, and starts, and wonders where he is—
> ('Winter', ll.253–5)

The common ground is easy enough to discern—the differentiation according to 'kind', the unity of all nature thrown into relief by the pressures of winter, the brisk realism of the lines on the robin which rivals that of Cowper's 'Half on wing,/And half on foot, they brush . . .', the scrupulous precision and suggestiveness with which stock terminology is used (Geoffrey Tillotson remarks on the brilliant transference of emphasis arising from the juxtaposition of the periphrasis 'bleating kind' and the carefully observed 'Eye . . . With looks of dumb despair'—'it is the dumb eye and *not* the voice that tells us of their despair').[4] But Cowper is in fact much more responsive than Thomson even to the opportunity for both accurate and animated delineation. His flair for vivid 'word-painting' is nowhere more obvious, not only in the graphic definition of such observed detail as 'Half on wing . . .' and 'peep', or the figurative aptness of 'gossip'd, 'trooping', or 'thievishly', but also in the mildly inflated, 'mock heroic',

formulations which lend a humorous colouring to the whole.
The conventionality of 'pure convention' is everywhere out-
flanked by the dexterity with which Cowper puts it to work,
whether as a general aid to this last-mentioned effect ('smiling
day', 'the fair occasion') or in the subtler moment of 'pert
voracious kind', which is introduced virtually as an afterthought, a conscious and slightly comic alternative for describing 'sparrows'. Paradoxically, the passage is a pure 'original'.
And its originality arises from something more than a skilful
deployment of an inherited style. It has what we call 'character', which resides in this instance in a sustained expression of
glee—that is, Cowper's delight both in his subject, the curious
happenings around him, and in the process of composition
itself.

   This is equally true of the descriptions on either side of this
vignette, though they differ from it, and from one another, quite
radically in style and perspective. The first concentrates on a
single animal, while the second contemplates the general effects
of winter on wild birds. In the first 'the eye' dominates, in the
second 'the mind':

> Shaggy, and lean, and shrewd, with pointed ears
> And tail cropp'd short, half lurcher and half cur—
> His dog attends him. Close behind his heel
> Now creeps he slow; and now, with many a frisk
> Wide-scamp'ring, snatches up the drifted snow
> With iv'ry teeth, or ploughs it with his snout;
> Then shakes his powder'd coat . . .
>
> (V,45–51)

> The very rooks and daws forsake the fields,
> Where neither grub, nor root, nor earth-nut, now
> Repays their labour more; and, perch'd aloft
> By the way-side, or stalking in the path,
> Lean pensioners upon the trav'ler's track,
> Pick up their nauseous dole, though sweet to them,
> Of voided pulse or half-digested grain.
> The streams are lost amid the splendid blank,
> O'erwhelming all distinction.
>
> (V,89–97)

The brilliance of the first passage is of the kind that is 'given' rather than, as in the farmyard scene, 'worked for', though we may note Cowper's command now of an overwhelmingly Anglo-Saxon vocabulary—the rapid succession of brusque but finely pointed epithets and verbs, settling in the second half of the passage into the rhythms of the animal's scampering, snatching, and finally more deliberate movements. The poet offers no interpretation on the event, and the language holds no particular associations: we are aware only of the dog himself and his unusual vitality, and of the observer's answering pleasure. In the other passage Cowper is less the involved spectator and more the distant interpreter of winter, reflecting on the debilitating influence of the same power that had magically invigorated the woodman's 'cur' but realizing that desolation has its own mystery and appeal, in the numberless rituals of death and survival, deprivation and compensation— thornberries feeding the thrush yet denying 'smaller minstrels' their 'supply', 'Ten thousand . . . self-buried ere they die', rooks and daws forsaking their normal foraging-ground for the way-side and finding 'sweet' what is 'nauseous' to man. Here the language is more dignified and the syntax more elaborate than elsewhere in the panorama. Latinate words ('pensioners', 'nauseous', 'voided' . . .) come suddenly to the fore, suggesting a much more rational and considered point of view. Neither this, however, nor the implied philosophical concern with the 'balances' of a perfectly adjusted Creation, makes the passage any less a personal act of 'seeing' and embodiment of specific individual perceptions.

Now, the simpler psychological benefits, of joy and unself-consciousness, that usually come to Cowper from contemplating nature are as apparent in this section of *The Task* as anywhere in his poetry. Indeed, the induction to Book V brings them very much into focus, by indicating the therapeutic value of even the most straightforward perceptual experience—that resulting from the casual operation of the outer eye. Incipient thoughts of transience and death—Cowper's sensation of being but 'a fleeting shade'—are diverted as soon as they arise through the influence of pleasing sights, firstly the comic grotesqueness of the poet's own shadow 'spindling into longitude immense' and then the more absorbing miracle of nature's unexpected beauty:

> Mine, spindling into longitude immense,
> In spite of gravity, and sage remark
> That I myself am but a fleeting shade,
> Provokes me to a smile. . . .
> The verdure of the plain lies buried deep
> Beneath the dazzling deluge; and the bents,
> And coarser grass, upspearing o'er the rest,
> Of late unsightly and unseen, now shine
> Conspicuous, and, in bright apparel clad
> And fledg'd with icy feathers, nod superb.
> (V, 11–14, 21–6)

The point is not merely that Cowper is capable only of light-heartedness in the presence of nature. The danger of tragic apprehension and inward-turning is there all right but is counteracted by outgoing response to the appeal of an external phenomenon, the strange appearance of his shadow, and then displaced entirely by concentration on the objects of the natural world. The moment of Cowper's original awareness of the shadows cast by the sun is a precarious one which could lead either way, into self-conscious and elegiac reflection or into unselfconscious encounter with the wonders of the transfigured landscape. The eye, triumphant over mind, ensures the latter direction, which itself issues in the fuller perceptual experience and activity of the passages we have already considered. Once underway, the act of perception—which eventually includes visual, intellectual, imaginative, and (in the humour) emotional energies—yields full and undisturbed recreation, a dynamic, varied, and stable involvement in a vital, various, and ordered world.[5]

But the significance of perception in Cowper always of course goes deeper than the level of immediate therapeutic gain, and it does so especially in Books V and VI of *The Task*. In his work perception is crucial to the whole question of the health or sickness of the psyche. We may recall that in the autobiographical *Memoir* disease of the mind and spirit—Cowper's own madness—is everywhere understood and portrayed in terms of 'seeing'. His pathological fear of the forthcoming examination of his suitability for the position of parliamentary Keeper of the Journals, for example, readily transforms the world around him into a prison-house of absolutely hostile things (his candidacy for the post was the beginning of his road to literally suicidal despair):

> I expected no assistance from anybody there, all the inferior clerks being under the influence of my opponent, and accordingly I received none. The journal books were indeed thrown open to me—a thing which could not be refused, and from which perhaps a man in health and with a head turned to business might have gained all the information he wanted—but it was not so with me.[6]

Vision is here malign, projecting back upon the seer a landscape analogous with and supportive of the daemonic force that inwardly possesses him. The 'hell within' creates a 'hell without' whose bounds then further close up the self. Cowper's intercourse with nature is the direct reverse of this—benign and beneficent vision, vision produced by and productive of interior well-being. Yet it cannot be taken simply as testifying to his continuing health—the continuing reality of his 'recovery'. For Cowper could never take for granted either his sanity or (and it is in essence one and the same thing) the 'reborn' state in which he had eventually come forth from the madhouse, 'rejoic[ing] day and night'—a fact made clear not only by the direct evidence of such letters as that (quoted earlier) in which he complains to Newton, even as he is writing *The Task*, of an intense spiritual 'gloom', but also by the sheer persistence of his preoccupation with the processes, nature, and signs of rebirth, not least in the 'stricken deer' passage of Book III. His contemplations of the natural world are trials of the spirit against a background of potential despair. It is an appropriate and pleasing irony that 'the journal', which had been the cynosure of his maniacal depression, should have become, in the form of a poem, the medium of both joy (however provisional) and personal spiritual affirmation.

In the later stages of Book V, Cowper insists more comprehensively than ever on the links between heightened perceptual capacity and the state of grace, developing at length a statement that God is both the source and the end of a true appreciation of 'delightful' scenes. In fact, this stress upon the primacy of God represents a new emphasis within *The Task*, a return to an earlier and more orthodox position than that of Book I, where faith in the renovating influences of nature itself had effectively displaced faith in the Deity, whether as the agent of redemption and healing or as the power within and behind the natural world. It is notable that the account in that Book of the prisoner who emerges from darkness into 'liberty and light', 'wing'd with joy' and rioting in the 'sweets of ev'ry breeze' (I,436–44), is introduced purely to illustrate the soul's appetite for nature's 'feast', without any of the reference to God-directed 'conversion' and 'uplifting' that lies at the centre of Cowper's use of exactly the same *exemplum* in *Hope*.[7] In Book I it is the experience of Nature's miracles and holy places that forms the positive antithesis of the negative sacrament, the downward viaticum into a world of malign presences, exemplified in the 'journal books' episode in the *Memoir*; but now Nature is subordinated to its Maker, and liberty becomes a matter of knowing God rather than simply seeking and receiving nature's food:

> His are the mountains, and the vallies his,
> And the resplendent rivers. His t'enjoy
> With a propriety that none can feel,
> But who, with filial confidence inspir'd,
> Can lift to heaven an unpresumptuous eye,
> And smiling say—My father made them all! . . .
> > . . . ye will not find,
> In feast or in the chase, in song or dance,
> A liberty like his, who, unimpeach'd
> Of usurpation, and to no man's wrong,
> Appropriates nature as his father's work,
> And has a richer use of yours than you.
> > (V,742–7,757–62)

Yet it is very clear from these lines that Cowper's interest in God is not limited to an assertion of His power over nature and over man. The really important thing is the special, and innocent, 'possession' of nature that comes from a proper relationship with God, which he defines as a relationship between father and son. Although he has relinquished a degree of autonomy, the ability to make an existential harmony and stability out of an unmediated intercourse with the natural world, his return to orthodoxy is not the radical retreat that it may appear to be. He has given up neither nature nor self; rather, the two-fold relationship of Book I has become three-fold.

The reason for this adjustment of position is to be found in the *Memoir* itself, where Cowper describes how he was suddenly refreshed during the visit to Southampton which his friends had arranged to help him escape his panic at the prospect of having to undergo the public examination for the post of Keeper of the Journals:

> Here it was that on a sudden, as if another sun had been kindled that instant in the heavens on purpose to dispel sorrow and vexation of spirit, I felt the weight of all my misery taken off; my heart became light and joyful in a moment; I could have wept with transport had I been alone. I must needs believe that nothing less than the Almighty fiat could have filled me with such inexpressible delight, not by a gradual dawning of peace, but, as it were, with a flash of his life-giving countenance. . . . But Satan and my own wicked heart quickly persuaded me that I was indebted for my deliverance to nothing but a change of scene and the amusing varieties of the place. By this means he turned the blessing into a poison. . . .[8]

Acknowledgement of God—'the Almighty fiat'—was ultimately necessary to Cowper's peace of mind; to rely on self and nature, to the exclusion of the Almighty, would be to commit the same unpardonable sin as was committed at Southampton, which had been 'corrected' in the light of subsequent knowledge. Book V reaffirms the enlightened state, the state of grace, that Cowper felt was his when writing the *Memoir* and rejecting the poisonous influence of demonic persuasion. It is noticeable, however, that the uncompromisingly reductive attitude apparent in the phrases 'my own wicked heart' and 'amusing varieties of the place' has no presence in *The Task*, where 'heart' and 'place' become essential ingredients in a conception of ideal 'being' that includes God at its centre and circumference. Nature is no longer a locus of temptation, the feelings are no longer in league with Satan, and there is no conflict between the natural and the Divine as objects of contemplation. In other words, *The Task* sees a modification as well as a recall of the earlier position: a split personality and a philosophy of exclusion have been replaced by an integrated personality and philosophy of inclusion.

But this harmonizing of self, nature, and God, this three-fold 'balance' on which Cowper's theory and practice as contemplative poet both finally rest, is by no means a foregone conclusion even within Book V itself. It is something reached for and established during an extended process of formulation. For a time all praise *is*, at least explicitly, given to nature, whose Energy becomes for example the main theme of the passage immediately following the panorama of animal life. Beneath the stillness of the 'snowy weight' the current of the stream flows on, silently and 'unperceiv'd', until, gathering force, it shatters the stasis of the winter landscape—

> scornful of a check, it leaps
> The mill-dam, dashes on the restless wheel,
> And wantons in the pebbly gulf below;
> No frost can bind it there; its utmost force
> Can but arrest the light and smoky mist
> That in its fall the liquid sheet throws wide.
> And see where it has hung th'embroider'd banks
> With forms so various, that no pow'rs of art,
> The pencil or the pen, may trace the scene!
>
> (V, 101–9)

Thus the celebration of nature's inherent power, symbolized in the stream, leads on to an assertion of her superiority over art—a point then further underlined by the impact of her 'inimitable feats' of creation:

> Here glitt'ring turrets rise, upbearing high
> (Fantastic misarrangement) on the roof
> Large growth of what may seem the sparkling trees
> And shrubs of fairy land. The crystal drops
> That trickle down the branches, fast congeal'd,
> Shoot into pillars of pellucid length . . .
> The growing wonder takes a thousand shapes
> Capricious, in which fancy seeks in vain
> The likeness of some object seen before.

Thus nature works as if to mock at art,
And in defiance of her rival pow'rs . . .
             (V, 110–15, 119–23)

This reminds us of the Lockean version of 'fancy' as an agent
that can produce nothing entirely new but only 'new combinations or interpretations of objects (or parts of objects) previously perceived',[9] and of where Thomson protests the
hopelessness of trying to emulate nature's canvas, the 'hues'
and 'matchless skill' that no imagination can boast: '. . . If fancy
then/Unequal fails beneath the pleasing task,/Ah, what shall
language do?'.[10] But of course such apparently negative
attitudes to poetry and the status of the poet-artist do have
positive repercussions. The homage paid to nature is, both in
Thomson and Cowper, at the same time a plea for recognition
of the excellence of their own chosen subject, which supplies an
incomparable challenge and an incomparable fund of material
for the aspiring imagination. They bathe, as it were, in nature's
reflected glory. From Cowper's lines, moreover, there emerges
a striking paradox. He says that 'no pow'rs of art . . . may trace
the scene' and that art and nature are 'rival pow'rs', yet
throughout the passage there is nothing but successful tracing
and conspicuous harmony. The verse movement and echoic
effects of the lines on the current that 'leaps/The mill-dam,
dashes on the restless wheel,/And wantons on the pebbly gulf
below' are a perfect example of the 'marriage' of 'poetic' and
'natural' energies so characteristic of *The Task*. The landscape
of 'th'embroider'd bank' pushes us even further into recognition of the claims of art *where art is trained on and prompted by nature*.
The active verbs—'rise, upbearing high . . . trickle . . . Shoot
. . . prop . . .'—fix attention on nature's interior, autonomous
processes, but the fabric is nevertheless of the poet's making.
The phrase 'what may seem . . .' (l. 112) signalizes overtly what
the application of architectural terminology more continuously
implies—a receptive and constructive self tracing the untrace-
able and otherwise unperceived, giving shape to, and embel-
lishing, matter in its envisioning of 'glitt'ring turrets', 'pillars of
pellucid length', 'grotto within grotto'. Cowper's poetic performance modifies the thought of his theoretical assumptions of
the inadequacy of the 'pen' so as to present a partially elevated

idea of the poet-artist, very like that of Addison's contribution
to a long and eloquent tradition which saw the poet as much
more than the receiver and imitator of external images: 'We
cannot indeed have a single image in the fancy that did not
make its first entrance through the sight; but we have the power
of retaining, altering and compounding those images which we
have once received into all the varieties of picture and vision
that are most agreeable to the imagination', or again, '[im-
agination] has something in it like creation; it bestows a kind of
existence . . . It makes additions to nature, and gives a greater
variety to God's works.'[11] Cowper's practice and Addison's
remarks are the closer for making art and nature interdepen-
dent powers, rather than insisting, as others (including Bacon)
had done,[12] upon the independence of the greater 'spirit of
Man' from the lesser 'Nature of things'. Their ideal is of a
process of 'getting' and 'making' in which supremacy falls to
neither side—and in which both 'parties' are active.

Where Cowper does conclusively devalue art is in the sphere
of *human* artefacts, which he sees as worthless in themselves and
inferior to nature as objects of contemplation. The central
image here is the Empress of Russia's ice-palace, symbolizing
both 'the work of man' and the 'estate' of princes. This
monument to man's ingenuity at first clearly fascinates Cowper
and wins from him the tribute of some of his own most
ingenious craftsmanship, the well-adjusted unnaturalness of
the Miltonic style making a perfect medium for describing the
strange and mighty structure:

> Silently as a dream the fabric rose;—
> No sound of hammer or of saw was there:
> Ice upon ice, the well-adjusted parts
> Were soon conjoin'd; . . .
> Lamps gracefully dispos'd, and of all hues,
> Illumin'd ev'ry side: a wat'ry light
> Gleam'd through the clear transparency, that seem'd
> Another moon new risen, or meteor fall'n
> From heav'n to earth, of lambent flame serene.
>
> (V, 144–7, 149–53)

The urge to celebrate is no less apparent in the care Cowper
brings to producing such effects as the astonishingly graceful

'lambent flame serene' than in the overt admiration expressed through the comparison with a 'moon new risen' and 'meteor fall'n/From heav'n'. Yet the reservations that are obvious from the first mention of the ice-palace, which he calls not only a 'wonder' but a 'freak' (ll.130–1), easily overcome his approval and delight, so that he talks at last of a 'brittle prodigy' and—

> scene
> Of evanescent glory, once a stream,
> And soon to slide into a stream again.
> (V,166–8)

The stream, already an emblem of nature's never-ceasing life, now also becomes a means of underlining the transience of human achievement; the grandeur and permanence and worth of the palace were but an illusion:

> 'Twas transient in its nature, as in show
> 'Twas durable: as worthless, as it seem'd
> Intrinsically precious; to the foot
> Treach'rous and false; it smil'd, and it was cold.
> (V,173–6)

These final comments reflect back upon what Cowper has himself 'achieved' earlier in the passage. In so far as he had felt the attractions of the gleaming 'fabric' he had fallen victim to the outward show of beauty, the intrinsically worthless. As its celebrant he had validated the 'treacherous' and 'false'. He rejects his own 'creative' engagement with the world of man-made objects: the light shining through the 'clear trans-parency' suggests the 'light' of imagination, which embellishes the object, making of it something 'natural' (a new moon) and holy (from 'heav'n'), but all that had been a deception and 'evanescent glory', and the poetry, once a 'stream' running in harmony with nature, must return again to its proper and worthy channel, 'slide into a stream again'.

Thus, Cowper enforces his previous elevation of the art that looks to the natural world—that may add to its beauties and give them existence but never, like those who hew the slabs of the ice-palace, murders by dissecting or appropriates its materials for the purposes of self-aggrandizement. But he doesn't stop there. There are higher things to contemplate and

more important sources of bliss. In the final analysis, nature is
itself transient:

> the visible display
> Of all-creating energy and might,
> Are grand, no doubt, and worthy of the word
> That, finding an interminable space
> Unoccupied, has fill'd the void so well
> And made so sparkling what was dark before.
> But these are not his glory. Man, 'tis true,
> Smit with the beauty of so fair a scene,
> Might well suppose th'artificer divine
> Meant it eternal, had he not himself
> Pronounc'd it transient, glorious as it is . . .
> These, therefore, are occasional, and pass;
> Form'd for the confutation of the fool,
> Whose lyeing heart disputes against a God;
> That office serv'd, they must be swept away.
> Not so the labours of his love . . .
>   . . . There is a paradise that fears
> No forfeiture, and of its fruits he sends
> Large prelibation oft to saints below.
> Of these the first in order, and the pledge
> And confident assurance of the rest,
> Is liberty:—a flight into his arms
> Ere yet mortality's fine threads give away . . .
>   (V,553–63,566–70,572–8)

The Creation, 'so fair a scene', *is* there to be enjoyed, as well as
to glorify the Creator and rebuke the instincts of the unbelieving 'fool' (a contention that places Cowper distinctly within the
ranks of Newtonian, anti-mechanistic thinkers, who, as Voltaire puts it, 'accepting the vacuum and finite nature of matter,
accept as a result the existence of God').[13] Yet its 'sparkling'
beauty is potentially even more misleading than that of the
ice-palace, for it may trap the perceiver, especially one who
'believes', in the most dangerous illusion of all, the supposition
that it is coterminous with the Everlasting. The true paradise is
the heavenly paradise, the immortal joy foreshadowed by the
inward 'liberty' of the recipients of divine grace, that freedom
'Bought with HIS blood who gave it to mankind' (l.546).

Entering a new dimension, Cowper places greatest value on a spiritual condition above all endeavour in, and all the satisfactions of, this world—while keeping faith with the pleasures and sacramental purposes of informed contemplative endeavour in the presence of nature.

So thorough is this conspicuous shift of emphasis that 'liberty of heart derived from heav'n' is deliberately placed above the one aspect of civil life which Cowper always continues to prize—the liberty of the individual as guaranteed by the institution of Whig constitutional monarchy:

> We love
> The king who loves the law, respects his bounds,
> And reigns content within them; him we serve
> Freely and with delight, who leaves us free . . .
>
> (V,331–4)

The poet of Book V of *The Task* has not lost interest in political affairs. He justifies the 'decollation' of Charles I who would have made men 'slaves' (ll.337ff.), praises 'our Hampdens and our Sidneys' who bled in freedom's cause (the latter, Algernon Sidney, for his martyr's opposition to Charles II), and above all passionately laments what he sees as England's present disgrace, not only its 'loss of empire' but the apparently endless upheaval and ineptitude of the years following the separation of the American colonies, which saw the fall of Shelburne, the Fox-North coalition, and the King's fierce counter-attack against Fox's administration which many interpreted as an attempt to revert to the 'arbitrary rule' of his Stuart predecessors (though it in fact opened the way, after the general election of 1784, for the stabilizing Pittite regime).[14] What must have made matters worse in Cowper's eyes was that Fox, champion of 'liberty', was a notable profligate: 'when was public virtue to be found/Where private was not?' (ll.502–3). Yet for all its faults—the 'factious fumes' that threaten the 'gen'ral weal' (where Cowper seems to be responding to the rising importance of opposition within the parliamentary system and the growing significance of extra-parliamentary agitation), the weakness, the lack of private and corporate decency—he accounts England 'still happy' and 'chief' among the nations, 'seeing thou art free' (ll.446ff.). This is the patriotic Cowper,

the Cowper whose humane and powerfully imaginative indict-
ment of the horrors of Absolutism, in the lines on the Bastile,
were quoted in the Commons by Fox himself:[15]

> ... life stands a stump,
> And, filletted about with hoops of brass,
> Still lives, though all its pleasant boughs are gone ...
> To turn purveyor to an overgorg'd
> And bloated spider, till the pamper'd pest
> Is made familiar, watches his approach,
> Comes at his call ...
> To wear out time in numb'ring to and fro
> The studs that thick emboss his iron door ...
> Moves indignation; makes the name of king
> (Of king whom such prerogative can please)
> As dreadful as the Manichean god,
> Ador'd through fear, strong only to destroy.
>   (V,379ff.)

Yet superior to all is the soul-liberty that is the gift of God,
which grants 'full immunity' in the face of any oppression
whatsoever, the freedom 'Which monarchs cannot grant, nor
all the pow'rs/Of earth and hell confed'rate take away'
(ll.540–1).

Now, this and the subsequent sections of Book V are, it is
clear, a promulgatory act—Cowper writing from and arguing
for particular positions. With the introduction of the direct
reference to the Atonement—'Bought with HIS blood who
gave it to mankind'—the issue becomes no longer that of good
and bad government but of the world versus the spirit,
soul-experience as against the experience and needs of man in
society. We have, what might be expected from Cowper, a plea
for 'personal', 'experimental', and 'revealed' religion. The
images of enchainment shift from a socio-political register to a
religio-philosophical one as he launches into a prolonged
restatement of the 'facts' of the Fall and 'the slavish state of man
by nature'. 'Chains are the portion of revolted man,/Stripes
and a dungeon', the body is a 'sickly, foul,/Opprobrious
residence', man is the prisoner of death and every sin from 'lust'
to 'self-congratulating pride' (ll.58off.). 'Grace'—and grace
alone—'makes the slave a freeman' (l.688). If one wonders *why*

Cowper should thus insist on such cardinal points of religious belief, his lengthy condemnation of Deism reminds us that they were by no means secure in his time. He proclaims orthodoxy with the urgent enthusiasm of one who knows that it is under threat, and attacks with all the harshness of one who secretly respects the strength of the opposition. As I suggested earlier, his insistence on the 'truth' of God's abiding control of nature, His Creation—'that unwearied love/That planned, and built, and still upholds, a world/So cloth'd with beauty for rebellious man'—is in tune with a widespread contemporary resistance to the atheistic implications of Cartesian, 'mechanistic', inter-pretations of the universe. Although the latter gained new ground in the mid-eighteenth century—Norman Hampson cites for example the proto-evolutionary theories of Buffon, who wrote that 'Life and movement, instead of being a metaphysical degree of existence, are physical properties of matter'[16]—it was not they that really worried Cowper; he merely adds his voice, as it were, to the many who found in Newton the scientific proof of a Supreme Being:

> If matter gravitates, as has been proved, it does not do so by virtue of its very nature . . . Therefore it received gravitation from God. If the planets rotate through empty space in one direction rather than another, their creator's hand . . . must have guided their course in that direction.[17]

What troubles Cowper is 'natural religion' itself, the deistic vision of a providential order in which Original Sin and Salvation, Christ and a personal God, have no place, and in which man is innately good, a benevolent and rational character in the drama of a beneficent and reasonable Deity. Some of the severest words in *The Task* are reserved for the philosophy that would smooth 'The shag of savage nature', presuming to deliver fallen humanity from the burden of its sinful state by granting it the all-sufficient gift of—

> moral sense how sure,
> Consulted and obey'd, to guide his steps
> Directly to the FIRST AND ONLY FAIR.
>
> (V,673–5)

All 'rhapsody in virtue's praise', the 'most sublimely good, verbosely grand', is but a 'tinkling cymbal' that can do nothing to eradicate either vice or the darkness of a 'wide-wand'ring soul'; the 'STILL SMALL VOICE' is wanted, the *miracle* of grace, God in his *mysterious* aspect (rather than God as First Cause and Perfect Being)—

> transformation of apostate man
> From fool to wise, from earthly to divine,
> Is work for Him that made him.
>   (V,695–7)

Does Cowper have any particular 'tinkling cymbal' in mind? There were philosophers enough pleading the assumptions represented in Cleanthes, the Deist of Hume's *Dialogues concerning Natural Religion*, who secularizes religion so thoroughly as to make it a matter of social utility, its proper office being 'to regulate the hearts of men, humanize their conduct, infuse the spirit of temperance, order and obedience';[18] and discourses enough in favour of the theory that a principle of *bienfaisance* animates both man and the order around him—a view put with the minimum of fuss in Morelly's *Code de la Nature* of 1755, which begins with an outright rejection of the belief that 'Man is born wicked and vicious', for 'In the natural order the idea of active or passive benevolence precedes every other idea, even that of the Divinity'.[19] But Cowper's phrasing— 'sublimely good, verbosely grand'—suggests of course Pope's *Essay on Man*. The poet of revealed religion is taking on the poet of natural religion who had reduced the Fall to an episode in prehistory when human society emerged from a shadowy Golden Age, assigned to reason the place traditional Christianity assigns to grace, and announced how Providence ensures the earthly bliss of the physical man, especially the virtuous.[20]

These more polemical parts of Book V, both the 'political' and 'religious-philosophic' sections, are good examples of Cowper's lively involvement in contemporary issues. They are just as surely, however, strong instances of his essential inability to see the stability and purposes of the individual life, his own or any other, in terms of available corporate structures and goals. Though he loves his country, 'being free', its present situation—imperial defeat and the emergence of a politics of 'faction' and 'cold pretence'—points finally all in one direction, to catastrophe and the collapse of the 'castle of the state' whose 'tempest-beaten turrets shake' while men 'Stand motionless expectants of its fall'. This image reminds us that Cowper is not simply the man of religion turning his back upon worldly supports and interests. Castles are things to respect; but one cannot place much hope in them when there are rumblings in the foundations. They are archetypally secure places, but not when the cracks appear and there is fighting within. Evidences from the public world tilt the balance with a mind only half inclined to reject it as a 'home'. But the balance is tilted so far that the rejection becomes complete; political systems and the triumphs of a nation are, at last like ice-palaces, mere passing shows:

> We build with what we deem eternal rock:
> A distant age asks where the fabric stood;
> And in the dust, sifted and search'd in vain,
> The undiscoverable secret sleeps.
>
> (V,534–7)

And Cowper's response to contemporary religious thinking is in its way equally full of a sense of dissolution. He sees around him only 'philosophic eyes' that dishonour God, viewing His miracles, whether of grace or humanization ('... humanizing what is brute/In the lost kind . . .'), as 'Trivial and worthy of disdain' (ll.697ff.). Blind or not, these eyes were real and manifold—as Cowper's own concern acknowledges. This acknowledgement, together with the fact that Cowper writes, not, as Butler had done in the *Analogy of Religion* (1736), with a conviction of redeeming the deviant, but rather with the determined opposition which consigns error to the futility of its ways, places him, both personally and historically, in the position of a defiant rearguard, more an adherent to one particular faith than the champion of a shared orthodoxy. The integument of a truly collective wisdom lies as much out of his reach in the religious as in socio-political terms.

But out of the hard-pressed Christianity to which he holds in these passages of discursive argument Cowper does evolve a Faith and 'philosophy of being' sufficient to his needs. That very point in *The Task* where he is most alienated from the political and religious 'values' of his society sees his most developed account of the bliss, security, and freedom of the 'individual reborn', the man 'Whom God delights in, and in whom he dwells' (l.778). It becomes clear that 'Liberty of heart, deriv'd from heav'n' is to Cowper really nothing so simple as being 'saved' from sin and made conscious of future rewards, but means a comprehensive liberty in this world, an unchallengeable inward strength and happiness in this life:

> He is the freeman whom the truth makes free, . . .
> His freedom is the same in ev'ry state;
> And no condition of this changeful life,
> So manifold in cares, whose ev'ry day
> Brings its own evil with it, makes it less:
> For he has wings that neither sickness, pain,
> Nor penury, can cripple or confine.
> No nook so narrow but he spreads them there
> With ease, and is at large. . . .
> $(V,733,767-74)^{21}$

In Book VI Cowper will spread his wings in some very narrow nooks indeed, but even now he lays claim to the blessedness he celebrates. We have another Cowper altogether than the 'biographical' Cowper who felt that he was damned, for such an enthusiastic glorification of the privileges of God-given heart-liberty presupposes a confidence in the exponent himself: the impersonal 'he'—'He is the freeman whom . . .'—includes the personal 'I'. And the greatest of these privileges is the power to enjoy the 'varied field'. It is here, in the final section of Book V, that Cowper makes his most assured statement of the interdependence of spiritual well-being and a capacity for appreciating nature. Not only is natural beauty God's gift to 'rebellious man' (l.754), it is the special possession of him 'whom the truth makes free' and 'Whom God delights in'; he 'Calls the delightful scen'ry all his own', his 'by a peculiar right,/And by an emphasis of int'rest his' (ll.741,745-9). To enjoy nature to the full one must first be admitted to God's embrace:

> Acquaint thyself with God, if thou would'st taste
> His works. Admitted once to his embrace,
> Thou shalt perceive that thou wast blind before:

Thine eye shall be instructed; and thine heart,
Made pure, shall relish, with divine delight
Till then unfelt, what hands divine have wrought.
(V,779–84)

He now rebukes the praise and admiration that stops at nature itself, as in his own prospect of the Ouse Valley: man 'views' and 'admires' the 'scene outspread/Beneath, beyond, and stretching far away', but he should not rest content with what he views:

The landscape has his praise
But not its author. Unconcern'd who form'd
The paradise he sees, he finds it such,
And such well-pleas'd to find it, asks no more.
Not so the mind that has been touch'd from heav'n . . .
(V,792–6)

In thus correcting his earlier position, however, he only increases the significance of his powers of perception. Re-incorporated into a religious perspective, his 'relish of fair prospect' becomes more than ever a proof of a personal state of grace, of divine favour and closeness to God.

One is tempted to say a proof of *election*. But Calvinist doctrine is in fact bypassed in the religious philosophy of *The Task*. Its God is a welcoming and available God, not the stern and arbitrary Deity who rules a bleak world of reprobate and justified souls. To seek Him is to be received: 'Aquaint thyself with God' and He will admit you to his 'embrace'; all that is needed to be a 'freeman' of grace, inheritor of earth and heaven, is to let in the light of 'the lamp of truth'. Cowper's doctrine of grace, though retaining the idea of some mysterious working, some sudden influx from without (a mind 'touch'd from heav'n'), everywhere transfers the initiative to the individual himself—to a concern with Him 'who form'd/The paradise he sees', or to 'worthy thoughts' of the 'unwearied love' that planned and still upholds the world. He roots salvation in right-mindedness and a sense of priorities—the recognition of God and a desire to know God which lead *inevitably* to fuller enlightenment and its rewards. He constructs a system in which belief itself is an unfailing channel to and from God, in which 'liberty' is the worthy pilgrim's certain possession, and in which proper 'seeing'—response to the Creation and to its spiritual meanings—is at once the badge and occupation of that proud, serious-happy traveller.

The enlightened man, as represented by and in the poet at the end of Book V, is no passive spirit. He 'receives sublim'd/ New faculties', discerning what the impure cannot see—a numinous world, the supernatural behind, within, and beyond nature:

> A ray of heav'nly light, gilding all forms
> Terrestrial in the vast and the minute;
> The unambiguous footsteps of the God
> Who gives its lustre to an insect's wing,
> And wheels his throne upon the rolling worlds.
>
> (V,810–14)

The drift of these lines was not itself new. The point had been made, for example, by the Abbé le Pluche, prominent among those orthodox Christians who appropriated the advances of science to the cause of religion (he is writing at this stage of *Spectacle de la Nature* about the wonders revealed by the microscope):

> We will not begin then with taking a survey of those glorious orbs that roll above us ... we'll take the minutest objects ... [Insects] ... though their minuteness ... may seem a just argument for that contemptible idea which the vulgar entertain of them ... yet he that views them with due attention ... cannot but discover an all wise Providence.[22]

But Cowper vivifies the idea. Within the process of his own writing, as well as in comparison with le Pluche's demonstrative prose, authorial statement about something is displaced by authorial apprehension of something so as to produce an epiphany-experience, a visionary 'seeing' in which the physical lustre of an insect's wing shades into a heavenly radiance and the planets take on the aspect of a palpable mystery, a wondrous mechanism bearing round the throne of a vastly majestic God. The lines are no mere assertion of preconceived knowledge of God's wisdom and presence in the Creation; the

uplifted and uplifting rhythms, the solid lucidity of 'unambiguous footsteps', 'lustre', 'wheels', the impression of a felt and
seen magnificence are registers of immediate encounter with a
manifest Divinity, and with the manifest glory of all forms,
great or small (though 'gilding' and 'gives' remind us of
Cowper's traditional priorities—that he reaches towards
rather than achieves the Wordsworthian, and Joyceian, sense
of the 'divineness' of objects themselves, 'the soul that leaps to
us from the vestment of . . . appearance' in more modern
epiphanic experience).[23] There follows accounts of how the
wise and pure 'soul', holding converse with the stars, 'beacons
in the blue abyss', is visited by both powerful longings and
intimations of immortality—

> Love kindles as I gaze. I feel desires
> That give assurance of their own success,
> And that, infus'd from heav'n, must thither tend.
> $$(V,842-4)$$

and how the Creator himself will be disclosed in an instant of
profound revelation:

> a flash from heav'n
> Fires all the faculties with glorious joy . . .
> In that blest moment Nature, throwing wide
> Her veil opaque, discloses with a smile
> The author of her beauties, who, retir'd
> Behind his own creation, works unseen
> By the impure . . .
> Thou art the source and centre of all minds,
> Their only point of rest, eternal Word!
> $$(V,884-5,91-7)[24]$$

In these passages self, nature, and imagination are all active,
though within limits. Superior perception derives from God but
resides within and emanates outwards from the self, while
nature becomes the superior object of that perception—a world
of lovely forms shot through with divine radiance, a beacon-
light helping the aspiring soul heavenwards, a plenum in which
God moves and is discovered. And the seeing that is informed
with a 'clearer light' is itself a species of imagination (not
imagining, or invention), which penetrates nature's 'veil

opaque'. By this metaphor Cowper signifies, not nature *per se*, but what Blake calls 'apparent surfaces', the face ordinarily seen by impure, 'physical' man: 'If the doors of perception were cleansed . . .'—well, for Blake 'every thing would appear to man as it is, infinite', while for Cowper the only Infinite, God, is revealed.[25] The distinction is important. Though god-like as well as God-granted ('pure as thou art pure'), Cowper's higher liberated perception is given definite bounds. He binds imagination without binding it down; it must operate within a closed universe circumscribed by God, but within those confines its freedom is total. He has developed not only proof of a personal state of grace but a model of faith and 'being' that preserves conventional religious concepts of the Divine and the Creation, yet redeems them by reference to human creative potential—higher forms of 'seeing'—working with and through the familiar world.

Now Cowper's sense of the spiritual value and content of perceptual acts in the presence of nature—and indeed, of the simpler aesthetic, emotional and psychological benefits—owes much to the tradition of what has been recently called 'natural Methodism'.[26] Here is James Hervey in *Theron and Aspasio* (1755):

> . . . the whole earth, and all that replenishes it, all that surrounds it, are full of his presence . . . An habitual belief in this truth gives Nature her loveliest aspect, and lends her the most consummate power to please. The breath of violets, and the blush of roses; the music of the woods, and the meanders of the stream . . . then appear in their highest attractiveness; then touch the soul with the most refined satisfaction; when God is seen—when God is heard—and God enjoyed in all.[27]

This might serve as a summary of the final argument of Book V of *The Task*: awareness of God heightens the pleasures of contemplating nature, and contemplating nature heightens awareness of God, who may be 'seen', 'heard', and 'enjoyed' in all. And there are examples enough in Hervey's 'Reflections on a Flower Garden' of the beauties of the Creation, which 'transfuse a sudden gaiety through the dejected spirit and dissipate the gloom of thought':

> ... when the air was cool; the earth moist; the whole face of the Creation fresh and gay. The noisy world was scarce awake ... All was serene, all was still. Everything tended to inspire Tranquillity of Mind, and invite serious thought.
> Only the wakeful lark had left her nest, and was mounting on high ... Abundance of ruddy streaks tinge the fleeces of the firmament ...[28]

It was probably such images as these which first encouraged Cowper to see a 'relish' of nature as a sign of grace, to find in nature a source both of pleasure and useful meditation, and to seek inspiration in a response to its life, the 'breath', 'blush', and 'music' of its objects. And Hervey's own meditations stand in a long line of 'Puritan' writings based on the belief that 'if [the heart] be sanctified, it ordinarily distils holy, sweet and useful meditation out of all objects.'[29] '*All* objects', since everything was specifically ordered by God (Joseph Hall includes 'an arme benumbed' and 'the sight of a left-handed man'); but above all the Creation, in which God's wisdom, beneficence, and purposes were revealed with a power second only to that of the Bible.[30] As far back as Thomas Sherman's *Second Part of The Pilgrim's Progress* (1684)—a 'reply' to Bunyan—we get the same morning walk amidst the plenitude of divine creation as we encounter in Hervey's 'Reflections' ('... the healthful air rendered more pleasing and delightful by the gentle winds then breathed from the south, impregnated with the exhilarating fragrancy of the variety of flowers ...'), followed by a direct statement of the 'obligation upon heavenly minds to spiritualize the several objects they behold, and satiate their happy souls with heavenly meditation, ... contemplating the divine goodness'.[31] The eighteenth-century apostles of 'natural religion' also, of course, spiritualized the several objects they beheld. Basil Willey quotes a passage from Addison ('that most accurate reflector of contemporary moods'), which contains all the components that we have just identified in Cowper's debt to Hervey—delight, instruction, the necessity of habitual belief in God's 'presence' for the full enjoyment of the rewards of being with nature:

> It does not rest in the murmur of brooks ... but considers the several ends of Providence ... and the wonders of Divine Wisdom ... Such an habitual Disposition of Mind consecrates every field and wood, turns an ordinary Walk into a morning or evening Sacrifice, and will improve ... the Soul on such Occasions, into an inviolable and perpetual State of Bliss and Happiness.[32]

Moreover, Cowper was obviously influenced by Thomson's classic 'deist' address to the 'Inspiring God' who 'boundless spirit all/And unremitting energy, pervades,/Adjusts, sustains, and agitates the whole'—the informing Author who 'though concealed, to every purer eye/... in his works appears'.[33] But the difference is that Thomson relinquishes the central tenets of Christianity, while Sherman's dawning of the day is the return of the 'shining bridegroom', Hervey's rising sun becomes at once 'the emblem of Christ' (the Son of Righteousness), and both raise their thoughts through nature's delights to 'those sublimest delights which are above, which will yield, not partial but perfect felicity'.[34] Cowper is with them: he insists, as we know, that there is a 'paradise' beyond nature, 'that fears no forfeiture' (V,572–3), and when he talks later of the God that presides over nature he enters an explicit Christian reference—'One spirit—His/Who wore the platted thorns with bleeding brows—/Rules universal nature' (VI,238–40).

But the nature of this reference gives pause for thought. Christ comes in as an afterthought—a parenthesis. The passage in question, which closes off 'the winter walk at noon' in Book VI, is otherwise indistinguishable from Deist statement:

> The Lord of all, himself through all diffus'd,
> Sustains, and is the life of all that lives.
> Nature is but a name for an effect,
> Whose cause is God. He feeds the secret fire
> By which the mighty process is maintain'd,
> Who sleeps not, is not weary; in whose sight

Slow circling ages are as transient days . . .
. . . all are under one. One spirit—His
Who wore the platted thorns with bleeding brows—
Rules universal nature. Not a flow'r
But shows some touch, in freckle, streak, or stain,
Of his unrivall'd pencil . . .

(VI,221–7,238–42)

In a way, Sherman and Hervey themselves dilute the Christianity they so deliberately uphold, by partially transferring emphasis from Christ and God to nature, from Truth to the contemplative self, and above all from Word to word, Scripture to text. John Newton perhaps recognized this danger in meditative writing when arguing that the Bible must always be the 'key' to interpreting 'the book of Nature', and that the objects of the Creation are useful for leading our thoughts to Jesus or *illustrating* 'some scriptual truth or promise'.[35] If Newton did feel this way about works like Hervey's *Meditations*—which remains a great *omnium gatherum* of not only natural and experiential delights but 'lively sermons' (the 'redeemed *look unto Jesus*' as the sunflower looks to the sun)—Book VI of *The Task* would have seemed positively pernicious. In spite of the 'stricken deer' passage in Book III, where he thinks of Christ as his saviour ('There was I found by one . . .'), Cowper displays very little real interest in the Redeemer; in Book VI it is a palpably interpolated interest. Nor does he read nature as a fair cypher of which the Bible is the key. Certainly *God* is real and substantial to him—He that 'feeds the secret fire' and encompasses the 'Slow circling ages'. But in reading *The Task* we encounter this God, not as *logos*, something outside the authorial consciousness, but as something envisioned, a perceptual and imaginative apprehension; in the long run it is the mind and not the Word, author and not Author, that commands the centre. This is the more apparent when we compare Cowper's relation to the Creation with the more conservative 'Puritan' stance as exemplified in Edmund Bury's meditation 'Upon sweet smelling flowers' (1677), where the appeal of nature (such 'poor objects') is positively resisted in favour of more practical, *logos*-oriented thoughts—'the sight, the smell and savour delighted me, the melodious harmony of

birds delighted me . . . till upon consideration I checkt myself
for my folly . . . [and] began to screw my thoughts a little higher;
. . . what sweetness then is in the Creator'.[36] Cowper, like
Hervey and Addison, closes the gap between nature and God,
carnal and spiritual acts—the same dichotomy that had
troubled him in the Southampton episode in the *Memoir*: since
God is 'through all diffus'd' (as well as being separate, the
circumference and originator of all), and since perceptual
pleasure and insight are God's gift, contemplation of nature is
both allowed and *in itself* a spiritual exercise. The doctrines of
purer 'seeing' and God's immanence free him from doctrine.
They put him at complete liberty to explore and engage
creatively with the rich life of his closed world; they turn an
ordinary walk into a sacrifice; they make a superior felicity
available in the here-and-now—whatever the joys of heaven
may be. The religious philosophy of the later parts of *The Task*
thus finally leads back to and revalidates the intercourse
between self and nature which Cowper had always practised—
and which he practises most fully in Book VI itself.

The long 'winter walk at noon' in Book VI is the most varied
and exalted of all Cowper's 'interchanges' with the natural
world—full of confidence, wide-ranging, encompassing all
aspects of the inner self, of intellect and feeling, while embracing the whole space of the Creation between the kindred points
of heaven and earth, the vast and the minute, the sky's 'vault'
and 'the meand'ring veins/Of leaf and flow'r'. As so often in
The Task, however, the mind's journey originates in a mood of
subdued and melancholy reflection; the act of outgoing perception springs from, and is a reaction to, the pressure of a still,
faintly troubled, inward-turning consciousness. Whatever it
may say of God's creativity and gifts, the poem never allows us
to forget for long where its own sources lie—its psychological
basis, the subjectivity of its landscapes, the relativity of its
truths, the making and the shaping from within. With 'easy
force' the distant music of village bells 'opens all the cells/
Where mem'ry slept', and where the feelings of the past, linked
to this particular spot, await always their release:

> Wherever I have heard
> A kindred melody, the scene recurs,

And with it all its pleasures and its pains.
(VI,12–14)

The prospect that opens up before the recollecting mind is
initially one of 'pain' rather than 'pleasure', as Cowper turns
backwards and inwards to retrace 'The windings of [his] way
through many years', seeing himself, as he so frequently does in
his melancholy moments, as a lonely and forlorn traveller:

> the rugged path,
> And prospect oft so dreary and forlorn,
> Mov'd many a sigh at its disheart'ning length.
> (VI,20–2)

The reflex movement into an opposite mental state—joyful,
unselfconscious, open to the influence of *happy* memories—is·
delayed by the claims of elegiac sentiment, slow musings on
loss, mortality, and our making 'the world the wilderness it is'
(through a failure to understand 'a treasure's worth' till time
has stolen it away). But when it does come, the reversal is
strikingly complete. Dark thoughts give way to bright, enervation to excitement, as unequivocally as day follows night:

> The night was winter in his roughest mood,
> The morning sharp and clear. But now at noon
> Upon the southern side of the slant hills,
> And where the woods fence off the northern blast,
> The season smiles, resigning all its rage,
> And has the warmth of May. The vault is blue
> Without a cloud, and white without a speck
> The dazzling splendour of the scene below.
> (VI,57–64)

This is as much a psychological event as a description of events
in nature. Rebirth, spaciousness, calmness and warmth, a
'speckless' purity—such terms are applicable to the poet's
present self no less than to the scene portrayed. Indeed, there is
in a sense no real landscape at all, only the creation of a
regenerated mind—a mind that has found the vigour to renew
itself, driving onwards into a paradisal world of its own making.
　In this, and the 'blest moments' that are to follow, the mind is

truly lord and master. The 'sublime' experience described at the end of Book V—a heightening of perceptual faculties and enjoyment of a second Eden (Edward Young puts it succinctly in the lines, '... what a world, an Eden; heightened all;/It is another scene! another self!')[37]—becomes a repeated, unexceptional action. There is no 'flash from heaven', no *'glorious* joy', no disclosing of the divine Author. The process of meditation brings its own simpler pleasures and its own revelations— revelations of the life of nature itself and of the perfect felicity to be found in the presence of that life:

> I again perceive
> The soothing influence of the wafted strains,
> And settle in soft musings as I tread
> The walk, still verdant, under oaks and elms,
> Whose outspread branches overarch the glade.
> The roof, though moveable through half its length
> As the wind sways it, has yet well suffic'd,
> And, intercepting in their silent fall
> The frequent flakes, has kept a path for me.
> No noise is here, or none that hinders thought.
> The redbreast warbles still, but is content
> With slender notes, and more than half suppress'd:
> Pleas'd with his solitude, and flitting light
> From spray to spray, where'er he rests he shakes
> From many a twig the pendent drops of ice,
> That tinkle in the wither'd leaves below ...
>
> (VI,67–82)

The most familiar scenes are transformed in the mind's eye into a *locus amoenus*, so vividly envisoned that the poet feels himself to be there, a privileged inhabitant for whom the branches have kept a path, charmed by the soft sounds and light motions of swaying roof, warbling redbreast, and tinkling drops of ice. This a happy waking dream of a singular happy state. As in a dream, all distinction between the imagining and the imagined self dissolves, so that Cowper enters his creation, experiencing the landscape from the inside, a quiet but sensitive spirit within a calm, active, and beneficent world. If the stricken deer is an image of the unhappy, vulnerable Cowper, the redbreast mirrors his happiest self—pleased with his solitude, at home in the recesses of nature, contentedly warbling 'slender notes', flitting light in a controlled and instinctive movement from object to object and point to point, releasing without deliberate effort the intrinsic life of things (the 'pendent drops of ice' suggest only a temporary stasis, nature in suspended animation).

A composed and sensitive spirit within a benign and active world: that is the relationship on which Cowper's finest moments depend. 'These shades are all my own', he asserts—confident, as he is throughout these last stages of his mental pilgrimage, of the 'peculiar right' of one who acknowledges the indwelling God and of the 'liberty' of the 'freeman' of grace, but thinking also of his special relations with the life around him. He wanders 'unmolested, through whatever sign/The sun proceeds', nothing 'checking' him or hindering his pleasure. Used to his regular visits, the birds and animals set aside their usual fear of man:

> The tim'rous hare,
> Grown so familiar with her frequent guest,
> Scarce shuns me; and the stock-dove, unalarm'd,
> Sits cooing in the pine tree . . .
>
> (VI,305–8)

Even the squirrel, venturing forth to bask in the warm sun, displays only a mock dismay:

> there whisks his brush,
> And perks his ears, and stamps and scolds aloud,
> With all the pettiness of feign'd alarm,
> And anger insignificantly fierce.
>
> (VI,317–20)

Realistic detail ('cooing', 'whisks', 'perks') blends with the creation of a larger image; Olney has become indeed 'an Eden', with Cowper its 'new-made [and self-appointed] monarch' (l.353). The connection is enforced by the next section of the poem, which describes the first Paradise where all was 'universal love' and 'fear . . . was not, nor cause for fear' (ll.360,367).

In his psychoanalytical study of Cowper's personality, H. K. Gregory argues that poetry, like his other hobbies of gardening

and painting, provided him with an escape from the 'depressive' condition of abnormal terror and passivity by allowing him
illusions of mastery over his environment.[38] Certainly there is
something of this in the passages we have just considered: he
makes nature both his retreat and his kingdom. Important as it
is, however, this particular therapeutic aspect is of course only
one aspect of Cowper's landscapes even at the level of
subjective involvement and goals. Before summarizing, there is
a final passage to take into account:

> Laburnum'rich
> In streaming gold; syringa, iv'ry pure;
> The scentless and the scented rose; this red
> And of an humbler growth, the other tall,
> And throwing up into the darkest gloom
> Of neighb'ring cypress, or more sable yew,
> Her silver globes, light as the foamy surf
> That the wind severs from the broken wave;
> The lilac, various in array, now white,
> Now sanguine, and her beauteous head now set
> With purple spikes pyramidal, as if,
> Studious of ornament, yet unresolv'd
> Which hue she most approv'd, she chose them all;
> Copious of flow'rs the woodbine, pale and wan,
> But well compensating her sickly looks
> With never-cloying odours, early and late;
> Hypericum, all bloom, so thick a swarm
> Of flow'rs, like flies clothing her slender rods,
> That scarce a leaf appears; mezerion, too,
> Though leafless, well attir'd, and thick beset
> With blushing wreaths, investing ev'ry spray;
> Althaea with purple eye; the broom,
> Yellow and bright, as bullion unalloy'd,
> Her blossoms . . .
>   (VI,149–72)

This, the pageant of spring and summer glories that follows on
from Cowper's mind-picture of the 'naked shoots' and 'cold
stagnation' of the winter scene, is perhaps his most remarkable
display of dynamic interchange with the 'given' life of nature, of
self-expression and discovery of the external world.

The range of perceptions is startlingly wide for a catalogue of nature's 'charms'. There are references to colour, shape ('streaming', 'globes', 'pyramidal'), generic characteristics (from the racemes of the laburnum to the hypericum's thick mass of stamens), high and low, delicate and heavy, the round and the sharp, dark and bright, the scented and the scentless. The cool sensuousness of the perfumed honeysuckle contrasts with the more flamboyant attractions of the lilac, the lilac's 'iv'ry' richness with the brilliant 'gold' of the laburnum. All is diversity, and yet all is related; the dominant metaphors of wealth and ornament connect the human and the natural words—'purity', humility, and pride are there, and the blooms are various belles—while the association of 'silver globes' and 'foamy surf', the hypericum flowers and a swarm of flies, and later (ll.173–6) the jasmine and 'scatter'd stars', insist on relationships among the parts of the created universe. The image of the surf and 'broken wave' introduces an elegiac note, implying evanescence and transience even in the face of an overwhelming impression of abundant life; and, on the other hand, the sickliness of the pale woodbine, suggestive of death, is compensated by the idea of unfailing continuity in 'never-cloying odours, early and late'. There is even an element of eroticism in Cowper's response: the lilac raises 'her beauteous head', the jasmine emerges 'luxuriant above all ... throwing wide her elegant sweets'.

Thomson and Hervey both employ similar catalogues, the former taking us through the seemingly endless variety of spring and summer ('hyacinths, of purest virgin white,/Low bent and blushing inward', 'jonquils of potent fragrance' ...) in celebration of the 'Essential Presence', the latter applying his 'Evangelical telescope' to God's workmanship, distinguishing the airs, habits, and lineaments of non-sentient nature as a basis for moral and religious commentary.[39] Preceding both is Milton's account of the Creation—'humble shrub,/And bush with frizzled hair implicit: last/Rose as in a dance the stately trees'.[40] Cowper personalizes the convention in the fullest sense; it expresses an entire sensibility. His landscape pulsates with life. Effects and meanings collide and fuse, forming, under their own pressure, a concentrated whole—an image of na-ture's organic profusion and God's plenty (there is no distinction) and an active embodiment of organic personality, 'Cowper's desire for peace, for beauty, for piety; his emotional and religious yearnings, his intellectual convictions'.[41]

These earlier portions of Book VI mark the peak of the involvement with nature which had begun for Cowper in *Retirement*, an involvement that made possible a sense of well-being, the discovery and channelling of creative power, the satisfaction of special psychological needs, an integration of the demands of 'self' and the demands of religion. Religious faith is as much a part of the final vision of *The Task* as of any poem by Cowper, witness the calm exhilaration of the following lines, which are at once an encouraging address to the reader and the poet's personal summary of his own feelings as he contemplates the winter landscape:

> Happy who walks with him! whom what he finds
> Of flavour or of scent in fruit or flow'r,
> Or what he views of beautiful or grand
> In nature, from the broad majestic oak
> To the green blade that twinkles in the sun,
> Prompts with the remembrance of a present God!
> His presence, who made all so fair, perceiv'd,
> Makes all still fairer. As with him no scene
> Is dreary, so with him all seasons please.
>
>   (VI,247–55)

To walk with nature *is* to walk with God; nature's beauty and grandeur prompts the contemplative spirit to a renewed sense of the Deity, and the apprehension of a divine Presence in turn heightens the appeal of nature. As for Coleridge—who was as much indebted to this passage as to any in *The Task*—all seasons are sweet to him that sees and hears the lovely shapes and sounds of the God who teaches 'Himself in all things, and all things in himself';[42] and Cowper, on the indisputable evidence of his own recorded experience of winter at noon, includes himself among those who enjoy this happy state. And there are, as we know, simpler registers of fundamental religious motivation throughout Book VI. Nature's changes are all 'prodigies . . . divine' (l.118). Her constant progress from 'dearth to plenty, and from death to life' is a lecture in 'heav'nly truth': '. . . there lives and works/A soul in all things, and that soul is God' (ll. 181–5). The drama of mind, of inward renovations and psychological progression from 'dearth' to 'plenty', is not the only drama articulated in *The Task*. We are asked to join the poet in witnessing a timeless pageant—the 'renovation of a faded world'—of which God is the only begetter.

Yet careful reading of the poem leads always to the conclusion that its faith and religion are hardly the Christianity of Newton or the Wesleys—or indeed Cowper's Olney hymns. Cowper does precisely what Spacks, and Huang, and Gilbert Thomas insist that he doesn't do—that is, absorb God into Nature.[43] That Cowper also upholds the tenets of revealed religion—the primacy of redemptive grace in particular— makes no difference to the fact that he cultivates a faith and spirituality rooted in response to a divinized natural world. In this cultivation, and indeed everywhere in *The Task*, he undermines the claims of Christian orthodoxy; everywhere, because when he is not 'naturalizing' Faith he is at least 'poetizing' it, transmuting it into text. Bunyan was careful to gloss his allegorical pilgrim's progress with references to the relevant Biblical texts; in *The Task* all is interiorized as mind-journey and part of the authorial consciousness, and there is no Truth or Reality—even the existence of God— independent of the experiencing, perceiving, affirming, arguing, contemplating, desiring self. Cowper's great capacity for creating change extends even to his relations with the sacred and inviolable.

Finally, this capacity is brought into very sharp focus by the influential passage lying between his 'soft musings' within the bower of oaks and elms and the imagined pageant of spring and summer flowers:

> Meditation here
> May think down hours to moments. Here the heart
> May give an useful lesson to the head,
> And learning wiser grow without his books.
> Knowledge and wisdom, far from being one,
> Have oft-times no connexion. Knowledge dwells
> In heads replete with thoughts of other men;
> Wisdom in minds attentive to their own.

> Knowledge, a rude unprofitable mass,
> The mere materials with which wisdom builds,
> Till smooth'd and squar'd and fitted to its place,
> Does but encumber whom it seems t'enrich . . .
> Books are not seldom talismans and spells,
> By which the magic art of shrewder wits
> Holds an unthinking multitude enthrall'd . . .
> But trees and rivulets whose rapid course
> Defies the check of winter, haunts of deer,
> And sheep-walks populous . . .
> Deceive no student. Wisdom there, and truth,
> Not shy, as in the world, and to be won
> By slow solicitation, seize at once
> The roving thought, and fix it on themselves.
>   (VI,84–95,98–100,109–11,114–17)

The point is not, of course, simply that nature leaves the mind free to discover 'wisdom' and 'truth'; to 'Deceive no student' is also to co-operate, actively but without undue force, in the process of enlightenment. Nature's role is that of an unrivalled and kindly teacher, working in unison with the intuitive powers of heart and head; *there*, amidst the quiet life of trees and rivulets and peeping primrose (l.113), true knowledge comes unsought and unawares to the unfettered spirit. It comes so to Cowper in this very passage, which it itself an example of 'truth' breaking in upon the meditating mind.

Here, if anywhere, is the immediate source of Wordsworth's early lyrics in praise of 'natural education':

> Enough of science and of art;
> Close up those barren leaves;
> Come forth, and bring with you a heart
> That watches and receives.
>   ('The Tables Turned', ll.29–32)

But what is really in question in relating these two poets is not any simple distinction between the 'dull and endless strife' of worldly, intellectual knowledge and the 'spontaneous wisdom' to be caught from 'one impulse from a vernal wood' but a shared ontology and version of 'individuated' selfhood. Though consciousness of God plays no such major part in

Wordsworth's poem as it does in Cowper's, it is by means so absent, even from the 1805 text, as is often assumed:

> I am content
> With my own modest pleasures, and have liv'd,
> With God and Nature communing, remov'd
> From little enmities and low desires . . .
>
> (*Prelude*, 1805, II,444–7)

In basing his ideal of 'calm existence' and of poetic creation on responsiveness to the 'one life' of 'all things', the privilege of standing 'In Nature's presence . . /A sensitive, and a creative soul' (without those vistings of imaginative power which obliterate self and nature), Wordsworth trod a path Cowper had trod before. And so it is when he values the 'healing and repose' that come from nature, and her gift of 'that happy stillness of the mind' which fits man to receive 'truth' when 'unsought'.[44] What 'truth'? we may ask. In a sense it is an unreal question, for the important thing is the 'revelation' itself, the moment of perception: in Cowper's passage on meditation 'wisdom' and 'truth' simply fix the mind '*on themselves*', in an instant of perfect poise that has no reference beyond itself, to any specific insight gained. At the same time, however, there is a simple answer—the 'truth' of the object, the 'soul' in all things that is apprehended in the act of beholding. It is true that Cowper does have the conventional idea of God's workmanship in mind when proceeding to talk of 'agency divine', and say 'All we behold is miracle; but, seen/So duly, all is miracle in vain' (ll.132–3). Yet this does not make his poetry or its message only a lecture in 'heavenly truth'—a sermon on the wisdom and might of the Creator. The language of religion—sometimes preacherly and 'biblical' ('. . . Should God again,/As once in Gideon, interrupt the race/Of the undeviating and punctual sun')—is the outside of a position which is at its heart firmly comparable to Wordsworth's great assertion of the twin principles of 'being' and 'Being':

>   only then
> Contented when with bliss ineffable
> I felt the sentiment of Being spread
> O'er all that moves, and all that seemeth still,

O'er all, that, lost beyond the reach of thought
And human knowledge, to the human eye
Invisible, yet liveth to the heart . . .
                    (*Prelude*, 1805, II,418–24)

Of the future history of this philosophy of 'heart-knowledge', heightened 'perception', 'reciprocity', and 'wonder' something was said in the last chapter, with reference to Carlyle. Its further investigation would take in the epiphany-poems of Yeats, Williams, Stevens, Lawrence, Edward Thomas, and would involve too the shadow side of the same philosophy, our sense of lost potential in an age of almost limitless potentialities for materialistic and utilitarian mass-production.

   Wordsworth opposed his faith in 'the life of things' not only to the viewpoint of science but to the seeming decay of humane and religious sensibility at large—to the 'indifference and apathy/And wicked exultation' that infected the social and public worlds, and the rising disease of life in cities, 'where the human heart is sick,/And the eye feeds it not, and cannot feed':

                    in this time
Of dereliction and dismay, I yet
Despair not of our nature . . .
                    (*Prelude*, 1805, II,456–8)

His defence of 'our nature' includes affirmation of the dignity of man objectively perceived, in the character poems of *Lyrical Ballads*. The life of a Michael or an Idiot Boy is as much a miracle to behold as any miracle in nature. The nearest Cowper comes to 'love of man' is the humanitarianism of such sketches as that of Crazy Kate or the poor cottagers of Olney, and general pleas for 'human fellowship, . . . love and friendship' (*Task*, VI,321ff.). So far as the human world is concerned, his interest is much more in the condition of the age, the 'dereliction and dismay' itself. It is in this subject that our discussion of *The Task* will end.

6

Public Poet and 'Self-sequester'd Man': Cowper's Search for Repose

The beginning of Book IV of *The Task* finds Cowper in his sitting-room, listening to the post-horn, reading the newspaper, taking a vicarious pleasure from the numberless goings-on of 'the busy world' beyond the shutters of his retreat—imagined love-letters, tidings of the budget, the jockeying for political office, advertisements for wigs and false teeth, the fall of stocks, even voyages of discovery:

> I tread his deck,
> Ascend his topmast, through his peering eyes
> Discover countries, with a kindred heart
> Suffer his woes, and share in his escapes;
> While fancy, like the finger of a clock,
> Runs the great circuit, and is still at home.
> (IV, 114–19)

Post and newspaper, the sofa and the famous 'cups,/That cheer but not inebriate': Cowper was not averse to the little luxuries of modern 'consumerist' society, made possible by increased trade and improved communications (the post-boy, 'Cold and yet cheerful', is the sturdy swain of pastoral tradition transformed into a service-worker, and his safe arrival, though with 'spatter'd boots' and 'frozen locks', bears witness to the recently redoubled efforts of the Turnpike Trusts).[1] This is

Notes and References begin on page 340.

clearly the same man who had, in Book I, rejected the
attractions of the secluded 'low-roof'd lodge', the *peasant's nest*,
because it lacked the ordinary conveniences of a handy
water-supply and 'baker's punctual call': 'If solitude make
scant the means of life,/Society for me!' (I,248–9). And the
same man who had, again in Book I, felt pity for Omai 'the
gentle savage', whom he imagines pacing the shore of his native
island after his return from England, waiting for a ship to take
him back to the 'sweets' he has left behind—'sweets' which
include the more splendid ingredients of cultivated life, 'all that
science traces, art invents,/Or inspiration teaches', 'palaces,
. . . pomp, . . . gardens, . . . sports, . . . music' (I,663–8,642–
53,626–8).

Cowper, then, both praises and enjoys 'The manners and the
arts of civil life'. But this is only one side of the picture. Even in
Book I he is more likely to condemn what is going on in the
world than he is to approve of it, especially where the world is
that of the town or of commerce. The *peasant's nest* may be finally
undesirable as a permanent abode but it is definitely preferable
to any dwelling within the industrialized landscape of 'clinking
hammers, grinding wheels,/And infants clam'rous whether
pleas'd or pain'd' (I,231–2). It was perhaps lucky after all that
Omai went home, for the metropolis would soon have tempted
him to 'squander life'; and there is in any case no chance of
another ship visiting his land, when it is void of 'bait' and
'Doing good,/Disinterested good, is not our trade' (I,672–6).
While London is undeniably the 'fairest capital of all the
world', it is also, like every city, a place of 'Rank abundance',
'gain-devoted', a 'sew'r' running with the 'dregs' of humanity
(I,681ff.). In the light of these images of gross excess and
debasement, we can hardly view the following lines as an
altogether safe compliment:

> Where has commerce such a mart,
> So rich, so throng'd, so drain'd, and so supplied,
> As London—opulent, enlarg'd, and still
> Increasing, London?
>
> (I,719–22)

The urge to celebrate is neutralized by Cowper's apprehension
of the moral and social dangers of a world built upon the

'principle' of satisfying ever-increasing desires. It is worth saying straight away that this critical response is not determined simply by the biblical, and Puritan, sense of the city as the seat of profligacy and temptation—Bunyan's City of Destruction and Vanity Fair, very much, of course, 'gain-devoted' and, to use words from elsewhere in Cowper's passage, the breeding-place of 'sloth', 'lust', and 'wantonness'. That response is part and parcel of his wider immediate, and realistic, reaction to what Richard Feingold terms 'the very palpable and demanding facts of his day', the facts of 'New forms of commerce, new methods of industrial and agricultural production, new patterns of population, new habits of consumption, new international commitments, new and growing military might'.[2]

A *realistic* reaction? Yes, in spite of the troublesome moral exaggeration apparent in the preacherly tones of 'Rank abundance . . . sloth and lust . . .'. If we compare Thomson's exultation over the energy, growing wealth, and imperial designs of the English nation—

> Full are thy cities with the sons of art;
> And trade and joy, in every busy street,
> Mingling are heard: even Drudgery himself,
> As at the car he sweats, or, dusty, hews
> The palace stone, looks gay. . . .
> Bold, firm, and graceful, are thy generous youth,
> By hardship sinewed, and by danger fired,
> Scattering the nations where they go . . .
> ('Summer', ll. 1457–61, 1467–9)

who could deny that Cowper has the surer instincts and better judgement, when eschewing pastoral and heroic idealization, seeing a fundamental dichotomy between 'business' and 'goodness' ('Doing good,/Disinterested good, is not our trade'—how well 'Disinterested' points the essential '*self-*interestedness' of commercial and imperial 'doing'), and recognizing that where wealth and people accumulate men may well decay? Given our knowledge of subsequent history, and our own ambiguous relationship with 'progress' and 'consumption', we cannot but conclude that he has got things fairly right while Thomson has got them plainly wrong.

Criticism of the outside world, done in many voices from playful to coldly censorious, grows more persistent after Book I. The famous passage in Book II—'England, with all thy faults, I love thee still—/My country! and, while yet a nook is left/Where English minds and manners may be found,/Shall be constrain'd to love thee' (ll.206–9)—leaves us in no doubt that Cowper was a patriotic Englishman but impresses us at the same time with his difficulty in finding much to be patriotic about. He has earlier put on record his pride in the fact that England has no slaves—'They touch our country, and their shackles fall./That's noble . . .' (II,42–3); yet his recommendation that she spread the blessing through her empire, so that where 'Britain's pow'r/Is felt, mankind may feel her mercy too' (II,46–7), immediately betrays his suspicion of imperialist energies, which apparently generate no export in freedom or virtue. Look where he will, it is the faults that strike him. True Englishness seems to have retreated already to narrow nooks, if indeed it still exists at all outside the poet himself. He swings relentlessly through the landscape of political, religious, and 'higher' social life, introducing the imagery, of 'play', ostentation, disease, madness, monstrousness, dissolution, and the like, which he uses throughout the poem to describe the present state of men and manners. Preachers perform their 'histrionic mumm'ry', while politicians 'tender as a girl, all essenc'd o'er/With odours, and profligate as sweet' let pass 'the perfidy of France' (her alliance with the American Colonies) as but 'a trick of state', and transform the duties of their offices into 'superior jockeyship' (ll.221ff.). 'Expenditure' wastes the vitals of the upper classes; 'Dress drains our cellar dry'; the ritual of social pleasure becomes a dance of lunatics, a *danse macabre*:

> So many maniacs dancing in their chains.
> They gaze upon the links that hold them fast
> With eyes of anguish, execrate their lot,
> Then shake them in despair, and dance again.
>
> (II,663–6)

Yet no brief quotation can give a fair impression of the vigour, intensity, and bleakness of Book II of *The Task* as a whole. In a unique blend of Juvenalian savage indignation and Hebraic apocalyptic vision, with an admixture of the politer satiric animus of Pope's *Moral Essays* and the prophetic toning of Book IV of *The Dunciad*,[3] moral and imaginative pressure constantly rises and bursts forth, culminating in denunciations of the source of all the evils that infect the land, Profusion:

> Profusion is the sire.
> Profusion unrestrain'd, with all that's base
> In character, has litter'd all the land . . .
> It is a hungry vice:—it eats up all
> That gives society its beauty, strength,
> Convenience, and security, and use:
> Makes men mere vermin, worthy to be trapp'd
> And gibbeted as fast as catchpole claws
> Can seize the slipp'ry prey: unties the knot
> Of union, and converts the sacred band
> That holds mankind together to a scourge. . . .
> The country mourns—
> Mourns, because ev'ry plague that can infest
> Society, and that saps and worms the base
> Of th' edifice that policy has rais'd,
> Swarms in all quarters; meets the eye, the ear,
> And suffocates the breath at ev'ry turn.
> Profusion breeds them . . .
> So, when the Jewish leader stretch'd his arm,
> And wav'd his rod divine, a race obscene,
> Spawn'd in the muddy beds of Nile, came forth . . .
> the streets were fill'd;
> The croaking nuisance lurk'd in ev'ry nook;
> Nor palaces, nor even chambers, 'scap'd;
> And the land stank—so num'rous was the fry.
> (II,674–6,680–7;814–20,825–7,829–32)

The climactic allusion to the plague in Egypt reminds us that the early part of Book II had been concerned with the way God shows his 'hot displeasure against foolish men,/That live an atheist life' (ll.178–80). There had seemed a simple explanation for the calamities that befell nations, and an obvious remedy. By the end of the Book the problem is cast in much more complex and challenging terms. England is the victim of an apparently unstoppable force—no less rampant and vicious than its predecessor, Pope's Dulness—which devours everything of worth in society, dehumanizes man, transforms social 'union' into the chaos of verminous existence, rots the fabric built by good polity, and fills every corner of the land with its contagion and obscene progeny. Profusion is as unaccountable and irresistible as the Deity himself (one effect of the closing smile is to accredit it with godlike power), but is man-made and everywhere present. There would seem now to be no solution to England's situation; the enemy has been born from within and ranges at large under its own momentum.

Such passages do raise the question of whether Cowper is indeed representing actuality or inventing a world out of an imagination influenced above all by the Old Testament *mythos* of the decadent, luxury-ridden, and idolatrous nation.[4] Clearly he is doing both. Feingold, attacking Raymond Williams's view of eighteenth-century 'pastoral' as a device for evading the harsh results of capitalist enterprise, remarks that 'It is not a mystification of capitalism that we see in [Cowper and Dyer], but a prescient approach towards and bewildered withdrawal from the larger phenomenon of which capitalism is a part.'[5] Cowper's account of the conquest of Profusion can certainly be understood as a 'prescient approach towards' the emergent autonomy and triumph of 'consumption', the inexorable process of getting and spending. He is strongly aware, too, of the psychological realities of a commercial and materialist society—how tailors, for example, trade on changes in fashion and 'With our expenditure defray [their] own' (for now 'Variety's the very spice of life,/That gives it all its flavour'),[6] or how in extreme cases 'Wives beggar husbands, husbands starve their wives' by worshipping compulsively at 'fortune's velvet altar' (II,656ff.). Yet these materials and truths are accommodated within a particular imaginative ambit, an ambit so totally dominated at times by instinctive moral horror that, as in the lines on Profusion, the verse swells with a profusion of its own, a kind of visionary disgust and despera-tion, and Cowper's countrymen became a race of odious little vermin worthy only to be trapped and gibbeted. (Mandeville's well-known paradox—private vices make public virtues—was plainly anathema to this writer).[7] Book II is powerful poetry which embodies astute insights into the direction of a changing world; but its power, like parts of Swift and Book IV of *The Dunciad*, is that of the deeply pessimistic and abundantly negative. It is in the end as if Cowper has got into the dark metropolitan sewer, which is a structure partly of his own making, and can't see or climb out of it.

The recognition of 'negative vision', however justifiable such vision might be in purely poetic terms, usually sends the critic in search of compensating 'positives'—some set of values that redeems the work of satire from hopelessness or the spirit of rejection. Cowper's own standards are obvious enough: the Augustan ideals of moderation, 'use', order, discipline, sobriety. On close examination, however, *The Task* is not so much a defence of these virtues as a lament for their vulnerability and decline, especially if we leave aside for the moment their importance within its conception of the sequestered life. When talking of politics in Book II, for example, Cowper makes the qualities of 'soldiership and sense'—best interpreted by reference to the classical ideas of *virtus* and *gravitas*—the exclusive possession of the *last* generation, of Chatham and Wolfe. 'Those suns are set', and the present is all 'effeminates' and 'dishonour' (II,221–54). He introduces a description of the true preacher, based upon the 'design' of St. Paul and imagining the man 'simple, grave, sincere;/In doctrine uncorrupt; in language plain,/And plain in manner'; but there are no such apostles in all the church, only odious 'things' that prostitute and shame their noble office (II,395ff.). Although Cowper's satire is admirably consistent and impressively belligerent, it presents at bottom a rather alarming impasse, with the poet and his beliefs on the one side and on the other a world from which those beliefs are radically, terminally absent, a world forming itself on frighteningly strange and immoral assumptions.

The gulf is an ever-widening one, so that in Book III a note of puzzled resignation enters his attacks upon the industrial and commercial landscape of the city. Are not the pleasures of the country to be preferred to

> the eclipse
> That Metropolitan volcanos make,
> Whose Stygian throats breathe darkness all day long;

> And to the stir of commerce, driving slow,
> And thund'ring loud, with his ten thousand wheels?
>
> (III,736–40)

But there is a 'madness' and a 'folly' abroad in England, which drives men into the 'crowded coop'. By calling the movement from the country to the town 'madness' Cowper expresses his disapproval yet admits that the process cannot be arrested. It is a deplorable but indisputable reality—like the demise of Old England itself, once 'plain, hospitable, kind,/And undebauch'd'

> But we have bid farewell
> To all the virtues of those better days,
> And all their honest pleasures.
>
> (III,744–6)

The 'better' way of life Cowper has in mind at this point seems to be that of the patriarchal rural community as celebrated in Dryden's 'To my Honour'd Kinsman' and Pope's lines on the Man of Ross, or in heartier vein by Crabbe's Benbow in *The Borough*.[8] The myth of a virtuous and coherent social order, rooted in idealization of squirearchal rule, still survives; only, however, as the faint prelude to a further register of the evils of wealth and consumption. 'Mansions once/Knew their own masters' and 'laborious hinds/Who had surviv'd the father, serv'd the son'. Those times are dead and gone, and estates bought, sold, and altered with incredible rapidity. Everything is consumed—'patrimonial timber' by the heir eager to realize his assets, the heir by 'some shrewd sharper' or else the gaming-tables, another by 'Improvement . . . , the idol of the age', the natural beauties of the countryside by the 'improver' himself, the bankrupt by political usurers who buy his vote (III,751ff.). It is worth noting that, although Cowper is taking his cue from Pope's Moral Essays on 'the Use of Riches' in parts of this section of *The Task*, and especially from the satire on the ignoble waste of Timon's lavish villa, he introduces no such optimistic philosophy as Pope's proposition on the underlying productiveness of senseless expenditure—'Yet hence the Poor are cloath'd, the Hungry fed;/. . . What his hard Heart denies,/His charitable Vanity supplies'.[9] The nearest he comes to an idea of just order and providential patterning is the observation that he who destroys the country by selling off or 'improving' his patrimony will himself be destroyed:

> The country starves, and they that feed th' o'ercharg'd
> And surfeited lewd town with her fair dues,
> By a just judgment strip and starve themselves.

> (III,757–9)

To Cowper all are victims, at times of self-love and private vices but always of an impersonal process, a vicious and incurable contagion.

This dark, alienated, essentially desperate view of England's course and condition finally deepens and intensifies in Book IV, taking in all classes of society and the country as well as the town:

> Pass where we may, through city or through town,
> Village, or hamlet, of this merry land,
> Though lean and beggar'd, ev'ry twentieth pace
> Conducts th'unguarded nose to such a whiff
> Of stale debauch, forth-issuing from the styes
> That law has licens'd, as makes temp'rance reel.
> There sit, involv'd and lost in curling clouds
> Of Indian fume, and guzzling deep, the boor,
> The lackey, and the groom; the craftsman there
> Takes a Lethean leave of all his toil;
> Smith, cobbler, joiner, he that plies the shears,
> And he that kneads the dough; all loud alike,
> All learned, and all drunk! The fiddle screams...
> Dire is the frequent curse, and its twin sound
> The cheek-distending oath, not to be prais'd
> As ornamental, musical, polite,
> Like those which modern senators employ,
> Whose oath is rhet'ric, and who swear for fame!
> ... 'tis here they [plebeian minds] learn
> The road that leads, from competence and peace,
> To indigence and rapine...
> But censure profits little: vain th'attempt
> To advertise in verse a public pest,
> That, like the filth with which the peasant feeds

His hungry acres, stinks, and is of use.
Th'excise is fatten'd with the rich result
Of all this riot; and ten thousand casks,
For ever dribbling out their base contents,
Touch'd by the Midas finger of the state,
Bleed gold for ministers to sport away.
Drink, and be mad, then; 'tis your country bids!
(IV,466–78,487–91,495–7,500–9)

With the reference to 'styes/That *law has licens'd*' a link is immediately established between rural debauchery and the workings of the state, which is later elaborated and explained as—in Feingold's well-chosen phrase—'a perverse harmony' between dehumanizing excess and the interests of a corrupt polity.[10] In the preceding passage Cowper had designated poverty a 'self-inflicted woe', the effect of 'laziness and sottish waste' (ll.430–1), and the images of swinish behaviour near the beginning of the present quotation ('styes', 'guzzling deep') seem merely to sustain this puritanical attitude. Within the more complex overall picture, however, that behaviour is seen, astutely, as an integral part of a system that encourages and has grown dependent upon vice. The rural community—and practically the whole range of occupations is represented, from labourer to baker—have become the bloated creatures, not of some mythic seductress or wizard, a Circe or a Comus, but of the latter-day monster, the State. They live unknowingly in its service, swilling and swelling so that the excise may be 'fatten'd'; their licensed depravity is its gain. In a grotesque conjunction of images, which concentrates all Cowper's caustic vituperation and all his imaginative horror of the situation, 'ten thousand casks,/For ever dribbling out their base contents,/Touch'd by the Midas finger of the state' are transformed at once into barrels of gold and a host of bodies slobbering, bleeding, and (perhaps) urinating to fill the coffers of the exchequer; and in another metaphorical conflation the manured fields of agricultural England, the 'hungry acres', merge with the fattened treasury in an emblematic representation of the countryside's participation in the economy—and the corruptness—of the nation (ll.500–3). Just previously, too, the country and the city have been brought together, this time as the twin extremes of a debasement that stretches horizontally across the land and vertically from the lowest to the highest rungs of the social ladder; for the vices of rural debauchees differ from the vices of 'modern senators' only in style—the ignorant 'cheek-distending oath' as against the musical phrases of those whose 'oath is rher'ric, and who swear for fame'. The tavern scene is an analogue not only to what goes on in parliamentary debates but also to what is happening in the schools, and indeed in politer society at large: the rituals and talk of the public-house educate 'plebeian minds' in 'arts/ Which some may practise with politer grace', and teach them the road from 'competence and peace' to 'indigence and rapine'. Cowper's sense of a horrifyingly amoral and monstrously voracious economic system is one with his sense of a wider activity, a headlong progress into ruin and chaos. It is not stagnation or passivity that he sees and worries about, but a peculiar vitality and expenditure of energy—which he can apprehend, however, only in negative terms, as elsewhere he apprehends the expansion and life of the metropolis.

All the salient features of Cowper's vision of the national life are prominent in this passage. Of these, his unsentimental and thoroughly anti-pastoral view of the countryside is something we have not met with before. The scene of rural debauchery is a very far cry from the georgic concept of the virtuous and frugal peasant, as expressed in Thomson's famous lines in praise of '... plain innocence,/Unsullied beauty, sound unbroken youth/Patient of labour—with little pleased', and it seems fair to say that Cowper is, like Crabbe in *The Village*, intent on exploding the myth by an assertive appeal to reality. Sure enough, in the very next passage of Book III he describes those 'golden times' and 'Arcadian scenes' of 'innocence' and 'simplicity' which Maro had sung, or Sidney, as an illusion even then: '... those days were never: airy dreams/Sat for the picture; and the poet's hand,/Imparting substance to an empty shade,/Impos'd a gay delirium for a truth' (ll.525–8). Yet the truth is that the myth, and above all its moral content, still hold powerful sway over Cowper's own mind and imagination, providing the measure against which the present state of the country and its inhabitants is judged. When he goes on to say that the town has 'tinged' the country, he automatically uses imagery that suggests the purity and absolute innocence of the latter: the stain appears 'a spot upon a vestal's robe,/The worse for what it stains' (ll.554–5). When depicting how the habits of the town have invaded the country, he does so in terms of the transformation of an old type into a new, the 'rural lass', half graceful Arcadian shepherdess and half the feminine counterpart of the honest labourer of georgic tradition (all 'virgin modesty and grace', 'artless manners and ... neat attire'), into the woman of fashion, 'Indebted to some smart wig-weaver's hand/For more than half the tresses [she] sustains' (ll.534ff.). Or again, his critique of the evils of 'universal soldiership' is a lament for the corruption of the rugged but simple husbandman of Vergil and Thomson; after three years of 'heroship' the 'child of nature, without guile'

> Returns indignant to the slighted plough ...
> T'astonish and to grieve his gazing friends,
> To break some maiden's and his mother's heart;
> To be a pest where he was useful once ...
> (IV,645,655–7)

Behind these lines, strongly felt by its absence, is the Vergilian image of the husbandman in whom martial prowess, virtue, and a capacity for useful toil are aspects of the same independent character.[11]

There is a realism in such passages, but it is a realism delimited by the influence of those very ideals which Cowper has earlier said are impossible even to dream of 'in days like these ... when virtue is so scarce' (IV,529–31). This is an important point, for it does much to explain the nature of his response to the contemporary world and especially his failure to reach any accommodation with it, any serviceable compromise on the question of values, principles, and goals. He tends to perceive, define, and experience the real world as a reverse image of the moral world to which he is inwardly habituated and intellectually committed. The force and originality of his insights are beyond dispute, not least where the *invisible* facts of the political and economic environment are concerned: for all the sarcasm and virulent censure of the 'merry England' passage, Cowper lays the blame at no-one's door, but sees, quite rightly, that 'the system' is a law unto itself, and that within the system there does exist a productive relationship between individual consumption and the needs of government. But he is no pragmatist—no Mandeville or Adam Smith, ready to recognize the public utility of private desires, the contribution of private vices to the greater good.[12] The perspectives of *The Task* are always in the final analysis controlled by the straightforward assumptions of the Christian and rural moralist, by ideals of 'good' and 'order' which are intrinsically hostile to any form of comprehensive political and social organization, and could never themselves be the basis of any such organization. It was never virtue, or frugality, or quietness, or simplicity that made the world go round or held it together—even in Vergil's Rome, though his mythopoeic imagination might make it seem so.

Cowper does finally come out against all forms of political union—administrative, commercial, military:

> Man in society is like a flow'r
> Blown in his native bed: 'tis there alone
> His faculties, expanded in full bloom,
> Shine out; there only reach their proper use.
> But man, associated and leagu'd with man
> By regal warrant, or self-join'd by bond
> For int'rest-sake, or swarming into clans
> Beneath one head for purposes of war,
> Like flow'rs selected from the rest, and bound
> And bundled close to fill some crowded vase,
> Fades rapidly, and, by compression marr'd,
> Contracts defilement not to be endur'd.
> Hence charter'd boroughs are such public plagues;
> And burghers, men immaculate perhaps
> In all their private functions, once combin'd,
> Become a loathsome body, only fit
> For dissolution, hurtful to the main.
> Hence merchants, unimpeachable of sin
> Against the charities of domestic life,
> Incorporated, seem at once to lose
> Their nature; and, disclaiming all regard
> For mercy and the common rights of man,
> Build factories with blood, conducting trade

> At the sword's point, and dyeing the white robe
> Of innocent commercial justice red.
> Hence, too, the field of glory, as the world
> Misdeems it, dazzled by its bright array, . . .
> Is but a school where thoughtlessness is taught
> On principle, where foppery atones
> For folly, gallantry for ev'ry vice.
>   (IV,659–85,688–90)

In *The Wealth of Nations*, published less than a decade before *The Task*, Adam Smith had attacked the then accelerating process of 'incorporation', and the 'corporation spirit' itself, because it prevented 'free competition'. He was sceptical of the advantages of factories, since routine daily labour might debilitate both mind and body, leading to dexterity in one particular trade 'at the expense of . . . intellectual, social, and martial virtues' (and so the state would do well to provide the labouring poor with mental and gymnastic instruction).[13] Cowper's objections are of course altogether more thorough. It is not what happens in factories that concerns him, but the fact that they are built 'with blood'; mercantile corporations are seen, not as a clog on trade, but as the source—and emblem—of rampant institutionalized greed; private and domestic virtue ('private functions . . . the charities of domestic life') ceases to influence men once they are associated, either under regal warrant or by mutual consent for 'int'rest-sake'; and, in spite of Cowper's earlier respect for 'soldiership', there is no such thing as martial virtues or warlike 'glory', only a perverse education in empty-headedness and superficial elegance (which follows on consistently from his recent condemnation of military training, where the country boy is returned 'a pest' to the fields he should cultivate—and a drunkard who will provide more wealth for the exchequer).[14] As always, it is impossible not to admire Cowper's radical criticism of the brutal realities of organized power and bold assertion of the conflict between virtuous and political action. The trouble is, however, that the verdict is absolute—a rejection, on closed moral grounds, of a central, unalterable fact of life, the political impulse itself. The condemnation of corporate enterprise, as the cause of folly, inhumanity, and all loss of decency, is so clear, so complete, that no room is left either for adapting to it or (which is the direction Smith takes) for improving it.

We are given at the beginning of the passage, of course, an image of a very different kind of community, a 'society' in which human faculties may 'shine out' and 'reach their propse use', but this is, precisely, an *image*, a theoretical conception of some perfectly natural order of things which loses all force and relevance before the evidences of actual circumstance, the ineluctable *un*naturalness of real human society. Similarly, Cowper talks of 'innocent commercial justice' in its 'white robe', but he never tells us what this truly is, where it might be found, in which sort of situation it would flourish or go unviolated. He could not tell us, for it is not of this world, but the phantom-figure of an impossible dream. 'Man incorporated', power, self-interest and the mutual pursuit of profit, political organizations are the inescapable features of collective life in the modern state. Cowper sees but cannot accept them; reality itself is for him an incurable ill.

The Task does not, and could not, offer models of collective life other than those it condemns in its survey of city and countryside, state and corporation. What it does give is the model of an alternative existence—the life of rural and domestic retreat.

*   *   *   *   *

If we return to the opening of Book IV, it will be immediately obvious that Cowper's relation to the subject of secluded domesticity involves the union, so characteristic of his work, of personal and didactic impulses. 'I behold/The tumult, and am still' (ll.99–100): retirement is a welcome repose, or, more accurately, a locus for activity-in-repose since the poetry everywhere articulates a lively movement of the mind. One way of interpreting this movement would be to stress its moral content and elements of public statement. Even where it is playfully observed, metropolitan life is condemned as a poor worthless thing—an absurd farce, amusing perhaps yet senseless and contemptible:

> So let us welcome peaceful ev'ning in.
> Not such his ev'ning, who with shining face

        Sweats in the crowded theatre, and, squeez'd
        And bor'd with elbow-points through both his sides,
        Out-scolds the ranting actor on the stage:
        Nor his, who patient stands till his feet throb,
        And his head thumps, to feed upon the breath
        Of patriots, bursting with heroic rage,
        Or placemen, all tranquillity and smiles.
                                        (IV,41–9)

Over against these scenes are set the scenes of the poet's
domestic world, distinguished at first by their comforts but also
before long by their qualities of orderliness, quiet industry,
frugality, and piety:

        Now stir the fire, and close the shutters fast,
        Let fall the curtains, wheel the sofa round . . .
                                . . . the threaded steel
        Flies swiftly, and, unfelt, the task proceeds.
        The volume clos'd, the customary rites
        Of the last meal commence. A Roman meal;
        Such as the mistress of the world once found
        Delicious, when her patriots of high note,
        Perhaps by moonlight, at their humble doors,
        And under an old oak's domestic shade,
        Enjoy'd—spare feast!—a radish and an egg!
        Discourse ensues, not trivial, yet not dull . . .
                                . . . Themes of a graver tone,
        Exciting oft our gratitude and love,
        While we retrace with mem'ry's pointing wand,
        That calls the past to our exact review,
        The dangers we have 'scap'd, the broken snare,
        The disappointed foe, deliv'rance found
        Unlook'd for, life preserv'd and peace restor'd—
        Fruits of omnipotent eternal love.
        Oh ev'nings worthy of the gods! exclaim'd
        The Sabine bard.
                        (IV,36–7,165–74,181–90)

The light-heartedness towards which the passage veers at times
(a radish and an egg!) does nothing to undermine the basic
seriousness of Cowper's claims for the superiority of the

sequestered life. Conflating his own way of life with a venerable *topos*, the Roman and Horatian ideal of retirement, he recommends a model existence, a corporate selfhood opposed to the communal 'insanity' on the outside.

But the public and ethical ingredients are not the only ingredients in the poetry of Cowper's 'Winter Evening'. The typical private motives are also present. Plainly, one of the great advantages of retirement for Cowper is that it frees him from the demands and stresses of 'the peopled scene', and not a little of what he says on the subject reflects the worryingly abjurative attitude, 'To fly is safe'. Yet it is hard in practice to take exception to this escapism because Cowper is so open about it, and so readily prepared to take us into his confidence:

> 'Tis pleasant through the loop-holes of retreat
> To peep at such a world; to see the stir
> Of the great Babel, and not feel the crowd;
> To hear the roar she sends through all her gates
> At a safe distance, where the dying sound
> Falls a soft murmur on th'uninjur'd ear.
> Thus sitting, and surveying thus at ease
> The globe and its concerns, I seem advanc'd
> To some secure and more than mortal height,
> That lib'rates and exempts me from them all.
> It turns submitted to my view, turns round
> With all its generations; I behold
> The tumult, and am still. The sound of war
> Has lost its terrors ere it reaches me;
> Grieves, but alarms me not . . .
>
> (IV,88–102)

Very special needs are evident in this—for safety, security, a shelter from 'the crowd'. Retirement offers refuge without isolation. More, it is a position from which the world may be reduced to an object of contemplation, a 'globe', a source of pleasure and play. The sequestered man can be involved without fear of injury, can experience conflict ('war') with god-like ('more than mortal') immunity from danger; without moving from his armchair he can travel the seas, 'While fancy, like the finger of a clock,/Runs the great circuit, and is still at home' (ll.118–19). *Stillness* is important to Cowper. But activity is just as necessary to him, and in the hand of the clock, moving yet not moving, fixed yet free, is the perfect image of his ideal state, and the perfect image too of the situation afforded by poetry and contemplation, where seclusion and stasis—being shut up in Olney—is no bar to far-resonant action.

The therapeutic effort so central in *Retirement* thus continues, though in a lower key, in *The Task*. It would be a mistake to think of 'The Winter Evening' as simply a record of what Cowper's retirement was like. We have all the selectivity of a construct, determined partly by moral presuppositions and objectives but also by an urge to justify himself to the world (in stressing the superior merit of his latter-day 'Roman' life) and to establish and make trial of the singular privileges of existence behind 'the loopholes of retreat'. The shadow of darker thoughts flickers across the imagined landscape in metaphors of confinement—'Fast bound in chains of silence', the pensive cell from which is heard 'the faint echo of . . . brazen throats' (ll.53,104)—but there is now no real threat of psychic reverse: Cowper's energies flow all in the direction of affirmation and the framing of a personal bliss. So, at the end of Book IV, directly after the passage on 'incorporated man', he asserts his long-standing, indeed lifelong, enjoyment of the pleasures of the country—

> I never fram'd a wish, or form'd a plan,
> That flatter'd me with hopes of earthly bliss,
> But there I laid the scene. There early stray'd
> My fancy, ere yet liberty of choice
> Had found me, or the hopes of being free.
>   (IV,695–9)

and goes on to describe how no bard could ever please him but those whose lyres were tuned to Nature's praise, ending with an address to 'Ingenious Cowley':

> I still revere thee, courtly though retir'd;'
> Though stretch'd at ease in Chertsey's silent bow'rs,
> Not unemploy'd; and finding rich amends
> For a lost world in solitude and verse.
>   (IV,727–30)

His apartness is no failure or defeat, but what he has always wanted; not enforced, but made by 'liberty of choice'. It is, moreover, an honourable station, endorsed by the great example of the occupant of Chertsey's 'silent bow'rs'. Clearly, Cowper is re-enforcing that 'fiction' of freedom and good fortune by which he consistently stabilized his life and identity; but the process of stabilization now more than ever involves cutting a figure in the eyes of 'the world' from which, he declares, he is lucky to have withdrawn. There is an inherent problem in his necessary commitment to sequestration: he values its 'safe distance' and solitary, easeful benefits, yet desires to be of some use and consequence. The claims of being born to a love of the country, schooled in the rural poetry of Milton and the classics, and comparable to at least one great light—and indeed his subsequent contention that all men seek what he possesses, witness the gardens that spring up 'in the stifling bosom of the town' (ll.734ff.)—are a way, not only of reassuring himself of his happiness, but of offering his credentials to those he has left behind, as a well-qualified poet writing on a significant theme and within an important tradition.

Cowley, we notice, was 'not unemployed'. Employment, the responsible business of being useful, is always a matter of great concern, and difficulty, to Cowper. It had emerged early in Book III. The poet feels himself 'at large' and 'refresh'd for future toil' after his struggles in the 'miry ways' of metropolitan corruptness ('half despairing of escape'—how honest Cowper is about the danger of terminal arrestment within the confines of a desperately censorious and apocalyptic imagination). But what form is that 'future toil' to take? Not that of satire, for, if pulpits fail to reform men, what chance that a mere unknown poet should 'speak to purpose, or with better hope/Crack the satiric thong?' (III,21–6). The temptation for Cowper, as for Wordsworth in the not dissimilar induction to *The Prelude*, is to rest and do nothing, taking repose 'Where chance may throw me, beneath elm or vine', or confining his criticisms of society to fireside conversations with his 'partners in retreat' (ll.27–40).[15] His sense of the ineffectualness of poetic censure has led him seriously to doubt the point of writing poetry at all. The poem then, however, immediately renews itself, in an address to 'Domestic happiness . . . the nurse of virtue' (ll.41ff.), as if Cowper foresees a useful future for himself after all, as the celebrant of purity and ease. Yet that impetus itself soon fades before thoughts of how the world has turned its back on domestic virtue, making a shipwreck of 'honour, dignity, and fair renown',

> Till prostitution elbows us aside
> In all our crowded streets; and senates seem
> Conven'd for purposes of empire less
> Than to release th'adultress from her bond.
>
> (III,60–3)

We are back with the 'satiric thong' whose application has already been pronounced pointless. Thus the poem proceeds in fits and starts, circling back upon itself. Cowper cares about the state of the world but feels he can do nothing about it. He wishes to recommend virtue but the world cares nothing for it. He cannot beat them—and certainly can't join them.

The deadlock is never broken, but side-stepped. *The Task* settles down only when Cowper decides to make himself and his occupations the subject of his verse, and apparently leave the world to its own devices:

> How various his employments, whom the world
> Calls idle; and who justly, in return,
> Esteems that busy world an idler too!
> Friends, books, a garden, and perhaps his pen,
> Delightful industry enjoy'd at home,
> And nature in its cultivated trim
> Dress'd to his taste, inviting him abroad—
>
> (III,352–8)

It is obvious, however, from what follows next in this prologue to the famous 'georgic' on greenhouse and gardening that the problem of usefulness has not altogether disappeared. 'Can he want occupation who has these?' (l.359). The answer must in fact be yes, unless one takes a very restricted view of 'occupation'. For friends, books, a garden, and a pen seem to have more to do with leisure, personal satisfaction, and passing the time than with being productive. Cowper appears to realize this, since he proceeds at once to grope, rather incoherently, for some less fragile line of self-justification, some explanation of how and why his life is fruitful. 'Bus'ness' finds him 'ev'n here':

> while sedulous I seek t'improve,
> At least neglect not, or leave unemploy'd,
> The mind he gave me; driving it . . .
> To its just point—the service of mankind.
> He that attends to his interior self,
> That has a heart, and keeps it; has a mind
> That hungers, and supplies it; and who seeks
> A social, not a dissipated life;
> Has business; feels himself engag'd t'achieve
> No unimportant, though a silent, task . . .
> . . . wisdom is a pearl with most success
> Sought in still water, and beneath clear skies.
>   (III,367–9,372–8,381–2)

This makes the mind itself a centre of production, working somehow in 'the service of mankind'. Whether Cowper has it precisely in view or not (he may be thinking of serving others in some other way through his 'heart' and intellect), the poem, suggested finally by the word *task*, is his best defence against idleness and the best way forward in achieving a worthy purpose—but a poem that now focuses upon the sequestered poet himself, his pursuits, his wisdom and character, his relationship with his environment, his special sympathies. If the forthcoming 'georgic' episodes *do* serve mankind it is because there is some 'use' in contemplating this particular man's particular business and disposition.

These episodes are among the very finest combinations in *The Task* of realism and metaphor, and of self-reference and the creation of an exemplary *ethos*. The activities of the retired poet, described with humour and in loving detail, develop effortlessly into an emblem of possible harmony between man and his environment, between art and nature. We have, as it were, a bucolic, and more outward, representation of the same ideal relationship that is expressed and pursued in Cowper's experiential engagements with the natural world.

The impression of harmony is apparent from the start: the garden with its many cares 'demands' the poet and he 'attends/The *welcome* call' (ll.398–9). The hand of 'lubbard labour' is rejected in order to differentiate the labour which may violate nature from that which respects and aids it—'force' from 'skill' (ll.399–407). Skill, which may itself include necessary force, is the subject of the whole first section of 'The Garden':

> What is weak,
> Distemper'd, or hast lost prolific pow'rs,
> Impair'd by age, his unrelenting hand
> Dooms to the knife: . . .
> . . . The rest, no portion left
> That may disgrace his art, or disappoint
> Large expectation, he disposes neat
> At measur'd distances, that air and sun,
> Admitted freely, may afford their aid,
> And ventilate and warm the swelling buds.
> Hence summer has her riches, autumn hence,
> And hence ev'n winter fills his wither'd hand
> With blushing fruits, and plenty, not her own.
> Fair recompense of labour well bestow'd,
> And wise precaution; which a clime so rude
> Makes needful still, whose spring is but the child
> Of churlish winter, in her froward moods
> Discov'ring much the temper of her sire.
> For oft, as if in her the stream of mild
> Maternal nature had revers'd its course,
> She brings her infants forth with many smiles;
> But, once deliver'd, kills them with a frown.
> He, therefore, timely warn'd, himself supplies
> Her want of care, screening and keeping warm
> The plenteous bloom . . .
>   (III,414–17,421–41)

As Feingold says, the emphasis falls repeatedly on the successes of art, which are shown even 'to withstand the defects of nature'.[16] Not only must the weak and old wood be cut out, but also the large and barren shoots that feed 'at th'expence of neighb'ring twigs' (ll.417–21); and the children of spring must often be defended against their own unnatural mother. The disorders of the natural world are thus corrected by art, in acts, of rearrangement, incision, and intervention, that also suggest a certain opposition between the powers of man and the energies of nature. Yet the opposition is no discord, and the triumphs of art are no affront to natural order. The gardener disposes the plants neatly so that 'air and sun' may do their proper work more freely; he is 'timely warn'd' by nature herself to come to nature's aid; he intervenes, not as a usurper, but as a kindly nurse and protector who returns the delicate progeny of spring to their parent's rightful care, 'As the sun peeps and vernal airs breathe mild' (ll.442–5). Though art is primary, its relation to nature is entirely harmonious and wholly fruitful.

In the cucumber passage the balance is to some extent altered—redressed. Here nature has a kind of primacy:

> when summer shines,
> The bee transports the fertilizing meal
> From flow'r to flow'r, and ev'n the breathing air
> Wafts the rich prize to its appointed use.
> Not so when winter scowls. Assistant art
> Then acts in nature's office, brings to pass
> The glad espousals, and ensures the crop.
>
> (III,537–43)

Taught by her example, art becomes nature's 'assistant', helping her to her own 'glad espousals'. And there is a greater sense in this passage of nature's autonomous power, which has to be carefully watched and which always exists as a potentially decisive threat to human plans, however well laid and expertly carried out:

> Warily, therefore, and with prudent heed,
> He seeks a favour'd spot; that where he builds
> Th'agglomerated pile his frame may front
> The sun's meridian disk . . .
>
> (III,470–3)

> Moisture and drought, mice, worms, and swarming flies,
> Minute as dust, and numberless, oft work
> Dire disappointment that admits no cure,
> And which no care can obviate.
>
> (III,555–8)

Cowper views the relationship between art and nature as a complex one, and he views it comprehensively; if in the previous section of the poem we see, despite the assertion of harmony, a final subordination of nature to man, the poet organizing his little kingdom, we encounter in the present section the apprehension that man can never gain full mastery over nature. Rather, he must submit himself to its rhythms in order to receive its fruits:

> Thrice must the voluable and restless earth
> Spin round upon her axle, ere the warmth,
> Slow gathering in the midst, through the square mass
> Diffus'd, attain the surface . . .
>
> (III,490–3)

Earth, we notice, is 'voluable' and 'restless'; it cannot be controlled. But experience and respect for nature's powers and favours do lead on to achievement:

> Experience, slow preceptress, teaching oft
> The way to glory by miscarriage foul,
> Must prompt him, and admonish how to catch
> Th'auspicious moment, when the temper'd heat,
> Friendly to vital motion, may afford
> Soft fermentation, and invite the seed.
> The seed, selected wisely, . . .
>
> (III,505–11)

The concept of nature as master ('assistant art . . .') and threat does not preclude the idea of fertile co-operation: the 'temper'd heat', a natural element but created in this spot by human labour, *invites* the seed; the seed, though natural ('plump' and 'smooth'), is *selected* by the experienced gardener. The whole process of growing the unseasonable fruit is a triumphant conjunction of complementary forces—a sort of 'glad espousal' in itself.

Out of the projects of the self-sequestered man, then, Cowper has fashioned a rounded and complete image of optimal relationship, the marriage of art and nature; an image that is 'moral' and 'useful' in the broadest sense, as a concentration and resolution of a fundamental human concern rooted in essential facts of the human condition. Yet it is not only this relationship that is expressed, but also images of optimal *social* order. Within the garden—

Few self-supported flow'rs endure the wind
Uninjur'd, but expect th'upholding aid
Of the smooth-shaven prop, and, neatly tied,
Are wedded thus, like beauty to old age,
For int'rest sake, the living to the dead.
Some clothe the soil that feeds them, far diffus'd
And lowly creeping, modest and yet fair,
Like virtue, thriving most where little seen;
Some, more aspiring, catch the neighbour shrub
With clasping tendrils, and invest his branch,
Else unadorn'd, with many a gay festoon
And fragrant chaplet, recompensing well
The strength they borrow with the grace they lend.
All hate the rank society of weeds,
Noisome, and ever greedy to exhaust
Th'impov'rish'd earth; an overbearing race,
That, like the multitude made faction-mad,
Disturb good order, and degrade true worth.

(III,657–74)

Beside this may be placed the equally beautiful lines from the preceding greenhouse interlude:

Plant behind plant aspiring, in the van
The dwarfish, in the rear retir'd, but still
Sublime above the rest, the statelier stand.
So once were rang'd the sons of ancient Rome,
A noble show! while Roscius trod the stage;
And so, while Garrick, as renown'd as he,
The sons of Albion; fearing each to lose
Some note of Nature's music from his lips,
And covetous of Shakespeare's beauty, seen
In ev'ry flash of his far-beaming eye.

(III,593–602)

This is more than a simile; for a moment the poetry flairs into vision.

Both of these passages display—noble show!—ideal worlds which are the perfect opposite of the contemporary world as Cowper sees it in *The Task*. All is proportion, no profusion or excess. 'For int'rest sake' catches the eye in the first quotation: this is not the 'interest' of men self-joined for profit and power but that of more 'natural', organic interdependence between the weak and the strong, young and old, beauty and wisdom, the present generation and the past. Those that clothe the soil, 'lowly' yet 'fair', suggest not only the virtuous (who have a place in *this* social order) but also an uncorrupted peasantry. 'Strength' and 'grace' blend and complement one another (reminding us of Dryden's image of a consummate art and perfected civilization: 'Thus all below is Strength, and all above is Grace').[17] Even the 'weeds' are there, an image combining reference to acquisitive greed that would exhaust 'the land' ('improvers', speculators in agriculture, the lord realizing his assets to pour them down the drain of investment and metropolitan pleasure?), to politicians (an 'overbearing race'), and to the popular mob (reminding us again of Dryden, as well as Shakespeare, though perhaps reflecting above all Cowper's memory of the Gordon Riots). But these are all hated by the rest—a separate colony that threaten and disturb the prevailing 'good order' but do not destroy it. Cowper's imagination here relegates the disturbing realities of the contemporary world to a decentralized role, the position of a peripheral sub-culture.

Not the least remarkable aspect of the other passage is the fact that the metaphors of theatre and military array (the 'sons' of Rome and Albion suggest heroes as well as an audience, and the plants are just afterwards called 'marshall'd ranks'), which are among Cowper's most familiar means of criticizing the present state of English life, have become a mode of celebration, the medium in which he envisions civilization in its most noble and achieved form. This is Cowper's model of the good society, the land of 'sublime' and stately heroes dedicated to 'soldiership and sense', 'honour, dignity and fair renown'; a society graceful, strong, and well ordered, which both respects and mirrors in itself the qualities of great art, the art that is also Nature. Cowper's own art—instinct with the same qualities— momentarily gives substance and shape to values which have previously in *The Task* been merely words ('soldiership' etc.) or merely implicitly present in his censure.

Now, Feingold relates the vision of Book III, 'the good work of the gardener, the marriage of art and nature, and ... the social potential of man', to the celebrative 'bucolic' poetry of Vergil's *Georgics* and the English Augustans, notably Pope, where these concerns and metaphors are the means of organizing a coherent response to national life. It is true that the greenhouse and garden episodes of *The Task* express an 'imaginative understanding of optimal civilization', an 'emblematic fusion that celebrates the harmony a poet perceives in the natural and social orders of experience';[18] and true that the understanding and celebration rest upon, and continue, traditional values and poetic affirmation. We need only to remind ourselves that the harmonies of Cowper's 'social shade', and of the relationship of his sequestered man to his tasks and environment, are in essence those of Pope's great address to Burlington:

> Still follow Sense, of ev'ry Art the Soul,
> Parts answ'ring parts shall slide into the whole,
> Spontaneous beauties all around advance,
> Start ev'n from Difficulty, Strike from Chance;
> Nature shall join you, Time shall make it grow ...
> ('Epistle to Burlington', ll.65–9)

Yet the comparison is of course an uneasy one. Pope's vision rises above the felt energies of a mad, dull, morally purposeless society whose motivation is the engrossment and ill-use of wealth—'At length Corruption, like a gen'ral flood,/... Shall deluge all; and Av'rice creeping on,/Spread like a low-born mist, and blot the Sun'[19]—in an act of imaginative resolution that incorporates a sense of the public world, of power and politics:

> You too proceed! ...
> Till Kings call forth th' Idea's of your mind,
> Proud to accomplish what such hands design'd,
> Bid Harbors open, public Ways extend, ...
> Back to his bounds their subject Sea command,
> And roll obedient Rivers thro' the Land;
> These Honours, Peace to happy Britain brings,
> These are Imperial Works, and worthy Kings.
> (Ibid., ll.191,195–7,201–4)

Cowper's vision has neither the structural status nor public content and reference of Pope's. His apprehensions of the good society, indeed this whole celebrative section of Book III, represents a localized success within a dialectic dominated by a sense of dissolution, change, and the growth of a 'decivilized', unnatural world. The sense of this world even intrudes at the very heart of the celebrative vision itself, in recognitions of the 'rich' who (like a 'rank society of weeds') thoughtlessly consume the produce of the earth, all the more eagerly when (like cucumbers) it is 'costly yet and scarce': those who 'little know the cares,/The vigilance, the labour . . . exercised . . . That ye may garnish your profuse regales/With summer fruits brought forth by wintry suns' (ll.544ff.). For a brief yet pointed moment Cowper comes close to realizing that he and his poem, the labour of his mind and hand, are themselves bound up in the process of production and consumption, when he talks of how his 'pow'rs' pant for 'the praise of dressing to the taste/Of critic appetite . . . no sordid fare' (ll.460–61); the humour, which continues into the georgic interlude ('The stable yields a stercoraceous heap,/Impregnated . . .), is all part of the 'play' between the entertainer and the entertained.

But this is an underdeveloped perception, and a passing accommodation with the cultured world beyond the innocent and idyllic garden. What really compromises the force of Cowper's celebration of elegance, moderation, order, the union of art and nature is the powerful consciousness of doom and malignancy which floods back into the poem directly after the lines imaging good social order: 'vicious custom, raging uncontroll'd/Abroad, and desolating public life', commerce 'driving slow,/And thund'ring loud, with his ten thousand wheels', cities that attract us while 'neglected Nature pines', the metropolis that 'ingulphs' all. The idea of a fair community completely vanishes, leaving the poet in retreat, celebrating only his own private bliss and convinced that its example will reclaim no one:

> Health, leisure, means t'improve it, friendship, peace,
> No loose or wanton, though a wand'ring, muse,
> And constant occupation without care.
> Thus blest, I draw a picture of that bliss;
> Hopeless, indeed, that dissipated minds,

And profligate abusers of a world
Created fair so much in vain for them,
Should seek the guiltless joys that I describe . . .

(III,691–8)

Civilization has shrunk to civility, society to friendship, ambition to peace, the public poet to a man sitting behind his 'faithful barrier'.

We may recall that Cowper's dark response to a changing world was by no means an isolated or eccentric phenomenon. It but confirms the direction of Pope's poetry if we take Pope's career as a whole; and even Johnson, who loved the city and once got very excited at the prospect of someone making a fortune 'beyond the dreams of avarice' out of Thrale's brewery, wrote his greatest poem *de contemptu mundi*.[20] There were also the enthusiasts like Dyer; but *The Fleece*—'And ruddy roofs, and chimney tops appear,/Of busy Leeds, up-wafting to the clouds/ The incense of thanksgiving'[21]—seems to us no less naive (probably more) than Thomson's images of gay Drudgery. We are more at ease with the prose writers whom Feingold talks about, Arthur Young and Paolo Balsamo, whose attitudes are at times the direct opposite of Cowper's: 'To satisfy more wants increases man's happiness'; 'political bodies, and with more reason great cities, are better calculated . . . to procure man's happiness than deserts and petty villages'; moderation 'may be good for the people of the moon'.[22] But we accept from the economist and sociologist what would seem out of place in the poet: Cowper's view of the world is historically the emergent representative view of the artist, who is concerned with value rather than practical gain. In the landscape of *The Task* may be read the rough features of future cities of Dreadful Night, Dickensian valleys of the Shadow, and waste-lands, where the imagination feeds (more or less willingly) on forbidden fruit.

Yet we are no less aware in Book III of that important corollary in Cowper to the split between 'value' and 'world'— the deepening centrality of the consciousness and resources of the individual. For all the emblematic content of the georgic episodes, we never do lose a strong sense of a particular man with a particular business and disposition. The distinctiveness of style and locale constantly turns moral standards into preference:

> Strength may wield the pond'rous spade,
> May turn the clod, and wheel the compost home;
> But elegance, chief grace the garden shows,
> And most attractive, is the fair result
> Of thought...
>
> (III,636–40)

There is a constant emphasis on the process of construction—the 'master's' hand shaping the poem, summoning the beauties on the page:

> They form one social shade, as if conven'd
> By magic summons of th' Orphean lyre.
> Yet just arrangement, rarely brought to pass,
> But by a master's hand...
>
> (III,586–9)

These are significant ingredients: they personalize the poetic statement. Nor is it possible to miss the customary evident satisfaction of psychological need—the illusion of privilege and greatness, the transformation of Cowper's garden into a demi-paradise tended by another Adam:

> each odorif'rous leaf,
> Each op'ning blossom, freely breathes abroad
> Its gratitude, and thanks him with its sweets.
>
> (III,621–4)

Rather than the expression of an idealism based in hopes for the larger community, the poetry is a poetry of personality and private ideals. Although the difference between the prophecy of Old Father Thames at the end of 'Windsor Forest' ('Behold! th'ascending Villa's on my side,/Project long shadows o'er the crystal side./Behold! Augusta's glitt'ring spires increase ...)[23] and Pope's accounts of the just harmonies of Burlington's estate represents a precarious decentralization of the locus of value, which has shifted from city to countryside, yet the bucolic vision of art and nature functions still in relation to civilizing potential and social order. In Cowper the locus of value has narrowed to the space behind the walls of the poet's garden, 'blest seclusion from a jarring world'; emblems of social order have retreated into mind-space; the celebration of balanced interrelationship between art and nature operates in terms of the relation of an identifiable person to his manifestly immediate surroundings.

It would be wrong, however, to see this only as reduction and loss; for it offers fresh possibilities and goals for poetry. There is a paradox about all that Cowper is doing here, which may be highlighted by reference back to the very last lines of 'Windsor Forest', where the figure of the sequestered poet enters with a humble farewell:

> My humble Muse, in unambitious strains,
> Paints the green forests and the flow'ry plains,
> Where Peace descending bids her olives spring,
> And scatters blessings from her dove-like wing.
> Ev'n I more sweetly pass my careless days,
> Pleas'd in the silent shade with empty praise . . .
> (ll.427–32)

In this brief coda the retired poet appears as an appendage to his own poem, situated at the edge of the world he has celebrated, though also sharing in the benefits of the public Peace. His life and mind are closed off from view, being subordinated to the claims of mythopoeic and socio-political mission. While Cowper too stands at the periphery of the public world, yet the situation is in an important sense the reverse of that appertaining to Pope's poem. Cut off and shut in he may be, but Cowper's self-sequestered man, who is no other than Cowper himself, is liberated from a marginal and secret role. The outsider has become very much the inside of the poem, his world—both physical and mental—the heartland to which the public world is a circumference. The moral and practical focus of Art has, as it were, swung over, to an extent previously unknown in eighteenth-century poetry: the nostalgic self of Goldsmith's *The Deserted Village* and the self-contemplating poet of Gray's more personal moods are as faint shadows beside Cowper's substantial model of active and entire apartness, or (as Wordsworth phrases it) 'genius, under Nature, under God,/Presiding'.[24]

*   *   *   *   *

Cowper never does, however, wholly renounce an interest in society. Returning late in Book VI to the theme of corporate identity, he still apparently has hopes for mankind, as a race 'Distinguish'd [and bound together] much by reason, and still more/By our capacity of grace divine' (VI,601–2). But the familiar pattern emerges. The ideal of a rational community united under the banner of Christ soon fails before a surging realization of what man is and does in the unideal present. One remarkable passage deserves lengthy quotation:

> Man praises man. Desert in arts or arms
> Wins public honour; and ten thousand sit
> Patiently present at a sacred song,
> Commemoration-mad; content to hear
> (Oh wonderful effect of music's pow'r!)
> Messiah's eulogy for Handel's sake!
> But less, methinks, than sacrilege might serve—
> (For, was it less, what heathen would have dar'd
> To strip Jove's statue of his oaken wreath,
> And hang it up in honour of a man?)
> Much less might serve, when all that we design
> Is but to gratify an itching ear,
> And give the day to a musician's praise.
> Remember Handel? Who, that was not born
> Deaf as the dead to harmony, forgets,
> Or can, the more than Homer of his age?
> Yes—we remember him; and, while we praise
> A talent so divine, remember too
> That His most holy book from whom it came
> Was never meant, was never us'd before,
> To buckram out the mem'ry of a man . . .
> —Man praises man; and Garrick's mem'ry next,
> When time hath somewhat mellow'd it, and made
> The idol of our worship while he liv'd
> The god of our idolatry once more,

Shall have its altar; and the world shall go
In pilgrimage to bow before his shrine.
The theatre, too small, shall suffocate
Its squeez'd contents, and more than it admits
Shall sigh at their exclusion, and return
Ungratified. For there some noble lord
Shall stuff his shoulders with king Richard's bunch,
Or wrap himself in Hamlet's inky cloak,
And strut, and storm, and straddle, stamp, and stare,
To show the world how Garrick did not act—
For Garrick was a worshipper himself;
He drew the liturgy, and fram'd the rites
And solemn ceremonial of the day,
And call'd the world to worship on the banks
Of Avon, fam'd in song. Ah! pleasant proof
That piety has still in human hearts
Some place, a spark or two not yet extinct!
The mulb'ry tree was hung with blooming wreaths;
The mulb'ry tree stood centre of the dance;
The mulb'ry tree was hymn'd with dulcet airs;
And from its touchwood trunk the mulb'ry tree
Supplied such relics as devotion holds
Still sacred, and preserves with pious care....
—Man praises man. The rabble, all alive,
From tippling-benches, cellars, stalls, and styes,
Swarm in the streets. The statesman of the day,
A pompous and slow-moving pageant, comes.
Some shout him, and some hang upon his car,
To gaze in's eyes, and bless him. Maidens wave
Their 'kerchiefs, and old women weep for joy: . . .
Thus idly do we waste the breath of praise,
And dedicate a tribute, in its use
And just direction sacred, to a thing
Doom'd to the dust, or lodg'd already there!
      (VI,632–52,664–90,694–700,711–14)

This refers of course to actual events: the Handel Commemoration at Westminster Abbey in the summer of 1784, and
Garrick's Shakespeare Jubilee held at Stratford in 1769 and
later the Drury Lane Theatre (Cowper's details of suffocated

and disappointed crowds are taken from reports of the Stratford occasion, which was something of a fiasco).[25] To Cowper they symbolize not just how 'man praises man' (that sonorous repetition which holds the long passage so superbly together), but the whole moral chaos and profaneness of the age. The immediate past had customarily been for Cowper a kind of golden age of dignity, honour, and virtue—as it is in the lines in Book III on the grace and nobility of Albion's sons when Garrick trod the stage. Not so here. That time, and Garrick's generation specifically, combines with the very immediate present of 1784 in a landscape of perverse, unChristian ritual, vast corporate pageants that are travesties not only of religious worship but also of cultural and social decorum. Art—still clearly respected by Cowper (Handel is 'the more than Homer of his age', Shakespeare and Garrick himself will be debased by the strutting actors of the imagined Garrick Commemoration)—is tainted by its usurpation of the place and function of religious rites, while God and religion are dishonoured in their association with, and displacement by, art. The house of God is appropriated for the purposes of eulogizing Handel, the Bible 'buckram[s] out the mem'ry of a man', Garrick acts like a divine—even like God himself—in drawing up the 'liturgy' and calling mankind to 'worship' on the banks of Avon. In some of Cowper's most scathing, and yet strangely beautiful, lines the image of the mulberry tree and its devotees—priests, worshippers, pilgrims at a shrine gathering relics of the saint—concentrates all his tragic sense of the time's impiety and inverted values. It is very much to the point that snuff-boxes and other mementoes cut from Shakespeare's tree were freely sold at the Jubilee, which would have suggested to Cowper the encroachment of the commercial spirit into every branch of ceremonial life, artistic and religious; and he may also have known of the entrepreneurial side of the Handel festival, as well as Garrick's financial stake in the proceedings at Stratford.[26] But it is the emblems of paganism that matter most: Cowper's apprehension of the collective life of no backward but an ungodly people. There are images of confusion and disarray in the passage as a whole, in the picture of the interior of the theatre and later (ll. 701–3) of the rabble untying the horses of the statesman's carriage so that they may pull it themselves, usurping (so Cowper says) 'a place they well deserve'; yet the significant thing is that the 'madness' is largely intentional and organized, less a *de*rangement than a total *re*arrangement of culture and belief on aberrant and impure principles. Various sections of the nation are involved: the clergy who 'hired out' Westminster Abbey, artists, polite society, money-makers, the statesman, and the mob who fête him in a gross parody of a military triumph and Christ's entry into Jerusalem ('Doth he purpose its *salvation?*', asks Cowper). The poet sees not only dissolution but a perverse reformation of the national life.

The marvellously sustained indignation of this passage, solid, controlled, measured, is perhaps the most achieved expression of that chasteness and masculine strength to which Cowper's finest satirical writing always to some extent approximates—the familiar Augustan socio-literary virtues of which Cowper is a late and notable exponent. The lines are also, however, his most passionate, inclusive, and complete rejection of contemporary society; even those on 'merry England' cover fewer aspects of the social order, and cover them with a less clear sense of the way things 'downward tend'. In facing the world so squarely he, as it were, turns his back upon it, making a clean break from thoughts of its redemption, giving up all faith in the corporate life of the nation which he apprehends more than ever as a perversion of true corporate ideals. It comes as no surprise that his mind moves next to the Day of Doom and Restoration, when all things will be destroyed and remade anew. The perfect world to which Cowper is committed can exist only in the hereafter:

> The various seasons woven into one,
> And that one season an eternal spring,
> The garden bears no blight, and needs no fence, . . .
> All creatures worship man, and all mankind
> One Lord, one Father. Error has no place:
> That creeping pestilence is driv'n away;
> The breath of heav'n has chas'd it. In the heart
> No passion touches a discordant string,
> But all is harmony and love.
>
> (VI, 769–79, 783–8)

The general lack of vigour and intensity in Cowper's account of the Earthly Paradise Regained has been often noted by critics.[27] How are we to explain it? Perhaps the simple answer is that Cowper intended it, out of respect for the inherent sufficiency and efficacy of scriptural truth, which needs no dress to recommend it: 'I have admitted into my description no images but what are scriptural, and have aimed as exactly as I could at the plain and simple sublimity of the Scripture language'.[28] And this thoroughly Puritan attitude, earnestly regardful of the primacy of *logos*, may be said to combine here with the bent of Cowper's genius, which was never that of the mystic, finding its fulfilment in transcendent revelation. But there is, I think, another factor to be taken into account. There is little excitement in his Earthly Paradise because there is little new. His vision of things to come is to a large extent his vision of how things are, put in reverse—a state where there is no State, no politics, no pestilent excess, no discordant passion, and where 'meek and modest truth' may be the norm, thriving at the centre of a community of believers:

> Oh for a world in principle as chaste
> As this is gross and selfish! over which
> Custom and prejudice shall bear no sway,
> That govern all things here, should'ring aside
> The meek and modest truth, and forcing her
> To seek a refuge from the tongue of strife
> In nooks obscure, far from the ways of men: . . .
> (VI,836–42)

Cowper's millennium is not so much scriptural as subjective. It is his dream of the England he would like to see and be in, to which he and his values might fully belong.

Pressure of a kind does of course exist in *these* lines, due to the influx of Cowper's underlying consciousness of his real isolation, moral and physical, from the rest of mankind. The *apologia* with which *The Task* concludes is full of this consciousness and may in part be understood as an attempt to overcome it:

> He is the happy man, whose life ev'n now
> Shows somewhat of that happier life to come;
> Who, doom'd to an obscure but tranquil state,

Is pleas'd with it, and were he free to choose,
Would make his fate his choice; whom peace, the fruit
Of virtue, and whom virtue, fruit of faith,
Prepare for happiness; bespeak him one
Content indeed to sojourn while he must
Below the skies, but having there his home.
The world o'erlooks him in her busy search
Of objects, more illustrious in her view;
And, occupied as earnestly as she,
Though more sublimely, he o'erlooks the world.

(VI,906–18)

There are apparent echoes here of Nahum Tate, Pope's lines on Sir William Trumbull in 'Windsor Forest' and his 'Lines on Solitude and Retirement', and of Goldsmith's praise of 'blest retirement' in *The Deserted Village*—all of which recall the Vergilian–Horatian celebration of rural innocence, ease, and contemplative spirituality.[29] As usual, however, we are more aware of how Cowper is using the *topos* itself—of psycho-drama rather than convention. The 'happy man' is Cowper's familiar self-consoling image of himself, content, occupied, advantaged beyond the fortune of other men, lucky in his fate, contemptuous of the world and its contempt. Yet as the passage continues it becomes clear that he is not in fact altogether happy in this role of 'happy man'—not content, at least, to overlook the world or to be overlooked by it. Not for the first time, the desire to be thought of as 'useful' pulses through the verse, in a whole series of protestations:

Not slothful he, though seeming unemploy'd,
And censur'd oft as useless.

(VI,928–9)

Perhaps she owes
Her sunshine and her rain, her blooming spring
And plenteous harvest, to the pray'r he makes,
When, Isaac like, the solitary saint
Walks forth to meditate at even tide,
And think on her, who thinks not for herself.

(VI,945–50)

His sphere though humble, if that humble sphere
Shine with his fair example, . . .
He serves his country, recompenses well
The state, beneath the shadow of whose vine
He sits secure . . .

(VI,960–1,968–70)

By no stretch of the imagination can we really see *The Task* and
its author as useful in such ways: priestly mediator between 'the
tribe' and its 'God', or serving his country by his 'fair example'
in virtuously 'aiding helpless indigence' (he probably has in
mind here his benevolent response to the plight of the poor
cottagers, recorded earlier in the poem).[30] The poet's own
insistence, however, is a signal response to, and illustration of, a
major 'truth' of his poem: the separation of poet from public
life, the divorce of poetry and the practical world. *The Task*
continues to teach a morality to the very last, in pleading the
virtues of 'good sense', 'decorum', and 'true worth'—'She
judges of refinement by the eye,/He by the test of conscience,
and a heart/Not soon deceiv'd . . .' (ll.987–8). Yet these are
now emphatically the possession of the solitary self, with little
or no relevance to the life of the greater community. And
Cowper knows it: his 'fruit' will be grateful to *some* palates,
'Insipid else, and sure to be despis'd' (ll.1014–15). At the same
time the *apologia* brings home with particular force the positive
side of this defeat of the public poet:

Ask him, indeed, what trophies he has rais'd,
Or what achievements of immortal fame
He purposes, and he shall answer—None.
His warfare is within. There unfatigu'd
His fervent spirit labours. There he fights,
And there obtains fresh triumphs o'er himself,
And never with'ring wreaths, compar'd with which
The laurels that a Caesar reaps are weeds.

(VI,932–9)

The 'labours' in question here are of course specifically
spiritual. Those of *The Task* are more various; but they are
always labours from 'within', whether the subject is nature,
God, society, or the self. It is, triumphantly, a great public

drama of mind; it makes the bright and dark side of individual 'being' into a public theme.

In these last sections of *The Task* confession and psycho-drama come manifestly to the fore. There is another way of interpreting them, most recently represented by James D. Boulger, who sees them as a public exposition of fundamental Calvinist–Puritan ideas which managed to find in Cowper 'an intelligent spokesman in verse and thus be given serious attention among the cultivated classes for another generation'.[31] The *apologia* presents familiar conceptions of the 'saint' and his vision in accordance with the general position of the Georges, Pettit, New, Knappen, and other commentators on the Protestant tradition—the 'saint' who isolates himself from the world but does not avoid its demands completely like the Catholic hermit, who looks beyond the natural to the heavenly realm yet must continue to act out his quest for sanctity, who elevates the pursuit of 'the paradise within' above the pursuit of worldly glory.[32] Boulger reminds us that all of this applies no less to the concluding passages of *The Task* than to *Paradise Lost*, XI–XII, Taylor's *Meditations*, Baxter's *Saints Everlasting Rest*, Bunyan, Law, Watts. And to his evidences we may add the echoes of *The Pilgrim's Progress*, as well as the Bible, in Cowper's glimpse of future joys—

> Oh scenes surpassing fable, and yet true,
> Scenes of accomplish'd bliss! which who can see,
> Though but in distant prospect, and not feel
> His soul refresh'd with foretaste of the joy?
> Rivers of gladness water all the earth,
> And clothe all climes with beauty; the reproach
> Of barrenness is past. . . .
>
> (VI,759–65)[33]

or the evidently Puritan aspiration and imagery of his view of the Celestial City:

> See Salem built, the labour of a God!
> Bright as a sun the sacred city shines;
> All kingdoms and all princes of the earth
> Flock to that light; the glory of all lands

Flows into her; unbounded is her joy,
And endless her increase. . . .

(VI,799–804)

This will return a potent feeling to the bosom of anyone who has
ever been at all experientially interior to the Puritan tradition,
as will Cowper's impressive picture of the coming apocalypse
and the majesty of God:

what remains
Of this tempestuous state of human things
Is merely as the workings of a sea
Before a calm, that rocks itself to rest:
For He, whose car the winds are, and the clouds
The dust that waits upon his sultry march,
When sin hath mov'd him, and his wrath is hot,
Shall visit earth in mercy; . . .

(VI,736–43)

Thus *The Task* may, with good reason, be said to culminate in
a great restatement of the millenarian *mythos* and contemplative ideals of traditional Puritanism. But that view will not
quite do. To talk of Cowper as the intelligent spokesman for
and preserver of religious ideas misses the effect of poetization,
which inevitably secularizes the ideas, undermining their
claims as unquestionable, 'absolute' truth, especially when,
like *The Task*, the poetic text is one that persistently locates
them within a specific individual consciousness. In reading *The
Task* we are always aware of its own internal structures and
logic, which are those of Cowper's mind and imagination. In
the lines recently quoted, for example, the concept of Salem,
heavenly City of God, has been, as it were, removed from the
ambit of objective belief and placed within a particular
psychological landscape: the glory of all lands flowing into her,
the unbounded joy and endless increase, suggest this celestial,
Bunyanesque City as the determining source of Cowper's view
of the earthly metropolis, whither flow the dregs and feculence
of every land, the breeding-place of rank abundance (I,682ff.),
but it also expresses his desire for a world of perfect felicity,
which he envisions in terms conditioned by his mode of
apprehending the world around him. As a whole the episode of

the Earthly Paradise Regained is Cowper's flight from his own
dark, uncompromising vision of a hell-on-earth of corruptness
and ugly profusion; a vision ultimately so all-embracing that
the end of all things becomes an urgent, deeply personal hope:

> Haste, then, and wheel away a shatter'd world,
> Ye slow-revolving seasons! we would see
> (A sight to which our eyes are strangers yet)
> A world that does not dread and hate his laws
> And suffer for its crime; . . .
>
> (VI,823–7)

Then follows the *apologia*. That too is deeply personal, not least,
as we have seen, in its expression of Cowper's persistent
concern about the extent of his usefulness. But we should not,
finally, make too much of this element of anxiety. *The Task* does
end happily and successfully in spite of it, or rather because it is
integrated within, and authenticates, an achieved poise and
calmness. The coda supplies a relatively restful ending to a
restless poem, not quite with 'all passion spent' yet with passion
contained and stilled. The voice is that of a man assured within
himself, though sensitive to the limitations of his position
vis-à-vis the outside world: assured above all of the 'bliss' of
'contemplation', which has in the course of the poem offered us
more than he realizes of both private-therapeutic and public-
exemplary value:

> He cannot skim the ground like summer birds
> Pursuing gilded flies; and such he deems
> Her honours, her emoluments, her joys.
> Therefore in contemplation is his bliss,
> Whose pow'r is such, that whom she lifts from earth
> She makes familiar with a heav'n unseen,
> And shows him glories yet to be reveal'd. . . .
> . . . Stillest streams
> Oft water fairest meadows, and the bird
> That flutters least is longest on the wing. . . .
> Perhaps the self-approving haughty world,
> That as she sweeps him with her whistling silks
> Scarce deigns to notice him, or, if she see,
> Deems him a cypher in the works of God,

Receives advantage from his noiseless hours,
Of which she little dreams.

> (VI,921–7,929–31,940–5)

It is remarkable how many of the preoccupations, tensions, and moral and emotional energies of *The Task* are included, resolved, and harmonized in its conclusion, this temperate expression of a balanced mind. The obsession with the death-in-life of worthless, atrophied passivity, which we first met in the sketch of the paralytic, that 'sad and silent cypher', is submerged here in a controlled concession to the world's viewpoint: 'or, if she see,/Deems him a cypher in the works of God'. Earlier, too, there had been a conflict between his desire for solitude and need for 'society'. He had rejected the *peasant's nest* as an 'abode' in spite of its attractions:

> Here, I have said, at least I should possess
> The poet's treasure, silence, and indulge
> The dreams of fancy, tranquil and secure.
>
> (I,234–6)

and had similarly been troubled by the deprivations of Omai's primitive island-prison despite the many 'charms' of an uncorrupt existence:

> But comes at last the dull and dusky eve,
> And sends thee to thy cabin, well-prepar'd
> To dream all night of what the day denied.
>
> (I,669–71)

In the lines on Crazy Kate solitude had actually been associated with madness, in a puzzled imaginative encounter with the riddle of human vulnerability and survival, and the fate of the eternal, haunted wanderer:

>   And now she roams
> The dreary waste; . . .
>   A tatter'd apron hides,
> Worn as a cloak, and hardly hides, a gown
> More tatter'd still; and both but ill conceal
> A bosom heav'd with never-ceasing sighs.
> She begs an idle pin of all she meets,
> And hoards them in her sleeve; but needful food,

Though press'd with hunger oft, or comelier clothes,
Though pinch'd with cold, asks never.—Kate is craz'd!
(I,546–7,549–56)

All such 'unease' has disappeared in the final section of the poem, with its consistent vision of a life that is at once 'apart' and 'social', sophisticated without being luxurious, peaceful yet not silent, still but active, inward-looking but at the same time never solipsistic or broodingly introspective, secure but no prison, 'free' but not exposed to the dangers of unlimited or downward imaginative flight. The formulations are endless: it is Cowper's perfectly stable vision of a perfect stability, incorporating all he longs for and all he approves. Personal impulse and a concern with self blend easily with moral statement; for the bliss peculiar to Cowper's individual needs is also an image of the moderation, virtue, and piety for which he constantly pleads.

So Cowper makes a peaceful exit, thinking

So life glides smoothly and by stealth away,
More golden than that age of fabled gold
Renown'd in ancient song; not vex'd with care
Or stain'd with guilt, beneficent, approv'd
Of God and man, and peaceful in its end.
So glide my life away! and so at last,
My share of duties decently fulfill'd,
May some disease, not tardy to perform
Its destin'd office, yet with gentle stroke,
Dismiss me, weary, to a safe retreat,
Beneath the turf that I have often trod.
(VI,995–1005)

The Task ends then in composure; but not, we notice, in certainty. 'So glide my life away!': Cowper goes out with a prayer, a wish. And in that so pleasant dream of a smooth passage ending in swift and gentle death is signalized the contrary nightmare of 'care', disapproval by God and man, slow torment, and premature, catastrophic ending. Even in this moment of quiet poise the happy, hopeful, solitary poet is accompanied still by the ghost of the unhappy, desperate, isolated prisoner of fate and a hostile world. The echoes will again become the living voice.

THE SHORTER POEMS

7

An Artless Song?
Poems 'Occasional'
and Comic

Cowper was never at a loss for the right poetic voice, a manner appropriate to any given event or task. Towards the end of 1787 he received a surprise visit from the clerk of the parish of All Saints, Northampton, with a request for some stanzas to affix to the forthcoming annual Bill of Mortality—the list of the parishioners who had died during the year:

> To this I replied—'Mr. Cox, you have several men of genius in your town; why have you not applied to some of them? There is a namesake of yours in particular, Cox the statuary, who everybody knows is a first-rate maker of verses. He is surely the man of all the world for your purpose.' 'Alas Sir! I have heretofore borrowed help from him, but he is a gentleman of so much reading that the people of our town cannot understand him.'[1]

In the event Cowper supplied material not just for 1787 but for five further years. As the letter playfully hints, Cox the statuary could hardly have been more 'a gentleman of ... reading' than the well-known author of *The Task* and translator of Homer; but being really a 'man of genius' rather than a 'first-rate maker of verses' the latter was able, when required, to write both with originality and so that 'the people of our town' understood him. Cowper's 'effusions in the mortuary style', as he terms them, show him in the role of 'popular' poet in a strict sense, writing for a literate yet uncultured audience:

Notes and References begin on page 343.

Could I, from heav'n inspir'd, as sure presage
To whom the rising year shall prove his last,
As I can number in my punctual page,
And item down the victims of the past;

How each would trembling wait the mournful sheet
On which the press might stamp him next to die;
And, reading here his sentence, how replete
With anxious meaning, heav'nward turn his eye.
                          ('For the year 1788', ll.1–8)

How well the *almost* prankish puns on 'sheet' and 'sentence'
contribute to the arresting blend of wit and aggressive sobriety
that Cowper so surprisingly, and so convincingly, develops as a
suitable form for the occasion. His shrewdest move is to take
advantage of the very custom and nature of the 'bill of
mortality', especially its anonymity and the apparent finality of
the printed word, by confronting the reader with the genuinely
shocking idea of a *predictive* list, playing on the impression of a
document self-written (is the 'I' of line three the poet or not?) or
the unalterable business-like declaration of some coldly impersonal force, like Death itself. There is something comfortable
and faintly comforting about purely retrospective bills of
mortality. What if they also foretold the future? It is a
fascinating yet unpleasant thought.

There is hardly a byway of Cowper's minor poetry where we
do not find this inventiveness and control. Beside the singular
brand of elegizing exemplified in the above stanzas may be
placed, for instance, a different sort of 'plain' sophistication and
'popular' writing—the full-bodied resonance of the verses on
the Royal George:

Toll for the brave—
The brave! that are no more:
All sunk beneath the wave,
Fast by their native shore . . .
                          (ll.1–4)

Or there is the disconcerting colloquial jauntiness of the
anti-slavery song 'Sweet Meat has Sour Sauce', which is
brilliantly cast in the grimly ironic form of a slave-trader's
horror at the prospect of giving up his long-studied 'art':

'Twould do your heart good to see 'em below
Lie flat on their backs all the way as we go,
Like sprats on a gridiron, scores in a row,
     Which nobody can deny, deny,
     Which nobody can deny.

                                        (ll.30–4)

We deny all the more firmly what the trader claims 'nobody can deny' by being reminded of that complacent fascination with suffering which is a part of human nature. And to the exploitation in this poem of the tension between idiom, which is buoyant, comic, and image (the human cargo), which resists comedy and transmutes it into the challengingly grotesque, can be added Cowper's gift, in less serious contexts, for using the disparity between elevated diction and trivial subject matter:

The honours of his ebon poll
Were brighter than the sleekest mole;
     His bosom of the hue
With which Aurora decks the skies,
When piping winds shall soon arise
     To sweep up all the dew.

('On the Death of Mrs. Throckmorton's Bulfinch', ll.13–18)

All these examples have two obvious but very important things in common: their deliberate artistry and strong sense of audience. Cowper is as much the cultivated and skilled poet when writing for 'the people' of Mr. Cox's parish or producing the clean, solid eloquence of 'Toll for the brave' as in the more obviously learned and agile presentation to Maria Throckmorton. He has the instinct for 'decorum', 'discipline', and 'communication' which goes with an awareness of poetry as a social craft, rather than solitary self-expression; and, as we shall see, even the most subjective of his poems benefit from that instinct, though they were composed without the slightest thought of publication. But the singularly effective alliance between Cowper the poetic craftsman and Cowper the lyricist of personal experience is apparent from the first, in the sequence of love poems to 'Delia' and in the relationship with Prior exemplified by these early yet remarkably distinctive and mature exercises.

From Prior, who was perhaps his favourite poet,[2] Cowper learned the basic art of steering and enriching human relations. Many of Prior's poems are perfect models of this art, whether in the fictional-dramatic form of the dialogue between a man of the world and a possessive husband in 'An English Padlock' or, more frequently, where he is cementing a personal friendship (the epistles to Fleetwood Shepherd), joking respectfully with a patron (Lord Buckhurst), soothing an angry lover:

> Dear Cloe, how blubbered is that pretty Face!
> Thy Cheek all on Fire, and Thy Hair all uncurled.
> Prythee quit this Caprice; and (as old Falstaff says)
> Let Us e'en talk a little like Folks of This World.
> ('A Better Answer', ll. 1–4)[3]

Cowper's manners are, to be sure, more uniformly 'provincial' than those of Prior, who retains a fair measure of the raffish gallantry of the Cavalier poets, but the fine tact and colloquial grace with which he addresses Mrs. Throckmorton, or consoles young Sally Hurdis on the loss of her tame robin:

> These are not dew-drops, these are tears,
>   And tears by Sally shed
> For absent Robin who, she fears
>   With too much cause, is dead . . .
> (ll. 1–4)

recall Prior just as surely as the witty octosyllabic epistles to Robert Lloyd and William Bull which were written in conscious imitation of 'Mat Prior's easy jingle'.[4] In all these pieces, both Prior's and Cowper's, the important thing is not so much what is said—which is normally slight and sometimes premeditated nonsense—as the way of saying it, the urbanity, the sympathetic or courteously bantering tone by which relationships are confirmed and nourished within the conventions of a civilized society. When the occasion arose, however, Cowper put Prior's example of how to talk 'like folks of this world' to conspicuously personal and independent use, adopting the style—and once or twice Waller's similar elegant colloquializing[5]—to conduct and speculate upon his difficult love-relationship with his cousin Theadora during the 1750s, when he was a frequent visitor at his uncle's house in

Southampton Row. 'This ev'ning, Delia, you and I' takes its
central idea—that lovers feign quarrels to be all the happier
when reconciled—from Prior's ode 'The Merchant to secure
his treasure', yet its tone is best described as a less playful
version of that employed by Prior in 'conversation' poems like
'A Better Answer':[6]

> This ev'ning, Delia, you and I
> Have manag'd most delightfully,
> For with a frown we parted;
> Having contrived some trifle that
> We both may be much troubled at,
> And sadly disconcerted. . . .
>
> Happy! when we but seek t'endure
> A little pain, then find a cure
> By double joy requited;
> For friendship, like a sever'd bone,
> Improves and joins a stronger tone
> When aptly reunited.
>
> (ll. 1–6, 19–24)

The second of these stanzas, which is the last of the poem, is in
fact much more reflective than anything in Prior's love lyrics,
and much more concerned with the emotional life of a
relationship—not only the increase of happiness and strength
that comes with 'reunion' but the pain, the *maiming*, of
'disunity'. Indeed, it is the latter that really stands out, through
the boldness of the strange physical image of the 'sever'd bone'
(no vague references to 'broken hearts' in Cowper, but the hard
specificity of 'broken bones'), and through the word 'aptly'
which reminds us at the last minute that loving, like healing, is
a precarious business and there is always the chance of being
permanently crippled. Though we still feel that the poem
belongs to a genre concerned with the rituals, refinements, and
nuances of behaviour, Cowper shifts the main focus squarely
onto the *experience* of love and what it means for the 'being' of the
individuals involved. It is a significant measure of the difference between Cowper and Prior that whereas the 'Ode' to
which Cowper's poem is related sustains a metaphor of
'commerce' or subtle 'dealing'—the poet sings Euphelia's
praise but fixes his 'soul' on his true flame Cloe, as 'The

merchant, to secure his treasure,/Conveys it in a borrow'd name'—the central image of 'This ev'ning, Delia' turns out to be one of 'suffering' and 'cure'.

That Cowper thus replaces the stress on 'play' with a stress on 'being' may be explained by the fact that his poems are the developing record of an actual situation—a profound 'affair' involving not only his love for Theadora but her father's relentless opposition to the match, the poet's first serious attack of melancholia, and the lovers' enforced separation. The history of one man's experience of love becomes a study in psychological experience itself. We begin with a brief tableau of the poet's initiation into the unknown ways of female company, which evokes, lightheartedly enough but with signal sugges-tions of vulnerability and too much self-consciousness, the feeling of being at once spectator and spectacle, 'hunter' and 'victim':

> ... The women said, who thought him rough,
> But now no longer foolish,
> The creature may do well enough,
> But wants a deal of polish.
>
> At length, improv'd from head to heel,
> 'Twere scarce too much to say,
> No dancing bear was so genteel,
> Or half so dégagé....
> ('Of Himself', ll.25–32)

The tone soon deepens and tension progressively mounts, as we move inwards from the pleasures and transient anxieties of courtship into elated visions of soul-union and nightmare premonitions of the anguish of parting:

> When lo! the force of some resistless weight
> Bears me straight down from that pernicious height;
> Parting, in vain our struggling arms we close;
> Abhorred forms, dire phantoms interpose;
> With trembling voice on thy lov'd name I call,
> And gulphs yawn ready to receive my fall ...
> ('In these sad hours', ll.21–6)

and finally to moods of half-bemused, half-resigned desolation:

Oh then! kind heav'n, be this my latest breath;
   Here end my life, or make it worth my care;
Absence from whom we love is worse than death,
   And frustrate hope severer than despair.
      ('Hope, like the short-liv'd ray', ll.33–6)

The poem we first discussed, 'This ev'ning, Delia, you and I', takes on a certain poignancy in the light of this recognition of the lingering torment of 'absence'. What could once be understood as a game, a contrivance to promote a 'double joy', is now a dreadful reality; separation is not something to be played with. And, vice versa, the later poem derives a sharper edge from what has gone before: hope, that flourished in thoughts of joy and firmer union, is known at last as a subtler, less bearable tyranny than despair. Cowper's progress in love was a progress into suffering, and into a knowledge of suffering.

The 'Delia' poems are a private drama of mind made representative in the act of poetic formulation. The *oneiros* of the above lines from 'In these sad hours' is the emergence, the initial surfacing into Cowper's waking life, of the obsession that will later familiarly take the form of religious terror. The prayer for release from uncertainty in the final stanza of 'Hope, like the short-liv'd ray' anticipates a characteristic position of the more personal hymns, where Cowper, however hard he begs or bids for his freedom, is left tugging frantically at the chains of irresistible hope—as in 'The Contrite Heart', where the pressure of confinement is compounded by the fact that the God whose absence tortures the poet is Himself the only source of assurance and peace, the God who alone can 'heal' or destroy ('break'), 'Decide this doubt for me'. But this is no 'closed', hyper-subjective poetry, though it is a poetry of the self. 'In these sad hours' discovers to us the night-world of our own fantastical lives, a world in which we take much the same fearful delight as in that compulsive–repulsive idea of peeping beforehand into Death's 'punctual' ledger. Cowper's prayer presents us with a truth that is at once new and 'normative': persistent, vain, unrealizable hope gnaws worse than despair. Dr. Johnson, one feels, would have approved of this stanza despite Cowper's impatient plea for death—because the sentiments are 'original . . . yet he that reads them here, persuades himself that he has always felt them'.[7] In Cowper the most singular experiences and insights are something 'to which every bosom returns an echo'.

'To Mary', Cowper's other and much later love lyric, is remarkable in this respect. Nowhere in English poetry is there a more dangerously private or more potentially disastrous enterprise—a sixty-year-old man's lament at the loss of the motherly affection of a woman who has just suffered her third paralytic stroke. The miracle is that we experience not the slightest embarrassment in reading the poem:

> The twentieth year is well-nigh past,
> Since first our sky was overcast;
> Ah would that this might be the last!
>   My Mary!
>
> Thy spirits have a fainter glow,
> I see thee daily weaker grow—
> 'Twas my distress that brought thee low,
>   My Mary!
>
> Thy needles, once a shining store,
> For my sake restless heretofore,
> Now rust disus'd, and shine no more,
>   My Mary!
>
> For though thou gladly wouldst fulfil
> The same kind office for me still,
> Thy sight now seconds not thy will,
>   My Mary! . . .
>
> And should my future lot be cast
> With much resemblance of the past,
> Thy worn-out heart will break at last,
>   My Mary!
>   (ll. 1–16, 53–6)

This pushes right at limits, risking sentimentality and self-pity even more than 'The Castaway' which has the advantage of the naturally virile and mythic theme of damnation. Of the reasons why the seemingly inevitable disaster does not occur, perhaps the most noticeable is Cowper's *honesty*: his relentless cleaving to the painfulness of the relationship and situation he seeks to

commemorate, not only his own distress at 'losing' his companion but her senile decay and physical paralysis, which he
acknowledges in a series of hard facts—the rusting needles, her
'silver locks' and 'indistinct expressions', the enfeebled hands
that 'Yet, gently prest, press gently mine', the observation that
every step she takes she takes 'Upheld by two'. Indeed, so
specific is the human drama referred to by the poem that the
commonest conventions are redeemed from cliché, as in the
detail of the gentle responsive pressure of Mary's weakened
hands, or the revivification of the image of the thread around
the lover's heart by its conflation with the real threads of
Mary's 'housewife's art':

> But well thou play'd'st the housewife's part,
> And all thy threads with magic art
> Have wound themselves about this heart,
>   My Mary!
>   (ll.17–20)

Donald Davie believes that this specificity also redeems 'a
stanza-form apparently foredoomed to ... monotony'.[8] This is
hardly fair to a stanza whose compactness, strong iambic
rhythm, and regular rhymes and refrain exert a necessary
discipline over emotion while allowing for the development of a
tone of personal sincerity, a speaking voice wherein matters of
fact blend easily, unpretentiously, into the flow of feeling and
immediate reflection. But Davie is right inasmuch as he is
placing emphasis firmly on Cowper's *art*. It is the use rather
than choice of stanza that matters, and an infinitely weaker
manuscript version of lines 9–16 shows well enough that
Cowper worked hard to improve and polish the poem, revising
as if with an audience in mind beyond the addressee herself and
beyond the present occasion (he does quite clearly think of
Mary as 'audience' in spite of the affliction that cuts her off from
normal intercourse, though part of the compelling individuality of the poem lies in the fact that she cannot hear and that the
reticence and sign-language of *this* 'wooed lover', with her
'indistinct expressions' and her 'smiles' [l.51], have a cause
very different from the usual shyness or lover's cunning):[9]

> Thy needles, once a shining store,
> Discernible by thee no more

Rust in disuse, their service o'er,
                My Mary!

But thy ingenious work remains,
Nor small the profit it obtains,
Since thou esteemst my pleasure gains
                My Mary![10]

Comparison with the printed version suggests that the qualities we have noted in the poem were not achieved without labour: increased self-reference in the change from 'Discernible by thee ...' to 'for my sake ...', which complicates our understanding of the relationship by introducing the idea of filial dependence; the shift, particularly in the second of the two stanzas, from an impersonal, somewhat discursive style to a 'conversational' idiom—the intimate 'talk' of 'folks of this world'; a finer concentration on concrete detail, the needles that 'Now rust disus'd, and shine no more' (for the less graphic 'Rust in disuse, their service o'er'), the failing sight that 'now seconds not thy will' (which makes a psychological point about Mary's condition as well as focusing unflinchingly on the reality of her blindness). The first and third of these features of the revision leave us in no doubt how far the artistry of the poem goes hand in hand with the honesty that most conspicuously raises it above the level of a sentimental exercise. And they return us, too, to the starting point of this discussion. For Cowper's quest for the literal and for accuracy of definition leads him also to the symbolic and the general; in centring on a single object, the rusty needles, in marking their function in relation to himself, and in describing so precisely the defeat of will by incapacity he creates a poetic statement that is not less but more universal in its appeal and meaning. The object becomes an *image*, of loss and ruin and the cruel indifference of time; the situation shades into *archetype*, of on the one hand total dependence and on the other premature decay—conditions which Cowper does not pretend are anything but desolate, yet which, in a way that is itself both intensely personal and representatively human, he mollifies by opposing to them both a sense of Mrs. Unwin's still-surviving love ('... yet still thou lov'st, My Mary!') and the invincible strength of his own affection which translates atrophy into beauty, the 'silver locks' into something lovelier than 'orient beams', the withered hands into a 'richer store' than 'gold'.

If 'To Mary' is a notable example of art controlling and generalizing personal experience and emotion, 'On the Death of Mrs. Throckmorton's Bulfinch' offers striking evidence of the difference made by the latter to the art of 'occasional' poetry as Cowper practises it. We noticed earlier the connection between the 'frustrate' lover of the last 'Delia' poem and the frustrated 'Calvinist' of 'The Contrite Heart'. Needless to say, every Calvinist is much aware of God's incontestable omnipotence, His complete freedom to act whenever and however He pleases: as Isaac Watts puts it, 'If He resolve, who dare oppose,/Or ask Him why, or what He does?'.[11] But for Cowper the inscrutable ways of Providence were an *idée fixe*, haunting both his waking and sleeping life, never more terrifying than in visions involving sudden violence or death. 'On the Death of Mrs. Throckmorton's Bulfinch', on one level a perfect performance in the art of sustaining friendly relations, is on another, deeper level a poem by one convinced that every moment was fraught with the most incredible danger—that the end could come at any time for caged birds and secluded poets alike.

But let us begin by taking the obvious way into this poem in company with William Norris Free, who sees it as simple mock-elegy, a satire on Mrs. Throckmorton's over-reaction to the death of her pet and an accomplished literary jest at the expense of the 'classical' and the 'heroic': 'It attacks Mrs. Throckmorton's sentimentalism, and it makes fun of the usual rhetoric of elegiac poetry'.[12] Clearly Cowper does use parody in this two-handed manner. Poetic conventions, especially mythological allusion and analogy, are given a mildly ludicrous turn as he invokes the minor deities to share Maria's grief ('Ye nymphs! if e'er your eyes were red/With tears o'er hapless fav'rites shed . . .'), offers a preposterously elaborate account of Bully's origins and education ('Where Rheus strays his vines among,/The egg was laid from which he sprung . . .'), and gives a last comical-tragical twist to the tale by likening poor Bully's beak (all that is left of him) to the head of Orpheus:

> He left it—but he should have ta'en.
> That beak, whence issued many a strain

> Of such mellifluous tone,
> Might have repaid him well, I wote,
> For silencing so sweet a throat,
>   Fast set within his own.
>
> Maria weeps—The Muses mourn—
> So, when by Bacchanalians torn,
>   On Thracian Hebrus' side
> The tree-enchanter Orpheus fell;
> His head alone remain'd to tell
>   The cruel death he died.
>   (ll.55–66)

Talking of 'the *absurdity* of Mrs. Throckmorton's behaviour' and considering her '*guilty* of misplacing values', Free seems at times to want to turn the poem into a much more cutting satire than it really is.[13] He is right to hold back. Although Cowper certainly draws attention to the fussiness and petty extravagances of well-cushioned provincial life, and of the female character itself, they appear as amusing foibles, not serious faults. He is careful to keep up a playful stance towards Maria's improvidence in having the cage made of 'smoothest-shaven wood' to save her favourite damaging its feathers:

> Not rough with wire of steel or brass,
>   For Bully's plumage sake,
> But smooth with wands from Ouse's side,
> With which, when neatly peel'd and dried,
>   The swains their baskets make.
>   (ll.26–30)

The humour discredits no one, but rather, as in Prior's epistle to Fleetwood and Cowper's own epistle to Robert Lloyd, serves as a vehicle for polite fun. In commemorating, and thereby sharing in, the occasion of poor Bully's death Cowper fosters the existing ties between the family at Weston Lodge (where he and Mrs. Unwin were now living) and their 'hosts' at the nearby Hall of Weston Underwood. The tragicomic toning, the genial sympathy, even the slightly audacious intimacy of using the first name Maria—everything is pitched at just the right level for familiar, but not too familiar, intercourse.

But there is much more to the poem than that. It is strange that Free should fail, in his five-page discussion, to make any comment on Cowper's manifest fascination with the manner of Bully's death, and with the agent of his destruction. In 'The Colubriad' the invading force, a viper that had strayed into the garden of Orchard Side, had been toyed with by the poet's imagination, just as it had been toyed with during the 'hunt' described in the poem, an inept quarry easily slain at the door and taught 'Never to come there no more'.[14] The grotesquely sinister 'long-back'd', 'long-tail'd' rat, on the other hand, goes inexorably towards its predestinated mark, fixed upon and tracked by the mind's eye:

> Night veil'd the pole—all seem'd secure—
> When led by instinct sharp and sure,
>   Subsistence to provide,
> A beast forth-sallied on the scout,
> Long-back'd, long-tail'd, with whisker'd snout,
>   And badger-colour'd hide.
>
> He, ent'ring at the study door,
> Its ample area 'gan explore;
>   And something in the wind
> Conjectur'd, sniffing round and round,
> Better than all the books he found,
>   Food, chiefly, for the mind.
>
> Just then, by adverse fate impress'd,
> A dream disturb'd poor Bully's rest;
>   In sleep he seem'd to view
> A rat, fast-clinging to the cage,
> And, screaming at the sad presage,
>   Awoke and found it true.
>
> For, aided both by ear and scent,
> Right to his mark the monster went—
>   Ah, Muse! forbear to speak
> Minute the horrors that ensued;
> His teeth were strong, the cage was wood—
>   He left poor Bully's beak. . . .
>
>   (ll.31–54)

The reason for this fascination and the significance of the poetic vision it generates are not easily determined. It may be, in fact, that the poem contains an element of revenge-fantasy: the ways of the mind are no less mysterious than the ways of Providence, and it is possible that, understood psychologically, the caged *Bully* represents the school *bully* that figures in the *Memoir* in one of Cowper's most lucid memories of persecution, or even the persecuting Deity himself.[15] That at least would be one way of explaining the subterranean pleasure that Cowper evidently takes in the horrifying event. The likelier interpretation, however, is that the poet saw in poor Bully's fate a mirror-image of his own foreseen destruction—which still leaves us with the expression of a concealed drive towards vengeful self-assertion, though this time in the muted defiance of that thought, in the penultimate stanza, of what might have happened had the rat taken his victim's beak.

The 'moral' of an earlier animal poem, in which a raven's new-laid eggs escape a storm only to be stolen next morning by Hodge as a gift for his pregnant wife, will remind us once more of Cowper's habitual sense, not so much of the quirks of fortune, as of the unpredictable but wholly deliberate workings of Fate (which it is impossible in Cowper to distinguish practically from Providence):

> An earthquake may be bid to spare
> The man that's strangled by a hair.
> Fate steals along with silent tread,
> Found oft'nest in what we dread,
> Frowns in the storm with angry brow,
> But in the sunshine strikes the blow.
>   ('A Fable', ll. 34–9)

This view of the world, chilling enough, is repeated in 'On the Death of Mrs. Throckmorton's Bulfinch': all seemed secure, cosy; the precaution of banning cats from Bully's room (ll. 19–21) succeeds in leaving the way open to rats. But the real nightmare, Cowper's nightmare, is when the individual is convinced that he himself is a destined target of the Fate which, rat-like, 'steals along with silent dread', or 'Wait[s], with impatient readiness, to seize my/Soul in a moment'.[16] That the doomed bird has some of the attributes of a poet (he is 'mellifluous', associated with Orpheus, and pipes like 'flagelet or flute'), that he is given to dreaming (Cowper later fell prey to a notorious interpreter of dreams), that he is a prisoner, that his position as plaything and his decked-out appearance resemble those of the 'genteel', 'dancing-bear' Cowper portrayed in 'Of Himself', all underline the identification of self and subject. This is not to say, though, that the poem is ever exactly dominated by fear—still less that it is hysterical; Bully's scream is a part of the poem not a parallel to it. There are places, it is true, where the vision operates on a knife-edge between terror and wit, notably in the final image of a severed head (a *bard's*, not a bird's) and in the prophetic nightmare itself, which is both clever parody of Adam's dream of Paradise and dread-full apprehension not only of the horrors of sleeping-life but of the fact that the reality may be no less catastrophic than they.[17] Here Cowper's irrational fears push to the surface of the poem and threaten to consume the comic detachment; like the rat in the action they emerge where all had seemed secure. Yet control is maintained. The laughter persists, though always under pressure, hesitant—'Ah, Muse! forbear to speak/Minute the horrors that ensued'.

Put another way, Cowper's 'good spirits' have sufficient resilience to absorb the challenge from within—to prevent a domestic it-tragedy from being altogether overturned into an I-tragedy of mental obsession, self-involvement in a horror-fable from becoming a horror-fable of self-involvement. This said, however, we cannot leave the poem without noting that its high-spiritedness is itself of a complex and shifting kind. The comedy does not give way but it does change; in the first half it is a comedy of relaxed good-humour, in the second there is a strong admixture not only of grotesqueness but of manic delight. It is not simply the fateful violence of the event that fascinates Cowper but its conclusiveness as well. Although the lesson of the tale, in so far as it has one, appears to be that birds had better be kept in wire cages, the poet who suffered the suspense of knowing that he like Kempenfelt, commander of the Royal George, might 'go down' even while his fingers held the pen, and who knew what it was like to be 'Buried above ground', derives a certain positive satisfaction from Mrs. Throckmorton's improvidence and the sad outcome. A wooden cage facilitates the issue; by letting Fate in it lets the victim out,

the swiftest route to the forgetfulness that can be his only
repose. 'On the Death of Mrs. Throckmorton's Bulfinch' is a
vision of cruel death, but it is also a gleeful dream of release.

So too is its more explicit companion-piece, 'On a Goldfinch
Starved to Death in his Cage'. Now even wire cages are no
barrier to death—thankfully so from the goldfinch's point of
view:

> . . . gaudy plumage, sprightly strain,
> And form genteel, were all in vain,
>   And of a transient date;
> For, caught and cag'd, and starv'd to death,
> In dying sighs my little breath
>   Soon pass'd the wiry grate.
>
> Thanks, gentle swain, for all my woes,
> And thanks for this effectual close
>   And cure of ev'ry ill!
> More cruelty could none express;
> And I, if you had shown me less,
>   Had been your pris'ner still.
>
> (ll. 7–18)

This weird little melodrama of confinement and release is
infinitely tougher in its texture and atmosphere than the fables
and poems of humanitarian sentiment to which it is generically
related. Instead of a narrative or debate followed by an
aphoristic, and often spurious, summary of meaning ('All that
glisters is not gold', 'Beware of desp'rate steps. The darkest
day/(Live till to-morrow) will have pass'd away'), we have a
psychological event which petitions from us a composite
response. We are not moved simply to indignation at the
swain's cruelty, for this turns out in a sense to be a kindness in
disguise; nor simply to pity for the captive victim, since he gives
thanks for his woes, assumes a position of superiority, and in
any case has lived to argue from the grave. Nor, though we feel
it as a possible reaction, can we quite shudder at the implicit
message, that death is preferable to life where life means
endless imprisonment; the well-bred rationality and cleverness
of the last ironic statement—'And I, if you had shown me less
. . .'—blunts the cutting-edge of this 'truth' even as it is
threateningly disclosed. Like 'On the Death of Mrs. Throck-

morton's Bulfinch', 'On a Goldfinch' has its origins in Cowper's darker feelings; the above-mentioned 'truth' is 'for real', not faked, in that it results from and projects lived experience. Yet it is easier to see from 'On a Goldfinch' that he makes excellent fictional play and artistic capital out of this experience and the insights it affords. In all poetry the act of formulation is an act of exploiting whatever is given, whether from within or from more deliberate searching, and Cowper's is no exception in spite of his singular reliance on what is thrust upon him.

'On a Goldfinch' is almost Blakeian in its taut and puzzling simplicity, and in the delight Cowper takes in complicating moral significance (cruelty is bad, birds have feelings) by the application of an astute psychological twist (in certain circumstances cruelty can bring relief from suffering, though in the desperately ironic form of death). There is nothing so gracefully incisive or so humanly—as well as humanely—meaningful as this last surprising point in Gray's somewhat comparable 'On the Death of a Favourite Cat':

> (Malignant Fate sat by and smiled) . . .
> Eight times emerging from the flood
> She mewed to every watery god,
>   Some speedy aid to send.
> No dolphin came, no Nereid stirred:
> Nor cruel Tom nor Susan heard. . . .
>   (ll.28,31–5)

The ruthlessness of Fate, the terror that exists in garden or drawing-room—these primary motifs of Cowper's poems are present already in Gray. But Cowper both feels them more urgently and as poet makes more of them. In Gray they are ideas disposed, the mechanics of a plot, a source of effect in a poem whose direction is towards light-hearted moralism in a mock-cautioning of the female sex ('From hence, ye beauties, undeceived,/Know, one false step is ne'er retrieved . . .'). To Cowper they are a compelling mystery in which he is personally implicated—'There is a mystery in my own destruction . . .'—but out of which emerge general truths and unique and testing artefacts.

Artefacts so distinctive that we think of analogies outside the context of petty-humorous, socio-satiric, or humanitarian verse. 'On the Death of Mrs. Throckmorton's Bulfinch' and 'On a Goldfinch Starved to Death in his Cage' could be described in some respects as proto-*surrealist* poems; that is, in their valuing of oneiric moods, reference to the mind's reservoir of less controllable forces, half-playful yet sinister images of violence (severed heads, clinging rats, pretty birds starved in a cage), combinations and juxtapositions of the commonplace and the uncommon and of the natural and the unnatural or supernatural (dead birds arguing gracefully from the grave, beasts prowling the study, pet birds screaming, beaks lying in latticed cages ...). I have in mind David Gascoyne's 'The Very Image'—and not only because of his concluding mention of bird-cages:

> An image of my grandmother
> her head appearing upside down upon a cloud
> the cloud transfixed on the steeple
> of a deserted railway-station
> far away

> An image of an aqueduct
> with a dead crow hanging from the first arch
> a modern-style chair from the second ...

> And all these images
> and many others
> are arranged like waxworks
> in model bird-cages
> about six inches high.

The differences are of course obvious: Gascoyne's poem is a lot more 'fantastical' than Cowper's poems, and a lot more calculated; and his feeling goes *all* into the making and contemplating of the verses, the images, rather than the apprehension or revelation of conditions of 'being'. For Cowper too, however, the making and the contemplating are important. 'On the Death of Mrs. Throckmorton's Bulfinch', too, is a cage, a model receptacle of images arranged with delight for our delight. Even as he extends the psychological content and ontological meanings of bourgeois 'social' and 'humorous' verse, then, Cowper also produces a kind of 'play' familiar to the modern reader. Shut-in he may have been, but he was able nonetheless, in his captivity, to write a poetry that we experience as superior *recreation*.

Recreation; fictional play; artistic capital wrung from darker feelings. *John Gilpin* is the supreme example of this. The poem was, so Cowper tells us, the product of 'the saddest mood',[18] and, as Morris Golden says, it embodies 'something of Cowper's attitude toward the rush toward death, the unreliability of God, the meaningless violence of the world': Gilpin is swept away by an uncontrollable force, no one can rescue him (we think of the plight of the Castaway, 'Deserted, and his friends so nigh'), his journey is like a bad dream and is accompanied by veritable madness ('The stones did rattle underneath,/As if Cheapside were mad'). But although Cowper's characteristic obsessions are thus traceable in *John Gilpin*, they take a purely benign form, having been entirely absorbed into a flow of creative good spirits. If Gilpin—like Mrs. Throckmorton's bulfinch or the ill-fated Kempenfelt—is a projection of the poet's self, then it is not only as a man carried helplessly on a chaotic journey but also as one who does come 'safe home again' and who can treat his own misfortunes in 'merry guise' (ll.169–76). Whether we see the famous ride as the author's view of what life is like or whether we see it as a mental process undertaken in a melancholy mood, there is finally nothing grim about it. It is Cowper's happiest poem.

It is the incredible buoyancy and sheer sportive zest of *John Gilpin* that above all account for its perennial freshness. Generations of readers, of all ages, have been happily diverted—carried away—by the non-stop swing of the jovial humour and inoffensive caricature, at a pace dictated by the varying gallop of Gilpin's steed and the relentless train of farcical events:

> Thus all through merry Islington
>   These gambols he did play,
> And till he came unto the Wash
>   Of Edmonton so gay.
>
> And there he threw the Wash about
>   On both sides of the way,
> Just like unto a trundling mop,
>   Or a wild goose at play.

At Edmonton his loving wife
    From the balcony spied,
Her tender husband, wond'ring much
    To see how he did ride.

Stop, stop, John Gilpin!—Here's the house—
    They all at once did cry;
The dinner waits, and we are tir'd:
    Said Gilpin—so am I!

(ll. 133–48)

Hardly a poetry to analyse perhaps; yet neither is it an artless
one. The care Cowper took in revising the poem for the press,
after first conceiving it during a single sleepless night, shows in
such expert effects as the deft understated comedy of Gilpin's
reply at the end of the quoted stanzas. The crudenesses of
style—for example the fatuous, rather inept laundry images
stirred up by the Wash—are all deliberate. And for many of
Cowper's contemporaries the amusement would have been
redoubled by their acquaintance with the street-ballad, of
which *John Gilpin* is part parody and part imitation. Successfully hawked around the streets of London as a chapbook long
before it appeared in solid covers, the tale of Gilpin seems to
have taken its place naturally among other examples of the
genre.[19] As A. B. Friedman demonstrates in the standard book
on the subject, notwithstanding Percy's *Reliques* the ballad was
commonly associated in Cowper's day with the unrefined taste
of the lower classes and the unmannerly exchanges of the
hustings, so that while the form did not easily lend itself to
serious literary purposes it was excellently adapted to humorous matter, since 'the very vulgarity of the model might be
counted on to import the desired tone of casualness or
frivolity'.[20] Cowper's 'diverting history' is undoubtedly the
masterpiece of all such humorous writing.

    There is, however, a further, unexpected, influence behind
the work—'Chaucer's merry page', for which Cowper admitted
his liking in another context.[21] Like Chaucer's Sir Thopas,
Gilpin is very much an unheroic hero, a middle-class knight
starring in a middle-class adventure; an adventure, moreover,
that is narrated in a manner strongly reminiscent of the
tongue-in-cheek 'drasty speche' and 'drasty ryming' of this

particular Canterbury tale. Both poets interweave two levels of
incongruity, the one resulting from the disparity between high
style and low subject-matter and the other from the disparity
between the heroic/romance pretensions of the style and the
rhythms, diction, and images actually employed. Cowper's
own mixture of mundane words and details with an idiom that
claims chivalric status for Gilpin and his exploits—a status
Gilpin also claims for himself ('I am a linen-draper bold,/As all
the world doth know')—goes a long way to making the poem, in
its author's words, 'a tale ridiculous in itself and quaintly told'
which raises 'a laugh that hurts nobody'.[22] We see Gilpin
'manfully' equipped from 'top to toe', calling for the belt that
usually holds his 'trusty sword' so that he can load it with his
wife's ample liquor-ration (ll.60–76). He mounts his 'nimble
steed', a 'snorting beast', only to be 'gall'd [rubbed sore] ... in
his seat' as soon as it begins, not to gallop, but to 'trot'
(ll.77–84). Thus, as in the later comparison of Gilpin to a
'trundling mop' or the horse's smoking flanks to a 'basted'
carcass (ll.127–8), Cowper's fine instinct for the absurd finds
expression not simply in references to Gilpin's behaviour but in
the juxtaposition of the language, customs, and objects of the
world of Romance and those of the Gilpins' practical and
prosaic world. In Chaucer the latter procedure is quite
definitely linked to the presence of an inept 'romancer', who
likens the bloody, sweating sides of Sir Thopas's horse to a less
than appropriate rag that 'men myghte ... wrynge'.[23] This, we
know, is also a feature of Cowper's poem. But William Norris
Free surely goes too far in suggesting that *John Gilpin* is mainly a
satire on bourgeois attitudes and speech as represented in the
characters of Gilpin and his wife and in a narrator who is
'overimpressed with their wit and prestige'.[24] According to this
view, it is 'to further discomfit Gilpin and the narrator' that
Cowper has the latter running out of ideas before a stanza is
complete or producing effects that are 'resoundingly anticli-
mactic':

> John Gilpin at his horse's side
> 　　Seiz'd fast the flowing mane,
> And up he got, in haste to ride,
> 　　But soon came down again.
> 　　　　　(ll.45–8)

This resounding anticlimax in fact has more the mark of a festive poet enjoying ringing the bell than of an unskilful narrator dropping a clanger. Yet even where we do get fumbling indiscretions—the crudeness already noted or the simpler incompetence of cliché, line-padding, and awkward syntax—the spirit is not really satiric, but rather one of good-tempered travesty as Cowper turns the Romance and ballad conventions to comic ends.

Some of Cowper's 'comic' and 'occasional' poems are distinctly coloured by the darker side of his interior life. Others, like *John Gilpin*, are a reaction against it. If dejection and troubled thoughts—'the saddest mood'—did play the alleged part in the genesis of the poem, it was not by forcing him to express or discipline them but by provoking him to dispel them. In the 'Epistle to Robert Lloyd' we find a record of this reactive process actually taking place. On Cowper's own admission the poem was germinated in a need to

> divert a fierce bandetti
> (Sworn foes to every thing that's witty),
> That, with a black infernal train,
> Make cruel inroads in my brain,
> And daily threaten to drive thence
> My little garrison of sense . . .
>
> (ll. 13–18)

Many are the biographers who have quoted this passage, written in 1754, to prove Cowper's early disposition to melancholia. And so they should. However, the poem itself, after this solid pointer to the therapeutic motives behind his large output of lighter verse, shows him at his most positively carefree. In the end 'Epistle to Robert Lloyd' is most important to the critic of Cowper as an example of his ability to make an art even of relaxed chit-chat.

The influence of Prior is once more in evidence. The above-mentioned lines are themselves an adaptation of the older poet's strategic mock-argument in favour of writing nonsense:

> thought is trouble to the head;
> I argue thus: the world agrees,

That he writes well who writes with ease;
Then he, by sequel logical,
Writes best who never thinks at all.
　　　　('Epistle to Fleetwood Shepherd', ll.36–40)

Cowper's muse continues to jingle smartly along at exactly this
steady rate of congenial and quick-witted pleasantry, taking in
the twin subjects of friendship and verse letters in a complaint
over the difficulty of repaying Lloyd's 'gold' with like coinage.
After one fifteen-line simile about Gammer Gurton's search for
her needle and one just as long about the trials of chasing
butterflies, which form what seems an inordinately roundabout
way of saying that ideas are hard to come by, Cowper settles at
last for a tribute to 'Friend Robert's' talent for dashing off
verses *en passant* and throwing his 'Helicon about/As freely as a
conduit spout' (ll.83–4). In all of this Cowper is of course being
flippant; but the flippancy serves the fundamentally serious
objective of cementing his 'bond' with a fellow gentleman-poet.

At the same time, moreover, a serious statement is being
made about the art of poetry itself, and about Cowper's own
art. As on other occasions, Cowper seizes the opportunity of
explicitly praising Prior's 'ease', but he now places most
emphasis on the art of concealing art, on the laborious process
of refinement that brings distinction to the meanest styles and
subjects;

> Matthew, (says Fame) with endless pains
> Smooth'd and refin'd the meanest strains;
> Nor suffer'd one ill-chosen rhyme
> T'escape him, at the idlest time;
> And thus o'er all a lustre cast,
> That, while the language lives, shall last.
> 　　　　　　　　　(ll.73–8)

This of course also achieves the result of drawing attention to
the finesse, the combination of 'ease' and 'art', with which
Cowper is himself handling the octosyllabic couplet and
reproducing the familiar Prioresque 'swagger' and ear-catch-
ing colloquialisms:

> Thus, the preliminaries settled,
> I fairly find myself pitch-kettled;

>   And connot see, though few see better,
>   How I shall hammer out a letter.
>   (ll.31–4)

The letter is hammered out with blows that are never
ill-chosen, either in sound or sense; it is as 'polished' as
anything of a similar kind in Prior—and Cowper knows it.
('Epistle to Fleetwood Shepherd' is indeed a good deal *less*
controlled.) By likening himself to the 'virtuoso' who pursures
'the gilded butterfly' (ll.149ff.) he points to the relative
slightness of the type of poem he is writing; but this admission is
itself a mark of confidence and discernment. His sense of
proportion in relation to what he is doing is no less than his
sense of proportion in relation to Lloyd's Helicon. Whatever
the inbuilt limitations of the genre, 'Epistle to Robert Lloyd'
operates on an altogether different level from the superficiality
to which genteel light verse can sink in the hands of second-rate
makers of verses—to which it did sink often with Lloyd himself,
whose 'Ode Secundum Artem' for example, once wrongly
attributed to Cowper, is a pretty good instance of what Cowper
condemns in *Table Talk* as 'whipt-cream' and 'gingerbread'
poetry.[25]

'Epistle to Robert Lloyd' is one of those pieces which could, if
cursorily read, set up a false impression of Cowper as an *amateur*
in shirt sleeves, tinkering with rhyme. He is never that, however
small his subjects and limited his horizons. Many of his slighter
lyrics display too his noted ability 'to project his good nature
into the structure of his poetry'[26]—a quality which he himself
valued in the poems of Vincent Bourne, along with the virtues
of seriousness and sharp, receptive observation:

> His humour is entirely original; he can speak of a magpie
> or a cat in terms so exquisitely appropriated to the
> character he draws, that one would suppose him animated
> by the spirit of the creature he describes. And with all his
> drollery there is a mixture of rational, and even religious,
> reflection at times; and always an air of pleasantry, good
> nature, and humanity.[27]

Add to this a readiness to take the utmost care with the
'meanest strains' and we have a description of Cowper's own

unrivalled excellence as lyricist of the domestic and provincial scene, as in 'Epitaph on a Hare'. The setting is Orchard Side, the subject the 'character' and death of Cowper's pet animal, Tiney:

> Old Tiney, surliest of his kind,
>   Who, nurs'd with tender care,
> And to domestic bounds confin'd,
>   Was still a wild Jack-hare. . . .
>
> A Turkey carpet was his lawn,
>   Whereon he lov'd to bound,
> To skip and gambol like a fawn,
>   And swing his rump around. . . .
>
> I kept him for his humour' sake,
>   For he would oft beguile
> My heart of thoughts that made it ache,
>   And force me to a smile.
>
> But now, beneath this walnut shade
>   He finds his long, last home,
> And waits in snug concealment laid,
>   'Till gentler Puss shall come.
>   (ll.5–8, 21–4, 33–40)

Yet here too there is something more than good nature, or humanity, or drollery. The emotional life of the poem has its heavier side, supplying a seriousness beyond that of humane sensibility. Tender feelings towards animate nature take the subtler form of vivid memories, and sadness at the passing of a 'good friend' becomes a deeper form of pathos. The melancholic Cowper's fondness for his 'wild Jack-hare' is, like his sense of loss, given a particular poignancy by his consciousness of how Tiney had brought him, not merely entertainment, but frequent relief from an aching heart. But neither is his sorrow unmixed with pleasure. His loss is not total, for Tiney can still beguile him and force him to a smile, in recollections of the same antics that once enthralled him—which is also to say in unselfconscious contemplation of a freedom, 'to bound,/To skip, to gambol', that is unavailable to man himself. The ambiguity of this act of contemplative retrospection, which is at once a release and an unspoken recognition of the lasting impossibility of liberty, is echoed throughout the poem, and not least in Cowper's final response to Tiney's death, in which he finds not only a personal deprivation but an image to delight in, a 'long, last home' and 'snug concealment' beyond the reach of 'shocks' and 'storm'.

There are still simpler examples: the genial nonsense of, for instance, 'Between Nose and Eyes a strange contest arose'—as to which should be the resting-place of a pair of spectacles; or, a mischievous verse-cartoon of tithing time at Stock parsonage, where robust observation of the rural 'character' and hearty distaste for the superior manner of the fastidious 'worthy priest' remind us of Burns:

> One wipes his nose upon his sleeve,
>   One spits upon the floor,
> Yet, not to give offence or grieve,
>   Holds up the cloth before. . . .
>
> Oh, why are farmers made so coarse,
>   Or clergy made so fine!
> A kick that scarce would move a horse
>   May kill a sound divine.
>   (ll.41–4,61–4)

Or the wide-awake, delicately adjusted affectation of 'The Colubriad':

> On to the hall went I, with pace not slow,
> But swift as lightning, for a long Dutch hoe;
> With which well arm'd I hasten'd to the spot,
> To find the viper. But I found him not, . . .
>   (ll.18–21)

These are what Norman Nicholson, in a nice turn of phrase, calls the 'little splashes and flashes of [Cowper's] shorter poems'.

The trouble comes, for the modern reader at least, when there is no splash or flash at all—when the verse is void of personality and character. Predictably this occurs most often, indeed almost exclusively, in the poems on public affairs. 'The Negro's Complaint' was an outstandingly influential anti-slavery song, being widely used by the Abolitionists and many

times reprinted in magazines;[28] but it does not take enduring
poetry to make successful propaganda:

> Forc'd from home, and all its pleasures,
>   Afric's coast I left forlorn;
> To increase a stranger's treasures,
>   O'er the raging billows borne.
> Men from England bought and sold me,
>   Paid my price in paltry gold . . .
>
> Still in thought as free as ever,
>   What are England's rights, I ask,
> Me from my delights to sever,
>   Me to torture, me to task?
> Fleecy locks, and black complexion
>   Cannot forfeit nature's claim;
> Skins may differ, but affection
>   Dwells in white and black the same.
>
>   (ll. 1–6, 9–16)

The 'movement' was no doubt greatly inspired by this clear
and in every respect 'solid' presentation of its radical ideals by a
leading poet; and even now we can only admire Cowper's
honest style and humanitarianism. Yet there is no depth to the
poem, whether as dramatic lyric, or the presentation of an
issue, or simply as manifesto. Blake's 'Little Black Boy', written
at about the same time, satisfies us where Cowper's lyric does
not, for while in Cowper the 'dramatic' mode is merely a
convenience for proclaiming the self-evident truth that all men
are equal because all men have feelings, Blake takes real
advantage of it to confront the reader with a reversal of the
usual roles of White and Black—the roles they have both in
slavery (master/servant) and, in practice, in abolitionist
Reform (guardian/guarded)—by making the Black Boy the
superior and protector of the White Boy: 'I'll shade him from
the heat till he can bear/To lean in joy upon our Father's knee'.
Cowper has left us the versified principles of the contemporary
Christian reformer, issuing rather incredibly from the mouth of
a Negro; Blake, in an audacious fiction that credits a Negro
child with a range of basic emotions and drives (love,
sympathy, belief, insecurity, aspiration), offers an aggressive
challenge to human complacency and an astute study in the

fundamental kinship, and artificial distinctions, between men.

It is not difficult to discover limitations within Cowper's 'occasional' and topical verse as a whole. In broad literary-historical terms, we are sometimes undoubtedly aware of a narrowing of poetic vision and purposes. There is, for example, a world of difference between Dryden's *Astrea Redux* or *Annus Mirabilis* and Cowper's 'Annus Memorabilis', on the King's 'happy recovery' of 1789—all the difference between soaring mythopoeic idealism and respectable, homely nationalism. Despite an early reference to 'poetry divine', the Muses appear more than content to quit their heavenly sphere for the 'frugal board' at which Cowper later describes himself as proudly sitting: the 'spring of eighty-nine' he, more the good citizen than the inspired poet, will 'joyful . . . oft record',

> For then the clouds of eighty-eight,
> That threaten'd England's trembling state
> With loss of what she least could spare,
> Her sov'reign's tutelary care,
> One breath of Heav'n that cry'd—Restore!
> Chas'd, never to assemble more . . .
>
> (ll.36–41)

Then after a brief celebration of the recontinuation of George's 'righteous reign' the poem chronicles, at much greater length, the renewed happiness of a Queen long troubled by the supposed loss of 'The good on Earth [she] valued most', and turns at last to the 'not unallied' joy of the people:

> Transports not chargeable with art
> Illume the land's remotest part,
> And strangers to the air of courts,
> Both in their toils and in their sports,
> The happiness of answer'd pray'rs,
> That gilds thy features, show in theirs.
>
> (ll.60–5)

Instead of the priest-king and saviour-monarch of Dryden's panegyrics, leading his people in a sublime cultural, martial, and commercial enterprise, we have a sovereign who is valued for his emphatically human virtues of justness, sobriety, moral strength ('a *righteous* reign') and for his practical, stabilizing guardianship ('tutelary care') over the nation's life, which for Cowper means ideally an ordinary life of 'toil' and 'sport' and the freedom of the individual to enjoy his 'frugal board'. 'Bourgeois' assumptions—much more our own assumptions than are Dryden's—come everywhere to the fore, and not least in the fact that the king actually figures less as a political force than as a husband. Family relations based in love eventually steal the show, along with social relations based in respect and sensibility: the bond between Queen and subjects is not one of fealty or even loyalty, but of feeling, of natural and shared 'tears' and 'smiles' that are the communal counterpart of such neighbourly sympathies as exist between the poet and Maria Throckmorton. And all is cast in rhythms normally used for less auspicious occasions involving less august personages; whereas Prior in a similar celebratory act of praise, 'To the Queen on the Glorious Success of her Majesty's Arms', chooses the 'heroic stanza' of *Annus Mirabilis*, Cowper selects the octosyllabic couplet, the 'easy jingle', of his own and Prior's epistles and lighter poems, with an inevitable lowering of tone from the level of rich and spacious solemnity of traditional 'high panegyric'.

That 'Annus Memorabilis' reflected and appealed to standard socio-political assumptions and taste is suggested by the fact that it was welcomed as a contribution to the popular *Morning Herald*. Two other similar poems were likewise framed for the press: 'On the Queen's Visit to London', which appeared in *The Times* and further underlines the 'cordial' ties between Queen, King, and nation; and stanzas on 'The Benefit Received by His Majesty from Sea-Bathing', which was published in both the *Whitehall Evening Post* and the *Public Advertiser* and links George's debt to the waves with the greatness of English naval power, her 'empire on the sea', thus reminding us that, although Cowper was so out of sympathy in *The Task* with the consumerist and commercial spirit of eighteenth-century England, yet he was altogether in favour of the armed imperialism in which that spirit in fact found its strongest outlet and, through trade, its basic means of practical realization.[29] This expansionist patriotism—which is declaimed with greater zeal in Boadecia's prophecy of how her British progeny 'Arm'd with thunder, clad with wings,/Sháll a

wider world command'—and the thoroughgoing preoccupation with domestic virtues are the twin emphases of Cowper's
representative Whig and bourgeois position. In so far as there
are ever beginnings and endings in history, the poems we have
been considering register the end of a process which had begun
exactly a century before, in the Act of Settlement, or 'Glorious
Revolution', of 1689—an event to which the first verse of 'On
the Queen's Visit' turns our thoughts directly by its pride in
England's possession of a constitutional monarchy:

> . . . George took his seat again,
> By right of worth, not blood alone,
> Entitled here to reign.
>
> (ll.2–4)

But the Glorious Revolution not only confirmed a system of
government, in inviting William and Mary to replace James II
'by right of worth, not blood alone'; it also, on a broader level,
'acknowledged that England had become or was fast becoming,
a bourgeois and merchantile society'.[30] Dryden's writings for
the most part assume a society which is aristocratic, and
monarchical in the fundamentalist sense that the monarchy is
taken to be naturally and essentially 'absolute'. In Pope the
desirability of such a society is still assumed. With Cowper's
patriotic lyrics and poems on the 'restoration' of George III,
and just as obviously with the clean, honest mirth of *John Gilpin*,
the amiable domesticity of 'Epitaph on a Hare', or the relaxed
civility and good nature of his epistles and elegies to friends and
neighbours, we are well and truly in a middle-class world. They
push to their logical conclusion the tendencies of those
enterprises—*The Spectator*, the sentimental comedies of Cibber
and Steele, the poems of Prior—in which literary historians
have traditionally seen that world forming and being instructed
and bound together.

And a falling-off in creative aspirations is in some respects
also obvious, whether we compare the poems with Dryden's
and Pope's or with 'Whiggish' Augustan literature itself. The
social responsibility that informs Cowper's exercises in the
conduct of human relations is not the missionary social
responsibility of Addison's and Steele's great design to teach

men how to behave in a changed economic and political climate, while 'On the Death of Mrs. Throckmorton's Bulfinch' is made to look decidedly 'provincial' in more than one sense by Pope's similarly ambivalent use of the mock heroic in *The Rape of the Lock*, where, instead of sympathy and mild reproof, we have the altogether richer veins of censure and celebration. And so it is if we glance forwards into the Romantic period: to Shelley's myth-making in *Prometheus Unbound*, which is to the idea of popular democracy what Dryden's *Astrea Redux* is to the idea of the sanctity of kingship, and which prompts us to recall that the year of George's 'restoration' was also the year of a Revolution which, though it did not affect Cowper's thinking at all, drove many to reassess the reality and comprehensiveness of the liberties ensured by the Glorious Revolution; or to Wordsworth's radical sense of the 'infinite complexity of pain and pleasure' that everywhere exists within and everywhere ennobles 'ordinary life', beside which Cowper's own unusual talent for finding a tale, and very often an emotional lesson, in the most common circumstances—in the death of a pet hare or a pet bulfinch, in the yearly crop of funerals in the parish of All Saints, in the predicament of a slave, in a lover's quarrel—seems limited by that 'certain tact' so admired by Wordsworth's detractor, Francis Jeffrey, which avoids being too earnestly moved by what 'must necessarily be despised . . . in all polished societies'.[31]

Nonetheless, Cowper's comic and occasional poems are a positive and, in certain ways, important achievement. His tact—his unwavering respect for an actual or notional audience—is, within the immediate context, a virtue, and is related to a flexible genius for hitting exactly the right note across a wide range of demands and possibilities. He is in every way a *responsible* poet—artistically, socially, morally, emotionally: never the poet in shirt sleeves. He is immensely resourceful, wresting significance from every available source in the world within his ken—whether serious truths about death, loss, 'acts of God', or the simple liberating truth that life can be comic, funny, farcical: after Cowper all objects and events are fair game for the poet, and all is potentially meaningful either as a comment on our humanity or as recreation. He brings a

singular personality, intelligence, and fund of feeling to the
contemplation of the commonplace and the uncommon alike.
Conventions are remade, normal objectives modified: a moral
fable and act of friendship becomes a personal-impersonal
tragicomedy of confinement, destruction, and release; a lyric on
a national disaster becomes an imaginative apprehension of the
ironies of Fate; a simple epitaph on a hare forms into a very
delicately shaded word-picture of a living, reflective consciousness. In these unique, oddly ambiguous poems, poetry as
psychological event blends with poetry as social and public
statement (for 'Epitaph on a Hare' does on the surface appeal
to standard sentimental attitudes, just as 'On the Loss of the
Royal George' appeals to nationalistic ones). They demand to
be experienced and understood as self-expression as much as
outgoing and outward-looking commemorations of happenings
external to the self; their meanings reside in, and emerge from,
the mind within—and not just biographically behind—the
lines. The works that remain to be considered are more
absolutely centred in and on 'the self': to adapt Arthur
Johnston's evaluation of Cowper, *their* triumph was in showing—more clearly than any shorter poem so far considered—
what 'the poets of the previous forty years had been unable to
accept, that individual human experience in the present was
still the best material for the poet and that out of it he could
make something new'.[32]

Let us make the transition to this concentratedly subjective
Cowper by re-viewing the essential difference between his love
poetry and Prior's. Here is the end of Prior's 'The Lady's
Looking-Glass':

> But when vain doubt, and groundless fear
> Do that dear foolish bosom tear;
> When the big lip, and watery eye
> Tell me, the rising storm is nigh;
> 'Tis then, thou art yon angry main,
> Deformed by winds and dashed by rain;
> And the poor sailor, that must try
> Its fury, labours less than I.
>
> Shipwrecked, in vain to land I make;
> While Love and Fate still drive me back;

Forced to dote on thee thy own way,
I chide thee first, and then obey.

(ll.31–42)

And here are further extracts from Cowper's obviously indebted 'Hope, like the short-liv'd ray':

> Oft I have thought the scene of troubles closed,
>   And hop'd once more to gaze upon your charms;
> As oft some dire mischance has interposed,
>   And snatch'd th'expected blessing from my arms.
>
> The seaman thus, his shatter'd vessel lost,
>   Still vainly strives to shun the threat'ning death;
> And while he thinks to gain the friendly coast,
>   And drops his feet, and feels the sands beneath:
>
> Borne by the wave, steep-sloping from the shore,
>   Back to th'inclement deep again he beats
> The surge aside, and seems to tread secure;
>   And now the refluent wave his baffled toil defeats . . .

(ll.9–20)

Prior, with all his usual colloquial eloquence, gives 'lustre' to a familiar love-situation; Cowper writes an earnest confessional poem powerfully realizing a psychological experience that, in the end, goes well beyond the context of 'the ways of love'. Whereas Prior uses sea and shipwreck imagery to 'talk' poetically and as an elaborative analogy for lovers' moods and behaviour, incorporating formal conceits into the gestures of the speaking voice (tears as storm, disdain as waves, etc.) and likening himself, the helpless lover, to a shipwrecked mariner, Cowper actually concentrates on what it is like, inwardly as well as physically, to struggle desperately and vainly for safety.

The stanzas on the seaman are a good example of the varied effects that Cowper can gain from 'prose' idiom dominated by verbs and participles. At the level of literal description, he defines the sailor's actions and predicament with exceptional accuracy, right down to his immediate thoughts (as when he 'thinks', makes a conscious effort, to gain the 'friendly' coast) and sensations (he 'feels' the sands beneath). But the style is also one that interprets, suggests, and symbolizes. 'Shatter'd', 'vainly', 'threat'ning', 'friendly', 'inclement', 'secure', 'baffled toil': the language is all a generalizing language, pressing us to think not only of the deluded hopes, futile struggle, and dreadful isolation of one man but, more conceptually, of the delusiveness of hope, the futility of struggle, man's embattled aloneness in a world of hostile forces. In the sharply specified physical event is a vivid statement of universal psychological and ontological truth.

The singularity of temper, concern, and perspective from which this and many other poems by Cowper derive is a valuable asset, accounting in no small degree for his particular contribution to what C. S. Lewis called 'the enormous extension of our being that we owe to authors'. An appropriate analogy is with dreams, for dreams, though strange, private, and selective, reveal truths that are no less valid than the insights or reasonings of waking life; and dreams, in laying bare the recesses of the mind, lay bare something of common interest. They can also, of course, be chaotic and esoteric. Cowper's poetry is never like that; it never degenerates into abnormity. Yet whereas 'On the Death of Mrs. Throckmorton's Bulfinch' owes everything in this respect to the 'common interest' that attaches to less conscious levels of mind, 'Hope, like the short liv'd ray' and the poems to which we now turn show a positive *self-possession*, an articulate self-consciousness which leads naturally on to coherent generalization.

In 'Hope, like the short liv'd ray' Cowper turns his own interior life out into image; for the seaman's experience is at bottom the poet's recurring dream. One of Cowper's greatest achievements was to translate nightmare into poetry, the 'threat'ning death' of autistic imagining into life-interpreting wisdom and imaginative creation. He not only imported confession into literary and social modes, he made of confession itself a literary and social mode.

8

'The Wings of Fancy'
'On the Receipt of
My Mother's Picture'

Hazlitt recommended 'On the Receipt of My Mother's Picture' as one of the most 'pathetic' poems ever written.[1] William Norris Free puts it happily aside as an example of the contemporary 'vogue for sentimentalism'.[2] Neither, however, gets the real measure of this fine and challenging poem, even in relation to its emotional content and effect. For we are struck as much by Cowper's controlling artistry as by his extraordinary daring and intimacy in laying open the secret recesses of the heart:

> Oh that those lips had language! Life has pass'd
> With me but roughly since I heard thee last.
> Those lips are thine—thy own sweet smiles I see,
> The same that oft in childhood solaced me;
> Voice only fails, else, how distinct they say,
> 'Grieve not, my child, chase all thy fears away!'
> The meek intelligence of those dear eyes
> (Blest be the art that can immortalize,
> The art that baffles time's tyrannic claim
> To quench it) here shines on me still the same.
>
> (ll. 1–10)

This is an 'excess' both natural and perfected. The whispering assonance, the liquid 'l's and soft 's's that gently accuse the silence of the picture, the fluent yet formal rhythms, the unforced but regular emphasis of the rhymes—all give shape

Notes and References begin on page 344.

and discipline to the feelings they simultaneously, and so faithfully, express. Cowper is pushing more than ever at limits, but his care and his evident sincerity win our assent for what would otherwise be an embarrassing moment of self-exposure. The audacity of the revelation is of course part of the appeal of 'On the Receipt of My Mother's Picture'—its peculiar fascination. Yet considering the difficulty of the theme—a man's love for his mother and the commonly repressed wish for the security of infantile dependence—it is also amazing how readable the poem is, how fit for an intelligent audience.

But there is much more to the work than that. Cowper's sudden reaction to the unexpected 'gift . . . out of Norfolk' is the starting point of a mental journey leading to a discovery of the restorative power of recollection and 'fancy'. Already in the opening passage he has made inward gains from the act of remembering and imagining: the first couplet is a cry of longing and absence but we soon recognize in the mountings and levellings of the verse a spirit both quickened and calmed, as the mind brings the picture 'to life' according to its needs, supplying a reassuring voice where there is none, renewing the benign influences and 'guiding light' of the past ('. . . here shines on me still the same'). By the end of the poem he becomes clearly conscious of what he has achieved:

> By contemplation's help, not sought in vain,
> I seem t'have liv'd my childhood o'er again;
> To have renew'd the joys that once were mine,
> Without the sin of violating thine:
> And while the wings of fancy still are free,
> And I can view this mimic shew of thee,
> Time has but half succeeded in his theft—
> Thyself remov'd, thy power to soothe me left.
>
> (ll. 114–21)

At first it had been the portrait that had been seen as 'baffling' time; now Cowper understands his own strength, acting on and through that lifeless 'mimic shew' to recover 'lost' joys in and for the present.[3] There is nothing sentimental about these lines: the impression is of a mind ready to accept the confinements of Time, Change, and Loss but confident in the knowledge, guaranteed by all that has gone before in the poem, that they

may be transcended by 'contemplation's help' and on 'the
wings of fancy'. Cowper values his wishes and his freedom to
satisfy them but respects the limits and limitations of reality.
And this, as we shall see, was no easy balance; the process of
'On the Receipt of My Mother's Picture' includes uncertainty
too, an effort to reconcile desire and acceptance, surmise and
rational 'knowing', poetry as therapeutic fiction and poetry as
wide-awake self-abnegation.

'On the Receipt of My Mother's Picture', then, is not only a
poem of emotion. It is a contemplative poem and a poem about
the uses of contemplation. It is also, thirdly, an elegiac tribute.
Virtually at the outset Cowper decides upon a double objective:
to seek the consolations of Fancy—

> Fancy shall weave a charm for my relief—
> Shall steep me in Elysian reverie,
> A momentary dream that thou art she.
>
> (ll.18–20)

and to 'honour with an artless song,/Affectionate, a mother lost
so long' (ll.13–14). In carrying out this latter aim he closely
follows the conventions of eighteenth-century verse elegy,
though with all his customary individuality of response. As it
turns out, however, the whole poem can be usefully approached
through reference to the tradition.

*   *   *   *   *

Some years ago James Sutherland realized that elegy was one
area of eighteenth-century poetry which immediately called in
question the assumption that the period was peculiarly reticent
about the individual's 'most private thoughts and feelings',[4] his
main example being Lyttleton's 'monody' on the death of his
wife, with its 'vein of unforced simplicity, which would be the
natural expression of sorrow in any age':

> In vain I look around
> O'er the well-known ground,
> My Lucy's wonted footsteps to descry;
> Where oft we used to walk,
> Where oft in tender talk
> We saw the summer sun go down the sky...
>
> (stanza IV)[5]

'Unforced' maybe, but not in fact unrestrained. 'Simplicity, if it does not descend into *vulgarism*, is the chief excellence of all kinds of writing, but above all of those in which the heart is to speak': as this, Lyttleton's own comment on the much-praised style of his poem, suggests, there is in the self-expression a certain tact, a regard for decorum, that sets it sharply apart from that advocated by Rousseau when complaining that 'Politeness requires this thing; . . . ceremony has its forms, fashion its laws, and these we must follow, never the promptings of our own nature'.[6] Similarly, Johnson's well-known attack on 'Lycidas' for its insincerity—'Where there is leisure for fiction there is little grief'—does not mean that he was in favour of informality and improvisation. The studied gravity of his own lines on Robert Levet proves that; as does his admiration (shared by Goldsmith and Edward Young) for Thomas Tickell's elegy on Addison, where the opening rejection of 'art' ('Grief unaffected suits but ill with art') is observed more in the avoidance of highly orchestrated conceits than in an absence of ceremony and measured eloquence:

> To strew fresh laurels let the task be mine,
> A frequent pilgrim at thy sacred shrine;
> Mine with true sighs thy absence to bemoan,
> And grave with faithful epitaphs thy stone . . .
>   (ll.23–6)[7]

This poem, moreover, is embellished with long patches of formal eulogy, always an ingredient of elegy, either, as here, in the high style of panegyric and *apotheosis* (the chief of 'arms' and 'arts' how dwells a 'guardian Genius' in 'th'ethereal sky') or, as was naturally more the case with 'personal elegies' on friends and relatives, in reference to the subject's humbler human virtues (Lyttleton's Lucy's 'modest beauties', 'virtuous heart', maternal 'love') and, often, attainment of heavenly rewards. It is in this last particular aspect that Cowper himself most obviously echoes the anonymous verses 'On the Death of a Beloved Mother', published in the same issue of *The Gentleman's Magazine* that reviewed *The Task*. He uses the same imagery to describe his mother's love, writing of its 'constant flow', never 'roughen'd' (ll.65–7) where the earlier poet had stated, 'Her bounty flow'd with one unruffl'd course'. In both poems the peace and glory of heaven is imagined as the end of a successful voyage—

> . . . the Elysian shore
> Where friends congenial join to part no more.[8]

> . . . the shore
> 'Where tempests never beat nor billows roar'
>   (Cowper, ll.96–7)

Beside Cowper's designation of his lines as an 'artless song' may be placed his predecessor's distrust of 'turgid strain' and 'learned pomp'; but the above brief quotations are enough to show that neither poet altogether relinquishes the usual poetic colouring and ritualism of elegiac praise. It is, however, Thomson's 'On the Death of His Mother' (1725),[9] a more ambitious instance of the genre, that supplies the best comparison.

Like Lyttleton and Tickell, Thomson combines lament with eulogy, and the display of feeling with decorous formality. After first entering the familiar claims of sincerity ('genuine woe . . . love . . . filial duty'), he moves constantly between grief, sometimes muted and sometimes passionate, and compensatory affirmations of his mother's triumphant release from earthly cares into 'yonder worlds of light'. Since it was never meant for publication, we may suppose that the poem was written on impulse, under the immediate pressure of bereavement and out of a need to make sense of, and thus alleviate, a deep distress. The very act of setting down his dereliction no doubt brought Thomson some relief; more clearly, he wills and discovers a measure of consolation through what he calls the 'waking vision' of *apotheosis*:

> Why was I then, ye powers, reserved for this,
> Nor sunk that moment in the vast abyss?
> Devoured at once by the relentless wave,
> And whelmed for ever in a watery grave?
> Down, ye wild wishes of unruly woe!
> I see her in immortal beauty glow . . .
> The exalting voice of Heaven I hear her breathe,
> To soothe her soul in agonies of death.

> I see her through the mansions blest above,
> And now she meets her dear expecting love.
>
> (ll.45–50,53–6)

Yet the fact is that in the final analysis Thomson can put little faith in the offerings of the 'mind's eye'. No 'Heart-cheering sight' can, he insists, redeem him from dark thoughts, 'the damp gloom of grief's uncheerful shade'—and he looks at last to a future based in 'reason' and submission to the will of God, 'the kind o'erruling power'. But in thus rejecting the vivifying force of contemplative experience Thomson is in a sense being true to the character of the whole poem, for his 'heart-cheering' visions are visions more in name than nature. 'Looks soft yet awful; melting, yet serene', 'I see her in immortal beauty glow …': these are images culled from without by the desperately contriving mind, not the genuine bright imaginings of an inwardly active, recuperated self. They are a failed strategy for inner restoration, rather than true moments of restorative creation and triumph.

If 'On the Death of His Mother' fails as a quest for consolation and trial of the redemptive imagination, it is hardly more successful simply as a sincere, 'natural', expression of feeling. Thomson lacks an appropriate medium for communicating his emotions. We are ready to accept in theory that 'the heart dictates every flowing line' (l.6), but in practice instead of fluent, heart-given spontaneity we have, especially in the passionate parts, a densely rhetorical poetry:

> May joy on it [the night of parting] forsake her rosy
>   bowers,
> And screaming sorrow blast its baleful hours!
> When on the margin of the briny flood,
> Chilled with the sad presaging damp I stood,
> Took the last look, n'er to behold her more,
> And mixed our murmurs with the wavy roar . . .
>
> (ll.35–40)

In the snatching at extremes of tone, diction, and image ('blast', 'baleful', 'Chilled'), the repeated stock phraseology ('screaming sorrow', 'briny flood', 'wavy roar'), and the later evident recourse to 'Lycidas' ('Nor . . . whelmed for ever in a

watery grave'), we contemplate not so much the real face of woe
as the search for terms in which to paint it—the struggle for
formulation. The feeling in which the poetry undoubtedly
originates has been lost to a process of articulating it.

In 'On the Receipt of My Mother's Picture', on the other
hand, the 'heart' does dictate every 'flowing' line. Emotional
process and the process of writing the poem are one process—
even when Cowper is following the most commonplace conventions. The elegist's claim to sincerity, for example, which
appears in Thomson or Tickell as overt statement and a generic
requirement, emerges in the middle of Cowper's poem as part
of an intimate display of feeling that is itself demanded by, and
evolves out of, recollections of early childhood:

> All this still legible in mem'ry's page,
> And still to be so, to my latest age,
> Adds joy to duty, makes me glad to pay
> Such honours to thee as my numbers may;
> Perhaps a frail memorial, but sincere,
> Not scorn'd in heav'n, though little notic'd here.
>
> (ll.68–73)

Or, similarly, the 'consolation' of the subject's heavenly repose
is charged with, and complicated by, the poet's own deep
longing for peace:

> But was it such?—It was.—Where thou art gone
> Adieus and farewells are a sound unknown.
> May I but meet thee on that peaceful shore,
> The parting sound shall pass my lips no more!
>
> (ll.32–5)

The uncertain hope of 'May I but ...'; the sense of heaven as
rest as much as reward; the generality of 'The parting sound ...
no more', which evokes a whole life of dereliction akin to that of
separation without dissipating the pressure of a specific
memory of pain and a specific desire to renew the innocence to
which he had bidden a premature farewell when he 'wept a last
adieu' behind his mother's hearse: all points a particular
personality, not only behind the poem but forming itself in the
course of the poem. The ingredients of a public rhetoric have
become the integral features of a drama of mind.

Clearly, then, Cowper carries the 'sincerity' and 'naturalness' of 'personal elegy' to fresh limits. The life and movement
of his poem is best described as 'organic', in accordance with
the Romantic theory that 'a poem is not a deliberate rhetorical
construction but a quasi-natural organism, a "birth" as
Nietzsche calls it, a kind of plant which the mind puts forth in
accordance with the laws of its own nature'.[10] Lyttleton's
'monody' is, in its unforced and unvulgar simplicity, more a
triumph of form than an outgrowth of the mind: as its
sub-title—'monody'—suggests, it is a literary performance (an
extremely fine one),[11] offering the affective melody and affecting gestures of loss and grief rather than any immediate, direct
contact with a developing inward experience—which is exactly
how Lyttleton's contemporaries saw it, to judge by the
controversy involving Gray, Walpole, Doddridge, and Lyttleton himself over whether the simplicity or the more ornate
sections, where we encounter for instance a long elaborate
simile of an orange-tree blighted like Lucy in its prime,
provided the best model for preserving pathos.[12] Up to a point
the 'organic' or 'expressive' theory is applicable to Thomson's
lines, in that they do manifest sudden inner promptings and
perceptions which form overall an interplay between disquiet
and affirmation, abruptly terminated by the shift into Christian
stoicism. But if they are thus a 'growth' rooted in the private
consciousness of the poet, it is a growth which fails to take a
coherent or convincing shape, issuing as it does in a series of
postures held loosely together by opposition and reaction—
'Yet fond concern recalls the mother's eye . . .', 'But ah! that
night . . .', 'Down, ye wild wishes . . .'. In Cowper, however, the
change from deliberate rhetorical construction to quasi-natural
organism is complete. We are aware always of continuum and
progression, of a unity developing from within: developing,
that is, simultaneously from within the mind of the poet and
from within the poem, since the poem is a flowing of the
consciousness. Each point is a growing-point contributing to a
larger unintentioned structure. That structure can now be
explored in detail.

*   *   *   *   *

'Poetry is the spontaneous overflow of powerful feelings; it takes its origin from emotion recollected in tranquillity: the emotion is contemplated till by a species of reaction the tranquillity gradually disappears, and an emotion, kindred to that which was before the subject of contemplation, is gradually produced, and does itself actually exist in the mind.'[13] Wordsworth's account of creative process accords very closely with the genesis of 'On the Receipt of My Mother's Picture'. A letter from Cowper to Anne Bodham, who had just previously sent him the gift of his mother's picture, records the germinal stage during which some past emotion is remembered in a state of relative calm but with a strong intermixture of excitement:

> I received it the night before last, and viewed it with a trepidation of nerves and spirits somewhat akin to what I should have felt had the dear Original presented herself to my embraces ... She died when I had completed my sixth year, yet I remember her well and am an ocular witness of the great fidelity of the copy. I remember too a multitude of maternal tendernesses which I received from her and which have endeared her memory to me beyond expression.[14]

The sudden 'trepidation of nerves and spirits', which is the initial catalysis in the chemistry of creation, has given way even now to a quieter but kindred reaction in which the distant past is called up with its 'multitude of maternal tendernesses'; and it is this mood that overflows into poetry in the opening lines of 'On the Receipt of My Mother's Picture' where the past becomes, so to speak, the living present—'thy own sweet smiles I see ...'. Although there is from the beginning a conscious artistry, the poem is in essence a spontaneous psychological event so fundamentally private and instinctive that to read it we must, by a willing trespass, involve ourselves in its momentum, must make it an out-growth of our own minds as well. But the spontaneous, the psychological, the instinctive, is not necessarily the patternless or purposeless. 'Life has pass'd/ With me but roughly since I heard thee last': as we saw earlier, Cowper's habitual sense of aloneness steers and determines the act of contemplation, sensitizing his perceptions of the past so that they burgeon into present consolations. This might be called a logic of recoil: sad thoughts prompt their own dissolution in countervailing moments of release; the conviction that life has been one long, continuous process of suffering leads on to, and is answered by, the forging of a very different continuity in a happy recovery of childhood happiness.

Now, the structure of 'On the Receipt of My Mother's Picture' consists very largely in this opposition between dark and bright continuities. Cowper does not immediately pursue the implications of the recognition that 'Fancy shall weave a charm for my relief—/Shall steep me in Elysian reverie'. That opportunity for escape is stored up for the future, and he returns squarely to the sense of self as a prisoner of time and circumstance, perceiving in his early loss of his mother the start of a destiny of unaccountable deprivation. He was 'Wretch even then, life's journey just begun':

> I heard the bell toll'd on thy burial day,
> I saw the hearse that bore thee slow away,
> And, turning from my nurs'ry window, drew
> A long, long sigh, and wept a last adieu!
> But was it such?—It was . . .
> Thy maidens griev'd themselves at my concern,
> Oft gave me promise of a quick return.
> What ardently I wish'd, I long believ'd,
> And, disappointed still, was still deceiv'd;
> By disappointment every day beguil'd,
> Dupe of *to-morrow* even from a child.
> Thus many a sad to-morrow came and went,
> Till, all my stock of infant sorrow spent,
> I learn'd at last submission to my lot;
> But, though I less deplor'd thee, ne'er forgot.
>
> (ll.28–32,36–45)

Biographers have often used this and other passages in the poem to show what Cowper's childhood was like. But there is really no way of knowing the accuracy, or even veracity, of his recollections—apart from the recorded fact that his mother died when he was seven. The 'authenticity' of the scenes depends, not on the precision of Cowper's memory, however precise it *might* be, but on the communicative power of his writing, the text with which we as readers form a productive relationship. In Thomson's elegy on his mother we *notice* personal detail because it has been strongly defamiliarized, made strange, by the adoption of a specialized poetic language and the pursuit of a tragic, 'sadly pleasing', sublimity. Thus Thomson assigns himself to 'the orphan train', his grief inspires his 'throbbing breast', the ship from which he last saw his mother becomes 'the bulging vessel' and the shore 'the margin of the briny flood', his predicament is to be 'So hardly left! so bitterly resigned', and so on. Eschewing the level of generality at which we ordinarily conceive and speak of our engagement with the world he eschews 'naturalism', verisimilitude (although we do 'naturalize' such texts, make sense of them, in the act of reading by functionally translating their terminology back to that level ['briny flood' = sea, 'throbbing breast' = excitement . . .]—which then in turn produces a surplus of potential meaning which must be justified and interpreted at another level).[15] In Lyttleton's 'Where oft we used to walk,/Where oft in tender talk/We saw the summer sun go down the sky', on the other hand, the unelaborated verbs, nouns, and syntactical units are sufficiently close to ordinary consciousness and usage to achieve an immediate *vraisemblance*. The same effect is conspicuously present in Cowper, in the naming of concrete objects (the bell, the hearse, the nursery window) and the straightforward signification of relation to those objects ('saw', 'heard', 'turning from', 'wept'). Not that this observance of what a writer on *vraisemblance* calls the normative 'middle distance . . . an optic which neither brings us too close to the object nor lifts us too far above it'[16] precludes subtlety. The simplicity of 'heard' and 'saw' and the exclusion of all but the most starkly relevant features of the landscape operate with extraordinary finesse to express at once both the poet's temporal distance from the event, which he can recall only in terms of the barest salient detail, and the child's raw, unreflecting, 'unmediated' engagement with *his* obscure, mysterious, but dynamically significant world. And the rhythms too are those of both then and now—of the adult mind in the process of remembering and of the boy's automatic (or only incipiently explorative) perceptivity and crude, repeated acts of response that give way after a brief hesitation and inevitable reaction ('And, turning . . .') to a long-drawn-out and irrepressible grief. My point is not that the passage is without sophistication but that it is a construct rather than a record—realism rather than reality. A construct, moreover, with which we co-operate not simply because it adheres linguistically to 'the level of generality' but because it satisfies our notion of what childhood is like. In *Tirocinium*, his poem on public schools, Cowper describes childhood as 'innocent sweet simple years'. In 'On the Receipt of My Mother's Picture' he goes infinitely deeper, acknowledging its traumas, compulsive self-delusion ('What ardently I wish'd, I long believ'd') and vulnerability (the innocence that allows us to be cruelly 'still deceiv'd'), and affirming the continuity of the individual life so as to make that life a destiny—'Dupe of *to-morrow* even from a child'.

Realism rather than reality. One type of modern criticism—Structuralism—would extend this emphasis to encompass the 'I' of the poem, and talk of a meditative persona instead of an empirical individual, the author, William Cowper. According to this approach, the question 'But was it such?—It was', with its indications of uncertainty and time, or the personal pronouns and particularized subject of 'Thy maidens griev'd themselves at my concern,/Oft gave me promise of a quick return', for instance, are 'orientational' devices within a fiction, a means of bringing a voice and a situation into being.[17] But while it is true that 'On the Receipt of My Mother's Picture' is, like all poetic discourse, a construct, there can be no sense in denying it an identifiable and subjective 'I'—that is, the same person who wrote the associated letter to Anne Bodham. Its realism is as it were a by-product of his earnest mental journeying; the structures, life, and purposes of the work must be seen, not as the constituents of a fictional project, but as the creation and definition of a structuring, living, and purposing consciousness. The lines in which Cowper describes the aftermath of his mother's death suggest the indubitably earnest procedures of Puritan meditation on the past, with, however, an inversion of motivation and result; for whereas the Puritan turned to personal history for evidences of election and in order to discover the underlying unity of his road to salvation, Cowper's encounters give rise, here, to the quite opposite, ironic *telos* of disappointment, deception, and unfulfilled hopes. The terms in which the events are portrayed are strongly interpretative: the adverbs of extended time ('long', 'still'), the switch from active to passive verbs ('I wish'd, I long believ'd'/ 'disappointed still, was still deceiv'd'), and the repeated but forward motion of the rhythm (each line consisting of two units of six and four beats) realize a ceaseless cycle in which the child is both chief actor, fuelling the process by his burning wishes, and only victim, 'caught' and acted upon. 'I learn'd at last submission to my lot': this memorable line implies a future to which childhood was an induction. 'Dupe of *to-morrow* even from a child': Cowper sees himself still in the role of Time's fool and slave to fruitless hopes. He wins from memory a confirmation of his tragic fate.

Cowper never breaks entirely free from this view of himself as passive victim, 'set ... distant from a prosp'rous course' (as he puts it later). Yet the claims of helplessness that underlie it are themselves belied. Circling back and outwards, he now extends the earlier recoil from dark obsession in answer to the confirmation of that obsession. Memory weaves its charm for his 'relief', as he moves beyond the time of his mother's death to the 'elysian' scenes of infancy:

> ... where the gard'ner Robin, day by day,
> Drew me to school along the public way,
> Delighted with my bauble coach, and wrapt
> In scarlet mantle warm, and velvet capt,
> 'Tis now become a history little known,
> That once we call'd the past'ral house our own.
> Short-liv'd possession! but the record fair
> That mem'ry keeps of all thy kindness there,
> Still outlives many a storm that has effac'd
> A thousand other themes less deeply trac'd.
> Thy nightly visits to my chamber made,
> That thou might'st know me safe and warmly laid;
> Thy morning bounties ere I left my home,
> The biscuit, or confectionary plum;
> The fragrant waters on my cheeks bestow'd
> By thy own hand, till fresh they shone and glow'd;
> All this, and more endearing still than all,
> Thy constant flow of love that knew no fall,
> Ne'er roughen'd by those cataracts and brakes

> That humour interpos'd too often makes;
> All this still legible in mem'ry's page,
> And still to be so, to my latest age,
> Adds joy to duty ...

(ll.48–70)

Norman Nicholson comments, 'When, over fifty years later, his cousin, Mrs. Bodham, sent him a copy of his mother's picture, he was able to recall, vividly and tenderly, the days at the Rectory.'[18] This, a good example of the 'biographical' approach, takes us nowhere unless to the question of what features of Cowper's writing account for the 'vividness'. Not, we might think, the decided literariness of much of the language—the Miltonic inversion in 'scarlet mantle warm', the curious exactness of 'confectionary plum', the periphrasis in 'morning boúnties', 'fragrant waters', 'past'ral house'. Yet we have only to set Cowper's literariness against that of Gray's account in the Eton College 'Ode' of the 'sprightly race' who 'now delight to cleave/With pliant arm the glassy wave' and 'chase the rolling circle's speed' to appreciate that in Cowper's case a formalizing and circumlocutory style is no barrier to graphic portrayal.[19] Gray's artifice brings into focus not 'careless childhood' itself, nor the perceiving mind, but the mechanics of swimming and playing with hoops. Cowper, on the other hand, gives, as usual, the distinctive 'feel' of an individual past as it is recovered in the adult consciousness— through the specificity of 'scarlet', 'velvet', or *public* way', the naming of the gardener Robin, the positioning of 'warm' so as also to suggest an adverbial meaning and draw attention to the 'texture' of childhood experience, and, by no means least, the conjunction of humour and poignancy that authenticates the whole recollection of so brief, so quaint, and so appealing a 'possession'. With the memories of 'maternal tendernesses' ('Thy nightly visits ...') we move from a remembered scene, a 'spot of time', to a flow of 'association', a mingling of sharp detail ('biscuit, or confectionary plum') and vaguer impressions ('nightly visits', 'fragrant waters')—the images of a dream, a reverie. What might be judged out of context an over-studied rhetoric—'chamber' and 'bestow'd' can also be mentioned—

becomes, within the inner monologue of which this passage is a part, a perfect means of fixing, memorializing, the past at the very instant that it is reborn in the imagination.

Again, however, we are aware not only of vivid representation but of psychological activity and significance—above all of the experiential gains of contemplation so characteristic of Cowper. It is not enough to say that he tastes the pleasures of memory; he is mentally 'wrapt up' in them, shut off from darker themes and absorbed in the paradise before his 'fall'—the guiltless 'fall' into self-consciousness and consciousness of a world beyond self, occasioned by the then but half-understood 'shock' of death and absence. The images that fill Cowper's mind are not random, even in the moment of reverie. Determined by that very sense of an unlovely present which they alleviate, they form, by a kind of psychic reaction, a direct inversion of his customary view of his existence. They are images of a *happy* prison, a safe and comfortable confinement, dominated by a 'constant flow of love' (not deceptions or hostility), full of simple satisfactions, a pleasurably passive life in which external influence is all benign and 'cycle' a matter of routine, ever-repeated, blessings: how the gardener Robin *drew* him *day by day* to school *delighted*, his mother's nightly protective visits, the daily bounties, the waters on his cheeks gently *bestow'd*, all is in marked contrast to the continuum apprehended in 'Life has pass'd ... but roughly' or 'Dupe of *to-morrow* ...'. The narrator of Sterne's *Sentimental Journey* (which Cowper refers to elsewhere) talks of the 'Sweet pliability of man's spirit, that can at once surrender itself to illusions, which cheat expectation and sorrow of their weary moments', and goes on to describe how 'when my way is too rough for my feet, or too steep for my strength, I get off it, to some smooth velvet path which fancy has scattered over ... When evils press sore upon me, and there is no retreat from them in this world, then I take a new course: I leave it ... I was never able to conquer any single bad sensation in my heart so decisively, as by beating up as fast as I could for some kindly and gentle sensation to fight it upon its own ground'.[20] But the enchanted ground on which this troubled traveller finds relief is that of great art. He has just been reading Shakespeare; and his regular abode is with Dido in Vergil's 'elysian fields'. Cowper is beguiled and strengthened by the 'spirit' of his own past—which is to say by experiences partly 'given' and partly of his own making, creations from and of the mind which answer the mind's creations and yield the sensation to fight sensation. Cowper's 'escape' in this passage is to a degree unintentioned, an 'absorption' in feeling, a loss of waking consciousness. Yet he sees, too, the special logic of what is happening: the disciplined maturity that can acknowledge change and transience—''tis now become a history little known ...'—can also comprehend the objectifying, shaping, and vivifying side of memory, which forms a 'record' that may efface the other themes, of 'storm' and adversity, a 'page' offering retreat from 'expectation and sorrow'.

It is clear, though, that this sense of recollection as self-justifying personal 'good' is held in check by the traditional sense of recollection as elegiac tribute. Cowper specifically aligns his 'mem'ry's page'—his poem—with the 'frail memorial' of conventional commemorative inscription. Like the 'tablet' on which Remembrance surveys maternal 'bounty' in 'On a Beloved Mother', it is both goal and motivation, eulogy and an inducement to eulogy; and it is not long before the poetry rises to a more formally celebratory level in a quasi-*apotheosis* that reminds us of Tickell and Thomson:

> Thou, as a gallant bark from Albion's coast
> (The storms all weather'd and the ocean cross'd)
> Shoots into port at some well-haven'd isle,
> Where spices breathe and brighter seasons smile,
> There sits quiescent on the floods that show
> Her beauteous form reflected clear below,
> While airs impregnated with incense play
> Around her, fanning light her streamers gay;
> So thou, with sails how swift! hast reach'd the shore
> 'Where tempests never beat nor billows roar,'
> And thy lov'd consort on the dang'rous tide
> Of life, long since, has anchor'd at thy side.
>
> (ll.88–99)

The epic simile, Latinate diction and personification, concentrated literary echoes (of James Hervey, Johnson, Samuel

Garth), and the elaboration of the concept of life as journey or
sea-voyage by its conflation with the *topos* of the heavenly
Paradise as a garden among 'the fortunate isles' produce 'notes
of gratulation high' (Thomson, 'To the Memory of Sir Isaac
Newton') equal in ceremonial stateliness to any in the elegiac
verse of the period.[21] Thus the less subjective of Cowper's two
original aims is brought to a climax in the 'figures, or
metaphors, or ... high colouring' which even Lyttleton,
staunch champion of simplicity, thought it proper to preserve,
'at ... intervals', in the poem on his wife.

But it is at this point that Cowper's poem takes, in fact, its
most acutely personal turn. At the end of 'Lycidas' ('Weep no
more, woeful shepherds ...'), the great example of *apotheosis*,
tribute and consolation blend, in a sustained leap of Faith and
Vision that restores Milton to a deeply felt belief in grace and
resurrection.[22] In Thomson, we remember, vision had been
reduced to image, and consolation had been finally comprom-
ised by the 'gloom' of 'grief's uncheerful shade'; but in Cowper
the imaging of a triumphant repose brings no consolation at all,
only an intensification of a tragic sense, of danger, perpetual
strife, and seemingly certain disaster:

> But me, scarce hoping to attain that rest,
> Always from port withheld, always distress'd—
> Me howling winds drive devious, tempest toss'd,
> Sails ript, seams op'ning wide, and compass lost,
> And day by day some current's thwarting force
> Sets me more distant from a prosp'rous course.
>
> (ll. 100–5)

The familiar refuge of the earth-bound spirit, the visionary or
merely cerebral contemplation of an exemplary fate to which it
might aspire, is not only closed to Cowper but re-opens in fuller
and sharper outline the bleak interior landscape of reality's
dark dream. He had of course used a similar imagery and
juxtaposition before to point the turmoil of his existence, in
lamenting to Lady Hesketh as early as 1765 his own 'world of
tempest and commotion' in contrast to her safe return from the
'storms' of Southampton,[23] and in the poem 'To Mr. Newton,
on his Return from Ramsgate'—

> Your sea of troubles you have past,
>   And found the peaceful shore;
> I, tempest-toss'd, and wreck'd at last,
>   Come home to port no more.
>   (ll. 13–16)

But there was never previously quite the urgency, the tension, of the present lines: the dislocated syntax, piling up of brief phrases, and the plangent violence of image and rhythm—all so conspicuous beside the smooth periodic flow of the preceding sentence—make them Cowper's keenest and fullest apprehension of his 'world' of turbulence and aimlessness. (That Cowper took the ideas and imagery of both sentences from Johnson's juxtaposition of calm and tempestuous voyage in his poem 'The Young Author' makes them no less sharply personal. Johnson (ll. 1–10) uses the contrast very differently, to illustrate the gulf between expectation and the realities of experience; and what we have is an example of Cowper's habit of recalling material long after he had encountered its source.)

Yet there are two journeys in 'On the Receipt of My Mother's Picture': life as journey and poem as journey. And the latter is even at this point by no means entirely an unprosperous course. It is true that Cowper is driven dangerously inwards to a solipsistic view of his being-in-the-world, completing his vision of a perverse 'unity' linking past, present, and future, and all the space between, in a chain of unbroken adversity, where the child who was 'disappointed still' and 'still deceiv'd' is father of the adult-victim, 'day by day', of some 'current's thwarting force', the man dispossessed of the heavenly paradise that is the mirror-image at the opposite end of life's ocean of the infant paradise which he prematurely lost. At the same time, however, the self as *me*—victim and object—is balanced by the self as *I*, the active 'I' who comes face to face with and embraces the shadow within, richly poetizing his 'fate', making of it something spectacular. Cowper's triumph in this poem is in part a triumph of tragic insight and tragic acceptance—a triumph signalized not only by the act of courageous self-confrontation and the 'realization' of self through exact metaphoric amplification of a felt predicament but also by the aspect with which he emerges on the other side of this precarious moment. For he 'breaks out' with:

> But oh the thought, that thou art safe, and he!
> That thought is joy, arrive what may to me.
> My boast is not that I deduce my birth
> From loins enthron'd, and rulers of the earth;
> But higher far my proud pretensions rise—
> The son of parents pass'd into the skies.
>
> (ll. 106–11)

There is no great liberation of spirit in this, but there is a firm effort of will and a genuine release. In the joy and pride he takes from the thought of his parents' possession of the haven from which, on all the evidence, he is excluded, in the selflessness of this recognition, and in the openness to an unknown and unpromising future of the cry 'arrive what may to me', we perceive not simply a capacity for making the best of things but also the 'stiffening', salutary, cathartic effect of the climactic vision of personal insecurity, exposure, and extreme distress.

It is, however, the other victory, of contemplative solace, that means most to Cowper in the final analysis:

> And now, farewell—time, unrevok'd, has run
> His wonted course, yet what I wish'd is done.
> By contemplation's help, not sought in vain,
> I seem t'have liv'd my childhood o'er again;
> To have renew'd the joys that once were mine . . .
>
> (ll. 112–16)

Thus the poetic journey ends in calm, all passion spent, and with a fresh insight into that journey itself. The *poem* becomes at last an object of contemplation and source of soothing thoughts—a 'memory's page' in its own right, in which, with a quiet satisfaction and philosophic mind, Cowper can read his success in renewing the joys of his 'innocent sweet simple years'. He draws as it were a secondary delight from the previous recollections, which have acquired the status themselves of a significant 'moment', a 'spot of time'. There is, moreover, a further advance in perception, as Cowper realizes that the Elysian reveries and momentary dreams that circumvent the laws and pressures of 'what here we call our life' will continue to be available to him. The concluding couplets—

> And, while the wings of fancy still are free,
> And I can view this mimic shew of thee,
> Time has but half succeeded in his theft—
> Thyself remov'd, thy power to sooth me left.

(ll. 118–21)

contain of course an implicit admission, honest and melancholy, that the 'wings of fancy' may not always be 'free', that
they are as vulnerable to loss and constraint as any human
possession. But the dominant note is of tranquil faith in the
routine accessibility of 'flight'. Ironically, Cowper's future
lay—in 'The Castaway'—amidst the furious currents of his
fate; yet not the least of his rewards in 'On the Receipt of My
Mother's Picture' rests in a prediction of a 'continuity' rivalling
both that of the Christian *mythos* of the voyage to Heaven, from
which he is shut out, and that of his perceived destiny, where he
is ever shut in by external and internal 'forces', hostile 'howling
winds', or fruitless 'ardent wishes', unfulfilled hopes. He
envisages a future in which a substitute h(e)aven is always
available from within—in which the provisional repose he has
won during the poem can be always repeated.

   Yet it is important finally to note that whatever their value
'contemplation' and 'fancy', 'reverie' and 'momentary dream',
are not given absolute precedence in 'On the Receipt of My
Mother's Picture'. The poem comes to rest in careful rationalization, with the realist in Cowper conceding time's 'course' and
'theft' even as he happily celebrates the fulfilment of his wishes
('what I wish'd is done . . .'). In this he reminds us of Keats,
who, though he cultivated Fancy's charms with a peculiar zest,
could not give himself wholeheartedly to them, feeling as he did
'the weariness, the fever and the fret', the 'giant agony', of life.
If, however, we think of 'Ode to a Nightingale' itself, it is at
once apparent that Cowper's is the more clear-cut and
satisfactory position. There is in him nothing of the often noted
frustration that dogs Keats at the frayed end of his poem: the
sad concession that Fancy is after all but a 'deceiving elf' who
cannot cheat so well as she is famed to do; the fact that flight on
the 'viewless wings of poesy' must issue in the 'sole self'

returning more desolate to earth, 'forlorn'; uncertainty as to which is the greater truth, 'the happiness of poetic reverie or the colder experience of everyday reality'.[24] For Cowper, as he bids 'farewell', both these 'truths' are equally valid: he balances contraries, Keats finds a problem and a conflict.

But Cowper's own well-adjusted compromise between colder reality and the claims of Fancy itself emerges out of conflict, for he has faced the very question so insistently raised in (and by) Keats's work: how far are fancy and reverie a mere indulgence, how far should the poet commit himself to them and the satisfaction of private longings? Immediately after the recollections of childhood he had turned to ask—

> Could time, his flight revers'd, restore the hours,
> When, playing with thy vesture's tissu'd flow'rs,
> The violet, the pink, the jessamine,
> I prick'd them into paper with a pin,
> (And thou wast happier than myself the while,
> Would'st softly speak, and stroke my head and smile)
> Could those few pleasant hours again appear,
> Might one wish bring them, would I wish them here?
> I would not trust my heart—the dear delight
> Seems so to be desir'd, perhaps I might.—
> But no—what here we call our life is such,
> So little to be lov'd, and thou so much,
> That I should ill requite thee to constrain
> Thy unbound spirit into bonds again.
>
> (ll.74–87)

Implicit in this rejection of the heart's wishes in favour of outgoing love, filial duty, and recognition of the world as a place of bondage is a hard-won refusal to pursue the 'happiness of poetic reverie' beyond reasonable limits, to the point where all disagreeables, whether of actuality or the imagination, might be entirely evaporated. The images of a world of unselfconscious delight—bright, soft, sensuous—now rise up more easily and vividly than ever, effortlessly and, in the parenthesis, uncalled, bidding for complete ascendency over the poet and his creation. But Cowper blocks in himself the almost irresistible desire to submit gratefully to their attractions; the idea of time being reversed, a proposition which poetry can make effective by its illusions, is conjured with and cherished ('I would not trust my heart . . .') but is seen at last as a temptation to be overcome ('But no . . .'). In assuming the more public role of elegist in the following paragraph, commemorating a life and a success other than his own, he endorses and confirms this victory over 'self', and though in the subsequent metaphoric amplification of a private affliction 'self-interest' (however richly poetized) again challenges, in opposite form, for the centre of consciousness and poem, this too, as we have seen, is broken through in a further act of will and self-abnegation.

In Keats's 'Ode' (and also notably in 'Lamia')[25] the retreat from pleasing illusion is forced upon the poet. In Cowper it comes more as a choice, which places him in fact closer to Milton in 'Lycidas'. Interestingly enough, Cowper's list of his mother's 'vesture's tissu'd flow'rs' is firmly reminiscent of that used by Milton when summoning nature to pay sympathetic heed to the death of Lycidas, a hypothesis Milton eventually judges a 'false surmise' as the thought returns of Lycidas's body being hurled beneath the 'whelming tide'.[26] Though (typically) transmuting the mythopoeic situation into a familiarly human one, Cowper follows his predecessor in rejecting poetic fictions except to 'interpose a little ease'. In the closing lines the balance is redressed in favour of that 'ease', yet the other attitude still stands: when Cowper says 'time, unrevok'd, has run/His wonted course' and 'Without the sin of violating thine' he draws attention to a core of hard sense and a by no means easy allegiance to 'other-centred' humane sensibility which are enough in themselves to make nonsense of the charge of 'sentimentalism', without reference to the greater poetic, and literary-historical, triumph of 'On the Receipt of My Mother's Picture' in the exposure, exploration, and dramatization of personal experience.

*   *   *   *   *

The literary-historical interest of Cowper's poem should now be obvious. It is not only a brilliant adaptation of Augustan elegy but a new species of confessional meditation—

... a varied but integral process of memory, thought, anticipation, and feeling which remains closely inter-volved with the outer scene. In the course of this medita-tion the lyric speaker achieves an insight, faces up to a tragic loss, comes to a moral decision, or resolves an emotional problem. Often the poem rounds upon itself to end where it began, at the outer scene, but with an altered mood and deepened understanding which is the result of the intervening meditation.[27]

This would make a perfect—or, as we shall see in a moment, almost perfect—description of 'On the Receipt of My Mother's Picture'. It is in fact M. H. Abrams's classic account of 'the greater Romantic lyric', of 'Frost at Midnight' and 'Dejection', 'Tintern Abbey', Shelley's 'Stanzas written in Dejection'.

The one designated constituent that does not quite 'fit' with Cowper's poem is the 'intervolvement' with 'the outer scene'; and that Cowper's opening and closing point of focus is a picture rather than a landscape or 'setting' draws attention, like the elegiac content, to the eighteenth-century roots of his meditation, reminding us of 'polite' occasional verse, his contemporaries' fondness for recording their responses to a gift or something casually found, often a portrait. Among eight-eenth-century 'picture' poems, as among the elegies, there are some with a degree of flexible self-reference and private reflection: Thomas Edwards's very fine sonnet 'On a Family Picture', for instance, where the group-portrait, a 'goodly monument of happier days', leads the author to thoughts of his lone survival and the final stroke of 'wasting Time', culmina-ting in metaphoric self-identification with a decaying column, 'single, unprop'd, and nodding to [its] fall'.[28] Like many a later, 'Romantic', lyricist, Edwards dramatizes and gives public status to a personal situation of isolation and stress through an interplay between speaker and object-as-image—that is the object-images of portrait and column, which serve basically the same function, of releasing and 'centring' the meditation, of modifying subjective consciousness and being a locus or 'habitation' for it, as Keats's urn and nightingale, or Shelley's West Wind, or indeed 'the outer scene' of Abrams's examples of the 'greater lyric'.[29] But 'On the Receipt of My

Mother's Picture' is an infinitely more developed and sustained version of this type of psycho-drama. While the theme of Romantic meditation—in essence always the life and death of the inner self—is present everywhere in Cowper, its form is predicted most precisely by this single remarkable poem. The picture is at once the inspiration and anchor of the poetic-reflective process, a bringer both of grace and melancholy convictions, a 'space' through which the poet moves inwards, a 'shew' into and from which is projected his own subjective life and spirit—a dynamic focal point with which the contemplation remains 'closely intervolved' in a series of promptings, returns, remembrances, interrogations, acts of interpretation. Abrams's circular structure, integration of the intellect and the feelings, and advance to 'an altered mood' and 'deepened understanding', all are applicable; and Cowper achieves psychologically everything that, according to Abrams, may be achieved—facing up to a tragic loss (the death of a mother, the death of innocence, the unaccountable 'loss' of Heaven), reaching a moral decision (setting limits to the claims of poetic illusion), resolving an emotional problem (coming to terms with his 'dereliction').

But the kind of meditation to which 'On the Receipt of My Mother's Picture' most exactly relates is what I would call the poetry of 'provisional self-stabilization', tragi-remedial dramas of mind where the poet may finally say, if rarely with the confidence of Coleridge in 'This Lime-tree Bower', 'have I not marked/Much that has soothed me'. To adopt the terminology of Jung's 'individuation' process,[30] such poems are not so much 'circular' as 'spiroid', since, in spite of there being always some residue of unanswered anxiety, sorrow, or despair at the end, there has just as surely been some genuine 'uplift'. In 'This Lime-tree Bower' Coleridge escapes his prison, one of gloomy thoughts no less than a physical space and condition, by an appeal to the powers of recollection, re-experiencing his own past comforts in the presence of nature: solace and ontological release derive from a mental journey-within-a-journey. In 'Dejection' they are effected by a different strategy—the prayer for Sara's well-being, arrive what may to him. Cowper's poem contains both sorts of stabilizing event—both the consolatory journey and the other-centred act of love which redeems self

from the bondage of selfhood, though not from the bonds of
affliction. Wordsworth's 'Resolution and Independence' suggests a less obvious but no less important connection. It would
be all too easy to associate the realistic attitude and clear-
sightedness which emerge towards the end of Cowper's poem
with an Augustan 'reasonableness' that naturally prevents him
from committing himself fully, like a 'Romantic', to fancy,
reverie, and imagination. But it would be wrong. Reason plays
as great a part in the final resolution of 'Resolution and
Independence' as in that of 'On the Receipt of My Mother's
Picture', for Wordsworth's rescue from despondency and 'dim
sadness' comes in a saving act of rationalization, whereby he
resists the 'fears and fancies' that present his 'mind's eye' with
the spectacle of a tragic destiny (both his own and that of the
leech-gatherer, whom he 'sees' as a figure of aloneness, silence,
and eternal wandering) in favour of a resilient compromise
with the difficulties of human existence—'I could have laughed
myself to scorn to find/In that decrepit Man so firm a mind'.[31]
The stronger the imagination and the emotions the greater the
need for wide-awake presence of mind.

Coleridge speaks of the importance of 'mind' from another
angle when stressing the major deficiency in the work of
Bowles, whom he otherwise greatly admired for his contribution to the poetry of personal reflection in the late eighteenth
century: 'Bowles has indeed the sensibility of a poet, but . . . he
is not a thinker.'[32] This is true even of the very best of Bowles's
verse, as 'To the River Itchin' where like Cowper he presents
himself in the role of lonely, fated wanderer, discovering the
bitter-sweet paradox that memory brings both sorrow and
solace: gone are 'Hope's delusive gleams' . . .

> upon thy banks I bend
> Sorrowing, yet feel such solace at my heart,
> As at the meeting of some long-lost friend,
> From whom, in happier hours, we wept to part.[33]

This is compellingly simple, direct, carefully modulated 'sentiment'. But there is more of the 'head' and of the 'heart' in
Cowper. And much the same conclusion will come of, finally,

comparing the reflective-recollective passages of *The Deserted Village*, another classic example of the developing poetry of subjective meditation:

> Sweet was the sound when oft at evening's close
> Up yonder hill the village murmur rose;
> There, as I passed with careless steps and slow,
> The mingling notes came softened from below;
> The swain responsive as the milkmaid sung,
> The sober herd that lowed to meet their young;
> The noisy geese . . .
>
> (ll. 113–19)

The 'sweet confusion' of sights and sounds rise from 'below' the conscious level, forming a reverie-like flow of associations, a 'growth' of individual but idealized impressions. The heroic couplet has shed the pointedness characteristic of the first half of the century: though the end-stopped rhyme is there, the overall effect is of slow, pensive reflection, the verses unfolding in accord with the poet's leisurely rediscovery of details from his past. The notes do indeed come 'softened', mediated through a muted, ruminative sensibility. We trespass upon an inner monologue, contemplate a landscape that is as much a landscape of mind and feeling as of place. Yet the difference between *The Deserted Village* and 'On the Receipt of My Mother's Picture' is the difference between an embryonic, 'postured' (and also nostalgic) meditative 'lyricism' and a mature, earnest, 'necessary' one.

9
'Which Way I Fly . . .'
'The Castaway', Hymns, and Other Poems

While conceding that 'The Castaway' is 'a very fine poem', F. R. Leavis criticizes it for what he terms 'some discrepancy between Cowper's emotion and the prose rationality and critical balance of the statement'.[1] Donald Daved has no such reservation. For him the acutely deliberate style, 'dry, chastening and logical', makes a perfect medium for expressing not only emotion but 'a whole view of human life and destiny'.[2]

Davie is right:

> At length, his transient respite past,
>   His comrades, who before
> Had heard his voice in ev'ry blast,
>   Could catch the sound no more.
> For then, by toil subdued, he drank
> The stifling wave, and then he sank.
>
> (ll.43–8)

Every phrase of this calculated understatement contributes something positive to the development of both narrative and the interpretation of narrative. The prosaic 'At length' becomes, within the poetic context, a piercing litotes, for the 'castaway' has struggled in the sea for the proverbially eternal 'hour' (l.37) of the drowning man. 'Transient respite' accurately suggests a passing reprieve, the mere postponement of a preordained sentence of destruction rather than the genuine possibility of survival. This is followed by one of the many ironies that emerge in Cowper's reading of the situation—

Notes and References begin on page 346.

ironies all the more potent for being left unelaborated, as literal ingredients of the mariner's predicament and the enigmatic workings of fate. The verb 'catch', a dead metaphor vivified, serves not only to enliven the 'scene' by its sudden graphic preciseness—the crew would *intercept* the sound of their comrade's voice as it reaches them on the wind—but also to press home the plain yet bitter fact that the gusts which have carried his cries for help to his ship-mates are the same gusts which have all the time been carrying the vessel away from him.

Cowper then proceeds to focus with extraordinary clarity upon the act of drowning itself, using a lucid progressive syntax that causes each main stage of the event to stand out. 'By toil subdued': again an implicit irony, that the mariner's effort to survive is in the end the immediate cause of his death—which suggests the larger 'view' that human strength is, however great and heroic, ultimately futile in the face of external forces that may lead him even to the point of having to co-operate in his own execution. Davie comments in detail on 'drank' and 'stifling'. The latter 'generalizes the fact of drowning, because "stifling" is equally applicable to all ways of dying'. We may add that this valuable generalizing effect, which gives the event the status of symbolic and universal truth, operates simultaneously with what can be termed a 'specifying effect', which communicates the very singular intensity, physical and emotional, of the experience described. For it is characteristic of the poetry of 'The Castaway' to combine powerful immediate definition with broader perspectives and meanings. 'Drank' too works in this way, but more remarkably than 'stifling'. We tend to think of drinking as a wilful imbibing for pleasure and/or nourishment, whereas Cowper uses it in the sense of all taking-in of liquid into the throat and at the same time applies it to circumstances where the liquid brings, not much-needed refreshment after 'toil', but suffocation. By overturning the normal associations of drinking he lends a notable emotive 'thrust' to his description of the castaway's death, but more importantly, his appeal to the word's figurative and generalizing potential, like the *meaningful* use of 'At length', 'respite', 'catch', and 'stifling', allows him to transcend narrative for vision—vision of being-in-the-world and of going-out.

In order to demonstrate just why the image of drinking

expresses a 'whole view of human life and destiny' Davie remarks that it 'takes up all the Calvinist arguments of free-will and fate'. Cowper the Calvinist believed that even in a world of rigid predestination the salvation or damnation of the soul was still the responsibility of the individual. He had affirmed in *Truth*, 'Charge not, with light sufficient and left free,/Your wilful suicide on God's decree'; to present the rush of water into the throat as a voluntary action is to bring this idea to appalling life; 'the death of the castaway is "wilful suicide"'.[3] Now, Davie puts his finger on a theological point worth noting, for the ontological anxiety that is a mark of so much Puritan writing derives as much from the burden of personal responsibility as from the idea of election and reprobation.[4] All the same, it is misleading to talk of the castaway's 'drinking' as if it represents some guilty abnegation of duty towards the state of one's soul. He is victim, not sinner. Free-will is conspicuous by its absence. Cowper's vision is of the alone individual in a hostile universe, acted upon by irresistible powers—'wash'd headlong' beneath the 'whelming brine', opposed by the 'furious blast', reduced by 'toil' into submitting to the 'stifling wave'. He is free only to realize the terrible extent of his aloneness—'Yet bitter felt it still to die/Deserted, and his friends so nigh' (ll.35–6)—or to take in the water of annihilation. And this is a view of human life that needs no theology to make it comprehensible and give it significance: a view that has all the 'chemical purity', the taut simplicity and frightening coherence, of Tragedy. Calvinist belief—the belief in 'rigid predestination'—is clearly there in 'The Castaway', but to say that it is the subject of the poem is to introduce an undue restriction of meaning. We must be careful not to concentrate too much here on questions of Cowper's religion.

But what then of the final stanza?—

> No voice divine the storm allay'd,
>   No light propitious shone;
> When snatch'd from all effectual aid,
>   We perish'd, each alone:
> But I beneath a rougher sea,
> And whelm'd in deeper gulphs than he.
>
> (ll.61–6)

These lines would seem to be the main reason for the usual assumption that 'The Castaway' has a specifically religious theme—that it expresses Cowper's conviction of being rejected, 'unchosen', by God. Two other poems lend support to this interpretation. In Addison's popular hymn 'How are thy Servants blest, O Lord!' the same storm imagery is used as a vehicle for confident celebration of God's mercies towards favoured 'souls': amidst waves, gulphs, and 'dreadful whirles' the believer's prayer is answered, and 'The Sea, that roar'd at Thy command,/At Thy command was still'.[5] Cowper, on the other hand, apparently sees himself as excluded from the Lord's 'blessings'. Then in Cowper's translation of Madame Guyon's 'Figurative Description of the Procedure of Divine Love' we have a dream-allegory showing how Divine Love leads the elect individual to (as the subtitle puts it) 'the point of self-renunciation'. One of many mariners is cast into the sea, where, the 'frail supports' of a few 'floating rushes' soon failing, he perceives the waves 'Yawn into a thousand graves': 'Down I went, and sunk as lead,/Ocean closing o'er my head'. But all this is a trial framed by Love to ensure child-like trust and submission. Out of tempest comes the calm of absolute faith: 'All is right that thou wilt do'.[6] In 'The Castaway' there is positively *no* divine intervention, no rescue, no loving and intimate relationship. The similarities between Cowper's poem and these representative psycho-dramas of soul-trial and repose suggest a reversal of position (the similarity extending in the case of Addison's 'Ode' to the use of 'common metre', the most familiar measure in English hymns). It is a song, not of hopeful thanksgiving, ultimate assurance, or (and Herbert's 'Love' also springs to mind) firmer acquiescence to the ways of Providence, but of desertion, doom, and damnation. Yet we also need some such phrase as 'terminal separation' from God; for Cowper's outright acceptance in 'The Castaway' of the fact that he has perished inwardly and spiritually is accompanied by a concomitant acceptance of a life and a world *without God*. There is nothing in the text, in fact, to hold it to the belief that the universe is God-directed; He is simply not present—'No voice divine the storm allay'd'. God, and the hymnology whose conventions and attitudes He rules, have a place still in the poet's consciousness, but as part of a vision that consigns Him to a now irrelevant heaven. 'The Castaway' is the work of one past worrying about whether Providence will aid or destroy him. It shows the God-abandoned self in the act of abandoning God.

We shall return to this later, but one related point requires stressing. Far from shunning the horror of his situation as 'destin'd wretch' and the inimical darkness of a world from which God (a *deus absconditus*) and all hope are absent, Cowper takes hold of them, from first to last, with deliberateness, zest, and sensitivity that raise him well above mere pessimism, self-pity, or blank despair. Nowhere does he display greater creative and psychological strength. From the beginning we are struck by his mastery of his subject and responses, which issues in a compact and frugal sublimity, a sublimity consisting, not of rolling periods and abundant figures of speech, but of brief, compressed statement instinct with feeling and metaphoric depth. 'Obscurest night involv'd the sky' (l.1): 'obscurest' establishes at once the singular fatefulness of this one 'night', a night of the soul as much as a phenomenon in nature, an ominous and extreme darkness resistant to any light—and any hope; the verb 'involv'd', carrying the latinate meaning of 'enfolding' or 'wrapping around' but suggesting also the modern meaning of 'to implicate in an event or action', personifies both 'night' and 'sky' (as 'roar'd ' in line two personifies 'billows') so as to locate the coming drama immediately within a field of active, indeed *conspiring*, powers and presences. What might seem preliminary scene-setting amounts, therefore, to a hard-hitting induction. The composure at the end of this same stanza—'Of friends, of hope, of all bereft,/His floating home for ever left' (ll.5–6)— is a tribute to Cowper's capacity for knowing immense pathos without yeilding to it. (The periphrastic 'floating home' may well be a difficulty for the twentieth-century reader, but we would pay for a less roundabout way of saying 'ship' with the loss of a telling image of an existence, like Cowper's own, in which rest and stability were always more apparent than real.) Or we might, finally, go again to the last stanza of the poem, to note how near Cowper does come to self-pity yet how emphatically it is resisted by his sense of the degree of all he has gone through, the specialness of his fate: 'And whelm'd in deeper gulphs than he'. There is a note of triumph in this, a proud feeling of uniqueness similar to that which had sometimes emerged, in the correspondence, in defiant rejections of spiritual comfort.[7] Cowper was never more certain of his tragic destiny than in 'The Castaway', and never did he get more out of it.

Though inclined to sentimentalize everything ('. . . it almost breaks one's heart to read it . . .'), Caroline Helstone in Charlotte Brontë's *Shirley* has a point when remarking that Cowper 'found relief in writing "The Castaway"'.[8] It must have alleviated the pressure of his melancholia, there at East Dereham where he had been taken in the grip of severest depression—alleviated it the more because in imagining the inevitable defeat of Anson's long-suffering mariner (whose struggles alone are the subject of the short record which John Johnson read out to him from Richard Walter's *A Voyage Round the World by George Anson*) he was also able to foresee the welcome finality of his own death and understand that to sink beyond recall is at least to be freed from the ordeal of staying afloat.[9] But we should always be wary of casting Cowper simply as a figure of despair and as a refugee from despair. He is altogether bolder and more positive than that. In a letter written shortly after his arrival in Norfolk he had identified himself with a 'solitary pillar of rock' along the coast, left at the high water-mark by the crumbling cliff:

> I have visited it twice, and have found it an emblem of myself. Torn from my natural connections, I stand alone and expect the storm that shall displace me.[10]

In 'The Castaway' the 'solitary pillar' miraculously still stands, and with it, writ large, the other prominent features of this impressive short statement—lucid imaginative intensity, resignation, personal experience stripped to its bare essentials and universalized through symbolic representation (the pillar symbolizes Cowper's isolation, his isolation symbolizes the grandeur and the pathos, the mixture of infinite strength and infinite vulnerability, potential in all men and their 'being'), the strange delight and satisfaction which poets can find and deliver in their sufferings.

*   *   *   *   *

On 19 March 1799, the day before he began 'The Castaway', Cowper finished the English translation of his Latin verses entitled 'Montes Glaciales'. 'On the Ice Islands, seen Floating in the German Ocean' is an obvious preliminary to his greatest lyric, and crucial to an interpretation of his mind during this last phase of his creative life.

The genesis of the poem closely resembles that of 'The Castaway'. A newspaper report on the sudden appearance of icebergs in the German Ocean, read out to him some weeks earlier,[11] fired Cowper's imagination in the same way as the incident related to him from Walter's *Ansons's Voyages*, though producing a less direct type of self-reference. In contemplating the strange occurrence, this unnatural natural phenomenon, he is, as so often in his poetry, 'spectator both and spectacle', seeing and reflecting himself in the object of his attention. The most important instance of this interplay between self and subject comes at the end of the verses, where he contrasts the icebergs with Delos, Apollo's wandering island, and then commands them back to the realms of Bleak Winter, their true abode:

> Delos bore
> Herb, fruit, and flow'r. She, crown'd with laurel, wore,
> E'en under wintry skies, a summer smile;
> And Delos was Apollo's fav'rite isle.
> But, horrid wand'rers of the deep, to you
> He deems Cimmerian darkness only due.
> Your hated birth he deign'd not to survey
> But, scornful, turn'd his glorious eyes away.
> Hence! Seek your home; no longer rashly dare
> The darts of Phoebus, and a softer air;
> Lest ye regret, too late, your native coast,
> In no congenial gulf for ever lost!

> (ll. 53–64)

In ordering those of 'hated birth', those scorned by the Deity, to their 'Cimmerian darkness' Cowper, at least subconsciously, chooses darkness as his own true home. Desire for that 'peaceful shore . . . "Where tempests never beat nor billows roar"', which had still remained in view in the poem on his mother's picture, has been displaced by outright recognition of

a very different 'native coast'. The sun and 'softer air' are now
designated as alien, 'uncongenial' ('no congenial coast'); and
by this assertion Cowper has taken a real step towards that
imaginative commitment to a harsher, turbulent sphere that
allows him in 'The Castaway' to win affirmation out of the very
jaws of disaster.

   'On the Ice-Islands' shows Cowper preparing to hug the
desolation and lasting strife of his existence to him. At the same
time he bids farewell to old joys and consolations, old selves, old
ways of experiencing the world. The references to the paradisal
fertility and brightness of Delos, laurel-crowned isle of pure
delight, recall the saving happiness and benign stimulation he
had once found in poetry and in nature—a nature which had in
Book VI of *The Task* actually worn for him 'under wintry skies,
a summer smile'. But that happy Muse of Cowper's earlier
career, that gift of Apollonian freedom and light, has departed,
and the imagination seizes upon, and is seized by, the 'uncouth
forms' and portentous creations of Bleak Winter:

> He [Winter] caught and curdled, with a freezing blast,
> The current, ere it reach'd the boundless waste.
> By slow degrees uprose the wondrous pile,
> And long-successive ages roll'd the while;
> Till, ceaseless in its growth, it claim'd to stand
> Tall as its rival mountains on the land.
>
> (ll.37–42)

There is nothing before in Cowper like this fascination with
Nature's sublime power, except in the description of the oak's
growth from 'embryo vastness' to 'matchless grandeur' in
'Yardley Oak' (which is in any case itself a fairly late poem,
written in 1791). In *The Task* the sterner aspects of nature—
storm and earthquake—had been manifestations of God's
anger at a faithless age;[12] here Nature is the presiding Presence,
to whose terrible beauty (we have 'Aetna's burning womb' as
well as the 'wondrous pile') the poet responds with awe,
enacting the primitive, or 'daemonic',[13] nature-worship which
his Christian conscience had caused him to reject at the
beginning of 'Yardley Oak':

Relicts of ages! Could a mind, imbued
With truth from heav'n, created thing adore,
I might with rev'rence kneel and worship thee.
                    ('Yardley Oak', ll.6–8)

In 'On the Ice-Islands' 'truth from heav'n' no longer holds
sway over Cowper's mind. Like Adam after he has tasted the
fruit he knows not God, let alone the atoning 'meed of blood
divine' ('Yardley Oak'), but unlike Adam he plunges 'gloomy
into gloom' (ibid.) without remorse, taking a delight in the
'portents' that 'ride . . . th'astonish'd tide' (ll.1–2), in the
apocalyptic disturbance suggested to him by their 'rivalry' with
the mountains, and in the primeval and pagan landscapes to
which they transport him (Delos and the perpetual night of the
Cimmerii are but two of the allusions in this—for Cowper—
exceptionally myth-crowded poem).[14] This is a new self, out of
which 'The Castaway' came: a self so far from the light of
hope—from God, Christ and grace, from the bosom of familiar
nature, from the help of friends and the shelter of home—as to
be past hopelessness, freed from uncertainty, unflinchingly
alert to the darkest mysteries. The intentness with which he
views the 'horrid wand'rers of the deep' is matched by the
intentness with which he views the no less disturbing wonder of
the castaway's fate.

        *   *   *   *   *

'The Castaway', however, stands apart only in this, the
completeness with which Cowper penetrates the theme of
darkness and destiny. Much of his poetry had rung the changes
on this theme—quietly in 'On the Receipt of my Mother's
Picture', obliquely in poems such as *John Gilpin*, forcibly in
'Lines written during a Period of Insanity', which foreshadows
'The Castaway' in its determined self-command and self-
assertiveness, though not the frenzy that is thereby just held in
check:

> *Him* [Abiram] the vindictive rod of angry justice
> Sent quick and howling to the centre headlong;

I, fed with judgment, in a fleshly tomb, am
                Buried above ground.
                    (ll. 17–20)

Like many of Cowper's 'works of affliction', these are the lines
of a resourceful and articulate poet—witness above all the final
climactic extension of the idea of 'living death' first introduced
by the play on 'quick' (which is of course both adverb and
epithet, *alive*). The sapphic metre places the experience as far as
possible from the representative and shared,[15] but it is
impossible all the same to consign it to the realms of case-
history, or be in any other way comfortably detached, when a
subjective condition is so powerfully objectified and generalized as in that trailing image of mental torment as physical
torture, where food becomes an instrument of punishment, the
flesh a burial-cell, and life an agony of confinement.

This poem is the perfect example of how potentially overwhelming affliction prompted Cowper to creative achievement.
'The Shrubbery', written at about the same time, presents its
other face—enervation, low vitality. At first in this poem he
seems to be complaining of inner turmoil, of too much energy
within—'How ill the scene that offers rest,/And heart that
cannot rest, agree!' (ll. 3–4)—yet it soon becomes clear that his
problem is really the lack of inward pressure, *too little* feeling.
The flat, unresponsive adjectives by which he picks out the
salient feautures of the landscape find their explanation, in
stanzas three and four, in his reference to an emotional
stasis—an undynamic melancholy—which casts its dim shadow over all things and cuts him off from the life around him:

    This glassy stream, that spreading pine,
        Those alders quiv'ring in the breeze . . .

    But fix'd unalterable care
        Foregoes not what she feels within,
    Shows the same sadness ev'ry where,
        And slights the season and the scene.

    For all that pleas'd in wood or lawn,
        While peace possess'd these silent bow'rs,

> Her animating smile withdrawn,
>> Has lost its beauties and its pow'rs.
>>> (ll.5–6,9–16)

Cowper talks specifically of his loss of 'peace' but in that loss is involved, more importantly, the loss of inspiration and active pleasure—the power to release nature's power. His 'care' is not so much restlessness as blankness, a dreary absence.

Here perhaps is the source of Coleridge's classic Romantic lament for lost reciprocity:

> My genial spirits fail;
> And what can these avail
> To lift the smothering weight from off my breast? . . .
> I may not hope from outward forms to win
> The passion and the life, whose fountains are within.
>
> O Lady! we receive but what we give,
> And in our life alone does Nature live . . .
>> ('Dejection', ll.39–41,45–8)

The same recognition is explicit in Cowper: 'the life' resides within, and once withdrawn leaves nature devoid of its 'beauties' and its 'pow'rs'. 'Ours is her [nature's] wedding garment, ours her shroud'. Yet this thematic correspondence between 'The Shrubbery' and 'Dejection' serves only to highlight in the present context a major distinction between the two poems. 'Dejection' is a self-contradictory work in that its sheer intellectual and perceptual vigour, apparent at every turn, belies the poet's surface-claims to a 'wan and heartless mood' of creative impotence. The 'dull pain' and 'unimpassion'd grief' *do* 'move' and 'live'; abundant life is created out of a condition of seeming lifelessness—a life extending even to a vivid sense of the joy-in-nature of which the poet himself stands dispossessed:

> To her may all things live, from pole to pole,
> Their life the eddying of her living soul!
>> (ll.135–6)

There is no such paradox about 'The Shrubbery'. Except for the fine prosaic strength of the odd phrase here and there ('fix'd unalterable care' . . .), the poetry all conforms to the sad unvital state that is being described. Cowper simply concedes his forlornness, a true victim of 'wan and heartless mood' whose instinct is to accept a cheerless confinement:

> Me fruitful scenes and prospects waste
>   Alike admonish not to roam;
> These tell me of enjoyments past,
>   And those of sorrows yet to come.
>
> (ll. 21–4)

He discovers no appetite for action—for contemplative 'roaming' in past and future, or for creative journeying of any kind. In a sense 'The Shrubbery', uninspired and leading nowhere, already follows the lines of the admonishment with which it concludes, 'not to roam', not to act, not to do. From beginning to end Cowper is bound down by his inescapable 'care'. To be 'buried above ground' did not always promote the poet in him.

Yet whatever their poetic success, their triumph in embracing and realizing individual human experience, the 'Lines' written during a time of insanity are themselves representative of a kind of paralysis, or non-progression, fairly typical of Cowper. There is no psychological advance: the poem ends where it began, in a completer sense of the 'wretchedness' from which it set out and with the poet more captive than ever, seeing himself as not just pursued but actually entombed (as in 'The Shrubbery' he finds himself admonished on all sides not to venture from the confines of his 'white', now faintly comfortable melancholy lest it be increased by reminders of 'enjoyments past' or predictions of 'sorrows yet to come'). No poet occupies the prison-house of the self more habitually or more variously than Cowper. Even 'The Castaway' is not altogether about being free, but rather about being so absolutely inured to the condition of the 'shut-in' that he is able as it were to stand on the outside of the walls looking knowledgeably in.

*   *   *   *   *

'Verses supposed to be written by Alexander Selkirk' is among the most interesting examples of this characteristic Cowperian confinement. '*Supposed*' is right. 'Negative capability', the power of denying self and inhabiting minds distinct from one's own, was never one of Cowper's gifts; and sure enough his personality and needs come everywhere to the fore in this monologue, sometimes threatening all semblance of dramatic objectivity. The reflections in stanza three are patently more applicable to Cowper than to a desert-island castaway like Selkirk:

> Society, friendship and love, . . .
> How soon I would taste you again!
> My sorrows I then might assuage
> In the ways of religion and truth, . . .
> (ll. 17, 20–2)

No real castaway would be likely to consider how he might calm his sorrows *after* he has returned to civilization—least of all a castaway whose main complaint has been the sheer loneliness, the 'solitude', of this 'horrible place' (ll. 5–8). Cowper, with his long-standing need for comfort even in the midst of 'Society, friendship and love', here intervenes directly in the poem, virtually displacing his 'supposed' character altogether. Elsewhere he speaks more in unison with the character, but no less personally: 'Ye winds that have made me your sport, . . ./O tell me I yet have a friend'. The voice is unmistakable.

Certain moments in the poem do, it is true, transport us unforgettably to Selkirk's island, to experience the strange, disconcerting effects of silence and desolation:

> I am out of humanity's reach,
> I must finish my journey alone,
> Never hear the sweet music of speech;
> I start at the sound of my own.
> The beasts that roam over the plain,
> My form with indifference see;
> They are so unacquainted with man,
> Their tameness is shocking to me.
> (ll. 9–16)

This would not be 'equally good whether in verse or prose' despite Wordsworth's assertion to the contrary when praising the 'natural language' of this and other parts of the poem.[16] The stanzaic form and anapaestic measure ('distant' and 'edgy' in itself and therefore all the more appropriate as a vehicle for abnormal impressions) are put to specially effective use in the fourth and last lines, where the sense is simultaneously rounded off, concentrated, and suddenly stretched—'wound up' in both meanings of the phrase—to create twin centres of focus, points of intensity. By so prominently coupling 'start' (a signal departure from the controlling trisyllabic rhythm), 'sound', and 'own' on the stress, the metre plays an important part in realizing the weird sensation of distinctly registering what is ordinarily so familiar as to be unnoticed. In the last line the perfect logicality of the experience, felt in the speaker's preceding straight statement of circumstance, is dramatically cut through by the unexpected illogicality of a 'shocking tameness'.

Yet still there can be no doubt that the monologue is, from start to finish, an utterance from, and definition of, Cowper's own island of isolation and self-consciousness; an island on which he was regularly marooned, and from which he ceaselessly reached out for solace. The 'ways of religion and truth', as in the Moral Satires, seem to offer a priceless support: 'Religion! what treasure untold/Resides in that heavenly word!' (ll.25–6). But that 'heavenly word', so over-enthusiastically proclaimed, rings hollow in the mind's emptiness, which is then moreover only increased by further thoughts of religion, as the imagined sound of 'the church-going bell' tolls the poet-outcast back to his sole self:

> . . . the sound of the church-going bell
> These vallies and rocks never heard,
> Ne'er sigh'd at the sound of a knell,
> Or smil'd when a sabbath appear'd.
> (ll.29–32)

The 'treasure untold' amounts to no more than the routine ceremonies of funeral and Sunday service but even these simple consolations, representing the normal round of social existence, are known merely as something absent, something lost. What does fill and electrify the void, of course, is the fantastical image of being broken in upon by the shattering sound of one's own voice, or of dwelling in a shockingly primitive and alien world. Cowper cannot, however, live by the subterranean side of his imagination, to which such images belong. Perhaps to do so would mean being, or going, mad; for there is something so intolerably real and immediate about the apprehensions of aloneness and disorientation in stanza two as to suggest how easily Cowper's waking life might turn to nightmare. Be that as it may, it is certain that he seeks the milder regions of community and faith, and equally certain that they are beyond his reach. Not only do the thoughts of religion rebound on the poet, but (in the penultimate stanza) belief in his capacity for creating imaginary joys—a sort of mental escape-route from his 'solitary abode'—fails before his more forceful sense of dereliction:

> How fleet is a glance of the mind!
> Compar'd with the speed of its flight,
> The tempest itself lags behind,
> And the swift wing'd arrows of light.
> When I think of my own native land,
> In a moment I seem to be there;
> But alas! recollection at hand
> Soon hurries me back to despair.
>
> (ll.41–8)

The latter part of this resembles an idea expressed in another poem about despair and the struggle to overcome it—Wordsworth's 'Resolution and Independence': 'As high as we have mounted in delight,/In our dejection do we sink as low'. The difference is, however, that Cowper's emotional reversals are inevitable and recurrent rather than arbitrary and sudden. The same pattern of action and reaction, movement-out and turning-back, repeats itself throughout the poem—from the very first verse, in which expectant claims to freedom, privilege, and command ('I am monarch of all I survey . . .') yield to dismay at the horror of solitude ('Better dwell in the midst of alarms,/Than reign in this horrible place'). Thus the processes of the poem, which are the processes of the poet's mind, are themselves like being on an island of extremely restricted bounds; an island where there is some room for manœuvre but no chance of journeying far, and none of breaking out.

One way of dealing with being shut in is to reconcile oneself to the confinement, to settle down with things as they are. This is what finally happens in these 'Verses':

> But the sea-fowl is gone to her nest,
> The beast is laid down in his lair,
> Ev'n here is a season of rest,
> And I to my cabin repair.
> There is mercy in every place;
> And mercy, encouraging thought!
> Gives even affliction a grace,
> And reconciles man to his lot.
>   (ll.49–56)

For once there is no recoil, but rather a steadying motion, a levelling into balance and rest. Heeding nature's lesson and discovering kinship with it, the mind now finds access to a condition of repose. Selkirk's comforting insights—that there is always a 'season of rest', that mercy exists everywhere, that the thought of mercy makes even affliction acceptable—are also Cowper's insights. But what do these insights amount to exactly? What kind of repose is being imagined and achieved? A temporary one—a *transient respite*, even though it may be enjoyed daily. Just as Selkirk goes off to his cabin-enclosure to receive the passing release of sleep, so Cowper extricates himself from restless thoughts *for the time being* by taking refuge in the encouraging recognition that no suffering is absolute or unbearable. He is left with his 'affliction' and 'lot', reconciled and at peace but not free of them.

*   *   *   *   *

In 'Verses supposed to be written by Alexander Selkirk' the consciousness of the shut-in poet becomes the subject of an apparently impersonal poem. Elsewhere in Cowper the psycho-drama of confinement is more directly expressed, and not least in certain of the Olney hymns. Religious poetry— Herbert's 'The Collar' or 'Affliction', Charles Wesley's 'Wrestling Jacob', Madame Guyon's 'A Figurative Description'— regularly brings into focus the tribulations of the soul, and not least the desire to burst free from psychic imprisonment, whether of unbelief ('My chains fell off' is how Wesley describes his discovery of Christ)[17] or of faith and subjection to God ('Forsake thy cage' is Herbert's rebellious cry in 'The Collar'). This aspect of the Christian experience is especially prominent in Cowper.

Lodwick Hartley discovers a definite sequence in Cowper's contributions to the *Olney Hymns*, representing the 'various stages of the poet's struggle for faith: an ebb and flow, but withal a progression'.[18] But while it is true that the series culminates in a cluster of hymns celebrating God and the rewards of Christian endeavour, this seems very much the result of formal arrangement and planned intent rather than a register of real spiritual change. 'The Christian' for example, which should according to Hartley's theory be a climactic triumph of confidence and joy, is typical of the cold (though by no means incompetent) conventionality of these later pieces:

> A kingly character he bears,
> No change his priestly office knows;
> Unfading is the crown he wears,
> His joys can never reach a close . . .
>
> (ll.5–8)

There is no majesty in this 'kingly character', no lustre in his 'crown', no feeling in his 'joys'. Cowper's true, convincing voice is to be found, almost without exception, in expressions of longing, uncertainty, desperation, weakness. What his hymns most powerfully realize is not so much even a 'struggle for faith', but the struggles of a mind for which assured faith, and the repose that goes with it, are impossible.

'Hark, my soul! it is the Lord', one of the very best of Cowper's hymns, is a good instance of this. The Lord speaks words of comfort and encouragement in the mind of the 'poor sinner', appealing first to the evidences of past experience:

> I deliver'd thee when bound,
> And when wounded, heal'd they wound;
> Sought thee wand'ring, set thee right,
> Turn'd thy darkness into light.
>
> (ll.5–8)

In the mind: for the poem is an inner monologue in dialogue form—the poet seeking reasons for loving and leaning on

Christ, which is to say for believing in the strength and profitability of his relations with the Saviour. The verse just quoted, not least its imagery of wounding and wandering, healing and setting right, brings straight to mind the 'stricken deer' passage in Book III of *The Task* where Cowper makes rather more obvious trial of the stabilizing possibilities of Christian faith (which stabilizes and gives direction to his existence) and of recollection (which stabilizes and revivifies his faith). This he follows up with what sounds like an argument in favour of trusting to the permanence of Christ's tender protection of those he has once delivered:

> Can a woman's tender care
> Cease towards the child she bare?
> Yes, she may forgetful be,
> Yet will I remember thee.
>
> Mine is an unchanging love . . .
>   (ll.9–13)

But of course this is actually no argument at all. It offers an unverifiable assumption, that whatever may happen in human relationships—and even the strongest love can fail—Christ will remain always constant. In fact, that Christ's is an 'unchanging love' and 'glory' a sure inheritance ('Thou shalt see my glory soon . . . Partner of my throne shalt be', ll.17–20) must be, for the individual concerned, an inner conviction which no amount of external comparison or logic can prove. (The classic dramatization of this fact of Puritan life is Christian's despondency and recovery at Doubting Castle, where reasoning from texts and the *exempla* of former deliverances cannot free him, only the 'key of Promise' that is *in his bosom*.)[19] And heart-felt conviction is precisely what Cowper lacks, not only at the beginning of the poem (hence the soul-debate, the pursuit of assurances) but at the end. The final stanza discovers a self which, despite the encouragements of the voice of faith, is still radically uncertain of its state and standing with Christ:

> Lord, it is my chief complaint,
> That my love is weak and faint;

Yet I love thee and adore,
Oh for grace to love thee more.
(ll.21–4)

All notion of continuing and everlasting peace collapses in a cry
of frustration.

We may contrast this with the end of Herbert's 'The Collar',
in which the irresistible claims of simple submission to the
Lord's paternal care arise suddenly to calm all passion:

But as I raved and grew more fierce and wild
        At every word,
Methought I heard one calling, 'Child',
        And I replied, 'My Lord!'.

Instead of supplying a point of rest, a welcome refuge from
doubt and constant questioning, the relationship between self
and Saviour is in Cowper a source of increased anxiety. He is
troubled above all of course by a sense of personal inadequacy—his love is 'weak and faint'. In the text for this hymn
(John xxi.16) Peter replies to the Lord's 'Lovest thou me?' with
a simple 'Yea, Lord, thou knowest that I love thee'. Cowper
cannot himself give the straight answer, Yea: although he
protests his love and adoration ('I love thee and adore'), he is
deeply conscious of his inability to measure up to the demands
of Christ's own Love. Needless to say, this is a perfectly proper
Christian frame of mind. How many have been as certain of
themselves as Peter? Yet the 'correctness' of Cowper's attitude
makes his condition no less a condition of stress, and no less a
condition of failure in relation to the preceding process of
attempted self-assurance. The evidences of the past, assertions
of Christ's faithfulness, promises of glory, come to nothing;
comforting words give way, powerlessly, to discomfort. On
careful inspection, moreover, it is clear that this discomfort
does involve much more than an apprehension of insufficiency.
That Cowper should cry out for 'grace to love thee more'
indicates just how helpless he is, and how distant from an ideal
state of grace, a true oneness with Christ. He does not love
Christ as he feels he should; but only Christ can do anything
about it, by a favour which he may or may not grant. All
Cowper knows for sure is the relative barrenness of his spiritual

life. There could be no more evident 'confinement' than is
expressed in this stanza: whatever may be said of God's service,
in which lies 'perfect freedom', to be in the Lord's keeping can
mean entrapment in the toils of insecurity, blindness, and
self-doubt. The poet's explicit complaint is against his own
weakness, but the poem itself is an implicit accusation of the
Faith that binds and torments him.

'Hark my soul' expresses spiritual unease. 'The Contrite
Heart', which will be our other example, explores it. The
essence of this poem is conflict, emerging first of all in a clash
between received knowledge—the scriptural promise that God
will 'revive the heart of the contrite ones' (Isaiah lvii.15)—and
an experiential bewilderment that makes the assurance of text,
or *logos*, the starting point, not for any easy or conventional
thoughts of redemption, but for a desperate confrontation with
personal doubt:

> The Lord will happiness divine
> On contrite hearts bestow:
> Then tell me, gracious God, is mine
> A contrite heart, or no?
>
> (ll. 1–4)

Isaiah's consoling and guiding words bring only confusion, like
those of Christ in 'Hark my soul' but sooner rather than later.
The certain fact, carrying all the authority of the Bible, that
God will bestow happiness where happiness is due breeds in
Cowper an immediate uncertainty as to his own position—and,
I think, not a little exasperation at being left unhappily in the
dark, extending even perhaps to a flicker of resentment in that
all too emphatic '*gracious* God'. (And if Cowper intends no irony
in this phrase, the nature of his condition as he communicates it
undoubtedly supplies one for the reader: how truly 'gracious'
can this God be who burdens the individual with suspense?)
Then begins a process of self-examination and meditation on
experience which leads the poet further into the morass of
discontent:

> I hear, but seem to hear in vain,
> Insensible as steel;

If ought is felt, 'tis only pain,
To find I cannot feel.

(ll. 5–8)

This could refer either to an habitual failure of response/ inward reward in hearing God's Word or to the present moment itself, his current inability to find much-needed comfort in the Word as mediated through Isaiah. But in any case it repeats, and defines with a rare deliberateness, an opposition wholly characteristic of Cowper: the opposition between, on the one hand, desire, correct procedure, favourable circumstance (he listens to and values the Word as 'believers' do and should) and, on the other, experience and emotion, the inner event that confirms, even intensifies (thus the 'pain'), the silence and emptiness from which he would escape. It is not simply that nothing happens when he hears God speak. Such numbness would be bad enough, but he also suffers the anguish of actually feeling that he 'cannot feel'. And not only is he talking about things that happen to him. They are happening to him as he writes the poem; his complaint of painful nonresponsiveness is, in its relation to the promise of 'happiness divine', an example of just the reaction of which he complains. Thoughts of a possible joy have led to joyless thoughts. He is hopelessly shut in.

But the poem is not yet half over, and perhaps Cowper does in turn reverse this spiritually negative direction, breaking through to a happier state of mind. Far from it. In the third stanza he focuses sadly upon a division in his personality, seeing himself as literally of two minds, one 'inclin'd' to love God and the other 'Averse to all that's good' (ll. 9–11). If (as with comparable sentiments at the end of 'Hark my soul') this seems no more than a conventional confession of unworthiness, then we must bear in mind Cowper's insistence, especially in the next two verses, that he tries his best to be 'at one' with God and goes readily through the prescribed procedures of a good Christian life—without, however, any return for his efforts and commitment. He supplicates, he says, for renewed spiritual strength ('. . . I cry, "My strength renew" . . .'), but is left feeling 'weaker than before' (ll. 15–16); his best intentions are consumed in unanswered prayers, his strength is ironically exhausted in fruitless appeals for greater strength. He describes how his attendance at the gatherings of God's people leaves him still comfortless:

> Thy saints are comforted I know,
> And love thy house of pray'r;
> I therefore go where others go,
> But find no comfort there.
>
> (ll. 13–16)

These movingly understated lines carry more conviction than any expression of joy in Cowper's hymns. How poignantly does the tired yet emphatic 'I know' concede the futility of mere knowing. How acutely do the direct, unelaborated second two lines echo the familiar disappointment, the flat routine of meaningless observance. And how much is said by being left unsaid; for there can be no severer privation than to find 'no comfort' where others are comforted, no greater isolation. Clearly, the self here expressed is a captive-victim, both of his feelings and his 'faith'. The latter yields only anxiety and desolation; God does not help him and he cannot help himself, his nobler energies are spent in appealing to apparently deaf ears or are changed to frustration, the meeting-house— standard refuge and required resort of the faithful—becomes for him a place of loneliness.

Now, the one remedy for a condition like this is an inward revolution, a radical change of heart. Theoretically it could take the form of breaking with God altogether and rejecting the religious prescriptions for living which have proved such a painful burden. Already we have noted a trace of exasperation, even accusation, that evokes this possibility. But it is no more of a *real* possibility for the author of the Olney hymns than it is for Mark Rutherford's Zachariah Coleman whose refusal to question Divine Authority, even in the midst of the most pressing sense of injustice and personal torment, is perhaps the finest imaginative rendering of the Calvinist's characteristic denial of self:

> [He believed] that the potter had power over the clay—. . .
> and that the thing formed unto dishonour could not reply
> and say to him that formed it, 'Why hast thou made me

thus?' . . . Darkness, the darkness as of the crucifixion night, seemed over and around him. Poor wretch! he thought he was struggling with his weakness; but he was in reality struggling against his own strength.[20]

For Cowper, as for Coleman, to 'protest' would be 'a sin'; he must go the way of God and Religion, and not his own way. The only acceptable solution to his uncertainty and inner conflicts is for belief/knowledge/understanding and feeling/experience/ instinct to be brought together *on the formers' terms*—for the latter to be transferred, as it were, to the proper side of the breach. But that change, like everything else, lies in God's hands alone; and so Cowper ends where he began, pleading now more desperately for God to decide his doubts for him by making him either joyful or sensible of a contrite state, by breaking his heart if needs be and, if necessary, healing it:

> Oh make this heart rejoice, or ache;
> Decide this doubt for me;
> And if it be not broken, break,
> And heal it, if it be.
>
> (ll.21–4)

The explosive imperative 'make' signals the fierceness of Cowper's desire for resolution, the subsequent passive verb-forms stress his helplessness, his inability to bring that resolution about. So acute is his frustration that he would willingly trade it for a shattered personality. Shattered, presumably, before it is remade. But can there really be any guarantee of remaking where God already seems indifferent (at least *that*) to the poet's well-being? 'Ache' and 'break', centralized by the rhyme and so tremendously literal, are the salient words in this act of self-expression. Aching and breaking are the fate Cowper can truly understand and envision; and indeed the emotional life of 'The Contrite Heart' is itself predictive of that fate. Between *thoughts* of being 'heal'd' and *felt apprehensions* of being painfully destroyed the imprisoned Cowper still restlessly, and very uneasily, swings.

Patricia Meyer Spacks rightly stresses the relative 'bareness' of style in this and others of Cowper's best hymns.[21] 'The Contrite Heart' has but one obvious metaphor, 'Insensible as

steel', which, like a brief Metaphysical conceit, uses provoca-
tive point-to-point comparison to specify and defamiliarize an
interior state—a cold, hard, unbending resistance to sensation,
an insensibility so extreme as to be distinctly felt. For the rest,
we have, in Coleridge's definition, 'the neutral style, or that
common to Prose and Poetry', a 'uniform adherence to
genuine, logical English'. Some of the effects gained from this
style, in conjunction with the operations of the stanzaic form,
have been noted during our interpretation of the poem.
Examples could be multiplied: the contrast-in-balance of 'I
sometimes think' and 'But often feel' in stanza three, for
instance, which gives so clear an impression of the endless
unequal strife that lies at the centre of the poet's experience; or
the epigrammatic compression and precarious, almost 'dislocated' syntax of the final two lines of the poem which makes
them so climactically pointed as an expression of a tension
bordering on distraction. 'Donnean' is Spacks's term for the
taut economy of the final verse, and we may recall that it was a
Metaphysical poet, Herbert, who, in his less 'conceited' and
'fantastical' mode, supplied Coleridge's main examples of 'the
neutral style'. But while Cowper's hymns were seemingly
influenced by the aggressive confessional toning and expressive
compactness, and the linguistic 'purity', to be found in
seventeenth-century devotional poetry, their more immediate
background and context is eighteenth-century hymnology
itself. Herbert is mentioned by Cowper but Isaac Watts
attracts high praise: '. . . a man of true poetical ability . . .
frequently sublime in his conceptions and masterly in his
executions'.[22] And if Watts's hymns do not possess the
psychodramatic texture we have encountered among Cowper's, then there is always Charles Wesley:

> Other refuge have I none,
> Hangs my helpless soul on thee:
> Leave, ah! leave me not alone,
> Still support, and comfort me . . .
>   ('In Temptation')

Wesley of course is never as introverted as Cowper. He
celebrates longing and delights in his helplessness. Yet much of
the work of these two poets stands in essentially the same

relation to the hymnological tradition that Watts did so much to establish. Both base their style in the virtues of 'prosaic strength, exactness and urbanity' (Donald Davie)—the energizing vigour of 'Hangs' and the revivified 'Still' are evidence enough of Wesley's superb control of just those poetic resources we have often distinguished in Cowper.[23] But more important, each in his way appropriated this style to the articulation of markedly individual and subjective states and experiences, though without compromising the function of the hymn as a vehicle for public, communal worship. They retain the impersonality of the 'tribal song' and at the same time personalize it in the strictest sense.

Not that this personalization always takes place in Cowper's hymns, or that Wattsian sobriety is always their root idiom. The language of the 'Dissenting' community emerges in other, stranger forms—not least the baroque sensuousness of hymns like 'Praise for the Fountain Opened':

> There is a fountain filled with blood
> Drawn from Emmanuel's veins;
> And sinners, plung'd beneath that flood,
> Lose all their guilty stains....
>
> (ll. 1–4)

Reflected here is the not uncommon readiness of those of Cowper's persuasion—amply sanctioned by the Old Testament—to press their enthusiasm for the Redeemer and redemptive experience to a level of extreme, even sensual physicality ('yearning bowels' was a favourite image).[24] It may be argued, as Norman Nicholson does, that the lines make us 'aware of rituals even older than the Old Testament: of the dying god of the fertility cults and of primitive symbols that probe deeply into the subconscious mind'.[25] And at the level of more civilized ritualism they served, and in the 'stricter' Dissenting chapels still serve, when sung, as a valuable means of 'rebinding' the congregation (or 'Church') through a shared act of dedication to a highly separate order of experience; they have, in other words, the force of a liturgy. For the uninitiated reader, however—even one as sophisticated as Spacks—the effect of the physical specificity of Cowper's imagery, with its insistence on the source of blood in *veins* and on the baptismal bath of purifying blood, is likely to be a 'shocking ... grotesquerie'.[26] Spacks in point of fact develops her criticism of this effect by reference to our probable difficulty in 'making the transition from image to meaning', due to Cowper's over-concentration on what *is* (Christ's body) at the expense of what it signifies or stands for ('*Redeeming love* has been my theme', says Cowper later). But the problem is, I think, one of religious sensibility rather than lack of tact or procedural/aesthetic awareness in the writer, for nobody steeped in the formulaic literalness of the Dissenting imagination in its dealings with the Redeemer would be concerned with 'meaning' in this context. Involvement in the 'image'—the form of words and the mode of apprehension they embody—would be total. 'Praise for the Fountain Opened' is a fine hymn—in an idiom that is alien to us.

On the other hand, there are passages which admit of no such appeal to the peculiar 'world' of the gathered church. The very last hymn of the Olney series, more a contemplative poem than a congregational 'song', offers clear examples of Cowper's occasional faults as a religious lyricist:

> What! has autumn left to say
> Nothing of a Saviour's grace?
> Yes, the beams of milder day
> Tell me of his smiling face.
>
> Light appears with early dawn,
> While the sun makes haste to rise,
> See his bleeding beauties, drawn
> On the blushes of the skies.
>
> ('I will praise the Lord', ll. 13–20)

The emblematizing of the first of these stanzas could hardly be flatter. The inertness of the personification of autumn and anti-climax of 'smiling face' can be safely put down to a straightforward failure to revitalize conventions without our looking for any deeper significance in Cowper's inability to be inspired in the presence of the Saviour, although that inability does remain relevant to our overall view of the Hymns as being 'unprogressive' and void of evidence of spiritual fulfilment. The other weakness is the lack of imaginative daring, in images like that of Christ's 'bleeding beauties, drawn/On the blushes of the skies'. Certainly, the image is also 'imperfectly controlled' (Spacks). Spacks's appeal to Johnson's stricture on Metaphysical wit is apt enough in relation to the clumsily paradoxical 'bleeding beauties' and concept of the dawn's 'blushes': 'heterogeneous ideas . . . yoked by violence together'. But her favourite criticism of Cowper's imagery, again based on Johnson, surely misses the point. The claim is that such images thrust themselves too concretely on our attention, drawing it 'inexorably to the "original" rather than the "secondary sense"'; or in Johnson's words, 'the force of metaphors is lost when the mind by the mention of particulars is turned . . . more upon that from which the illustration is drawn than that to which it is applied'.[27] In fact the lines in question have insufficient both of concrete particularity and figurative density, and inadequate fusing of the realms of the actual and the spiritual. We are made aware of the beauty of the dawn and the 'beauty' of Christ's wounds, the 'bleeding sacrifice'—but only vaguely, rationally, in one-dimensional linguistic signs. The major shortcoming of the piece is not Cowper's 'extravagances' (Spacks goes too far in likening his images to Cleveland's decadent Metaphysical wit, 'my pen's the spout/Where the rain-water of mine eyes runs out'), but the fact that he is too careful, too systematic, too detached in his spiritualization of landscape and response. So much so that we are as conscious of what he does not do as of what he does. What would Vaughan or Crashaw, or the Puritans Jonathan Edwards and Thomas Sherman, or the later Wordsworth ('Lines composed on an Evening of Extraordinary Splendour and Beauty' comes to mind) have made of the metaphoric potential, totally ignored by Cowper, of 'Light', 'sun' (= 'Son'), and 'rise'?[28] There is no sacramental vision in 'I will praise the Lord', merely a set of logical 'religious' equations.

'I will praise the Lord' can hardly be what Fausset had in mind when maintaining that 'of all the hymns Cowper wrote . . . those come nearest to pure poetry in which God is invoked through Nature'.[29] Perhaps he was thinking of the opening of one of Cowper's very finest hymns, which succeeds precisely where 'I will praise the Lord' fails:

> God moves in a mysterious way,
> His wonders to perform;

He plants his footsteps in the sea,
And rides upon the storm.
                    ('Light shining out of darkness', ll. 1-4)

The short, clipped 'common metre' of the old metrical psalms is
not easily made to 'move' with such stateliness, in cadences
that evoke the colossal majesty of an ubiquitous God. Scorning
the bounds of an inherently small and narrow measure, the
vowels ('moves', 'mysterious' . . .) draw themselves out in a
simultaneous embodiment of admiration and purposeful
Might, and also allow the weightier 'plants' and 'rides' to stand
out with peculiar distinctness. By attracting so much of the
reader's power of brief visualization these two single words
contribute no less to the memorability of Cowper's image of the
Deity—which has of course become part of the popular, and
not only religious, consciousness—than do the metre itself and
the epigrammatic cast of the opening formulation with its
appeal to man's abiding sense of the Incomprehensible. It is an
image, moreover, in which the realm of concrete actuality and
the realm beyond the physical are totally fused. God is
experienced as both nature and numinous force.

   To Johnson the idea of devotional poetry was a contradiction
in terms: 'the sanctity of the matter rejects the ornaments of
figurative diction'.[30] 'God moves in a mysterious way' both
supports and challenges this attitude, for, though not
'ornamented', it is *plainly* rich in figurative power and content.
Again and again the literal and the metaphoric—*logos* and
mythos—are inextricably one in Cowper's mode of perception.
'Deep in unfathomable mines/Of never failing skill', 'His
purposes will ripen fast,/Unfolding ev'ry hour', 'Blind unbelief
is sure to err,/And scan his work in vain' are not just 'homely'
or 'familiar' illustrations of religious truth; each is a concrete
apprehension of the physical world which is also, indivisibly,
an apprehension of the sacred and spiritually true. God's skill is
as man's but 'deeper' (*unfathomable*) and boundless; as well as
ripening like buds, His purposes unfold even Time itself (for
Unfolding is both transitive and intransitive); His work is there
for all to see, yet it requires an act of faith to see it aright. *This* we
may indeed call sacramental perception—not visionary and
transcendent as in (say) Blake's later 'prophetic Books', but

one in which the natural and supernatural are merged without yielding their separateness.

Now, we may obviously approach such hymns as rhetorical acts—attempts at communicating basic Christian truths, and at involving the believer, individually and as a member of a congregation, more fully in the emotions and experiences of a Christian life.[31] For this view we have the authority of Isaac Watts himself, who explained his own aim as that of appealing to, and defining, 'the Variety of our Passions ... as they are refined into Devotion', while also exercising 'the Mind ... that we might all obey the Direction of the Word of God, and *sing his praises with understanding*'.[32] In his discussion of Watts, Johnson contends that a hymn-writer is placed at an insuperable disadvantage by the very nature of his material—fixed, 're-vealed' Truth that cannot be added to or interpreted freely: 'The paucity of its topics enforces perpetual repetition. ... It is sufficient for Watts to have done better than others what no man has done well.'[33] But we do better, surely, to stress the artistic energy and quality of response that Watts, Cowper, Wesley, and the rest *did* bring to their limited and limiting subject-matter—if indeed it is all that circumscribed and restrictive when, as Watts remarked and even those selected hymns we have looked at from Cowper bear out, it includes not only doctrine but 'The most frequent Tempers and Changes of our Spirit, and Conditions of our Life, ... our Love, our Fear, our Hope'. Watts's own best hymns are less densely textured than Cowper's, nobly rather than intensely 'plain', but it is easy to see the connections, both of purpose and execution:

> Sweet fields beyond the swelling flood,
> Stand drest in living green;
> So to the *Jews* old Canaan stood,
> While Jordan roll'd between ...
>> ('There is a land of pure delight', ll. 9–12)

> A thousand ages in thy sight
> Are like an evening gone;
> Short as the Watch that ends the night
> Before the rising sun ...

> Time like an ever-rolling stream

Bears all its sons away . . .
('Our God, our help in ages past', ll. 17–20, 25–6)

Watts, we find, uses similes—there are four in these two and a
half stanzas—where Cowper (*moves . . . rides, Deep . . . unfathomable*, '. . . is sure to *err*') favours the more complex metaphoric
technique depending on the fusion of literal/physical and
figurative/spiritual meanings. There is, nevertheless, the same
sustained reliance upon brief visualization ('Sweet fields
beyond . . .'), the same appeal to basic emotions (in Watts
aroused and carried along especially by the lingering thrust of
the present participles) and to the reader's experience of the
concrete world, and the same gift for renewing familiar
religious sentiments and images without analysing or arguing
them, without questioning their inviolability as sacred truth.

'God moves in a mysterious way' is a notable success even at
the simplest level of 'church' use—the conveyance of tenet,
text, and didactic wisdom. The whole hymn is a persuasive
articulation of John xiii.7, 'What I do thou knowest not now;
but thou shalt know hereafter . . .'; and throughout it the most
commonplace sentiments concerning the hidden benignity of
God are given immediate freshness, whether in some sudden
audacity ('The clouds ye so much dread/Are *big* with mercy,
and shall break/In blessings on your head') or milder wit
('Behind a frowning providence,/He hides a smiling face').
And, as the first of these two examples makes particularly clear,
Cowper's province is as much experience as tenet, as much the
Christian's special 'Conditions of . . . Life, . . . our Love, our
Fear, our Hope'. Like Watts, he teaches 'being' no less than
'knowing', providing not only an ideology but also, in the range
of experiential reference in the series as a whole, an interpretation *and* model of existence. In the end, moreover, the
perceptual content—the chaste sacramental vision—of a hymn
such as 'God moves in a mysterious way' constitutes an integral
and primary aspect of that model. His apprehension of a soul in
yet beyond all things, which is the living, active God, operates
in fundamentally the same way as Watts's spiritual pictures of
the land of pure delight or of God's conquest of Time; it at once
reflects, improves, and fixes the 'practical imagination' of the
community. 'Teaching' is hardly satisfactory to describe a

function of this kind. The best hymns *nourish* and *purify* the life of the tribe. They are sacred texts of a secondary order, beneath the Bible but, like it, a collective 'possession' that is both repository and source of doctrine and existential wisdom.

Try as we may, however, we could never properly limit our interpretation of 'God moves in a mysterious way' to the hymnological and tribal context. It is also a text within the drama of mind formed by the major body of Cowper's poetic texts and letters, our experience of which will inevitably influence its meaning. As Samuel Greatheed, writing in 1800, seems to have perceived, the hymn is 'personal' in a very special sense: 'Our departed friend conceived some presentiment of this sad reverse [the breakdown of 1773]; and during a solitary walk in the fields, he composed a hymn'.[34] Greatheed, the Evangelical preacher, presumably intends to emphasize Cowper's faith in the ultimate 'rightness' of God's mysterious ways. If this is so, then we would need all Greatheed's own eagerness to make a point favourable to 'the cause' to be able to accept his reading with any degree of comfort. Considered more objectively, statements like 'He treasures up his bright designs' and 'Behind a frowning providence,/He hides a smiling face' take on a grim irony in the light of the coming 'sad reverse' and Cowper's past history of melancholia, whose symptoms had always included a paranoid fear of being singled out for some final and terrible fate, the victim of a decidedly *dark* design. But there is no need to invoke either biography or text-as-autobiography to appreciate the underlying precariousness of the individual's state of being-in-the-world as it is conceived and expressed in this poem. Cowper's insistence that everything will turn out for the best—'But sweet will be the flow'r'—stands in irreconcilable tension with the overall idea of 'sovereign will', of God's actions and purposes being God's own business. A tension peculiarly conspicuous in the final stanza, where the suggestion in the first two lines that there is something opposite from 'Blind unbelief' ('perceptive belief') which will *not* err or scan God's work in vain falls before the last emphatic declaration that 'God is his own interpreter,/And *he* will make it plain'. God may, quite logically, stay silent if He wishes or, more terrible, move positively against the individual's felt interests; which takes us back of course to the

unhappy shut-in of 'The Contrite Heart', the prisoner of
passiveness who is so tormented by suspense when God refuses
to act at all that his imagination grasps ultimately at the
perverse release of total inner destruction.

   In 'The Contrite Heart', at least, authoritative religious
truths, both the scriptural promise of happiness divine *and*
God's inalienable right to be His own Interpreter, are *in their
experiential consequences* severely questioned. The promise is in
the poet's experience (though not in his understanding) simply
untrue, and the necessity of waiting for God to 'make it plain' is
challenged by the impatient will to know and feel unambiguously, to be master of oneself, which surfaces from deep
within the very advocate of human frailty and subservience.
Understandably, this hymn appears (so far as I know) in no
collection other than the original one: it turns Belief into
prison-walls which it then undermines. 'God moves in a
mysterious way' emerges in practically every book of English
hymns, for it works magnificently on the levels of consolation
and straightforward celebration of Providence, even while
acknowledging the 'bitter taste' of a Christian's fears. But that
it can operate in this way—and that it can be seen in relation to
'The Contrite Heart' as a sign of victory over former doubts—
makes it no less expressive at bottom of the uncertainty of the
believer's situation and no less charged with ironic undercur-
rents that necessarily 'feed in' from the larger psycho-drama of
Cowper's works.

   It is difficult to see why Spacks should contend that 'the state
of "strength and peace", of enjoyment, calm, cheer, . . . is
Cowper's most potent vision' in his hymns.[35] There *are* sweet
memories: 'What peaceful hours I once enjoyed'. Intimations,
too, of some future repose: 'Calm and serene my frame'. And he
rises on occasion to a note even of present contentment:

> The calm retreat, the silent shade,
> With pray'r and praise agree;
> And seem by thy sweet bounty made,
> For those who follow thee.
>   (*Retirement*, ll.5–8)

Yet this simple, sincere hymn of thanksgiving to 'Author and
Guardian of my life', in which to be shut up in a world of silence

is indeed a blessed peace and to be dependent is to be the recipient of 'sweet bounty', and where desire (*pray'r*) and obedience (*praise*) exist in total harmony one with the other, is among four hymns written earlier than the rest—at the time of Cowper's conversion during the mid-1760s. Cowper's dream was of a return to the innocence and happiness of the new convert; the reality—his most 'potent vision'—was of strife, loss, insecurity, need, vulnerability, and of course (I think again of 'God moves in a mysterious way') such counterparts as courage and patience. The distinction is suggested in fact by one of his own later hymns, 'The New Convert', which acknowledges pain as the inevitable consequence of being a dedicated Christian. The new-born child of gospel-grace grows like 'some fair tree' beneath 'EMMANUEL's shining face':

> No fears he feels, he sees no foes,
> No conflict yet his faith employs,
> Nor has he learnt to whom he owes
> The strength and peace his soul enjoys.
>
> (ll.5–8)

but the realm of 'fears' and 'conflict' must soon be entered:

> Comforts sinking day by day,
> What seem'd his own, a self-fed spring,
> Proves but a brook that glides away.
>
> (ll.10–12)

The realization that 'strength and peace' spring from Christ/ God and not the self, which is valued as a necessary and major advance in the life of the Christian, also paradoxically means the *loss* of 'strength and peace', of simple instinctive confidence and all those comforts that fade day by day. The active happy child of grace, who '*Lifts up* his blooming branch on high' (l.4), becomes the helpless target of sin and guilt with no more control over his well-being than over the passing brook. To be a grown-up Christian and know the Lord more fully is to exchange unselfconscious joy-in-faith for self-conscious and God-conscious tribulation: it is to live out a painful second Fall.

And that is the focus, the lesson, the collective force, of Cowper's hymns. There can be no doubt that Cowper knows of an abundant recompense for his lost innocence. In 'The New

Convert' itself suffering is not seen as the terminus of maturation, but as a stage beyond which lies an alert and thankful
conviction of personal salvation. God draws our ebbing
comforts low—

> That sav'd by grace, but not our own,
> We may not claim the praise we owe.
>   (ll. 19–20)

Thus, like the Miltonic version of individual and human
history, Cowper's hymns do assume a divine plan which
includes earthly as well as heavenly joys and stability. The
point is, however, that 'the paradise within' is always for
Cowper purely notional. Experientially understood, the Olney
hymns of 1771–2 are nowhere a record of the third phase of the
divine plan. The condition that on the whole informs them is,
we might say, the reverse of that of Cowper's own Christian: his
anxious subjectivity 'can never reach a close'.

*   *   *   *   *

In moving to 'The Castaway' from the hymns the first thing we
notice is perhaps the stanza-form itself, consisting of the
familiar 'common metre' of eights and sixes—a favourite with
both Cowper and Watts—but extended by a final octosyllabic
couplet. We have seen already how the simple rhythmic and
rhyme pattern of the form allows individual words and phrases
to be given concentrated force. Here, however, there is a further
important effect. The relentless but hesitant pulse of the
four-line unit constitutes what might be termed the rhythm of
'stressful continuity', while the momentarily climactic (or
suspensive) emphasis of the couplets suggests, at the close of
each stanza, the constant possibility of sudden ending. The
'music' of the poetry enacts both the described event and the
poet's psychological involvement in it.

By 'described event' I do not mean just the repeated rise and
fall of the sea and the mariner's body, though this is always
present either in the background or, as the instant of drowning
approaches, in the fore:

> He long survives, who lives an hour
>   In ocean, self-upheld;

    And so long he, with unspent pow'r,
        His destiny repell'd;
    And ever, as the minutes flew,
    Entreated help, or cried—Adieu!
                    (ll.37–42)

In the split lines and recurrent 'up and down' of the iambic
measure the motions of wave and victim inextricably merge.
But physical phenomena are the least of what we witness. The
shape and movement of the verses also enforce a sense of the
mariner's shockingly basic situation and responses. The dominant, unstoppable rhythms of the poem are the rhythms of an
irresistible force, the energies of Nature and of Fate; their partial and temporary arrestment at 'self-upheld' (where the
preceding comma breaks up the flow of the verse) mirrors the
castaway's fundamental helplessness in the face of his destiny.
On another, more conspicuous level, however, they are the
rhythms of his own doings, sufferings, and reactions—above all
of a battle to sustain life, which at this point fades into desperate
entreaties for help and cries of farewell. All the flow and ebb of
slowly failing strength and hope is caught in the see-saw
balance of that last line: 'Entreated help, or cried—Adieu!'.
The verse endings often depict life in a symbolic attitude,
usually with the same mixture of pathos and respect for the
nobility of man: the mariner's romantic gesture of farewell—
Adieu—is in keeping with the heroism of his long fight against
destiny, and with the heroism of mind which allows him to
understand his ship-mates' haste to save themselves even
though . . . bitter felt it still to die/Deserted, and his friends so
nigh'.
    Yet our immediate concern is not with this representational
force and concentration but with the fact that each ending
could so easily be the last—is momentarily felt as terminus. It is
not simply that the protagonist could go under at any point. So
could the poet himself; for all his control, his mind and creation
are always at risk. In the 'stressful continuity' and potential
termini, the haltings and the willed forwards-thrust, of 'The
Castaway' we witness Cowper's own endeavour as he propels
himself among images of his life and death, his past and present
destiny, any one of which might 'sink' him. The insecurity of his

'floating home', the hostility of fate, the 'lasting strife' of solitary struggle against despair and spiritual death, the ineffectual aid of friends, the certainty of doom—Cowper re-views his whole sad existence in a brief span, breasting the dangerous surges of gloomy self-centred vision. Perhaps the best register of the tension involved in this encounter with the salient features of a *telos* of oppression and strife is the relaxation that comes, at length, with the perception of a final end, a completion:

> . . . and then he sank.
>
> No poet wept him: but the page
> Of narrative sincere,
> That tells his name, worth . . .

(ll. 48–51)

The relief is obvious: the 'lasting strife' of self-contemplation is over.

'The Castaway', then, operates on the same three levels that often, though never so overtly, intersect in Cowper: 'phenomenal'—the level of narrative, story, 'described event'; authorial psycho-drama—the process of self-contemplation and the contemplation of personal history; universalization—the level at which the specific events and subjective drama of mind take on general human significance. We have already considered the first stanza in some detail: preliminary scene-setting that becomes a figurative induction establishing both a private dimension—'such a destin'd wretch as I'—and a broader perspective, 'a whole view of human life and destiny'. Narrative appears to come emphatically to the fore in stanza two, which consists largely of circumstantial detail couched in an elevated language suggestive of romance:

> No braver chief could Albion boast
> Than he with whom he went,
> Nor ever ship left Albion's coast,
> With warmer wishes sent.
> He lov'd them both, but both in vain,
> Nor him beheld, nor her again.

(ll. 7–12)

Yet there is in the concluding couplet a reassertion of the claims of human interest, over those of narrative itself and of elegiac or patriotic tribute. As in *Lyrical Ballads*, 'the feeling ... developed gives importance to the action and situation, not the action and situation to the feeling ...'. The natural prominence and weight of a self-contained verse-unit thus positioned, together with the shift to a 'simple' style after the relative extravagance of the personification of the mythological Albion and the passive syntax of line four, promote a steady attention to the 'truth' and emotional lesson of the tale—to the cruelty of fate, the permanence of death the final parting. And personal history, too, is present even here. Cowper's identification of himself with his nominal subject in the previous stanza—'such a destin'd wretch as I'—and the framework of imagistic self-reference built up by the body of his poetry makes it impossible not to construct a mental equation between 'ship'/sea-voyage and the poet's own journey through life.

The next stanza is a comment by Cowper upon his whole past existence:

> Not long beneath the whelming brine,
>   Expert to swim he lay;
> Nor soon he felt his strength decline,
>   Or courage die away;
> But wag'd with death a lasting strife,
> Supported by despair of life.
>
>   (ll. 13–18)

Like the mariner Cowper had waged an unending struggle against death—death of the spirit. But as epitaphs generalize personal history and personal qualities, so does his poetry distil emblematic truth out of the particular experience of the 'castaway', who is now indivisibly both self and narrative subject. The style—lean, compressed, drily suggestive—owes much, obviously, to Cowper's practice in the art of hymn-writing (and something too, as we shall see, to Pope's *Homer*); nothing is superfluous, everything exact and potent. The negative grammatical structures at the beginning of the first and third lines, for example, are anything but a means of filling out the metre. They force us to register and to exclude alternatives. The castaway *might* have lain 'long' beneath the brine and so suffered a quick end, he *might* 'soon' have lost his strength and courage. But he does not: weight is thus thrown on the extraordinary length of his strife and upon the extent of his resistance. Cowper highlights, more fully than ever before, not simply human capacity or the instinct for survival, but the interplay of strength and vulnerability of which for him the individual's condition, his 'being-in-the-world', always essentially consisted.

There is of course a certain desperate irony even in Cowper's recognition of the individual's strength and courage. They serve but to prolong the agony of drowning. They are themselves elements in the field of forces that rule and imprison suffering man; 'felt' as something separate from the conscious will, things which come and go, 'decline' and 'die away', in their own good time, they are as much beyond his control as the external pressure of the 'whelming brine'. Yet this is to see only half the picture. Such chilling pessimism is not altogether the impression that the poetry leaves us with, for, however painfully ambiguous in their nature and result, strength and courage do retain their usual signification of nobility. Throughout the stanza, and nowhere more obviously than in the concluding couplet, the urge to celebrate is hard pressed by a sense of pathos but is never quite stifled. 'But wag'd with death a lasting strife,/Supported by despair of life': the pathos is that death will win anyway, and that the nearer death comes the more man clings to life ('despair of life' is a difficult formulation which suggests a foretaste of certain death as well as fear of losing life). But for all that the image remains one of heroism; there is a grandeur in the beat of the line and the 'plain and simple sublimity' of the phrasing that controls pity in favour of respect. Cowper's spectacles of affliction, impasse, strife, are never merely depressing, if only because he is so unerringly frank about the brutal facts of the situation, and so sensitive, too, to the very mysteriousness of why man should suffer and yet 'love life'. Nowhere, however, is there anything as inspirational as in 'The Castaway'. It is not only that Cowper keeps faith with the castaway's defence of life, but that he finds within himself the capacity to embrace all that is darkest in the darker side of existence. Stature in adversity is not just an attribute of the mariner-castaway, nor of a past self whose resilience Cowper unashamedly values; it belongs also to the poet-castaway of the continuous present whose vision of self and of life subdues all the pressure of negation, whether of despair, or self-pity, or the denial of hope, into its own positive, tersely rich perspectives.

So the poem continues to its climax, balancing pathos with celebration, recognition of man's imprisoned state with a tough respect for those qualities of mind and instinct by which his condition may be opposed though never escaped; and always the sober logicality and generalizing properties of the style turn the particular into the universal, to the point where we forget that we are witnessing what is after all an extreme and selective version of reality. In the fourth stanza one short phrase—'pitiless perforce'—is all Cowper needs to push home the wider implications inherent in his narrative:

> . . . nor his friends had fail'd
>   To check the vessel's course,
> But so the furious blast prevail'd,
>   That, pitiless perforce,
> They left their outcast mate behind,
> And scudded still before the wind.
>   (ll. 19–24)

The almost casual aside gathers all the latent suggestiveness of the surrounding words and phrases. 'Nor ... had fail'd': his shipmates *had* tried to help him (as Cowper's friends had and were still doing) but their generous impulses are useless against the determined hostility of Nature (where 'prevail'd' suggests warfare, the action of an adversary). Though 'outcast' reminds us that the story is of Fate's predetermined plan for the destruction of a single life, we are nevertheless brought to a sharp awareness of the limitations of all human action however nobly motivated—our weakness in a world that can itself be 'pitiless' in relation to our best desires. This same insight is then extended and complicated as attention swings to the point of view of the 'victim' himself:

> Nor, cruel as it seem'd, could he
>   Their haste himself condemn,
> Aware that flight, in such a sea,
>   Alone could rescue them;

Yet bitter felt it still to die
Deserted, and his friends so nigh.
                            (ll.31–6)

The force of the sea ('. . . in such a sea') is still the ruling
influence but to this is added the influence of self-interest.
Selflessness falls before the demands of self-preservation no less
than those of exterior phenomena—we are as much prisoners of
ourselves as of the world we inhabit. And the 'lesson' that we
thus perceive in the actions of the crew is mirrored in different
form in the mariner's own frame of mind. Neither can *he* avoid
thinking of himself, bitterly, in spite of his understanding; in his
case the prison-house of the self, the web within the larger web
of outer forces, takes the shape of an inner conflict in which
resentment clashes with acceptance and open-minded resignation. Or, to see it another way, the mind too is an eternal
battleground, a theatre of stress over which no man has the say.
Still, that moment of understanding stands to the castaway's
credit, just as surely as does his physical endurance 'self-
upheld'. His situation brings out the best in him.

The same can be said of Cowper. If he is 'broken-hearted' at
all when writing 'The Castaway',[36] it is the broken-heartedness
for which he longs in 'The Contrite Heart', the state of feeling
and knowing unambiguously, of being beyond doubt. The
stress of the emotions is everywhere met by a spontaneous
self-possession which allows him to bid a wise, impressive,
dignified, though moving, farewell to his life and art—a
farewell in which he sees his own 'melancholy' life as a species
of heroism. This will seem an odd word to apply if we share the
common assumption that Cowper takes a sentimental or
self-indulgent attitude towards his predicament in the closing
lines of the poem. But the assumption is wrong, especially when
we take the penultimate stanza into account. Here Cowper
declares that his purpose has not been to write an elegy on
Anson's mariner—to give the 'melancholy theme' of *his*
death-struggles 'a more enduring date'. Of course, in a sense he
does do precisely that. Who would have heard of the episode
had it not been for Cowper, despite the fact that in theory 'tears
by bards or heroes [Anson] shed/Alike immortalize the dead'
(ll.53–4)? 'The Castaway' is, whatever else, a memorial to a

nameless person, replete with the traditional elegiac ingredients of tribute and compassion. But no one could ever believe this to be the point of the poem. So why should Cowper raise the matter at all? In order, it seems, to stress by contrast his subjective motivation and concerns:

> But misery still delights to trace
> Its 'semblance in another's case.
>
> (ll.59–60)

The 'delight' that accrues from tracing the likeness of his own fate in the fate of another is more than the relief of pent-up feelings—the catharsis—to which Charlotte Brontë for one refers, although that is clearly an element in the poem. Nor is it merely the curious pleasure that sufferers find in measuring lots with fellow-sufferers. Cowper's delight includes finally a delight in the singularity of his case, the monumental proportions of his 'perishing'. In the end the difference between himself and the mariner-castaway becomes more important than the similarity:

> We perish'd, each alone:
> But I beneath a rougher sea,
> And whelm'd in deeper gulphs than he.
>
> (ll.64–6)

This is a much grander image of self than that of the boxed-in victim of 'Lines written during a Period of Insanity' or the crippled vessel of 'On the Receipt of my Mother's Picture'. The effect of the sudden reversal, 'But I', is to elevate the poet's own struggles, as well as his suffering—to make him the protagonist in a battle against incomparable odds, in the turmoil of inner strife, the depths of soul-anguish, the abyss of despair. The bareness of the style prevents any strain of self-pity but there is yet a note of relish in Cowper's sense of all he has gone through, unaided and 'alone'. It is impossible to say for sure whether by 'perish'd' Cowper means 'cast out', 'damned', in a specifically religious sense: perhaps so if we take the preceding 'No voice divine . . . No light propitious' to mean the Calvinist God's refusal to save him from the 'storm' the Calvinist God has created, perhaps not if we see these phrases as evidence of

Cowper's immersion in a pagan Homeric world of numinous powers and presences—a likelihood we shall note in a moment. Either way, what is clear is that Cowper's focus is all upon the 'roughness' and 'depths' of *his* life's journey, and that he draws a personal stature from them. If God is there at all in the poem, He is present only as the instrument of the situation: 'The Castaway' makes the self the centre of the universe. It is the self's tribute to its own suffering and to its own steadfast resilience and resourcefulness in facing the immense challenge of being-in-the-world and of going-out.

It has never been realized, I think, that in 'The Castaway' Cowper identifies not only with Anson's mariner but also with the Homeric Ulysses, 'much-afflicted, much enduring', whose battles with Fate, as described in Pope's translation, exercised almost as strong an influence on his imagination as the more obvious source-passage in the *Voyages*:

> Far on the swelling surge the chief was born: . . .
> At length emerging, from his nostrils wide
> And gushing mouth, effus'd the briny tyde.
> Ev'n then, not mindless of his last retreat,
> He seis'd the Raft, and leapt into his seat,
> Strong with the fear of death. The rolling flood
> Now here, now there, impell'd the floating wood. . . .
>   (Pope's *Homer's Odyssey*, V,405,411–16)[37]

No brief quotation can in fact do justice to the degree of Cowper's indebtedness (in other 'sea poems' besides 'The Castaway') to the style and content of Pope's *Homer*; in particular to the herio-romantic toning of the language ('chief', 'destin'd wretch', 'propitious', 'expert to', 'voice divine', 'adieu', '[lasting] strife', 'billows roar'd', for example, all appear in Pope) and the theme of the fated wanderer living strenuously in larger-than-life confrontations with the forces of Destiny and Providence, a theme articulated in the above passage, as it is in 'The Castaway', in the strain between verbs of personal 'doing' ('seis'd', 'leapt') and verbs signifying the action of impersonal and hostile forces ('was born', 'impell'd'). 'At length', 'not mindless': such inconspicuous formulations show just how far into detail the debt does penetrate (though the latter negative construction, which thrusts attention onto

Odysseus's extraordinary presence of mind, is much nearer to Cowper's astute usage, in 'not long' and 'nor soon', than the former phrase, which has none of the meaningfulness of 'At length' at line 43 of 'The Castaway'). But the one big difference between the Homeric and Cowperian narratives lies in the shape of the story itself, for Odysseus of course comes home safe again, having been rescued from the rage of the sea in the quoted episode by the intervention of the divine messenger, Leucothea, who foretells the future end of his torments—'Fate decrees thy miseries shall end'. The only message that comes to Cowper the convinced castaway is from his own memory of his fatal dream: '*Actum est de te, periisti*'—'We perish'd, each alone'. Yet this, the reverse-ending, merely turns the notes to tragic. Developing and coming face to face with the habitual 'truth' of his own dark imagination, the poet of 'The Castaway' found a last home within its confines. In solitary struggle and a solitary death he discovered not only horror but privilege; from the archetypal figure of the 'much-afflicted' and 'much enduring' hero-sufferer he took for himself a last positive identity.

An ageless identity, moreover. The dead 'immortalized' by 'The Castaway' is above all the poet himself. Cowper's fate is far from the kind Odysseus fears in a moment of despondency during the storm—to be 'un-noted, and for ever dead'.[38] By a familiar paradox, in recording how he perished he gives himself an enduring voice and presence. The hero of *The Pilgrim's Progress* had come to eternal life by passing through the River of Death; Cowper finds it by 'going under'. Never more than in 'The Castaway' does his poetry justify his destiny, affliction and all. By a superb irony, he achieved through art what he long felt was denied him by God—a life of value and a life after death.

Postscript

One recent reinterpretation of eighteenth-century English literature suggests a surprisingly apt historical context for at least one major theme of Cowper's poetry as we have experienced it, though Cowper figures all too fleetingly in its pages as the 'caged poet' of 'On the Death of Mrs. Throckmorton's Bulfinch'. W. B. Carnochan's *Confinement and Flight*[1] is an impressive and successful attempt to 'claim the eighteenth century for modernity' by identifying the twin concerns of 'entrapment and escape' within a wide range of texts from *Cooper's Hill* to *Rasselas*. While the question of what constitutes 'modernity' is both larger and more vexed than Carnochan ever admits, yet there can be no doubt that he brings something important to our attention: the metaphor of the prison, its variants and corollaries, are basic to our own way of understanding and experiencing the world. The opening words of Joseph Heller's *Something Happened* (1974), 'I get the willies when I see closed doors', are not so much a sign of madness as a sign of the times; times in which, to take an example from routine academic life, it requires a special effort of 'historical imagination' *not* to sympathize with the Satan who is his own dungeon—'Which way I fly is hell; my self am hell'. The 'prison-house of the self', what Victor Brombert terms 'the descent into a private hell, immurement within the confines of the mind, the oppression of madness, the experience of Time and Nothingness'—it is this (and certainly not God's 'infinite wrath') which casts it shadow over our sleeping and our waking lives.[2] But it is a destiny which fascinates as well as frightens us, which we delight to explore from the inside as well as flee from. Carnochan's literary criticism, and Brombert's, is no less an example of that fascination than Heller the novelist's sad, wise,

Notes and References begin on page 348.

but also seductively comic vision of circle upon circle of fear and frustration within the 'worlds' of work, family, love-rela-tionships, and above all inner personality.

Chandlerian knots of intrigue, 'midnight cowboys', Exor-cists and Omens, Star Treks to alien peoples whose lives turn out to be but versions of our own constrictions and aspirations can be safely let lie in favour of two further more literary examples. A major award for fiction was won not long ago by a novel that draws to an end as follows:

> Once in the street, however, he felt the certainty return; a cloud had lifted: the town, even the village when he finally arrived there, no longer held him. The shell had cracked.[3]

What the hero of David Storey's *Saville* has found release from is in fact not merely the restrictions of life in a small industrialized 'village' but the brooding, aimless, near-chaotic self which the pressures of home and community have fostered. 'The shell had cracked': he is 'reborn'. This is an apparently hopeful image, but the coda of the book then forces us to ask just what has been gained, if anything, by Saville's 'bursting out'—for all he seems to have won is the freedom to be carried along on the tide of events, to find life meaningless and without purpose. A 'faith in ... impossibility', he calls it; 'anything can happen'. The only 'salvation' the novel offers is an openness to an unknown and frankly unpromising future. In a sense the image of the shell cracking returns the work to its own beginning, the birth of the hero, and thus—perhaps—postulates a sequel that will be a repetition of the process of 'confinement and flight' already traced. The one positive thing we *can* acknowledge—the one reward and point of it all—is indeed the experience we have been taken through in reading the book, where we have inhabited an indisputably compelling world of psychic and social entrapment.

The Waste Land is not so far from *Saville* as might appear. There has been much argument about how pessimistic the end of Eliot's poem is, but it is a fact that, despite the 'damp gust/Bringing rain', his vision defies any attempt to perceive a future, a 'salvation', for the Individual and the Artist save that of a continual trafficking of self with self, sometimes lightheartedly and sometimes earnestly, amidst the ruins of a wrecked civilization. 'Each in his prison/Thinking of the key'—while the poet-speaker falls back into himself to contemplate unreal bats with baby faces, upside-down towers, reminiscent bells, or else moves headily outwards into a fragmented and dying landscape, becomes in Geoffrey Hartman's words 'solipsistic or seeming-mad'.[4] If we enjoy *The Waste Land*, then it is because, like the Saville who has emerged from his shell, we can enjoy the perverse liberty of knowing 'things are bad' and of having both everywhere and nowhere to go—especially when the space through which we pass is as richly and finely wrought as *The Waste Land* itself.[5]

On Eliot's own admission, *The Waste Land* was written under an impetus derived from the modern advance of psychology, the 'science of mind';[6] and the 'psychopoeic' drive of twentieth-century literature generally—its 'making' and exploration of interior landscape—is undoubtedly related to that advance. But of course our ambivalent relationship with 'the confines of the mind' can be tracked back much further into the past. It has become something of a critical commonplace to associate 'the weary genius of modernism' (Paul Zweig) with consciousness of self and to situate its first manifest stirrings in the Romantic assault on the deprivation that follows from Locke's version of mind as screened off from ultimate reality, receiving only shadowy projections of things as they are. The Romantic sought the distant ideal in the familiar face of things, relocating the attributes of godhead—Wordsworth's 'creation, power, divinity itself'—in the individual imagination as a prerequisite for restoring more than mechanistic value to the world and being-in-the-world. Yet that is to say that Romanticism is no less aware of the vulnerability of self than of its potentiality. No one, for example, pays more varied tribute to the vitality of the inner man than Coleridge, in oneiric visions, accounts of imaginative-organic form, celebrations of the interdependence of man and nature as counterparts in the One Life, or therapeutic journeys whereby the mind transforms prisons of its own making into spirit-healing nooks; but nowhere, either, are there clearer pictures of the inevitable shadow-side of this reliance on creative selfhood, the view of self as bereft of power to the point of death-in-life—or so helpless as to be in need of the supportive organization of an institution for the mentally unsound:

> ... a new charitable institution ... for lunacy and idiocy of the will, in which, with the full consent of, or at the direct insistence of the patient himself ... such a person ... might be placed under medical and moral coercion. I am convinced London would furnish a hundred volunteers in as many days.[7]

Nowhere clearer pictures of the shadow-side ... except in Cowper himself. Quoting also Goethe's belief that the world will turn into 'one huge hospital where everyone is everybody else's humane nurse', Philip Rieff finds in Coleridge's idea of 'a new charitable institution' a representative prefiguring of our favoured mode of social and cultural organization in our 'deconverted' state: 'it may not be possible to organize our culture again as an unwitting dynamic of moral demands claiming the prerogatives of truth ... Where family and nation once stood, or Church and Party, there will be hospital and theatre too'.[8] The derelict Coleridge who saw himself as a suitable case for treatment and the 'insane' Cowper who knew what an asylum was like are predictions of our commonest fears and fantasies. Their capacities for balancing, diverting, absorbing—and making capital out of—their anxieties foretell our more knowing, and more institutionalized, abilities for doing so.

Is it in Blake that feelings of entrapment first become those explicitly of the Poet?

> With sweet May dews my wings were wet,
>   And Phoebus fir'd my vocal rage;
> He caught me in a silken net,
>   And shut me in a golden cage.
>
> He loves to sit and hear me sing,
>   Then, laughing, sports and plays with me;
> Then stretches out my golden wing,
>   And mocks my loss of liberty.
>   ('How sweet I roamed', ll.9–16)

In this Carnochan observes 'one *topos* of the old world, that of the happy man, irresistibly yielding to one of the new, that of the captive artist', and goes on to remark that 'In God's service used to be perfect freedom, but no longer, especially not when the God is Phoebus Apollo'.[9] But anyone who has ever read Herbert or Donne, or Cowper or Bunyan, will know that God's service had been no sort of freedom at all—especially not when the God is the Calvinist God. There are at least two *topoi* in question, and that of the predestined solitary of Puritan tradition, so massively present behind Cowper himself, seems by far the more obvious and important. Even the evident sensuous pleasure that Blake finds in being 'played with' by his god was not unknown to a religion which produced Watts's 'The Church and Garden of Christ' ('I come, my Spouse, I come, he crys,/With Love and Pleasure in his Eyes'), or indeed to an Evangelical Anglicanism which offers us Wesley's 'Wrestling Jacob ('... touch the hollow of my thigh', 'I sink beneath thy weighty hand')—though it was unknown to Cowper, except in the ironic form of that serio-comic delight he takes in imagining the torture and deadly release of caged birds and shipwrecked mariners.

Thus can the theme of 'confinement and flight', being shut-in happily or unhappily or (more normally) both, be traced into the eighteenth century and beyond. Carnochan misses, I think, only one significant instance from that century: Gray, in whose work, as in Cowper's, the figure of the 'shut-in' looms strikingly large. Gray knew in his bones what Blake was to feel so exquisitely along the nerves in 'How sweet I roamed', and knew it as an interminable problem: that the Poet is doomed to perpetual isolation and confinement, free merely to sing of lost liberty and lost fellowship, of a bitter or bitter-sweet destiny. The eponymous hero of 'The Bard' can affirm his superiority over the conquerors of his race only by choosing to join his peers—who have all been put to the slaughter. 'Deep in the roaring tide he plunged to endless night.' It may be that, notwithstanding the irony of so truly pyrrhic a victory, the Bard's speech of defiance does offer a memorable celebration of the Poet's role as guardian of the spirit and aspirations of the nation. But the poem is set emphatically in an antique world, a bygone age; neither the role of national seer nor the grand heroic gesture—'To triumph and to die are mine'—is available to Gray as a justification for *his* existence in the mid-eighteenth century, although his envisioning of the former reflects his characteristic desire for positive ways of viewing poethood, just as the Bard's 'escape' into endless night represents an equally typical inability wholly to sustain the positive viewpoint, to leave it uncompromised and unimpaired. We remember that in 'Ode on the Spring' the retired poet, enthroned in 'rustic state', turns out on reflection to be after all but a 'Poor moralist . . . A solitary fly' whose life is wasted and empty; the knowledge of transience and mischance that is at first the measure of his superiority over the unthinking 'sportive kind' becomes in the end a means of degrading him, making him the sad and silent object of mild scorn, in a sudden switch to the values of *carpe diem*—'Thy sun is set, thy spring is gone—/We frolick, while 'tis May'. Such processes of negation are commonplace in Gray—as is the yielding of 'ethos' to 'psycho-drama' (involving here the perfect example of the loss of the *topos* of 'the happy man' to that of 'the captive poet'). The *locus classicus* is the *Elegy* itself: not content with a surpassingly eloquent statement of the great commonplaces of human life, he extended the poem to include that anxious portrait of the artist-outsider, 'listless', caught in the net of 'wayward fancies', and of inward-directed emotions, 'woeful wan', 'craz'd with care'.

In *The Romantic Poets* Graham Hough notes the centrality in Gray—and in Cowper—of 'negative' states of being, unrest, deficiency of joy, constriction, aloneness, 'despairs and frustrations'. To Hough, however, these states, these feelings, find at most a crude outlet, and are related to the difficulty of 'trying to be poets in a climate of feeling that did not suit what ought to have been their kind of poetry': 'When Shelley feels as Gray must often have felt, the result is "Stanzas written in Dejection". But the strong social sense of eighteenth-century poetry, its very good manners, made this kind of self-expression quite impossible. There was as yet no convention for communicating one's private griefs to the world'.[10] I would suggest of course that we reverse the emphasis: Gray, and especially the more lucidly and intently subjective Cowper, inaugurated the art of 'this kind of self-expression'. They were not so much poets with 'no convention' as the developers of a new one—the modern *topos* of the happy-unhappy 'shut-in'. They validated the isolated life of 'the sole self' as a poetic subject. Negative emotions and processes of negation do not necessarily mean inferior poetry: in so sadly discounting the consolations and kudos of the life of contemplative retreat in 'Ode on the Spring' Gray writes of course a poem at least as good as Pope's 'Happy the man', which warmly upholds them, while 'Ode on a Distant Prospect of Eton College' where he journeys from expectant feelings of rebirth—the 'gales' that blow across the landscape of memory seem to 'breathe a second spring'—to a 'paralysed' lament for the very fact of maturity ('Where ignorance is bliss,/'Tis folly to be wise') outlives literally hundreds of 'prospect' poems simply because it does realize an authentic human and psychological situation. And so it is with the 'despairs and frustrations' that pervade the poetry of Cowper. On the whole these are more compelling still, as well as more explicit, than Gray's projections of the captive self, developing at times indeed all the intensity of the satanic private hell. There is, surprisingly, no place in his work or vision for the conventional fire-and-brimstone Hell of Christian tradition: his 'deeper gulphs' and place of torment were above ground, a present reality. Whether directly ('The Castaway'), in acts of wide-awake self-consciousness ('The Contrite Heart'), in oneiric moods ('Lines written during a Period of Insanity'), or in dramatic form ('Alexander Selkirk'), he powerfully, variously articulates the dungeon-landscape of the most extreme of interior and lived confinements, making of it 'a poetry of life'—snatching affirmation from the jaws of denial.

The question of *why* western man should during the eighteenth century have become so acutely conscious of himself as a prisoner and of the world as a prison can hardly be addressed within the confines of this book. Were we to consider it, however, the first step might be to say that the fashionable approach, the 'structuralist' interpretation of history represented in the work of Michel Foucault and others, will bear little fruit in relation to Cowper; for how are we to understand Cowper's human and essentially religious imagination in terms of a language bent upon theoretical categorization of the concealed workings of a shift in society to a capitalist system of controls over the minds and actions of individuals—except that we might detect in Cowper's own apprehensions of the modern 'disease' of consumerism a traditional religio-moral response to the same restructuring that Foucault, with all the careful doubt and loving care of the enlightened empiricist, apprehends as an incipient machinery of subjection?[11] To Carnochan, the question directs attention primarily to 'the episode that more decisively than any other ushered in the modern world: the demolition of the closed world and its replacement by the infinite universe'—an episode issuing in the eighteenth century in God's retreat to the reaches of space and an accelerated change from a geocentric and anthropocentric cosmology to an awareness of an infinitude in some small corner of which man inhabits his '*petit cachot*', Pascal's 'little cell'.[12] It hardly needs saying that to this context of change Cowper can certainly be related, in a variety of interconnected ways. By locating 'pow'r divine' *in* nature, as well as behind and beyond it, he reconstitutes Divinity in a directly available form—and a form much more appealing to the modern mind, heir as it is to the scepticism of the Enlightenment, than the other major religio-philosophic effort of his poetry, the conservative defence of 'revealed religion', could ever engender. And by simultaneously cultivating the creative and spiritual potentialities of perception, which may reach from earth to heaven and transform this world too into another Eden, he participates in that project, so dear to one corner of modern consciousness, of transferring the limitlessness of the Creator to our own compound of body and imagination, substituting man for the retreating God. He makes his *petit cachot* a place of opportunity no less than of captivity, amplifying no less than regretting a tragic condemnation.

While stressing the poetization of the 'correspondence between imprisonment and the human condition' that took place in pre-Romantic and Romantic European literature, however, Brombert enters a salutary reminder of the antiquity of that correspondence itself: 'notions that the soul is tragically encaged in the body, that the body is tragically exiled in the world's prison, are commonplaces in the Gnostic, Christian, and Neo-Platonic tradition'.[13] With Cowper the relevant tradition is Calvinistic Christianity. Beside one of Brombert's main examples of the Romantic imaginative obsession—Alfred de Vigny's Pascalian lament for the terrible bondage of this life,

'Dans cette prison nommée la vie, d'où nous partons les uns après les autres pour aller à la mort'—we might place the opening words of *The Pilgrim's Progress*, 'As I walked through the wilderness of this world, I lighted on a certain place, where was a den ...'. The 'den' is glossed as 'gaol'. That Vigny's is a vision of a collective fate, a general 'tragic condemnation', where Bunyan knows a celestial world beyond the bounds of this wilderness and uses the den to envision the Christian's allegorical pilgrimage thitherwards, sets off the 'modern' mythopoeic imagination from a 'traditional' religious imagination; yet both conceive of life as privation and desolate confinement and equally both deny the implications of this conception by evoking, and themselves proving, the special creative possibilities of privation and confinement—the 'prison' that can be elaborately lamented, the 'wilderness' where one can lie down in a 'den' and dream one of the world's great books of spiritual endeavour. In Cowper, the Calvinist/religious viewpoint lies sometimes on the surface—the world as wilderness, subjection to the inscrutable will of God, the oppression of doubt—but more often it is submerged or altogether dissolved in imaginative readings of the world, revelations of the inner self, poetical dramas of mind, interplay between the haunted and the privileged imagination. In the light of Brombert's definition of Romantic and Modern by reference to 'favoured dialectical tensions between oppression and the dream of freedom, between fatality and revolt, between the finite and infinity',[4] Cowper stands out as Puritan but much more as Romantic and Modern.

Notes and References

INTRODUCTION

1. 'William Cowper', Boris Ford (ed.), *The Pelican Guide to English Literature: From Dryden to Johnson* (revised edn., London, 1968), p. 387.

2. Arthur Johnston, 'Poetry and Criticism after 1740', R. Lonsdale (ed.), *Sphere History of Literature: Dryden to Johnson* (London, 1971), p. 389.

3. Ibid., pp. 391–2.

4. Victor Brombert, 'Pétrus Borel, Prison Horrors, and the Gothic Tradition', *Novel*, ii (1969), pp. 151–2.

5. M. B. Forman (ed.), *The Letters of John Keats* (2nd edn., Oxford, 1935), p. 336.

6. *The Triumph of the Therapeutic* (Penguin University Books edn., London, 1973), pp. 4, 27, 34.

7. *Rambler*, no. 184; see also, *Rambler* 32, *Adventurer* 111, and *The Vanity of Human Wishes*, ll. 135–64, 343–68. One of the main themes of *Rasselas* is of man striving with difficulties in a life where 'all may suffer ... such maladies of the mind' as befall the astronomer, in whom solitude and fancy conspire to produce insanity (chaps. 43–4).

8. We may also note Eliot's accompanying apprehension of a collapsing civilization: *The Waste Land*, ll. 366ff.

9. Op. cit., p. 16.

10. Norman Nicholson, *William Cowper* (London, 1960), p. 18. This pamphlet in The British Council 'Writers and their Work' series should not be confused with Nicholson's book, *William Cowper* (London, 1951).

CHAPTER 1

1. *William Cowper* (London, 1960), p. 5.

2. *Memoirs of Cowper* (1803), p. 108.

3. Robert Southey (ed.), *The Life and Works of William Cowper*, 15 vols. (London, 1835–7), ii. 174; E. J. Morley, *Henry Crabb Robinson on Books and their Writers* (London, 1938), i. 72.

4. In *Letter on Bowles' Strictures on Pope* (1821); R. E. Prothero (ed.), *Works of Lord Byron: Letters and Journals* (London, 1898–1901), v. 558.

5. Francis Jeffrey, Review of Crabbe's *Tales*, *Edinburgh Review*, xx (July–Nov. 1812), p. 280; C. E. Norton (ed.), *Correspondence between Goethe and Carlyle* (London, 1887), p. 161.

6. See Norma Russell, *A Bibliography of William Cowper* (Oxford, 1963), p. xvii.

7. Letter to John Murray, 20 May 1820, in Prothero (ed.), *Letters and*

Journals, v. 25, and *Letter on Bowles' Strictures*, ed. cit., v. 556, 558.

8. For Hannah More's response to Cowper, see L. Hartley, *William Cowper: the Continuing Revaluation* (Chapel Hill, 1960), p. 5.

9. Russell, *Bibliography*, p. xvi.

10. *Critical Review*, liii (Apr. 1782), pp. 287–90.

11. *Monthly Review*, lxvii (Oct. 1782), pp. 262–5.

12. *Gentleman's Magazine*, lv (Dec. 1785), pp. 985–8.

13. *Monthly Review*, lxxiv (June 1786), pp. 416–25.

14. T. H. Banks Jr. (ed.), *The Poetical Works of Sir John Denham* (New Haven, 1928), p. 77. Various imitations of and references to these lines in the eighteenth century are recorded in this edition, pp. 342–50.

15. See J. O. Hayden, *The Romantic Reviewers* (Chicago, 1969).

16. *Gentleman's Magazine*, lv. 987.

17. *Gentleman's Magazine*, lix (1786), pp. 305–7.

18. J. D. Ferguson (ed.), *The Letters of Robert Burns* (Oxford, 1931), i. 260.

19. See Mary Lascelles, *Jane Austen and her Art* (Oxford, 1939), pp. 16–17, 43–6. A good example of the moral weight that Cowper possesses for Jane Austen is contained in Fanny Price's conservative reaction to 'fashionable' talk of 'improving' Sotherton in *Mansfield Park* (chap. 6): 'Cut down an avenue! What a pity! Does it not make you think of Cowper? "Ye fallen avenues, once more I mourn your fate unmerited."'

20. J. Shawcross (ed.), *Coleridge: Biographia Literaria* (London, 1907), i. 16.

21. L. H. and C. W. Houtchens (eds.), *Leigh Hunt's Literary Criticism* (New York, 1956), p. 150. For Byron's occasional use of Cowper, see Hartley, *Continuing Revaluation*, p. 5.

22. Compare, for example, Keats's 'To Charles Cowden Clarke', ll. 17–18 with 'On the Receipt of my Mother's Picture', ll. 100–6. T. O. Mabbott, *Notes and Queries*, clxxv (1938), p. 170, argues for the indebtedness of 'When I have fears' to Cowper's 'Stanzas subjoined to the yearly bill of mortality ... 1788'.

23. 'On Thomson and Cowper', *Lectures on the English Poets* (Everyman edn., London, 1964), p. 91.

24. *The Flapper*, xxx, xxxiv, xxxviii (May–June 1796); reprinted in S. Elledge (ed.), *Eighteenth Century Critical Essays* (Ithaca, 1961), ii. 1105–19.

25. 'The morning cheered, the moon lent pathos and sentiment ... in Cowfold, although it knew no poetry, save Dr. Watts, Pollok's *Course of Time*, ... and a little of Cowper' (*The Revolution in Tanner's Lane*, chap. 16).

26. T. S. Dorsch (ed.), *Longinus: 'On the Sublime'* (London, 1965), p. 100.

27. Joseph Warton, 'Reflections on Didactic Poetry', *The Works of Virgil* (London, 1763), i. 298; Johnson, 'Life of Cowley', *Lives of the English Poets* (Everyman edn., London, 1964), i. 12.

28. Preface to *Lyrical Ballads*; E. de Selincourt and H. Darbishire (eds.), *The Poetical Works of William Wordsworth* (Oxford, 1940–9), ii. 393.

29. *Biographia Literaria*, chap. 14.

30. Quoted from William Law in Nicholson, *William Cowper* (1951), p. 30.

31. W. L. Bowles, *Pamphlets on Poetry* (London, 1826), pp. 38–40, 116–17.

32. 'On Thomson and Cowper', op. cit., pp. 91–2.

33. R. H. Hutton (ed.), *Literary Studies by Walter Bagehot* (London, 1898), i. 87–143. Needless to say, there are some examples of the reverse position: for

instance, a writer in the *North American Review* in 1847 advised the admirers of Wordsworth 'to go and study Cowper, and to be ashamed of their mystic ravings and transcendental silliness'.

34. Quoted from Sainte-Beuve's *Notes Intimes* in B. Spiller (ed.), *Cowper: Poetry and Prose* (London, 1968), p. 27.

35. Enright, op. cit., p. 396.

36. For this early controversy, see Hartley, *Continuing Revaluation*, pp. 17ff.

37. Hugh I'Anson Fausset, *William Cowper* (London, 1928), pp. 223–49; Nicholson, *William Cowper* (1951), pp. 8–9; Thomas, *William Cowper and the Eighteenth Century* (London, 1948), p. 186. Fausset, however, did much to draw attention to the psychological tensions in Cowper's personality and writings, especially that darker side which was later brought right to the fore by Kenneth MacLean's excellent brief statement, 'William Cowper', in F. W. Hilles (ed.), *The Age of Johnson* (New Haven, 1949), pp. 257–67: 'Cowper's poems and letters are a record of a terror which must interest the modern reader ... Nothing has been faked. This is human terror. This is terror in a garden.'

38. France has again provided one of the most enthusiastic commentators: 'La littérature anglaise a l'enviable privilège de posséder deux œuvres infiniment originales, qui, l'une et l'autre, nous permettent de pénétrer jusque dans l'intimité la plus familière d'une vie humaine ... La première est ... Samuel Johnson ... L'autre ouvrage, ce sont ces lettres de Cowper' (Teodor de Wyzewa, Review of Sir J. G. Frazer's edn. of Cowper's *Letters*, *Revue des Deux Mondes* [15 July 1914], p. 467).

39. Enright, op. cit., p. 387.

40. *In Search of Stability* (New Haven, 1960), p. 169.

41. *Continuing Revaluation*, p. 70.

42. Ibid., p. 72.

43. Richard Feingold's chapters on Cowper's response to public life and traditional ideas of 'the good society', in *Nature and Society* (Harvester Press, Hassocks, 1978), are markedly original, though not altogether unindebted to Spacks and Golden. Among the occasional scholarly articles, I would mention David Boyd's 'Satire and Pastoral in *The Task*', *PLL*, x (1974) and T. E. Blom's 'Eighteenth-Century Reflexive Process Poetry', *Eighteenth-Century Studies*, x (1976), which contains interesting comments on 'spontaneous composition' in *The Task*. But my concern at this point is of course with the general situation—Cowper's status as poet—rather than with isolated critical statements.

44. A. Johnston, op. cit., p. 389; John Barrell, *The Idea of Landscape and the Sense of Place, 1730–1840* (Cambridge, 1972), p. 150. To these we may add the view of Cowper in John Dixon Hunt's *The Figure in the Landscape* (Baltimore and London, 1976): '... a lively and playful mind, sharply alert to natural phenomena, but not always able to sustain a poetry in which one is matched with the other'.

45. 'William Cowper: Harmonist of the Countryside', *The Times* (London), 13 Nov. 1931, pp. 15–16.

46. Spiller, *Poetry and Prose*, p. 15.

47. P. M. Spacks, *The Poetry of Vision* (Cambridge, Mass., 1967), p. 206.

48. *Purity of Diction in English Verse* (London, 1952); see also the annotated anthology, *Augustan Lyric* (London, 1974).

CHAPTER 2

1. Spacks, *Poetry of Vision*, p. 195.

2. Fausset, op. cit., p. 235; Johnston, op. cit., pp. 388–9.

3. John Aikin, *Letters to a Young Lady on a Course of English Poetry* (1804), p. 292. Cf. W. P. Ker, *Form and Style in Poetry* (London, 1928), p. 170: '. . . a vocabulary simple and clear. This sort of poetry is what Landor meant by "diaphanous" poetry, not "prismatic". A great deal of the beauty of Cowper is of this sort . . . The beautiful passages of *The Task* . . . seem to come upon the mind without the medium of language. Of course, it is not really so; the language is of the purest and finest, but it is not strikingly ornamental'.

4. *Essay on Taste* (London, 1759), pp. 3–4.

5. *Biographia Literaria*, chap. 4.

6. See, for example, 'I stood tip-toe', ll. 47ff.

7. '. . . the familiar style is of all styles the most difficult to succeed in. To make verse speak the language of prose without being prosaic—to marshal the words of it in such an order as they might naturally take in falling from the lips of an extemporary speaker, yet without meanness, harmoniously, elegantly, and without seeming to misplace a syllable . . .' (letter to William Unwin, 17 Jan. 1782; Thomas Wright (ed.), *The Correspondence of William Cowper*, 4 vols. (London, 1904), i. 430).

8. 'Life of Gray', *Lives of the English Poets*, ed. cit., ii. 391–2.

9. *Biographia Literaria*, chaps. 1, 4.

10. Hugh Blair, *Lectures on Rhetoric and Belles Lettres* (London, 1783), i. 390. Cowper had read this work carefully: see letters to Unwin, 5 Apr. and 25 Apr. 1783, *Correspondence*, ii. 188–9, 192–3.

11. I am indebted here, as at other points, to Spacks's analysis of the passage.

12. T. Haweis (ed.), *John Newton: Letters and Sermons etc.* (London, 1787), i. 210; quoted in Richard E. Brantley, *Wordsworth's 'Natural Methodism'* (New Haven, 1975), p. 144.

13. *The Poetry of John Clare* (London, 1974), p. 70.

14. In Brantley, op. cit., pp. 144–5.

15. 'Epistle to Bathurst', ll. 249–74.

16. To Unwin, 10 Oct. 1784; *Correspondence*, ii. 253.

17. Gay, *Rural Sports*, 1720 version, ll. 410–35, in J. Underhill (ed.), *The Poetical Works of John Gay* (London, 1893), i. 29–30; Edward Young, *Love of Fame*, Satire V, in *Poetical Works* (Aldine edn., 1867), ii. 109–10.

18. 'Epistle to a Lady', ll. 227–30; H. Davis (ed.), *Pope: Poetical Works* (Oxford, 1966), p. 297. All references to Pope are from this edition.

19. To Unwin, 6 Oct. 1781; *Correspondence*, i. 363.

20. Henry Morley, *Longer Works in English Verse and Prose* (London, no date), p. 254.

21. Maurice J. Quinlan (ed.), 'The Memoir of William Cowper', *Proceed-*

ings of the American Philosophical Society, xcvii (1953), pp. 376, 374. All references to the *Memoir* are taken from this text (hereafter *Memoir*).

22. See the excellent brief discussion of Cowper's *Memoir* in Frank D. McConnell, *The Confessional Imagination; a Reading of Wordsworth's 'Prelude'* (Baltimore, 1974), pp. 193–6.

23. To Newton, 13 Jan. 1784; Spiller, pp. 708–9.

24. At Doubting Castle the Giant Despair throws Christian and Hopeful into his 'dungeon'. The last word of *The Pilgrim's Progress* is not of Christian's salvation but of Ignorance's being cast down to Hell.

25. See Thomas Wright, *The Life of William Cowper* (London, 1892), pp. 205–9.

26. R. Sharrock (ed.), *Bunyan: The Pilgrim's Progress* (Penguin English Library, 1965), pp. 65–7.

27. *Memoir*, pp. 376, 378.

28. To Newton, 2 Sept. 1788; *Correspondence*, iii. 312.

29. To Mrs. Newton, 4 March 1780; *Correspondence*, i. 175.

30. *Poetry of Vision*, pp. 193–4.

31. To Mrs. Maria Cowper, 19 Oct. 1781; *Correspondence*, i. 368–9. To Newton, 27 Nov. 1784; Spiller, p. 726.

32. Spacks, *Poetry of Vision*, p. 201.

33. Ibid., p. 202.

34. Alfoxden Notebook (1798); de Selincourt and Darbishire (eds.), *William Wordsworth: The Prelude* (2nd edn., Oxford, 1959), p. xlii.

35. See note 7 (chap. 2) above.

36. Crabbe's remark (on Chaucer) is quoted in a relevant chapter in Davie, *Purity of Diction* (p. 31). For Goldsmith, see 'Hyperbole', *Essays* (Globe edn., London, 1871), p. 339. The writer of the memorial piece on Cowper in the *Monthly Mirror* (May 1800) shares Goldsmith's position—but fears that the battle for 'strength and vigour ... of thought' might be lost, since this virtue has everywhere been overlooked 'in the fondness for meretricious ornaments'.

37. '... the poet who undertakes to preserve or refine a poetic diction is writing in a web of responsibilities ... He is responsible to the community in which he writes, for purifying and correcting the spoken language. And of course he is responsible, as all poets are, to his readers; he has to give them pleasure, and also, deviously or directly, instructions in moral conduct' (Davie, *Purity of Diction*, p. 16). Later, with reference to the conservative 'sobriety' of Jane Austen and Wordsworth, Davie describes the breakdown, after Cowper, of the Augustan commitment to the principle of appealing to 'the good sense of "the best people" ': 'The centre fell apart ... the people with the money to command the best began to command something else; and taste and judgment no longer went with power and wealth ...' (p. 25). The intimate links between poetic style and social and moral values in the eighteenth century are also explored in M. R. Trickett, *The Honest Muse* (Oxford, 1967), pp. 275–82 especially.

It is worth emphasizing that Cowper's attack on 'theatrical' preaching is by no means the isolated grumble of a strict 'Evangelical'. Very much the same view emerges in a whole range of serious writers, including Goldsmith and Wordsworth: see Richard E. Brantley, *Wordsworth's 'Natural Method-*

ism', pp. 26–9. Jane Austen's earnest interest in Edmund's relationship with his vocation, and his involvement in the 'theatricals' organized by the fashionable Crawfords, in *Mansfield Park*, is of course highly relevant here.

38. The questions of literary taste and general morals are instinctively brought together by Cowper: 'It is a bold undertaking at this time of day . . . to step forth into the world in the character of a bard, especially when it is considered that luxury, idleness, and vice have debauched the public taste, and that nothing is welcome but childish fiction, or what has at least a tendency to excite a laugh' (letter to Mrs. Maria Cowper, 19 Oct. 1781; *Correspondence*, i. 368).

39. Paolo Balsamo, 'Thoughts on Great Cities', *Annals of Agriculture*, xiii (1790), p. 466; quoted in Feingold, *Nature and Society*, p. 62. Cf. Arthur Young, 'Importance of London to the National Husbandry', *Annals*, xxiii (1795), p. 273: 'the capital . . . cannot be too large; . . . its being an active market for every branch of distant industry, increases the national wealth, and quickens the population of the kingdom to a vastly greater amount than all the destruction we read of from abuses, ill health etc. etc.'. Cowper everywhere takes the opposite, gloomier view, hoping 'to combat that predilection in favour of a metropolis, that beggars and exhausts the country' (letter to Newton, 27 Nov. 1784; Spiller, p. 726).

40. J. H. Plumb, *England in the Eighteenth Century* (London, 1950), pp. 77–133, gives a succinct account of the political and social environment in which the 1782 poems and *The Task* were written; but see also, John B. Owen, *The Eighteenth Century* (London, 1974), Part Two, and the invaluable annotation in H. T. Griffith (ed.), *The Poems of William Cowper*, 2 vols. (Oxford, 1874).

Cowper's conception of 'virtuous politics' bears an extremely close resemblance to that of George III: 'Let the day come in which the banner of virtue, honour and liberty shall be displayed and prostitution of principle, venality, and corruption meet their just reward, the honest citizen, the zealous patriot, will lift up their heads, all good men will unite in support of a government on the firm foundations of liberty and virtue . . .' (quoted in J. Brooke, *George III* (London, 1972), p. 608). The currency of such attitudes is well illustrated by their inclusion in Richardson's *Pamela*, Part Two, letter xciv.

41. In his observation of life on the old commons Thomas Bewick, writing in 1820, similarly stresses the independent spirit of the peasantry, whose 'industry . . . made them despise being ever numbered with the parish poor' ('Memoir', quoted and discussed in Raymond Williams, *The Country and the City* (London, 1973), pp. 125–6). But Bewick is celebrating the prosperity of *his* cottagers in the golden age before 'enclosure'. Cowper focuses relentlessly on the stark details of deprivation:

> All the care
> Ingenious parsimony takes but just
> Saves the small inventory, bed, and stool,
> Skillet, and old carv'd chest, from public sale.

> They live, and live without extorted alms
> From grudging hands ...
>
> (IV, 399–404)

Cf. Cowper's harsh condemnation of the Poor Law in his letter on the outbreak of smallpox at Weston: to Lady Hesketh, 1 Jan. 1788; *Correspondence*, iii. 201.

42. *Table Talk*, ll. 670–89.

43. *The Country and the City*, p. 84.

44. Ibid., p. 91.

45. Roger Lonsdale gives an effective short account of Gray's dramatization of 'the poet as outsider' at the end of the *Elegy* but fails to note sufficiently the psychological, or 'subjective', dimension of the poetic event (*The Poems of Gray, Collins and Goldsmith* (London, 1969), pp. 115–16). The images of psychic and physical paralysis exemplify Gray's characteristic inability to find value and an acceptable personal identity in the role of isolated contemplative poet, though the role fascinates him; and in the Epitaph he attempts to re-locate himself in a useful relationship with society by claiming the virtues of pity and benevolence.

Raymond Williams (*The Country and the City*, p. 91) draws attention to the emergence in Thomson's *The Seasons* of the alienated poet meditating close to nature—the poet inhabiting 'twilight groves and visionary vales'. The concluding lines of *The Deserted Village* offer concentrated expression of the interrelated phenomena with which I am concerned—the poet driven over to the periphery of 'the world', from where he hopefully laments its passing or redemption, and the self as a new centre of power and value:

> trade's proud empire hastes to swift decay,
> As ocean sweeps the laboured mole away;
> While self-dependent power can time defy,
> As rocks resist the billows and the sky.

46. See Feingold, *Nature and Society*, pp. 31–44; and chapter 6 below.

47. See note 38 (chap. 2) above.

48. I discuss this aspect of Wordsworth in 'The Steadfast Self', in R. T. Davies and B. G. Beatty (eds.), *Literature of the Romantic Period* (Liverpool, 1976), pp. 36–55.

49. *The Late Augustans* (London, 1958), p. xxii.

50. See Cowper's letter comparing himself to a traveller through a wilderness, p. 30 above. Gray describes his life in similar terms, though different imagery: his days 'go round and round like the blind horse in the mill; ... my eyes are open enough to see the same dull prospect, and to know that having made 4 and 20 steps more, I shall be just where I was ...' (P. Toynbee and L. Whibley (eds.), *The Correspondence of Thomas Gray* (Oxford, 1935), i. 34).

51. *Table Talk*, ll. 652–5; Pope, *Essay on Criticism*, ll. 337–43.

52. To Unwin, undated; *Correspondence*, iii. 101.

53. *Late Augustans*, p. xxi.

54. See Introduction, note 7 above.

55. To Unwin, 10 Oct. 1784; *Correspondence*, ii. 252.
56. 9 Aug. 1763; Spiller, p. 553.

CHAPTER 3

1. The 'No Popery' riots led by Lord George Gordon, occasioned by a mild measure of Roman Catholic relief, had reduced the city to chaos during the first week of June, 1780, when the magistrates hesitated to read the Riot Act for fear of reprisals. Order was eventually restored by means of a royal proclamation. Cowper comments on the Riots in a letter to Maria Cowper, who was resident in London: 'The law was for a few moments like an arrow in the quiver ... now it is an arrow upon the string, and many who despised it lately are trembling as they stand before the point of it (20 July 1780; Spiller, p. 592).

Chatham was seized with an apoplectic fit during the Lords' debate on the proposal to surrender the American colonies, 7 April 1778. He did not die until 11 May but popular opinion, encouraged by poets and painters, identified the seizure with his death.

2. See pp. 37–41 above.

3. It is noticeable that the imagery Cowper here applies to a political situation is the same as that used to describe Charles Churchill's undisciplined poetic style in *Table Talk*.

4. Cf. Cowper's letter to his publisher, Joseph Johnson: 'Give me a manly, rough line, with a deal of meaning in it, rather than a whole poem full of musical periods that have nothing but their oily smoothness to recommend them' (Jan. 1781; Spiller, pp. 605–6).

5. One of the many recollections of Pope's *Essay on Criticism* in this part of *Table Talk*. Cowper's debt to the *Essay* is referred to later but we may conveniently note here not only Pope's praise of the bold expression that deviates, like Pegasus, from the common track so as to

> ... snatch a grace beyond the reach of art,
> Which without passing thro' the judgment, gains
> The heart, and all its ends at once attains.
>
> (ll. 155–7)

but also his attack on those who would judge by manner rather than substance:

> But most by numbers judge a Poet's song,
> And smooth or rough, with them, is right or wrong;
> In the bright Muse tho' thousand charms conspire,
> Her voice is all these tuneful fools admire ...
>
> (ll. 337–40)

And behind Pope lies of course Dryden's rejection of 'good numbers without good sense'—itself an appeal to the authority of Horace (see Preface to *Fables*, in G. Watson (ed.), *Dryden: Critical Essays* (London, 1962), ii. 274).

Wordsworth may in turn be recalling Cowper's defence of neo-classical tradition when condemning in the Preface to *Lyrical Ballads* 'arbitrary and capricious habits of expression, in order to furnish food for fickle tastes' and those who 'talk of poetry as a matter of amusement and idle pleasure'.

6. This theme is vigorously pursued, with reference to Collins, in Paul S. Sherwin's *Precious Bane: Collins and the Miltonic Legacy* (Austin, 1977). Collins's lament for the 'vain endeavours' of this 'laggard' age at the end of 'The Passions' is a simple instance of his pervasive sense of the burden of the past and the need to bring forth something new. Gray has a less driven but just as certain pessimism about the fate of literary enterprise: see, for example, 'Stanzas to Mr Bentley', ll. 17ff. ('But not to one in this benighted age/Is that diviner inspiration given ...') and the remark to Walpole that 'Litterature ... seems indeed drawing apace to its Dissolution' (*Correspondence*, ed. Toynbee and Whibley, i. 265).

7. The feeling can be tracked back indeed to Dryden and the earlier eighteenth century; as in Neander's unhappy comparison in *Of Dramatic Poesy* of the present age and that of the Elizabethans—'... all comes sullied to us: ... they could not make so plenteous treatments out of such decayed fortunes'—or Thomas Blackwell's comments on how the progress of society brings the regress of poetry, 'It is thus that a People's Felicity clips the Wings of their Verse' (*An Enquiry into the Life and Writings of Homer* (London, 1735), p. 28).

8. See *Essay on the Genius and Writings of Pope* (5th edn., London, 1806), ii. 402–3 ('Whatever poetical enthusiasm he actually possessed, he withheld and stifled'); Advertisement to *Odes* (1744), quoted in Sherwin, *Precious Bane*, p. 41.

9. Cowper, letter to Unwin, 17 Jan. 1782, 20 Oct. 1784; *Correspondence*, i. 430, ii. 257. Lord Kames, *Elements of Criticism* (1762), (11th edn., London, 1840), p. 236: '... communication being the chief end of language ... perspicuity ought not to be sacrificed to any other beauty whatever'. Blair, *Lectures*, i. 185: it must 'be our first object, to make our meaning clearly and fully understood, and understood without the least difficulty'. See also P. W. K. Stone, *The Art of Poetry, 1750–1820* (London, 1967), pp. 30–63.

10. H. Trowbridge (ed.), *Richard Hurd: Letters on Chivalry and Romance* (Los Angeles, 1963), p. 89. See also John Ogilvie's elevation of imagination in *Philosophical and Critical Observations* (1774), as discussed in Stone, op. cit., pp. 44–6.

11. See note 5 (chap. 3) above. One other parallel worthy of special mention is Pope's attack on 'vile Obscenity', the legacy of the Restoration, that 'fat age of pleasure' (*Essay*, ll. 526ff.), though Cowper does push moral disapproval much more to the limits.

12. 'The Critical Principles of William Cowper', *The Cambridge Journal*, vii (1953), p. 182.

13. 'On Dryden and Pope', *Lectures on the English Poets* (Everyman edn., London, 1964), p. 73.

14. For the Puritans' valuing of studied simplicity on both moral and practical grounds, see Perry Miller, 'The Puritans as Literary Artists', in Perry Miller and T. H. Johnson (eds.), *The Puritans* (New York, 1963), i.

64–79; also U. Milo Kaufmann, *The Pilgrim's Progress and Traditions in Puritan Meditation* (New Haven, 1966), passim.

15. Blair, *Lectures*, i. 217–18.

16. *Lectures on the English Poets*, ed. cit., p. 94.

17. Cowper names his prude 'Bridget' (l. 156), thus suggesting Fielding's character, Bridget Allworthy. Prudery was among the commonest subjects of eighteenth-century 'moral satire': e.g. *The Spectator*, nos. 208, 217, 496, etc.; William Law, *A Serious Call* (1728, Everyman edn., 1906), pp. 65ff.; Shenstone, 'On Hypocrisy'.

18. Especially *The Monthly Review*, lxvii (1782), pp. 262–5 and *The Gentleman's Magazine*, lv (1785), pp. 985–8.

19. Leslie Stephen, *Hours in a Library* (London, 1892), ii. 224.

20. The best example is Wordsworth's imitation of the semi-indignant mimicry of Book II of *The Task*, where Cowper brings the satire of *Conversation* to a very fine art:

> First we stroke
> An eye-brow; next compose a straggling lock;
> Then with an air most gracefully perform'd,
> Fall back into our seat, extend an arm,
> And lay it at its ease with gentle care,
> With handkerchief in hand depending low ...
>   (II,445–50)

> a comely Bachelor
> Fresh from a toilette of two hours, ascend
> The Pulpit, with seraphic glance look up,
> And, in a tone elaborately low
> Beginning, lead his voice through many a maze ...
>   (*Prelude*, 1805, VII,546–50)

21. As Gilbert Thomas argues (*William Cowper and the Eighteenth Century*, pp. 266–70), there is little or nothing in the way of doctrinal statement in Cowper to align him specifically with the Calvinists—Whitfield, Lady Huntingdon, Newton—who opposed the Wesleys on the issue of 'election' and 'predestination' to form a separate branch of the Evangelical movement (the Wesleys being 'Arminians', holding that grace was available to all true 'believers'). Nevertheless, Cowper shares the Calvinist's more strenuous sense of our fallen nature and the consequent primacy of 'soul-concern' and rejection of the world—while also, on the other hand, continuing, particularly in *Table Talk*, that interest in the conduct of 'business' and 'civil life' (Newton, *Cardiphonia*) which had been a feature of the Calvinist temper ever since Calvin's dedication to the *Institutes*, the 'Epistre au Roy'.

22. Revd. John Newton, *Cardiphonia, or the Utterance of the Heart* (Edinburgh, 1835), p. 466: hereafter *Cardiphonia*.

23. In addition to the example quoted, we may take one of the central passages of conceptual statement in *Hope*:

> Hope! let the wretch, once conscious of the joy,
> Whom now despairing agonies destroy,

> Speak, for he can, and none so well as he,
> What treasures centre, what delights, in thee.
>
> (ll.171–4)

24. See *Truth*, ll. 459ff.; *Truth*, ll. 1ff. as balanced by *Hope*, ll. 161ff. The imagery of sea-journey and of natural/unnatural growth is traditional: see, e.g. *Paradise Lost*, XI, 22ff.

25. Cowper's interest in such states of being link him to the 'graveyard school' of Young's *Night Thoughts* and Blair's *The Grave*, as well as to Prior's *Solomon* and Hervey's *Meditations*; but his apprehensions are on the whole very much sharper.

26. Reprinted in Milford (ed.), *Poetical Works* (revised edn., 1967), pp. 648–51.

27. Ibid., p. 649.

28. To Newton, 20 Apr. 1783; *Correspondence*, ii. 60.

29. See 'Letters to a Nobleman', letter II; *Cardiphonia*, ed. cit., pp. 41–5.

30. *Memoir*, p. 378.

31. Ibid., p. 379.

32. John Newton, *Autobiography* (Chicago, no date), p. 71. This is Newton's autobiographical *Authentic Narrative*, first published in 1764, two years before Cowper began his *Memoir*.

33. See Roderick Huang, *William Cowper, Nature Poet* (London, 1957), p. 24. This book deals in some detail with the influence on Cowper of Hervey's ideas about nature.

34. Revd. James Hervey, *Meditations and Contemplations* (1748, London, 1812), p. 241: hereafter *Meditations and Contemplations*.

35. Ibid., p. 364.

36. On this subject, F. C. Gill, *The Romantic Movement and Methodism* (London, 1937) and T. B. Shepherd, *Methodism and the Literature of the Eighteenth Century* (London, 1940) have never, to my knowledge, been superseded.

37. Oldham, 'A Satire (concerning Poetry)', in B. Dobrée (ed.), *The Poems of John Oldham* (London, 1960), p. 234; Pope, 'Epistle to Bathurst', ll. 299–314. It seems that Cowper's account of 'the sinner saved' may in fact owe something to Dr. Johnson's account of old age in *The Vanity of Human Wishes* (ll.255–90): there are common details (the failure of friends, music, and beauty to bring consolation) and both describe a figure half real and half deliberate personification. However, this may simply mean that Cowper and Johnson are allied to the same tradition of religio-moral *exempla*—rather than to the conventions of Augustan satire.

38. Cf. Newton's letter 'On the Benefits of Affliction', *Cardiphonia*, pp. 289–91; and Hervey's 'when misfortunes have eclipsed the splendours of our outward circumstances, how many important convictions present themselves . . . if tribulations tend to dissipate the inward darkness . . . welcome disappointment' (*Meditations and Contemplations*, p. 238).

39. Bunyan, Preface to *Grace Abounding*; Newton, *Autobiography*, ed. cit., p. 9. Cf. Richard Baxter's advice to the wavering convert: 'Call forth thy own recorded experience . . . Remember what discoveries of thy state thou hast

made formerly in the walks of self-examination' (*The Saints Everlasting Rest* (4th edn., London, 1653), Pt. IV, pp. 187–90).

40. This is very true to the spirit of Puritan mental pilgrimage, as expressed for example in the Apollyon and Doubting Castle episodes in *The Pilgrim's Progress*: see my 'Bunyan and the Confines of the Mind', V. Newey (ed.), *The Pilgrim's Progress: Critical and Historical Views* (Liverpool, 1980), pp. 21–48

41. Cowper has high praise for Prior's *Solomon* (letter to Unwin, 5 Jan. 1782), but his indebtedness lies all on the surface, in a general concern for 'the Vanity of the World'.

42. *Cardiphonia*, p. 467. Cf. Calvin's gruesome warning to those who would desire to be certain of their own election: 'But what proof have you of your election? When once this thought has taken possession of any individual, it keeps him perpetually miserable, subjects him to dire torment, or throws him into a state of complete stupor' (*Institutes*, Book III, chap. 24).

43. Newton's Preface, *Poetical Works*, pp. 649–50.

44. See note 38 (chap. 3) above.

45. To Lady Hesketh, 13 Oct. 1798; *Correspondence*, iv. 503–4.

46. I am thinking above all of the 'graver strains' of the letter to Newton of 13 Jan. 1784, where Cowper responds so urgently to the emblems in nature of his own interior 'cold gloom': 'A thick fog envelops everything, and at the same time it freezes intensely . . . The hedge that has been apparently dead, is not so; it will burst into leaf and blossom at the appointed time; but no such time is appointed for the stake that stands in it'.

47. I. A. Richards (ed.), *The Portable Coleridge* (New York, 1950), pp. 66–7. All quotations from Coleridge's poetry are from this edition.

48. *Biographia Literaria*, chap. 13.

49. For Johnson's attitude to solitude and preference for 'active life', see M. R. Trickett, *The Honest Muse*, pp. 233–4.

50. To Mrs. Newton, 4 March 1780; *Correspondence*, i. 175.

51. Cowper's allusion is to the remark, 'How sweet, how passing sweet, is solitude'. He wrongly attributes it, in a footnote, to 'Bruyere'; the true source is J. L. G. de Balzac's *Entretiens* (see *Poetical Works*, p. 654).

52. 'Ode on the Spring', ll. 31–50. Quotations from Gray's poems are taken throughout from R. Lonsdale (ed.), *The Poems of Gray, Collins and Goldsmith* (London, 1969).

53. To Unwin, 25 Aug. 1781; Spiller, p. 632.

54. Raymond Williams (*The Country and the City*, pp. 29–30) sees the general absence of Horace's irony—'The celebration . . . had been in Horace the sentimental reflection of a usurer, thinking of turning farmer'—as the register of at first conscious and then conventional idealization that replaced a 'living' with an 'enamelled' world. But this of course simply leaves out of account the positive moral weight, the valuable idealism, which the convention carries in writers like Jonson, Dryden, Pope, or Johnson. It is true, however, that Cowper does look at the common ideal with striking freshness, refusing to surrender to it without surrendering any commitment to its underlying values.

55. The tradition has often been expertly charted and described: see Maren-Sofie Røstvig, *The Happy Man* (Oslo, 1954–8) in particular.

56. See *Georgics*, II, 458–512; Horace, sixth Satire of the Second Book as well as the second Epode.

57. 'Of Obscurity', in A. R. Waller (ed.), *Cowley: Essays, Plays and Sundry Verses* (Cambridge, 1906), p. 339. Cowper's tribute to Cowley is at *Task*, IV, 718–30.

58. J. Logie Robertson (ed.), *The Poetical Works of James Thomson* (Oxford, 1965), pp. 177–8. All references to Thomson are from this edition.

59. 'Summer', ll. 465ff., 547ff.; 'Spring', ll. 897–903.

60. J. Chalker, *The English Georgic* (London, 1969), p. 116.

61. Ibid. I quote at this point from the 1727 text of *The Seasons*, as used by Chalker himself.

62. It is remarkable how far the components of Wordsworth's theme are concentrated here, though in more conventionally religious form: innocence, a return to nature, closeness to God, life as a play, 'the philosophic mind'.

63. For the ending of Gray's *Elegy*, see note 45 (chap. 2) above. Compare Cowper's anxiety over the publication of *The Task* (to Newton, 9 July 1785; *Correspondence*, ii. 335) with Gray's confession to Walpole, 10 Aug. 1757 (*Correspondence*, ed. Toynbee, ii. 513).

64. *Poems*, ed. cit., pp. 115–16.

CHAPTER 4

1. 1757 version, I, 1–4.

2. See Cowper's 'Advertisement', *Poetical Works*, p. 128.

3. To Newton, 27 Nov. 1784; Spiller, p. 726. *Retirement*, ll. 801–8.

4. 'Towards defining an Age of Sensibility', J. L. Clifford (ed.), *Eighteenth-Century English Literature* (New York, 1959), p. 318.

5. *William Cowper and the Eighteenth Century*, p. 263.

6. Frye, op. cit., p. 312.

7. Even Spacks (op. cit., pp. 179–81) sees the passages in question as 'visual' and 'aesthetic'. See also the discussion of the Ouse Valley 'prospect' by Myrddin Jones, 'Wordsworth and Cowper: the eye made quiet', *Essays in Criticism*, xxi (1971), pp. 236–45.

8. To Samuel Rose, 20 May 1789; *Correspondence*, iii. 376–7. Varro and Cowley are at least as likely sources: see H. T. Griffith (ed.), *Poems of Cowper* (1874), ii. 234.

9. To Newton, 3 May 1780; Spiller, p. 583.

10. *The Idea of Landscape and the Sense of Place* (Cambridge, 1972), pp. 22, 84 especially.

11. Ibid., p. 151.

12. See pp. 277–9 below.

13. Cowper's subject is the earthquakes that took place in Calabria and Sicily during 1783. Jeremiah is often echoed in Book II; and Cowper may also have in mind the anonymous *Verses on the Late Earthquakes* (1756).

14. See the final section of Part III of Burke's *Of the Sublime and Beautiful* (1756).

15. To Lady Hesketh, 9 Sept. 1792; Spiller, p. 968.

16. Barrell, *The Idea of Landscape*, p. 37.

17. Cf. pp. 19–21 above.

18. 'This Lime-tree Bower', ll. 68–76.

19. See 'Tintern Abbey', ll. 103–11.

20. I refer here of course to the whole central section of 'Tintern Abbey', ll. 58ff.

21. 'Tintern Abbey', ll. 112ff. Myrrdin Jones, op. cit., p. 236, suggests this and other similarities of detail.

22. These include Barrell and Spacks, as well as those referred to more specifically below.

23. Jones, op. cit., p. 238.

24. *Lectures*, ii. 371. The same attitude is expressed at length in John Aikin's poem 'Picturesque', *Poems* (1791), pp. 52–7. But the interrelating of poetry and painting was, needless to say, a very familiar concern, which has been amply documented by twentieth-century scholars: see, e.g., C. Hussey, *The Picturesque* (London, 1927) and Jean Hagstrum, *The Sister Arts* (Chicago, 1958).

25. *Aspects of Eighteenth-Century Nature Poetry* (London, 1935), pp. 93–4.

26. Lessing, *Laoköon* (1766); cited by Deane, op. cit., p. 87. Blair, *Lectures*, ii. 377–8.

27. Josephine Miles, *Renaissance, Eighteenth-Century, and Modern Language in English Poetry* (Berkeley, 1960), p. 23.

28. William Gilpin, *Observations on Western Parts of England* (London, 1798), p. 328.

29. See J. Arthos, *The Language of Natural Description in Eighteenth-Century Poetry* (Ann Arbor, 1949), p. 380 and Geoffrey Tillotson, *Augustan Poetic Diction* (London, 1964), pp. 32–3.

30. Warton, Dedication to *The Works of Virgil* (London, 1763), I. ii–iii; Aikin, *Essay on the Application of Natural History to Poetry* (Warrington, 1777), pp. 5–6, 57ff. Cf. Thomas Pennant's plea for a new detailed realism in the poetry of natural description; Preface to *British Zoology* (1766, 4th edn., London, 1776), I. xiii. Thomson was on the whole exempted from censure, and was often praised for his faithful representations.

31. It seems that Cowper's readers did recognize the 'prospect' delineated in the poem, for the poet's 'station' came to be known as 'Cowper's Eminence': see J. Bruce (ed.), *Poetical Works of Cowper* (London, 1865), note.

32. *The Idea of Landscape*, p. 24.

33. Ibid., pp. 17–22.

34. *Prelude* (1805), XII, 1–2; XI, 326–8, 258ff. I place the emphasis here on practice, for Akenside's *Pleasures of Imagination* provided a developed statement of the *philosophy* of creative and ennobling interchange between self and nature: see, e.g., 1757 version, II, 278ff. (Aldine edn., pp. 114ff.), to which Wordsworth may well have been indebted.

35. The allusion to *King Lear* at l. 162—'The sturdy swain diminish'd to a boy'—makes us realize that the plough is slow-moving because of its distance below us, not away from us. Compare the comment on the 'particular perspective' of 'Tintern Abbey' in Robert Langbaum, *The Poetry of Experience* (1957, Penguin University Books edn., 1974), p. 41.

36. Langbaum, op. cit., pp. 34–43.

37. Letter to Sotheby, 10 Sept. 1802; quoted by Langbaum, op. cit., p. 33.

38. Ibid.

39. *Paradise Lost*, IX, 783, 1001. Milton is much in Cowper's mind at this point: compare *Task*, I, 365 and *Paradise Lost*, X, 1053.

40. See Johnson, 'Life of Denham', *Lives of the English Poets*, ed. cit., i. 51.

41. *The Mirror and the Lamp* (New York, 1958), pp. 103–4.

42. Abrams, op. cit., pp. 30–5. Akenside, *Pleasures of Imagination*, II, 59–69, is among the clearest statements of the critical concept of 'the mirror of the mind'.

43. See Lady Hesketh's letter of 9 May 1799, in C. Bodham Johnson (ed.), *Letters of Lady Hesketh to the Rev. John Johnson* (London, 1901), pp. 86–7. Fuseli, Stothard, Greig, and Westall were among the artists who illustrated *The Task*. It is possible that Cowper based his vignette of gypsies in Book I of *The Task* (ll. 557–64) on a similar scene by Gainsborough (exhibited 1764, reproduced in C. B. Tinker, *Poet and Painter* (Cambridge, Mass., 1938), p. 79), while Gainsborough may be recalling Cowper's 'woodman' (V, 41–57) in his last picture (which was not publicly known when the painter died in 1788).

44. Shawcross (ed.), *Biographia Literaria*, ii. 16.

45. Romans I: 20.

46. Geoffrey H. Hartman, *Wordsworth's Poetry 1787–1814* (New Haven, 1964), pp. 152–4.

47. Wordsworth, 'The Tables Turned', ll. 15–16, 'It is the first mild day of March', ll. 27–8.

48. Carlyle, *Heroes and Hero Worship*, Lecture V; *Past and Present*, Book III, chap. 1. The relevant passages are quoted in Basil Willey, *Nineteenth-Century Studies* (Penguin Books edn., 1964), pp. 135–6.

49. See *Sartor Resartus*, Book II, chap. 7.

50. *Sartor Resartus*, Book II, chap. 9.

51. James Hurdis, *Poems* (Oxford, 1808), iii. 133.

52. 'Wordsworth's *Lyrical Ballads* in Their Time', F. W. Hilles and H. Bloom (eds.), *From Sensibility to Romanticism* (New York, 1965), p. 368.

53. See 'The Tables Turned', ll. 25–32; *Faust*, Part I, trans. C. F. MacIntyre (Norfolk, Conn., 1949), p. 60.

54. See Humphrey House, *Coleridge* (London, 1953), p. 79.

CHAPTER 5

1. *Poetry of Vision*, pp. 196–9.

2. Arthos, *Language of Natural Description*, passim.

3. Op. cit., pp. 196–7.

4. *Augustan Poetic Diction*, p. 42.

5. Wordsworth may well have the image of 'the bents,/And coarser grass' in mind when placing the tranquillity and beauty of the 'plumes' and 'high spear-grass' over against the 'sorrow and despair' of the young Poet who has

heard the tragic tale of Margaret in 'The Ruined Cottage' (*Excursion*, I, 924–55). In both cases gloomy thoughts are 'deflected' by a concentration on the permanent life of nature.

6. *Memoir*, p. 370.

7. See p. 65 above.

8. *Memoir*, p. 368.

9. Spacks, op. cit., pp. 189–90.

10. 'Spring', ll. 467–79.

11. *Spectator*, 411 (21 June 1712).

12. See Abrams, *Mirror and the Lamp*, p. 139; also Spacks, op. cit., pp. 222–3.

13. Quoted in Norman Hampson, *The Enlightenment* (London, 1968), p. 78.

14. See J. B. Owen, *The Eighteenth Century*, chap. 12.

15. For Fox's use of the passage, see Griffith (ed.), *Poems of Cowper*, ii. 262.

16. Hampson, *The Enlightenment*, p. 89.

17. Voltaire, *Éléments de la Philosophie de Newton* (1738); quoted in Hampson, op. cit., p. 79.

18. Ibid., p. 105.

19. Ibid., p. 99.

20. There is much in the *Essay on Man* with which Cowper is in agreement, both in *The Task* and the Moral Satires: notably the contention that happiness lies within rather than in the privileges of rank or wealth, and the opposition to over-confident reliance on the supposed certitudes of science and philosophy. But Cowper's conventional position in respect of sin and necessary grace places him in direct confrontation with Pope's idea of human nature and the providential plan, where 'Self-love and Social be the same'. Basil Willey, *The Eighteenth-Century Background* (London, 1940), p. 68, offers extremely relevant material from Shaftesbury's *Characteristicks*, when discussing the philosopher's view that true religion should be based on virtue and 'good nature' instead of upon Revelation: e.g. '... by building a future State on the Ruins of Virtue, Religion in general, and the cause of a Deity is betray'd; and by making Rewards and Punishments the principal Motives to Duty, the Christian Religion in particular is overthrown, and its greatest Principle, that of Love, rejected and expos'd' (Lord Shaftesbury, *Works* (1727 edn.), ii. 279).

21. 'This Lime-tree Bower' reads like a seeming expansion of Cowper's opposition of confinement and inviolable freedom, and there appears to be at least one direct echo: 'No plot so narrow, be but nature there,/No waste so vacant, but may well employ/Each faculty of sense ...' (ll.61–3). Cf. 'Tintern Abbey', ll.119ff.

22. Abbé le Pluche, *Spectacle de la Nature* (3rd edn., 1743), trans. John Kelly, D. D. Bellamy and J. Sparrow, pp. 3–5; quoted in John Holloway, *The Proud Knowledge* (London, 1977), p. 61.

23. I quote of course from Joyce's definition in *Portrait of the Artist*. It is the sense of a God separate from nature that makes Cowper's 'moment' emphatically traditional.

24. Cf. Akenside, *Pleasures of Imagination* (1744), III, 629–33.

25. Blake, *The Marriage of Heaven and Hell*, Plate IV, ll. 65–83; W. H. Stevenson (ed.), *The Poems of William Blake* (London, 1971), p. 114.

26. For Protestant 'meditation on nature', see Brantley, *Wordsworth's 'Natural Methodism'*, passim.

27. Revd. James Hervey, *Theron and Aspasio* (London, 1755), iii. 282.

28. *Meditations*, pp. 81–2.

29. Isaac Ambrose, *Prima, Media & Ultima* (London, 1654), ii. 68.

30. See Hall's *Occasional Meditations* (3rd edn., London, 1633). John Wesley, for example, instinctively compares the Volume of Creation to the Bible itself: ' "the Book of Nature" is written in an universal Character, which every man may read'; it consists 'not of words but Things, which picture out the divine Perfections' (T. Jackson (ed.), *Works* (3rd edn., 1831; rpt. London, 1872), i. 229).

31. 'T. S.', *The Second Part of The Pilgrim's Progress* (1684), para. 1.

32. *Spectator*, 393 (1712).

33. 'Spring', ll. 849–66.

34. Thus the sun becomes for Hervey 'The emblem of Christ': 'I have read of a person so struck with the splendours of this noble luminary, that he imagined himself made on purpose to contemplate his glories. O! that Christians would adopt his persuasion, and transfer it to the sun of righteousness' (*Meditations*, p. 85). This preserves the traditional Puritan–Evangelical elevation of 'spiritual' over 'carnal' perception.

35. Haweis (ed.), *Letters, Sermons etc.*, i. 210–11.

36. Edmund Bury, *Husbandmans Companion* (London, 1677), pp. 120–1.

37. *Night Thoughts*, IV, 504–5; ed. G. Gilfillan (Edinburgh, 1853), p. 82. We may note how much more intimate is Cowper's relationship with nature than that of the Methodists, John Furz and Thomas Olivers, whose conversion experiences have regularly been cited by critics as evidence of the spiritual and personal dimension brought by Evangelicalism to the treatment of the natural world. Here is Furz: 'I was in a new world. If I walked into the open field, everything showed forth the glory of God ... If I looked on the grass, the corn, the trees, I could not but stand and adore the goodness of God' (T. Jackson (ed.), *The Lives of Early Methodist Preachers* (2nd edn., London, 1846), ii. 333). Cf. Olivers' account of how he often 'received instruction ... even from a drop of water, a blade of grass, or a grain of sand' (*Lives*, i. 208).

38. 'The Prisoner and His Crimes', *Literature and Psychology*, vi (1956), pp. 53–9.

39. Thomson, 'Spring', ll. 526ff.; Hervey, *Meditations*, pp. 123ff.

40. *Paradise Lost*, VII, 309–38. This passage probably influenced Cowper directly, but elsewhere in *The Task* (IV, 311–32, V, 21–6).

41. Spacks, *Poetry of Vision*, p. 206.

42. See 'Frost at Midnight', ll. 58–65 ('Therefore all seasons shall be sweet to thee ...').

43. Spacks, op. cit., p. 194; Huang, *William Cowper, Nature Poet*, chap. 4; Thomas, *William Cowper and the Eighteenth Century*, pp. 283–7.

44. *Prelude* (1805), XII, 1–14, 180–1.

CHAPTER 6

1. The improvement of road engineering in the 1760s and 70s was one of the more obvious benefits of the industrial and agrarian revolutions (Plumb, *England in the Eighteenth Century*, pp. 80–1).

2. Feingold, *Nature and Society*, p. 6.

3. The Book opens with a reference to Jeremiah IX: 2; and there are clear echoes of Pope's Moral Essays (e.g. ll. 636ff. and Pope's 'Epistle II', ll. 235–40).

4. As expressed mainly in the Prophets: see J. Hastings *et al.*, *Dictionary of the Bible* (Edinburgh, 1914), pp. 761–2, 858, 966–7. Cowper wrote to Newton: 'The book ... is intended to strike the hour that gives notice of approaching judgment, ... dealing pretty largely in the *signs* of the *times*' (11 Dec. 1784; *Correspondence*, ii. 282).

5. Op. cit., p. 13.

6. ll. 599–607.

7. Mandeville's *Fable of the Bees* had of course argued that men are good from the worst of motives, and had developed on these grounds the expansionist economic doctrine that waste produces prosperity.

8. Benbow is himself looking back to a way of life that has passed—the 'Old England' of Fielding's Squire Western. Crabbe, writing in the first decade of the nineteenth century, brilliantly conveys, in this same section of *The Borough*, the changes that have come with 'improvement', 'enclosure', and the pursuit of economic advantage.

9. 'Epistle to Burlington', ll. 169–72.

10. *Nature and Society*, p. 141.

11. Vergil describes the farmer's tools as armaments: 'Now must I describe the armaments/Tough country-dwellers use, without which crops/Could not be sown nor raised; the ploughshare first ...' (Smith Palmer Bovie, *Virgil's 'Georgics': A Modern Verse Translation* (Chicago, 1956), Bk. I, p. 10).

12. Smith is much concerned with how man behaves from 'a regard to his own interest' (*Wealth of Nations*, Bk. I, chap. 2). The dissolution of the great feudal estates, an event wholly beneficial to the public good, was brought about because the proprietors spent to 'gratify the most childish vanity', while the merchants and artificers acted 'in pursuit of their own pedlar principle of turning a penny' (see E. Cannan (ed.), *Adam Smith: The Wealth of Nations* (London, 1950), i. 389). Elsewhere, far from seeing the town as a stain upon the country, Smith perceives only the fortunate side of its influences, for 'commerce and manufactures gradually introduced order and good government, and with them, the liberty and security of individuals, among the inhabitants of the country' (ibid., i. 384).

13. *Wealth of Nations*, ed. cit., i. 127–9, ii. 267.

14. Thus Cowper again perceives an irremediable process whereby the 'state' creates the means of its own further acts of corruption. He cannot break out from, so to speak, a 'circular' apprehension of a self-sustaining vicious 'circularity'.

15. Cf. *Prelude* (1805), I, 252ff.

16. *Nature and Society*, p. 161.

17. 'To my Dear Friend Mr Congreve', l. 19.

18. Feingold, op. cit., p. 176.

19. 'Epistle to Bathurst', ll. 135, 137–8.

20. For Johnson's comment, see J. W. Krutch, *Samuel Johnson* (New York, 1944), pp. 504–5.

21. John Dyer, *The Fleece*, III, 308–10; G. Gilfillan (ed.), *The Poetical Works of Armstrong, Dyer, and Green* (Edinburgh, 1858), p. 168. Dr. Johnson found Dyer's poem pompous and its subject 'uninteresting' (*Lives*, ii. 318–19). The modern reader may well find its subject—the growth of trade and the rise of industry—very interesting indeed, and recognize that the work is serious, highly moral, and observant; but we cannot help rejecting, or at least seeing as faintly ludicrous, the celebration and approval of a world which we (like Cowper) understand to be neither beautiful nor virtuous. Dyer's 'heroic' reads now as 'mock heroic'. Here are his lines on country workhouses:

> Even now the sons of trade,
> Where'er the cultivated hamlets smile,
> Erect the mansion: here soft fleeces shine;
> The card awaits you, and the comb, and wheel;
> Here shroud you from the thunder of the storm;
> No rain shall wet your pillow: here abounds
> Pure beverage ...
>
> (III,250–6)

22. Balsamo, 'Thoughts on Great Cities', *Annals of Agriculture*, xiii (1790), p. 480.

23. 'Windsor Forest', ll. 375–7.

24. *Prelude* (1805), VIII,394–5.

25. A full account of the Stratford Jubilee is given in Johanne M. Stochholm, *Garrick's Folly: the Stratford Jubilee of 1769* (London, 1964). Cowper also condemns the Handel centenary in letters to Newton and Unwin, 9 July 1785 and 20 Nov. 1784. For Unwin's benefit he composes a short dramatic scene in which an angel descends into the midst of hearers and performers: *Angel.* 'So then because Handel set anthems to music, you sing them in honour of Handel; and because he composed the music of Italian songs, you sing them in a church. Truly Handel is much obliged to you, but God is greatly dishonoured' (*Correspondence*, ii. 270).

26. For the sale of relics carved from the Mulberry Tree, see Stochholm, op. cit., pp. 6–10, 60–3. Garrick had to pay off a deficit of around £2,000 after the Jubilee but recouped the money from the subsequent Drury Lane reconstruction (ibid., pp. 173–4). There were over five hundred performers at the Handel Commemoration, and the five days' performances netted nearly £13,000 for the fund for 'decayed musicians' (see Griffith (ed.), *Poems of Cowper*, ii. 270).

27. See, e.g., Enright, 'William Cowper', in Ford (ed.), *From Dryden to Johnson* (1968), pp. 395–6.

28. To Newton, 27 Nov. 1784; Spiller, p. 724.

29. Nahum Tate's unassuming verses, 'Grant me, indulgent Heaven!', will serve to illustrate the conventions behind Cowper's 'retirement':

> Grant me, indulgent Heaven! a rural seat
>   Rather contemptible than great!
> Where, though I taste life's sweets, I still may be
>   Athirst for immortality!
> I would have business; but exempt from strife!
>   A private, but an active life!
> A conscience bold, and punctual to his charge!
>   My stock of health; or patience large!
> Some books I'd have, and some acquaintance too;
>   But very good, and very few!
> Then (if mortal two such gifts may crave!)
>   From silent life I'd steal into the grave.

All Cowper's emphases are here, in this representative example of the Augustan 'poetry of rural contentment', except for the link between retreat and fuller response to the Creation. The latter is present, for example, in Pope's 'Lines on Solitude': 'In safety, innocence, and full repose,/Man the true worth of his Creation knows./Luxurious Nature's wealth in thought surveys,/And meditates her charms, and sings her praise'. For further parallels, see 'Windsor Forest', ll. 235ff. and *The Deserted Village*, ll. 97–112.

30. At a point where Cowper is both humanitarian and a man drawing attention to his own usefulness:

> ye shall not want
> What, conscious of your virtues, we can spare,
> Nor what a wealthier than ourselves may send.
> (IV,424–6)

There is often an element of self-reference in Cowper's treatment of poverty and deprivation, which is thus more complex than an expression of merely 'a sense of duty' (as Spacks would have it, op. cit., p. 180). In another passage in Book IV he quite deliberately measures lots with the unfortunate waggoner struggling in the snow, on the assumption that by so doing 'We may with patience bear our mod'rate ills' (ll.336–40). But Cowper's response is uncertain. Instead of sustaining these consoling thoughts, he switches, under the influence of the georgic ideal of the rugged labourer, to a recognition of the waggoner's happy insensibility and freedom from care (ll. 357ff.). The wheel comes full circle: Cowper's reading of the image changes from an apprehension of the relative horror of an exposed existence to an apprehension of its relative privileges over the life of cultured retirement.

31. James D. Boulger, *The Calvinist Temper in English Poetry* (The Hague, 1980), p. 311.

32. Ibid., p. 326.

33. Cf. the foretaste of heavenly joys experienced by Christian and Hopeful along the road to the Celestial City, and especially in the land of Beulah: see Sharrock (ed.), *The Pilgrim's Progress*, pp. 195–7.

CHAPTER 7

1. To Lady Hesketh, 27 Nov. 1787; Spiller, p. 856.

2. See, e.g., Cowper's rejection of Johnson's criticisms of Prior (letter to Unwin, 5 Jan. 1782; Spiller, pp. 649–50).

3. A. R. Waller (ed.), *Matthew Prior: Poems on Several Occasions* (Cambridge, 1905), p. 77. Unless otherwise stated, all references are to this edition.

4. 'Epistle to Robert Lloyd', l. 4.

5. E.g., 'Did not thy reason and thy sense'.

6. Davie, *Augustan Lyric*, p. 168, points out that Cowper's poem is 'very clearly related to Prior's "Ode" '.

7. *Lives*, ed. cit., ii. 392.

8. *Augustan Lyric*, p. 173.

9. We may compare the 'cruel silence' and expressive 'eyes' of the lover to whom Prior is speaking in his lyric, 'To a Lady: She refusing to continue a Dispute with me, and leaving me in the Argument'.

10. Reprinted in Cowper, *Poetical Works*, p. 680.

11. 'God Incomprehensible and Sovereign', ll. 15–16. The next stanza is particularly relevant to Cowper's 'condition':

> He wounds the heart, and he makes whole;
> He calms the tempest of the soul;
> When he shuts up in long despair,
> Who can remove the heavy bar?

12. Free, *William Cowper*, p. 161.

13. Ibid., pp. 160–1.

14. Perhaps this poem is more precariously balanced between terror and comedy than my comment suggests. The mind of the 'inattentive' poet is, after all, suddenly arrested by the image of a sinister embodiment of violence and threat: 'When, lo! upon the threshold met my view,/With head erect, and eyes of fiery hue,/A viper, long as Count de Grasse's queue' (ll.9–11). But the joke at the end of this quotation, and the superbly controlled 'swagger' of the poem as a whole, do, I think, communicate a playful rather than troubled imagination.

15. For recollections of persecution at Dr. Pitman's school, see *Memoir*, pp. 366–7.

16. See 'Lines written during a short period of insanity', stanza 1.

17. For Adam's dream, see *Paradise Lost*, VIII, 292–314: 'I waked, and found/Before mine eyes all real ...'. Does Keats's famous statement—'The imagination may be compared to Adam's dream—he awoke and found it truth'—catch *Cowper's* phrasing?

18. To Unwin, 18 Nov. 1782; Spiller, pp. 677–8.

19. Written on the spur of the moment, after Lady Austen had told Cowper and Mrs. Unwin the linen-draper's tale one evening in October 1782, *John Gilpin* brought its anonymous author immediate fame when it appeared in *The Public Advertiser* for 14 November. Talking in 1784 of his publisher's request for information about any likely alterations to the poem, Cowper remarks that 'to print only the original again would be to publish what has

been hacknied in every magazine, in every newspaper, and in every street' (to Unwin, 8 May 1784; *Correspondence*, ii. 203). For the chapbook printing, see A. B. Friedman, *The Ballad Revival: Studies in the Influence of Popular on Sophisticated Poetry* (Chicago, 1961), p. 261. *John Gilpin* became so well-known that the reviewer of *The Task* in *The Gentleman's Magazine* could open with the simple recommendation that the poem was by the 'facetious and well-known author of *John Gilpin*'.

20. Friedman, op. cit., p. 260.

21. Two years earlier, in *Anti-Thelyphthora*, Cowper had parodied his cousin Martin Madan's defence of polygamy by casting the subject in the form of a medieval romance in the manner of 'Chaucer's merry page'.

22. To Unwin, 18 Nov. 1782; Spiller, p. 677.

23. Chaucer, 'Sir Thopas', stanza 11.

24. Free, *William Cowper*, p. 166.

25. The 'Ode' is reprinted in Cowper, *Poetical Works*, pp. 288–9. For Southey's erroneous assumption that it was by Cowper, see *Poetical Works*, pp. 659–60. The poem is an exercise in 'mock Pindarics', but a notably uninspired one.

26. Free, op. cit., p. 168.

27. To Unwin, 23 May 1781; Spiller, p. 618.

28. See *Poetical Works*, p. 674.

29. For the various printings of these poems, see *Poetical Works*, pp. 388, 677.

30. Davie, *Augustan Lyric*, pp. 1–2.

31. Review of *The Excursion, Edinburgh Review* (Nov. 1814); in G. McMaster (ed.), *William Wordsworth: a Critical Anthology* (London, 1972), p. 125.

32. Johnston, 'Poetry and Criticism after 1740', R. Lonsdale (ed.), *Dryden to Johnson* (1971), p. 392.

CHAPTER 8

1. 'On Thomson and Cowper', *Lectures* (Everyman edn., 1964), p. 95.

2. Free, *William Cowper*, p. 155.

3. Free says that Cowper makes 'nothing' of the idea that art may 'baffle' time. On the contrary, he makes a great deal of it, though with reference to poetry and his own poem.

4. *A Preface to Eighteenth Century Poetry* (Oxford, 1948), pp. 68ff.

5. 'To the Memory of a Lady' (1747); A. Chalmers (ed.), *The Works of the English Poets* (London, 1810), ix. 180.

6. For Lyttleton's remark, see R. M. Davis, *The Good Lord Lyttleton* (London, 1939), p. 138. Gray, among others, praised the simplicity of Lyttleton's 'truly tender and elegiac' verses (letter to Thomas Warton, Nov. 1747; *Correspondence*, Toynbee (ed.), i. 293). Rousseau's statement, from *A Discourse on the Arts and Sciences*, is discussed in Sutherland, op. cit., p. 69.

7. Tickell, 'To the Earl of Warwick, on the Death of Mr. Addison'; Chalmers (ed.), *Works of the English Poets*, xi. 122. For contemporary admiration of this poem, see Johnson, *Lives*, ii. 60; Goldsmith, appendix to

Beauties of English Poesy, in A. Friedman (ed.), *Collected Works of Oliver Goldsmith* (Oxford, 1966), v. 327; Young's imitation, 'A Letter to Mr. Tickell ...', *Poetical Works* (Aldine edn., 1867), ii. 194.

8. *Gentleman's Magazine*, lv (1785), p. 133.

9. *Poetical Works*, ed. cit., pp. 434–6.

10. Langbaum, *Poetry of Experience*, p. 230.

11. Dr. Johnson's definition of 'monody' as 'A poem sung by one person' suggests that the word, specifically chosen by Lyttleton as a sub-heading for his elegy, retained something of its original meaning of 'an ode performed by an actor'.

12. The exchanges are outlined by Sutherland, op. cit., pp. 73–4. On the whole the 'simplicity' was preferred, though Doddridge liked the orange-tree stanza best.

13. Preface to Lyrical Ballads; *Poetical Works*, ed. cit., ii. 400–1.

14. 27 Feb. 1790; Spiller, p. 917.

15. See Jonathan Culler, *Structuralist Poetics* (London, 1975), pp. 142–3.

16. J. P. Stern, *On Realism* (London, 1973), p. 121.

17. See, e.g., Culler, op. cit., p. 165.

18. *William Cowper* (1960), p. 6.

19. 'Ode on a Distant Prospect of Eton College', ll. 21–30.

20. Laurence Sterne, *A Sentimental Journey* (Everyman Library, 1927), p. 92.

21. Hervey, *Meditations*, p. 11—'But more eminently happy they who have passed the waves, and weathered all the storms of a troublesome and dangerous world'; Johnson, 'The Young Author', ll. 1–10; Garth, *The Dispensary*, III, 226—'Where billows never break, nor tempests roar'. The view of Paradise as a garden among the 'fortunate isles' reaches back to antiquity, but Cowper may have in mind *Paradise Lost*, IV, 153–65.

22. See Brian Nellist's succinct interpretative description of 'Lycidas', in B. Nellist (ed.), *Milton: Poems of 1645* (London, 1974), pp. 196–9.

23. 18 Oct. 1765; Spiller, p. 559.

24. Miriam Allott has some relevant comments on these aspects of Keats's poem; Miriam Allott (ed.), *The Poems of John Keats* (London, 1970), pp. 531–2.

25. In 'Lamia' by the crushing influence of 'bald-head' philosophy ('Lamia', II, 239–311).

26. 'Lycidas', ll. 132–53.

27. 'Structure and Style in the Greater Romantic Lyric', F. W. Hilles and H. Bloom (eds.), *From Sensibility to Romanticism* (New York, 1965), pp. 527–8.

28. In R. Dodsley (ed.), *A Collection of Poems by Several Hands* (London, 1763), ii. 326.

29. We may compare this dynamic interchange between consciousness and object with the moral or playful responses developed in so much eighteenth-century 'occasional' verse, conveniently exemplified in Cowper's early 'Verses, written at Bath on finding the Heel of a Shoe'.

30. See Frieda Fordham, *An Introduction to Jung's Psychology* (3rd edn., London, 1966), p. 79.

31. I argue for this view of Wordsworth's poem in 'Wordsworth, Bunyan and the Puritan Mind', *English Literary History*, xli (1974), pp. 219–24.

32. Letter to Sotheby, 1802; quoted in W. K. Wimsatt, 'The Structure of

Romantic Nature Imagery', M. H. Abrams (ed.), *The English Romantic Poets* (New York, 1960), p. 28.

33. G. Gilfillan (ed.), *The Poetical Works of W. L. Bowles* (Edinburgh, 1855), i. 11.

CHAPTER 9

1. *Revaluation* (London, 1936), p. 102.

2. *Purity of Diction*, pp. 52–3.

3. *Truth*, ll. 19–20.

4. The theme is 'responsibility'—of right knowing and right-mindedness—is, for example, at the centre of the conversations between Christian, Hopeful, and Ignorance on the Enchanted Ground in Part One of *The Pilgrim's Progress*.

5. See ll. 29–32 esp.

6. Cf. another of the translations from Madame Guyon, 'The Acquiescence of Pure Love'.

7. E.g. letter to Revd. William Bull, 27 Oct. 1782; Spiller, p. 673.

8. Quoted in Hartley, *Continuing Revaluation*, p. 6.

9. John Johnson was a subscriber to the 1798 edition of Walter's book, which had first appeared in 1748. The relevant passage ends:

> ... one of our ablest seamen was canted overboard; and notwithstanding the prodigious agitation of the waves, we perceived that he swam very strong, and it was with the utmost concern that we found ourselves incapable of assisting him; and we were the more grieved at his unhappy fate, since we lost sight of him struggling with the waves, and conceived from the manner in which he swam, that he might continue sensible for a considerable time longer, of the horror attending his irretrievable situation. (Bk. I, chap. 8)

10. To Lady Hesketh, 27 Aug. 1795; *Correspondence*, iv. 490.

11. '... a versification of a circumstance recorded in a newspaper, which had been read to him a few weeks before, without his appearing to notice it' (William Hayley, *The Life and Letters of William Cowper* (2nd edn., 1803), ii. 213).

12. See pp. 98–9 above.

13. I imply by this word the idea of compulsive-obsessive action suggested by 'daemon' in the context of pre-Olympian Greek mythology. Christianity tends always to associate such action with sin or guilt.

14. Whereas in the Olney hymn *God* rides upon the storm and plants His footsteps in the sea, vast 'portents' now occupy nature's space: Cowper takes a familiar view of the world but God is unfamiliarly absent.

15. Cowper's images, as well as his metre, derive substantially from Watts's 'The Day of Judgement: an Ode attempted in English Sapphick':

> Hopeless Immortals! how they scream and shiver
> While Devils push them to the Pit wide yawning
> Hideous and gloomy, to receive them headlong
>   Down to the Centre.

There is a stark contrast, however. While Cowper ends with a concentrated image of personal agony, a 'sentence/Worse than Abiram's', Watts can automatically switch from 'dark' to 'bright' imaginings:

> Stop here my Fancy: (all away ye horrid
> Doleful Ideas) come arise to *Jesus*,
> How he sits God-like! and the Saints around him
> Thron'd, yet adoring!

Watts concludes with a spacious sense of the Redeemer, Cowper with a narrow picture of his own terrible confinement.

16. Appendix to *Lyrical Ballads* (1802); *Poetical Works*, ed. cit., ii. 408. The same passage contains Wordsworth's criticism of the epithet 'church-going' ('But the sound of the church-going bell'), which he finds an unexpected 'abuse' in 'so chaste a writer as Cowper'.

17. Charles Wesley, 'Free Grace' ('And can it be, that I should gain'), stanza 4; Frank Baker (ed.), *Representative Verse of Charles Wesley* (London, 1962), p. 10.

18. 'The Worm and the Thorn: a Study of Cowper's *Olney Hymns*', *The Journal of Religion*, xxix (1949), p. 224. The theology of Cowper's hymns is described by H. Grant Sampson, *The Anglican Tradition in Eighteenth Century Verse* (The Hague, 1971), pp. 294ff., 303ff., but the best critical comments are in M. J. Quinlan, *William Cowper: a Critical Life* (Minneapolis, 1953) and 'Cowper's Imagery', *J.E.G.P.*, xlvii (1948), pp. 276–85.

19. *Pilgrim's Progress*, ed. cit., pp. 153–6.

20. *The Revolution in Tanner's Lane*, chap. 7.

21. Op. cit., pp. 165–6.

22. To Newton, 18 Sept. 1781; Spiller, p. 635. Cowper had read Herbert's poems to his dying brother in 1770, the year before he began the Olney hymns. They are also mentioned in the *Memoir*, p. 368.

23. Cf. the excellent critical description of the art of Wesley's hymns in Baker, *Representative Verse*, pp. xvii–xxxv.

24. See Davie, *A Gathered Church: The Literature of the English Dissenting Interest, 1700–1930* (London, 1978), pp. 31–2, 45–7.

25. *William Cowper* (1960), p. 16.

26. See Spacks, op. cit., pp. 169–70.

27. 'Abraham Cowley', *Lives*, i. 29–30.

28. Wordsworth's 'Lines' are an excellent late example of the tradition: the clouds that gather round the setting sun become a Jacob's ladder leading men's thoughts up to heaven.

29. Fausset, *William Cowper*, p. 79.

30. 'Isaac Watts', *Lives*, ii. 298.

31. See Rachel Trickett, *The Honest Muse*, pp. 246–7.

32. G. Burder (ed.), *The Works of Isaac Watts D.D.* (London, 1810), iv. 254.

33. *Lives*, ii. 298. See also Johnson's related remarks in the 'Life of Waller', *Lives*, i. 173–4. Cowper disagreed with Johnson's view of Watts, but gave no reason (though implying a more plainly admiring stance): see letter to Newton, 4 Oct. 1781, *Correspondence*, i. 361.

34. Memorial *Sermon* on Cowper, p. 18.

35. Op. cit., p. 172.

36. Caroline Helstone's remark to Shirley Keeldar in Charlotte Brontë's *Shirley*: 'Pity him, Shirley? What can I do else? He was nearly broken-hearted when he wrote that poem, and it almost breaks one's heart to read it'.

37. Maynard Mack (ed.), *Alexander Pope: the Odyssey of Homer* (London, 1967), p. 192.

38. Pope, *Homer's Odyssey*, V, 402.

POSTSCRIPT

1. University of California Press, 1977.

2. Quoted in *Confinement and Flight*, p. 2.

3. David Storey, *Saville* (London, 1976), p. 505.

4. Geoffrey H. Hartman (ed.), *William Wordsworth: Selected Poetry and Prose* (New York, 1970), p. xxx.

5. This aspect—the paradox of 'richness' and 'emptiness', 'fullness' and 'loss'—is admirably pointed by J. S. Cunningham, 'Pope, Eliot, and "The Mind of Europe"', A. D. Moody (ed.), *The Waste Land in Different Voices* (London, 1974), pp. 67–85.

6. Eliot, Review of Joyce's *Ulysses*, *The Dial* (Nov. 1923).

7. Quoted in Kathleen Coburn (ed.), *Inquiring Spirit: Coleridge from his Published and Unpublished Prose Writings* (New York, 1951), p. 36.

8. Philip Rieff, *Triumph of the Therapeutic*, pp. 21–2.

9. Carnochan, op. cit., pp. 23–4.

10. Graham Hough, *The Romantic Poets* (London, 1953), pp. 11–12.

11. See Michel Foucault, *Discipline and Punish* (*Surveiller et Punir*), trans. Alan Sheridan (Peregrine edn., London, 1979).

12. Carnochan, op. cit., pp. 8ff. See also A. Koyré, *From the Closed World to the Infinite Universe* (Baltimore, 1957).

13. 'The Happy Prison: a Recurring Romantic Metaphor', D. Thorburn and G. Hartman (eds.), *Romanticism: Vistas, Instances, Continuities* (Ithaca, 1973), p. 65.

14. Ibid., p. 64.

Index of Persons and Works

Works by writers other than Cowper are only selectively specified, with the remaining references being entered tacitly under the authors' names.